Professional
LINQ

Professional
LINQ

Professional
LINQ

Scott Klein

WILEY

Wiley Publishing, Inc.

Professional LINQ

Published by
Wiley Publishing, Inc.
10475 Crosspoint Boulevard
Indianapolis, IN 46256
www.wiley.com

Copyright © 2008 by Wiley Publishing, Inc., Indianapolis, Indiana

Published simultaneously in Canada

ISBN: 978-0-470-04181-9

Manufactured in the United States of America

10 9 8 7 6 5 4 3 2

Library of Congress Cataloging-in-Publication Data

Klein, Scott, 1966-
  Professional LinQ / Scott Klein.
    p. cm.
  Includes index.
  ISBN 978-0-470-04181-9 (pbk. : website)
  1. Microsoft LINQ. 2. Query languages (Computer science)   I. Title.
  QA76.73.L228K53 2008
  005.74'1--dc22

                                    2007045810

To Lynelle, Sadie, Forrest, Allara, and Shayna

About the Author

Scott Klein is an independent consultant with a passion for all things SQL Server, .NET, and XML. He is the author of *Professional SQL Server 2005 XML* and *Professional WCF Programming*. He also writes the biweekly feature article for the *SQL PASS Community Connector*, and has contributed articles to both Wrox (www.Wrox.com) and TopXML (www.TopXML.com). He frequently speaks to SQL Server and .NET user groups. Scott lives in Wellington, Florida, and when he is not sitting in front of a computer or spending time with his family, he can usually be found aboard his Yamaha at the local motocross track. He can be reached at ScottKlein@SqlXml.com.

Credits

Executive Editor
Bob Elliott

Development Editor
Maryann Steinhart

Technical Editor
Carl Daniel

Production Editor
Daniel Scribner

Copy Editor
Foxxe Editorial Services

Editorial Manager
Mary Beth Wakefield

Production Manager
Tim Tate

Vice President and Executive Group Publisher
Richard Swadley

Vice President and Executive Publisher
Joseph B. Wikert

Project Coordinator, Cover
Lynsey Stanford

Proofreader
Candace English, Nancy Riddiough,
Amy Rasmussen and
Jeremy Bagai

Indexer
Robert Swanson

Acknowledgments

First and foremost I'd like to thank Neil Salkind and everyone at Studio B for being who they are and for all that they do. They take care of all of the things I don't want to have to worry about and let me do what I like to do, which is working with the latest and greatest new technology. Without these people and their contributions, this book wouldn't be possible.

I'd like to give a huge thanks to the people at Wrox/Wiley for making this book happen. Maryann Steinhart, my development editor, was a delight to work with. Many, many thanks to Carl Daniel, the technical editor, for the time and energy he put into reviewing this book. His comments were invaluable.

Thanks to Jim Minatel, for accepting the book idea and letting me write it, and Bob Elliott for picking up where Jim left off after Jim went on to bigger and better things within Wrox. I appreciate your support.

As with my other books, having that "one person" who you could go to for whatever reason made life so much easier. Dave Remy, I cannot thank you enough! Your help was worth more than gold, and it sure made writing this book much easier.

A large dose of gratitude also goes out to Dinesh Kulkarni, Eric White, Erick Thompson, Lance Olson, Luca Bolognese, Mads Torgersen, Michael Blome, Ralf Lammel, Scott Guthrie, Luke Hoban, and Asad Khan. A thank you to each of you for letting me ask questions and providing excellent feedback.

It has been said that you are only as good as those with whom you associate. So enough cannot be said about the love and support of my family, for without them, this book, or anything else I do in life, would not be possible. My wonderful wife, Lynelle, who during these times is an anchor for this family, held the house together for the 8+ months I spent upstairs writing. And to my children, who were patient with their father knowing that they soon would get their dad back. I love you all. When did my eldest daughter turn old enough to start driving?

Contents

Contents

Contents

Contents

Contents

Introduction

It has been three years and I'm still trying to get the word "grok" into everyone's mainstream vocabulary (see the introductions to my last two books), and one of the things that I am "grokking" is the new LINQ technology coming out of the Microsoft campus.

Microsoft is touting LINQ as a "groundbreaking innovation" that promises to "revolutionize the way developers work with data." Like you, I was somewhat skeptical about these promises because similar comments have been funneled our way in the past, but these bold declarations would cause even the casual developer to stop and take notice.

Let me just say right here that the more I got into LINQ, the more excited I became (and the more guilty I felt about not believing the hype). And this isn't just any mere excitement; this is on par with a 10-year-old waking up Christmas morning to a pirate's share of loot under the Christmas tree.

Why? Because LINQ introduces queries (the concept of a query) as a first-class language construct in both C# and Visual Basic. No longer do you need to learn multiple technologies to query multiple data sources. It is a single query syntax for querying XML, SQL databases, ADO.NET DataSets, and other data sources.

LINQ simplifies how you will now write queries. If you use C# or Visual Basic, you will be able to start writing LINQ queries immediately because you know most of what you need. LINQ is a set of features built into Visual Studio 2008 that incorporates tremendous query capabilities directly into the language syntax of Visual Basic and C#. This provides the benefits of IntelliSense, compile-time type checking, and debugging support. How could life get any better?

Who This Book Is For

This book is for developers who want to learn about LINQ and how it can benefit and enhance their applications. Equally, this book is for those individuals who have spent at least a little time looking at LINQ, have done some experimental development with it, and want to delve deeper into the technology to see how LINQ can improve their applications.

A good understanding of Visual Studio and the C# language will be useful when reading this book and working with the examples, but it is not required. An understanding of SQL Server and T-SQL also would be useful but is not required.

What This Book Covers

Part I provides on overview of LINQ and of Visual Studio 2008, a look at many of the new and existing language-specific features that support LINQ, and a discussion of LINQ queries and the LINQ standard query operators.

❑ Chapter 1 provides an overview of LINQ and explains why there is a need for LINQ, and then takes a brief introductory look at the other LINQ providers.

❑ Chapter 2 affords a brief history of Visual Studio, and then takes a good look at Visual Studio 2008 and many of the .NET Framework language-specific features that will help you better understand LINQ.

❑ Chapter 3 examines LINQ queries, their overall concepts, and the syntax to use when writing LINQ queries.

❑ Chapter 4 provides a detailed discussion of the LINQ standard query operators.

Part II jumps right into LINQ to XML, providing an overview first and then showing you how to program with LINQ to XML with both C# and Visual Basic, and how to use LINQ to XML with other data models.

❑ Chapter 5 provides an overview of LINQ to XML, discusses many of the LINQ to XML concepts, and compares LINQ to XML with other XML technologies.

❑ Chapter 6 tackles many of the concepts, techniques, and programming fundamentals necessary to program with LINQ to XML.

❑ Chapter 7 compares LINQ to XML with the other LINQ data models such as LINQ to SQL.

❑ Chapter 8 explores some advanced LINQ to XML programming topics such as functional construction and working with events.

❑ Chapter 9 focuses solely on using LINQ to XML with Visual Basic .NET.

Part III focuses on LINQ to SQL, again providing an overview, and then tackling LINQ to SQL queries, advanced query concepts, LINQ to Entities, and LINQ to DataSets. It also introduces you to the visual tools provided by LINQ to automate many of the LINQ to SQL functions.

❑ Chapter 10 provides an overview of LINQ to SQL and its corresponding object model, as well as a discussion of attribute-based mapping and an overview of relational basics.

❑ Chapter 11 discusses LINQ to SQL queries and concepts, how to work with the `DataContext` class and entity objects, and how to manipulate data with LINQ to SQL.

❑ Chapter 12 explores concepts such as database relationships and LINQ query execution.

❑ Chapter 13 tackles many aspects of LINQ to SQL entities such as tracking changes and working with transactions.

❑ Chapter 14 focuses on using LINQ to DataSet to query the contents of an ADO.NET DataSet, and data binding with LINQ to DataSet.

❑ Chapter 15 discusses some advanced LINQ to SQL topics and tools such as multi-tier operations and the Object-Relational Designer.

Part IV, "Appendixes," provides a case study and a look at a couple of LINQ technologies that will be available post–Visual Studio 2008 but are sure to make an impact on the market: LINQ to XSD and LINQ to the ADO.NET Entity Framework.

❑ Appendix A walks you through building an application using LINQ and associated LINQ providers.

❑   Appendix B discusses the ADO.NET Entity Framework and associated objects as well as the Entity Data Model Generator tool.

❑   Appendix C discusses LINQ to XSD, a beta technology that allows you to work directly with XML in a typed manner.

What You Need to Use This Book

All of the examples in this book require the following:

❑   Visual Studio 2008 (Beta 2)

❑   .NET Framework 3.5 (Beta 2)

❑   LINQ to XSD Preview

❑   ADO.NET Entity Framework Beta 2

❑   ADO.NET Entity Framework Tools CTP

❑   SQL Server 2005 and the AdventureWorks sample database

Conventions

To help you get the most from the text and keep track of what's happening, a number of conventions are used throughout the book.

> **Boxes like this one hold important, not-to-be-forgotten information that is directly relevant to the surrounding text.**

Notes, tips, hints, tricks, and asides to the current discussion are offset and placed in italics like this.

As for styles in the text:

❑   New terms and important words are *highlighted* when we introduce them.

❑   Keyboard strokes look like this: Ctrl+A.

❑   Filenames, URLs, and code within the text are shown like this: `persistence.properties`.

❑   Code is presented in two different ways:

```
A monofont type with no highlighting is used for most code examples.
```

```
Gray highlighting to emphasize code that's particularly important in the present
context.
```

Source Code

As you work through the examples in this book, you may choose either to type in all the code manually or to use the source code files that accompany the book. All of the source code used in this book is available for downloading at www.wrox.com. Once at the site, simply locate the book's title (either by using the Search box or by using one of the title lists) and click the Download Code link on the book's detail page to obtain all the source code for the book.

> *Because many books have similar titles, you may find it easiest to search by ISBN; this book's ISBN is 978-0-470-04181-9.*

Once you download the code, just decompress it with your favorite compression tool. Alternately, you can go to the main Wrox code download page at www.wrox.com/dynamic/books/download.aspx to see the code available for this book and all other Wrox books.

Errata

We make every effort to ensure that there are no errors in the text or in the code. However, no one is perfect, and mistakes do occur. If you find an error in one of our books, like a spelling mistake or faulty piece of code, we would be very grateful for your feedback. By sending in errata you may save another reader hours of frustration, and at the same time you will be helping us provide even higher quality information.

To find the errata page for this book, go to www.wrox.com and locate the title using the Search box or one of the title lists. Then, on the book details page, click the Book Errata link. On this page, you can view all errata that has been submitted for this book and posted by Wrox editors. A complete book list, including links to each book's errata, is also available at www.wrox.com/misc-pages/booklist.shtml.

If you don't spot "your" error on the Book Errata page, go to www.wrox.com/contact/techsupport .shtml and complete the form there to send us the error you have found. We'll check the information and, if appropriate, post a message to the book's errata page and fix the problem in subsequent editions of the book.

p2p.wrox.com

For author and peer discussion, join the P2P forums at p2p.wrox.com. The forums are a Web-based system for you to post messages relating to Wrox books and related technologies and interact with other readers and technology users. The forums offer a subscription feature to email you topics of interest of your choosing when new posts are made to the forums. Wrox authors, editors, other industry experts, and your fellow readers are present on these forums.

At http://p2p.wrox.com you will find a number of different forums that will help you not only as you read this book but also as you develop your own applications. To join the forums, just follow these steps:

1. Go to p2p.wrox.com and click the Register link.
2. Read the terms of use and click Agree.

3. Complete the required information to join as well as any optional information you want to provide, and click Submit.

4. You will receive an email with information describing how to verify your account and complete the joining process.

You can read messages in the forums without joining P2P but in order to post your own messages, you must join.

Once you join, you can post new messages and respond to messages other users post. You can read messages at any time on the Web. If you would like to have new messages from a particular forum emailed to you, click the Subscribe to this Forum icon by the forum name in the forum listing.

For more information about how to use the Wrox P2P, be sure to read the P2P FAQs for answers to questions about how the forum software works as well as many common questions specific to P2P and Wrox books. To read the FAQs, click the FAQ link on any P2P page.

Part I
Introduction to Project LINQ

Project LINQ

I often hear the questions, "What is LINQ?," "What does it do?," and "Why do we need it?" The answer to the first question (and subsequently the other two questions) is that the Language Integrated Query (LINQ) is a set of standard query operators that provide the underlying query architecture for the navigation, filtering, and execution operations of nearly every kind of data source, such as XML (using LINQ to XML, previously known as XLINQ), relational data (using LINQ to SQL, previously known as DLINQ), ADO.NET DataSets (using LINQ to DataSet), and in-memory collections.

The best way to begin understanding this wonderful new technology is to take a look at some history and background on how and why LINQ came to be.

Although the public first became aware of LINQ early in the fall of 2005, LINQ had been in development since early 2003. The overall LINQ goal was to make it easier for developers to interact with SQL and XML, primarily because there exists a disconnect between relational data (databases), XML, and the programming languages that communicate with (that is, work with) each of them.

Most developers understand the concept of object-oriented (OO) programming and its related technologies and features, such as classes, methods, and objects. Object-oriented programming has evolved tremendously over the past 10 years or so, but even in its current state, there's still a gap when using and integrating OO technology with information that is not natively defined or inherent to it.

For example, suppose that you want to execute a T-SQL query from within your C# application. It would look something like this:

```
private void Form1_Load(object sender, EventArgs e)
{
    string ConnectionString = @"Data Source=(local);
     Initial Catalog=AdventureWorks;UID=sa;PWD=yourpassword";
    using (SqlConnection conn = new SqlConnection(ConnectionString))
    {
        conn.Open();
        SqlCommand cmd = conn.CreateCommand();
```

```
            cmd.CommandType = CommandType.Text;
            cmd.CommandText = "SELECT LastName, FirstName FROM
    Person.Contact";
            using (SqlDataReader rdr = cmd.ExecuteReader())
            {
                / / do something
            }
        }
    }
```

If you wanted to use the same code to execute a stored procedure that takes one or more parameters, it might look like this:

```
    private void Form1_Load(object sender, EventArgs e)
    {
        string ConnectionString = @"Data Source=(local);
          Initial Catalog=AdventureWorks;UID=sa;PWD=yourpassword";
        using (SqlConnection conn = new SqlConnection(ConnectionString))
        {
            conn.Open();
            SqlCommand cmd = conn.CreateCommand();
            cmd.CommandType = CommandType.StoredProcedure;
            cmd.CommandText = "uspGetBillOfMaterials";
            cmd.Parameters.Add("@StartProductID", SqlDbType.Int).Value =
    324;
            cmd.Parameters.Add("@CheckDate", SqlDbType.DateTime).Value =
    "07/10/2000";
            using (SqlDataReader rdr = cmd.ExecuteReader())
            {
                // do something
            }
        }
    }
```

While you and I have probably coded something like this many, many times, it isn't "friendly" on several levels. First, you are combining two languages into one. You have the language you are coding (in this case C#), plus you have the SQL language in quotation marks, which is not understood in the context of .NET. With the .NET language you have IntelliSense, but you don't get IntelliSense in the embedded SQL syntax.

More importantly, however, there is no compile-time type checking, which means you can't tell if something is broken until run time. Every line of code has to be QA'd just to see if it even begins to work.

Microsoft also packed a lot of features into the .NET Framework that enable developers to work with XML. The .NET Framework contains the System.Xml namespace and other supporting namespaces, such as System.Xml.XPath, System.Xml.Xsl, and System.Xml.Schema, which provide a plethora of functionality for working with XML. The namespaces contain many classes and methods that make up the XML .NET API architecture. The main classes are the XmlDocument, XmlReader, and XmlWriter.

To add to the complexity of working with different technologies, parsing an XML document isn't the easiest thing to do, either. Your tools of choice to work with XML are the Document Object Model (DOM),

XQuery, or Extensible Stylesheet Language Transformations (XSLT). For example, to read an XML document using existing technology, you would need to do something like the following:

```
XmlTextReader rdr = new XmlTextReader("C:\Employees.Xml");
while (rdr.Read())
{
    XmlNodeType nt = rdr.NodeType;
    Switch (nt)
    {
        case XmlNodeType.Element:
            break;

        case XmlNodeType.Attribute:
            break;
        case XmlNodeType.Comment:
            break;

        case XmlNodeType.Whitespace:
            break;


    }
}
```

That's a lot of code just to read an XML document (and it isn't even complete). Writing XML isn't any less confusing, as illustrated here:

```
XmlTextWriter wrt = new XmlTextWriter("C:\Employees.Xml");
wrt.WriteStartDocument;
wrt.WriteComment("This is an example");
wrt.WriteStartElement("Employees");
wrt.WriteStartElement("Employee");
wrt.WriteStartElement("FirstName");
wrt.WriteString("Scott");
wrt.WriteEndElement();
wrt.WriteEndElement();
wrt.WriteEndElement();
```

Visually, you don't know if this will work until you compile the project. Likewise, it is hard to see what the resulting XML will look like.

XML is great and its use continues to grow; you can expect it to be around for a long time. Yet, truth be told, XML is still hard to work with.

In dealing with these hurdles, Microsoft considered two paths. The first path would have required the company to build specific XML or relational data features into each programming language and run-time. That would be a major undertaking and an even bigger hassle to maintain. The second option was to add more general-purpose query capabilities into the .NET Framework—in other words, a framework of all-purpose querying facilities built into the .NET Framework that both C# and VB.NET could easily take advantage of.

Luckily, Microsoft chose the later option, creating a unified query experience across objects, XML, collections, and data. It accomplished that by taking query set operations, transforms, and constructs and bringing them to the surface, making them high-level concepts within the .NET Framework (for example, on the same level as objects and classes). So, you can now enjoy the benefits of a single declarative pattern that can be expressed in any .NET-based programming language.

The result of making these set operations, transforms, and constructs first-class operations is a set of methods called the standard query operators. These operators provide query capabilities that include sorting, filtering, aggregation, and projection over a large number of different data sources. The standard query operators are the focus of Chapter 4, "LINQ Standard Query Operators."

Think about it for a minute. A single set of query operators that work within any .NET-based programming language, enabling you to write a query against a database, XML, or an in-memory array using the same syntax? How cool is that? And you get the added benefit of IntelliSense and compile-time type checking! Somebody pinch me.

To illustrate this great technology, take a look at an example that queries the directories of your C drive and writes them to a list box:

```
DirectoryInfo di = new DirectoryInfo("C:\\");
var dirQuery =
    from dir in di.GetDirectories()
    orderby di.Name
    select new { dir.Name} ;

foreach {var item in dirQuery)
    listBox1.Items.Add(item.Name);
```

This code uses some of the standard query operators to create a LINQ query. In essence, Microsoft has taken the concept of query set operations and made them first-class operations within the .NET Framework.

Here's another example. This one queries all the system processes on your PC using the `Process` class, but notice that it uses the same query syntax as the previous example:

```
var procQuery =
    from proc in Process.GetProcesses()
    orderby p.WorkingSet64 descending
    select new { p.Id, p.ProcessName, p.WorkingSet64} ;

foreach (var item in procQuery)
    ListBox1.Items.Add(item.Id + "   " +
        item.ProcessName + "   " +
        item.WorkingSet64);
```

When you run this code, all the processes on your system will be listed in descending order by memory usage.

Simply put, LINQ enables you to query anything that implements the `IEnumerable<T>` interface. If you can loop through the contents using the `foreach` statement, then you can query it using LINQ.

The following example illustrates how LINQ works querying relational data, using a database as the source of data.

```
var conQuery =
    from c in contact
    where c.FirstName.StartsWith("S")
    orderby c.LastName
    select new { c.FirstName, c.LastName, c.EmailAddress} ;

foreach (var item in conQuery)
    ListBox1.Items.Add(item.FirstName + "  " +
        item.LastName + "   " +
        item.EmailAddress);
```

This previous example queries the `Person.Contact` table in the AdventureWorks database for all contacts whose first name starts with the letter "S".

The purpose of LINQ is to provide developers with the following benefits:

❏ A simplified way to write queries.

❏ Faster development time by removing run-time errors and catching errors at compile time.

❏ IntelliSense and debugging support for LINQ directly in the development language.

❏ Closing the gap between relational data and object-oriented development.

❏ A unified query syntax to use regardless of the source of data.

What is important to notice is the same syntax that you used to query the system processes was used query a SQL data source. Both of these topics will be discussed in much more detail, including how to easily connect and map to the source database.

So, with that primer, this chapter introduces the following topics:

❏ LINQ

❏ LINQ to XML

❏ LINQ to SQL

LINQ Overview

LINQ is a set of standard query operators that brings powerful query facilities right into the .NET Framework language such as C# and VB.NET. The LINQ framework brings together the capability of data access with the power of data manipulation. This section provides an overview of the capabilities of LINQ and the standard query operators, but Chapters 3 and 4, respectively, will discuss in great detail the LINQ query operators and language features that contribute to LINQ's direct, declarative style of queries.

The term Language Integrated Query signifies that the standard query facilities are architected directly into the developer's .NET-supported programming language of choice. These query facilities, known as the standard query operators, expose general-purpose query mechanisms that can be applied to many facets of information, such as in-memory constructs as well as information retrieved from external sources such as relational data or XML.

These operators provide the capability to express query operations directly and declaratively within any .NET-based programming language. What makes all of this possible is the simple application of the query operators to an IEnumerable<T> source of information.

Found in the System.Collections.Generic namespace, the IEnumerable<T> interface, a new addition in version 2.0 of the .NET Framework, supports a simple iteration over a collection of a given (specified) type. The IEnumerable<T> interface provides a slick mechanism to iterate through an arbitrary collection of strongly typed objects using the C# foreach statement or the Visual Basic FOR EACH statement. To utilize the foreach semantics, this interface must be implemented.

So the question is, what does this mean for LINQ? It means that a query that implements this interface can be a source for the corresponding query expression. You saw several examples of this at the beginning of this chapter, and the best way to understand the LINQ technology is to see it in action.

The following example utilizes LINQ, a few standard query operators, and the IEnumerable<T> interface to query and process the contents within a defined array:

```
private void ShowLINQ()
{
  string[] firstnames = { "Scott", "Steve", "Ken", "Joe", "John",
                    "Alex", "Chuck", "Sarah"};

  IEnumerable<string> val = from fn in firstnames
                        where fn.StartsWith("S")
                        select fn;

  foreach (string name in val)
  {
    Console.WriteLine(name);
  }
}
```

The first statement defines an array of first names. This should not be new to any developer. The next statement, however, is new. A local variable, val in this case, is initialized with a Language Integrated Query expression. The query expression contains two query operators taken from plethora of standard query operators. In this example, two operators are used: where and select. The local variable val exposes the IEnumerable<string> interface, which provides the capability to iterate through the collection. The results are actually created as you start to iterate through them via the foreach statement.

From here, the query can be modified to add sorting or additional filtering as well as many other options, but that will be expanded on in later chapters. For now, suffice it to say that via LINQ you can query various source data types, such as XML and relational data, through a standard and consistent query model and related query operators.

To illustrate this, let's modify the directory example from earlier in this chapter. One of the great things about LINQ is that it enables you easily to "map" object-oriented objects within your .NET programming language to a database and the objects within a relational database. That means you can access those relational objects in a strongly typed, object-oriented manner.

To do this, a mapping to the database needs to be made, and that is accomplished by creating and declaring two classes. Those classes map the relational objects into the object-oriented world. The first class maps the actual database:

```
[Database(Name="AdventureWorks")]
public class AdventureWorks : DataContext
{
    public AdventureWorks(string connection) : base(connection) {}
    public Table<DirectoryInformation> DirectoryInformation;
}
```

The second class maps the table and columns of the table you want to access:

```
[Table(Name="DirectoryInformation")]
public class DirectoryInformation
{
    [Column(DbType="varchar(50)")]
    public string DirectoryName;

    [Column(DbType = "varchar(255)")]
    public string DirectoryDescription;
}
```

The class name maps to the table in the database you want to access, and the columns are mapped by adding metadata to a couple of variables.

This example is just to whet your appetite. There's not a lot of explanation here because there are more than a handful of chapters that discuss object mapping and querying in much greater detail.

Once the mapping is complete, the data can be queried. And not just queried, but queried using strongly typed syntax.

The first line of the following code accesses the database as an object, creating a new instance of the class previously defined, a strongly typed connection. Once you have the connection, you can access the table and data in a strongly typed fashion, as shown in the second and third lines. Notice that the columns in the table are accessed via dot notation directly in C#.

```
AdventureWorks db = new AdventureWorks("Integrated Security=sspi");

foreach (var item in db.DirectoryInformation)
    listBox1.Items.Add(item.DirectoryName + "   " +
item.DirectoryDescription);
```

Executing this code returns the data from the DirectoryInformation table and lists both the directory name and description in a list box.

To make it more interesting, take the directory example from the beginning of the chapter and modify it to join to this query. You'll recall that the code in the earlier example simply queried the DirectoryInfo class to return the directories on your local C drive. Combining it with this query, you join the Name property of the DirectoryInfo class to the DirectoryName column from the DirectoryInformation table to return the `DirectoryDescription` information from the table. Just add the following highlighted code to the earlier query:

```
DirectoryInfo di = new DirectoryInfo("C:\\");

var query =
    from dir in di.GetDirectories()
    orderby di.Name
    select new
    {
        dir.Name,
        DirectoryDescription = (
        from d in db.DirectoryInformation
        where d.DirectoryName == di.Name
        select d.DirectoryDescription).FirstOrDefault()
    };

foreach (var item in query)
    listBox1.Items.Add(item.Name + "   " + item.DirectoryDescription);
}
```

To run this example, you first need to create a table in a database. The example used the AdventureWorks database and the following code to create the table:

```
CREATE TABLE [dbo].[DirectoryInformation](
    [DirectoryName] [varchar](50) NULL,
    [DirectoryDescription] [varchar](255) NULL
) ON PRIMARY

GO
```

You can use the following `INSERT` statement to add data to the `DirectoryInformation` table:

```
INSERT INTO DirectoryInformation (DirectoryName, DirectoryDescription)
    VALUES ('Windows', 'My Windows Directory')
GO
```

Before continuing, think about the amount of code you would have had to write to accomplish the same type of query in pre-LINQ technology. In the space of about two dozen lines, you were able to access data, query that data, and loop through that data simply and efficiently. In other technologies, you would have had to create a connection to the database, create an instance of a `SqlCommand` object and any other objects needed to execute a query, and write T-SQL code in your .NET code enclosed in quotation marks And that's not to mention all the work that has to be done once you get the data back—casting to the appropriate data types, and so on.

The good news is that LINQ does all of that for you. Sweet! And we haven't even covered XML yet.

Standard Query Operators

The LINQ standard query operators make up an API that provides the means of querying various data sources, such as arrays, collections, and even XML and relational data. They are a set of methods that are implemented by each specific LINQ provider (LINQ to SQL, LINQ to XML, LINQ to Objects, and so on). The operators form a LINQ query pattern that operates on a sequence (an object that implements the IEnumerable<T> or IQueryable<T> interface).

There are two sets of standard query operators—one operates on objects of the IEnumerable<T> type and the other operates on objects of the IQueryable<T> type. The operators are made up of methods that are static members of the Enumerable and Queryable classes, allowing them to be called using static method syntax of instance method syntax. You will learn all about this in Chapter 4.

The standard query operators can be categorized by their operation "type." For example, there are aggregate, projection, ordering, and grouping operators, among others. Take a look again at one of the examples used earlier in the chapter (repeated here for your convenience):

```
private void ShowLINQ()
{
  string [] firstnames = { "Scott", "Steve", "Ken", "Joe", "John",
                 "Alex", "Chuck", "Sarah"};

  IEnumerable<string> val = from fn in firstnames
                 where fn.StartsWith("S")
                 select fn;

  foreach (string name in val)
  {
    Console.WriteLine(name);
  }
}
```

The actual LINQ query is the middle part:

```
val = from fn in firstnames
  where fn.StartsWith("S")
  select fn;
```

In this example, several query operators are utilized from different operation types. The select query operator falls into the category of projection operators, and performs a projection over a sequence, an object that implements the IEnumerable<T> for a given type. In this case, the select operator enumerates the source sequence of first names.

```
select fn;
```

The where query operator is of the restriction operator type—in fact, it is the only operator of that type. Just like T-SQL, the LINQ where operator filters a sequence. In the preceding example, it filters the sequence by limiting the results returned to only those whose name begins with the letter S.

```
where fn.StartsWith("S")
```

If you are trying this example out yourself, create a new Windows Forms project and place a list box on the form. In the Load event of the form, place the following code:

```
string [] firstnames = { "Scott", "Steve", "Ken", "Joe", "John",
               "Alex", "Chuck", "Sarah"};
```

```
IEnumerable<string> val = from fn in firstnames
                         where fn.StartsWith("S")
                         select fn;

foreach (string name in val)
{
  listbox1.Items.Add(name);
}
```

Press F5 to run the app. When the form loads and is displayed, the list box should be populated with the names of Scott, Steve, and Sarah. Now try changing the where clause, change the capital *S* to a lowercase *s* and rerun the app. Do you get results? Why not? If you haven't figured out why, Chapter 3, "LINQ queries," will explain it.

Chapters 3 and 4 go deeper into LINQ and the standard query operators, so don't worry about understanding everything there is to know about LINQ just yet. This section was simply to whet your appetite. The following sections discuss LINQ to XML, which uses LINQ to query XML data, and LINQ to SQL, which uses LINQ to query relational data.

LINQ to XML Overview

LINQ to XML, or XLINQ, is the XML integration of the Language Integrated Query. LINQ to XML utilizes the standard query operators to provide the ability to query XML data. Also at your disposal are operators that provide functionality akin to XPath, letting you navigate up and down and navigate XML tree nodes such as descendants and siblings seamlessly and efficiently.

If you have ever used, and disliked, the DOM, you will love LINQ to XML. The great thing about LINQ to XML is that it provides a small-footprint, in-memory version of the XML document that you are querying. LINQ to XML utilizes the XML features of the System.Xml namespace, specifically the reader and writer functionality exposed by the System.Xml namespace.

LINQ to XML exposes two classes that help LINQ integrate with XML: XElement and XAttribute. The XElement class represents an XML element and is used in LINQ to XML to create XML element nodes or even to filter out the data you really care about. XElement ties itself to the standard query operators by enabling you to write queries against non-XML sources and even persist that data to other sources.

The XAttribute class is a name/value pair associated with an XML element. Each XElement contains a list of attributes for that element, and the XAttribute class represents an XML attribute. Within LINQ, both the XElement and XAttribute types support standard syntax construction, meaning that developers can construct XML and XML expressions using the syntax that they already know.

The following example uses the XElement to construct a simple XML document. The first XElement defines the outer node while the two inner XElement parameters define the two inner nodes of FirstName and LastName.

```
var x = new XElement("Employee",
          new XElement("FirstName", "Scott"),
          new XElement("LastName","Klein"));

var s - x.ToString();
```

Here are the results of this code:

```
<Employee>
  <FirstName>Scott</FirstName>
  <LastName>Klein</LastName>
</Employee>
```

You'll notice the use of var in the previous example. The var keyword tells the compiler to infer the type of the variable from the expression on the right side of the statement. The var keyword will be discussed in detail in Chapter 2, "A Look at Visual Studio 2008".

Also notice in the previous example how much easier the code is to read. The code actually follows the structure of an XML document, so you can see what the resulting XML document will look like.

The next example uses the XAttribute type to add an attribute to the XML:

```
var x = new XElement("Employee",
            new XAttribute("EmployeeID", "15"),
            new XElement("FirstName", "Scott"),
            new XElement("LastName","Klein"));

var s - x.ToString();
```

And here are the results from it:

```
<Employee Employee="15">
  <FirstName>Scott</FirstName>
  <LastName>Klein</LastName>
</Employee>
```

While the capability to easily define the contents of the XML is cool, the real power comes from the ability to pass an argument that is not user-defined but in reality comes from an outside source, such as a query, which can be enumerated and turned into XML via the standard query operators. For example, the following takes the array of names from the first example and uses that as the source of the query for which to construct XML:

```
string [] firstnames = { "Scott", "Steve", "Ken", "Joe", "John",
                         "Alex", "Chuck", "Sarah"};

var r = new XElement("Friends",
            from fn in firstnames
            where fn.StartsWith("S")
            select new XElement("Name", fn))
textbox1.Text = rToString();
```

Here are the results from this code:

```
<Friends>
  <Name>Scott</Name>
  <Name>Steve</Name>
  <Name>Sarah</Name>
</Friends>
```

This isn't to say that I only have friends whose first names begin with the letter *S*, but you get the idea. This query returns a sequence of XElements containing the names of those whose first name begins with the letter *S*. The data comes not from a self-generated XML document but an outside source, in this case the array of first names. However, the data could just as easily come from a relational database or even another XML document.

What XElement enables you to do is query non-XML sources and produce XML results via the utilization of the XElements in the body of the select clause, as shown earlier. Gnarly.

The object of these simple examples is to illustrate the basic concepts of LINQ to XML and the great power, flexibility, and ease with which XML can be manipulated. Note that the same standard query operators were used to generate the XML document in this example as in the first one. Nothing had to be changed in the query really, other than using the types to help integrate LINQ with XML to build the resulting XML. Yet the query operators remained the same, as did the overall syntax of the query expression. This way is much better than trying to figure out XQuery or XPath, working with the DOM or even XSLT. Chapters 10 through 13 cover LINQ to XML in much greater detail.

LINQ to SQL Overview

LINQ to SQL, or DLINQ, is another component in the LINQ technology "utility belt." It provides a mechanism for managing relational data via a run-time infrastructure. The great thing about this is that LINQ still keeps its strong points, such as the ability to query. This is accomplished by translating the Language Integrated Query into SQL syntax for execution on the database server. Once the query has been executed, the tabular results are handed back to the client in the form of objects that you as a developer have defined.

If you have been following the LINQ talk, you already know that LINQ to SQL is the next version of ADO.NET. This is great news, and by the time you are done with this section and the section on LINQ to SQL later in the book, you will surely know why. LINQ takes advantage of the information produced by the SQL schema and integrates this information directly into the CLR (Common Language Runtime) metadata. Because of this integration, the definitions of the SQL tables and views are compiled into CLR types, making them directly accessible from within your programming language.

For example, the following defines a simple schema based on the Person.Contact table from the AdventureWorks database:

```
[Table(Name="Person.Contact")]
public class Contact
{
  [Column(DBType = "nvarchar(50) not null")]
  public string FirstName;
  [Column(DBType = "nvarchar(50) not null")]
  public string LastName;

  [Column(DBType = "nvarchar(50) not null")]
  public string EmailAddress;

}
```

Once this schema is defined, a query can be issued. This is where LINQ comes in. Using the standard query operators, LINQ translates the query from its original query expression form into a SQL query for execution on the server:

```
private void button5_Click(object sender, EventArgs e)
{
  DataContext context = new DataContext("Initial
Catalog=AdventureWorks;Integrated
    Security=sspi");

  Table<Contact> contact = context.GetTable<Contact>();

  var query =
      from c in contact
      select new { c.FirstName, c.LastName, c.EmailAddress} ;

  foreach (var item in query)
  listBox1.Items.Add(item.FirstName + " " + item.LastName + " " +
    item.EmailAddress);

}
```

Following are partial results from the query:

```
gustavo Achong gustavo0@adventure-works.com
catherine0@adventure-works.com
kim2@adventure-works.com
humberto0@adventure-works.com
pilar1@adventure-works.com
frances0@adventure-works.com
margaret0@adventure-works.com
carla0@adventure-works.com
jay1@adventure-works.com
```

Obviously there is much more to LINQ to SQL, but the examples here illustrate what it can do and the basic features and fundamental concepts of LINQ to SQL.

If you were to query this table via SQL Query Analyzer or SQL Server Management Studio, you'd know that the Person.Contact table in the AdventureWorks database is 28 rows shy of 20,000, so the preceding list is only the first nine, but you get the idea. How would you filter this query to return only a specific few rows?

Typically I like to wait until the third or fourth chapter to start handing out ''homework assignments,'' but with the background presented in this chapter you should be able to figure this out quite easily. The Person.Contact table has some additional columns that you can use to filter the results. For example, it has a column named Title, which contains values such as ''Mr.'' and ''Ms.'' It also has a column named EmailPromotion, an int datatype with values of 0 through 2.

Your exercise for this chapter is to filter the query on either the Title column or the EmailPromotion column, using a standard query operator, so that the results returned are much less that 20,000. FYI if you are going to use the Title column: some of values of the column are null, so don't query where Title is null.

The goal of LINQ to SQL and its related tools is to drastically reduce the work of the database developer. Chapters 9–13 will discuss LINQ to SQL in much more depth.

Summary

This chapter introduced you to the LINQ project, a set of .NET Framework extensions that extend the C# and Visual Basic .NET programming languages with a native query language syntax that provides standard query, set and manipulation operations.

This chapter began by discussing LINQ and the set of standard query operators that is a combination of SQL query capabilities with the power and flexibility of data manipulation. From there, the topics of LINQ to XML and LINQ to SQL were discussed, which take the power and flexibility of LINQ and apply it to the querying of relational data and XML documents using the same syntax provided by LINQ.

With this foundation, the next chapter will take a look at the next release of Visual Studio by looking at the specific features LINQ supports for Visual Basic 9.0 and C#.

A Look at Visual Studio 2008

Many of the new language features and enhancements in Visual Studio 2008—both in Visual C# and Visual Basic .NET—make many of the LINQ features possible and enable you to take advantage of some of the LINQ capabilities.

Included with the new Visual Studio release are a number of designers that can help developers visually create many aspects of their SQL entity classes and associations. For example, the Object Relational Designer (O/R Designer) provides a visual interface for creating and designing LINQ to SQL entity classes and associations of database objects. The O/R Designer is discussed in Chapter 15, "Advanced LINQ to SQL topics."

Visual Studio 2008 also comes with the DataSet Designer, a visual tool used for creating and manipulating typed DataSets and the associated items of which the datasets are made, providing a visual image of the objects within the DataSets.

LINQ will be released in the next version of Visual Studio and the .NET Framework, currently slated for version 3.5. Because much of the LINQ functionality is based on the new features of the .NET Framework, this chapter explores those features and enhancements that help support LINQ and provide LINQ with the foundation it needs from a language perspective. It looks at the new language-specific features in both C# and Visual Basic .NET.

Visual Studio 2008

Visual Studio has come a long way since its inception in 1997. Visual Studio 97 hit the street with the goals of enabling developers to share and see large projects through a complete development cycle regardless of the different languages and deployment schemes.

That was followed up by Visual Studio 6.0 with its integrated development environment and built-in data designers for architecting large-scale and multi-tier applications, with the goals of supporting distributed and heterogeneous environments and architectures.

Early 2002 saw the launch of the .NET Framework 1.0 and Visual Studio .NET, built on the foundation of XML. Visual Studio .NET was a breath of fresh air with its tool integration, multiple languages, and handful of services and tools all housed within a single development environment, all for the purpose of building and delivering reliable, secure applications in distributed environments. One of the goals with this release was to enable integration with legacy applications so that developers could embrace new tasks while continuing to work and support old projects. With its emphasis on XML, Visual Studio .NET focused extremely hard on gathering and massaging data from a variety of sources independent of the platform.

Within 12 short months developers saw the release of Visual Studio .NET 2003 and the .NET Framework 1.1. This release included support for more data sources and new Internet protocols and an improved framework for architecting and delivering mission-critical systems. New and improved features supporting a myriad of access devices were also included to help solidify a "one-stop-shop" environment for building large-scale applications.

Microsoft then went to work on the next version of Visual Studio, which was released to the public in the fall of 2005. This release included the .NET Framework 2.0, which, together with Visual Studio 2005, focused on developer productivity and flexibility by including tools and mechanisms for building web, Windows, mobile, and Office applications faster and more efficiently than before.

Late in 2006 the .NET Framework 3.0 was released, which boasted a new managed code programming model for Windows. The .NET Framework 3.0 combined the strength of the .NET Framework 2.0 with four new technologies:

- **WPF (Windows Presentation Foundation)**—New technology for building rich content, "Windows Vista"–type user interfaces, and experiences combining application UI and media content.

- **WCF (Windows Communication Foundation)**—New technology for building and deploying reliable, secure, and interoperable connected systems across distributed systems and environments.

- **WF (Windows Workflow Foundation)**—A programming engine for building workflow-enabled applications.

- **WCS (Windows CardSpace)**—Microsoft's technology for managing digital identities.

Today, Visual Studio 2008 focuses on providing developers with a rich experience for Windows Vista, the web, and Office 2008, while continuing to improve its development languages and innovations. Visual Studio 2008 contains a number of new features, including C# and Visual Basic .NET language features, improved data features such as multi-tier support for typed datasets and hierarchical update capabilities, and a web application project model.

However, the most exciting new feature of Visual Studio 2008 (in my opinion) is LINQ, Microsoft's new Language Integrated Query, which extends powerful query capabilities into your favorite .NET programming language.

When you first start Visual Studio 2008 (see Figure 2-1), it looks much like the previous versions of Visual Studio.

On the surface, this might not be very impressive, but did previous versions of Visual Studio let you pick which version of the .NET Framework you wanted to create your projects with? No!

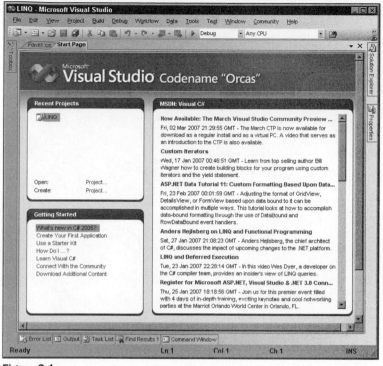

Figure 2-1

When you create a project in the new Visual Studio, you will notice something different in the New Project dialog box (see Figure 2-2), the addition of a "version" button in the top right.

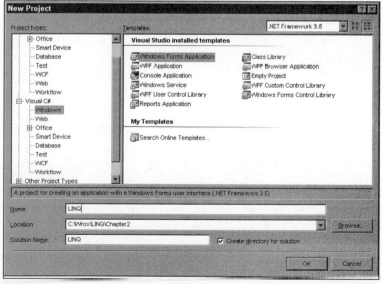

Figure 2-2

This button displays a small context menu that lets you select which version of the .NET Framework you want to create your projects with, as shown in Figure 2-3. How cool is that! As you know, it is possible to have multiple versions of the .NET Framework on your computer, and because different functionality is provided within Visual Studio per the version of the .NET Framework, Microsoft decided it would be extremely helpful to provide a single environment with which to create your applications.

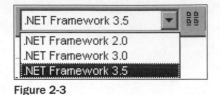

Figure 2-3

Visual Studio 2008 targets .NET 2.0 and later, which means that you won't have to open an instance of Visual Studio 2005 to work with Visual Studio 2005 projects and another instance of Visual Studio 2008 to work with Visual Studio 2008 projects. You can use Visual Studio 2008 to work with both.

To work with .NET 1.1 applications, you will still need to use Visual Studio 2003, since it was targeted for version 1.1 of the .NET Framework.

What is really nice about Visual Studio 2008 is that the appropriate templates change based on the version of the .NET Framework you select. Figure 2-4 shows the templates listed when the .NET Framework 2.0 is selected.

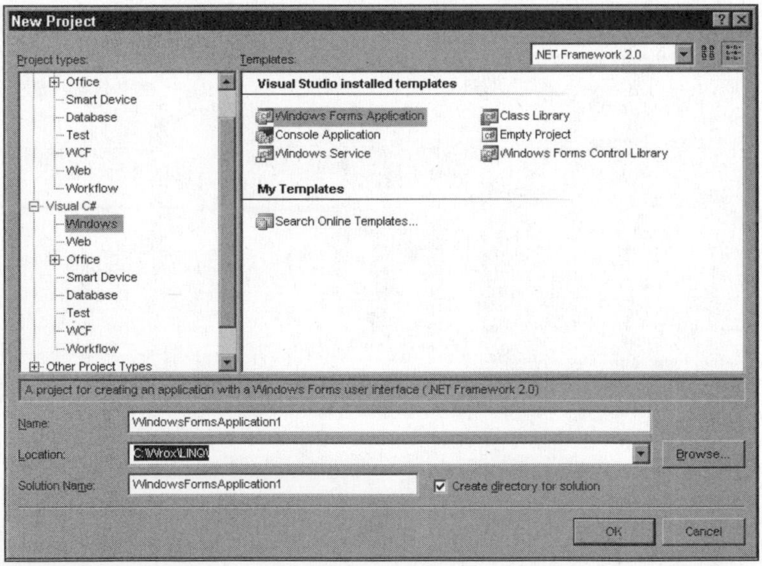

Figure 2-4

As a help, the New Project dialog shows the project description and .NET Framework version directly above the project name box and the list of Project types and Templates. For example, Figure 2-4 lists templates for the .NET Framework 2.0 and lets you know that the Windows Forms Control Library for the .NET Framework 2.0 is selected. Compare that to Figure 2-2, which shows the Windows Forms Application project template selected for the .NET Framework 3.5. Very helpful.

This chapter won't discuss installing Visual Studio, but if you would like to download it and go through the installation yourself, the latest Community Technology Preview (CTP) build can be found at the following location:

```
http://msdn2.microsoft.com/en-us/vstudio/aa700831.aspx
```

Now let's take a look at the new language specific features found in Visual Studio 2008.

Language-Specific LINQ Features

As stated previously, Visual Studio 2008 supports the Language Integrated Query, which is the capability for C# and Visual Basic .NET to support query syntax and supported constructs directly in the programming language. There are many benefits to this, including compile-time checking, elimination of syntax errors, and type safety.

The new language constructs found in both the C# and Visual Basic .NET languages make a lot of the LINQ functionality possible. Therefore, before this book really digs into the LINQ query language and standard query operators, the rest of this chapter discusses these new language features to better help you understand LINQ.

Query Expressions

Query expressions are the heart and soul of the LINQ technology. They are what describe the operations on the data source. Chapter 3, "LINQ Queries," tackles LINQ query expressions in great detail, so this section provides an overview of query expressions so that you can understand the full breadth in the next chapter.

Query expressions are the code that you write, using the standard query operators, to access, sort, and filter data, regardless of where the data comes from. They are written using a declarative query syntax, which was introduced in C# 3.0.

The data can come from an in-memory source, a relational database, or XML, as you saw in the examples in Chapter 1, "Project LINQ." If you've worked with SQL syntax, query expressions should look familiar to you simply because declarative syntax looks very reminiscent of SQL syntax.

From the example in Chapter 1, look at the following highlighted query expression:

```
DataContext context =
  new DataContext("Initial Catalog=AdventureWorks;Integrated Security=sspi");

Table<Contact> contact = context.GetTable<Contact>();

var query =
    from c in contact
    select new { c.FirstName, c.LastName, c.EmailAddress} ;
```

Query expressions must follow a specific format for specific reasons. Those reasons are explained in detail in Chapter 3; for now, suffice it to say that a query expression must begin with a `from` clause and end with either a `select` clause or a `groupby` clause.

C#

In C#, a query expression is written as follows:

```
IEnumerable<string> val = from fn in firstnames
                          where fn.StartsWith("S")
                          select fn;
```

In this example, the query expression starts with the `from` clause informing the query expression where to retrieve its data. It includes a filter expression (the `where` clause), and ends with a `select` clause, which projects (selects) the data gathered in the `from` clause.

Visual Basic

The following shows the previous example in Visual Basic .NET syntax:

```
Dim val As IEnumerable(Of String) = From fn in firstname _
                                    Where fn.StartsWith("S") _
                                    Select fn
```

Implicitly Typed Variables

Finally! Where has this been, I have to ask! Until now, you have had to explicitly specify a type when declaring and initializing a variable. No more. Now you can infer the type assignment by simply using the `var` keyword, as shown in the following examples.

C#

In C#, variables are implicitly typed as follows:

```
var firstname = "Scott";
var age = 28; //I wish!
var startdate = DateTime.Today;
```

So, why is this important, you ask? Because any variables declared as `var` are equally strongly typed as their explicitly declared counterparts. And, even more importantly, this includes LINQ query expressions. Stay tuned.

Visual Basic

Visual Basic also lets you implicitly type variables, but it does this by inferring the type of the variable from the type of the initialization expression. This is called type inference, which lets Visual Basic 2008 determine the data type of variables that are declared without the `As` clause.

The following shows the previous example in Visual Basic .NET syntax:

```
Dim firstname = "Scott"
Dim age = 28
Dim startdate = DateTime.Today
```

Anonymous Types

Anonymous types, class types made up of one or more public properties, provide a handy way to temporarily group sets in a query result, eliminating the need to create a named type for each set. Anonymous types are built as you go, built by the compiler with the typed name available only to the compiler.

In LINQ, anonymous types come in handy in the `select` clause of a query expression, returning a subset of properties from each element in the query sequence. They are created via the `new` operator with an object initializer.

C#

This query expression uses the `new` operator along with an object initializer to initialize a new type containing only three properties (`FirstName`, `LastName`, and `EmailAddress`) from the `Contact` object.

```
from c in Contact
select new { c.FirstName, c.LastName, c.EmailAddress};
```

Anonymous types derive directly from the `Object` class as reference types. A compiler assigns the anonymous type a name, and it is not available at the source code level. Anonymous types are no different from any other type as far as the CLR (Common Language Runtime) is concerned.

This might seem a little confusing, but it will all be cleared up when LINQ and query expressions are discussed in detail in Chapter 3.

Visual Basic

Anonymous types, new to Visual Basic for 2008, let you create objects without needing to write a class definition for the data type. In Visual Basic 2008, the compiler generates the class for you. A LINQ query expression uses anonymous types to join or combine columns from a query.

The great thing about anonymous types is that they let you write queries that return any number of columns in any order. The compiler has the responsibility of creating the data types that correspond to the specified properties (columns).

Here's the previous anonymous type example in Visual Basic .NET syntax:

```
From c In contact Select c.FirstName, c.LastName, c.EmailAddress
```

Initializers for Objects and Collections

Initializers for objects and collections provide the capability to initialize objects and collections without the need to explicitly call a constructor. You can use initializers to assign values to an object's properties and fields when the object is created without needing to invoke a constructor first.

Object initializers can be utilized in various forms, including with anonymous types, named types, and nullable types. Here is where LINQ comes into play because LINQ utilizes anonymous types greatly for the simple reason that anonymous types can only be initialized with an object initializer. Why does this come in handy? Because query expressions can manipulate objects of a sequence into an object of a different shape and value.

C#

The following example, taken from Chapter 1, defines a simple schema based on the `Person.Contact` table, consisting of five fields, from the AdventureWorks database.

```
[Table(Name="Person.Contact")]
public class Contact
{
  [Column(DBType = "nvarchar(8) not null")]
  public string Title;

  [Column(DBType = "nvarchar(50) not null")]
  public string FirstName;

  [Column(DBType = "nvarchar(50) not null")]
  public string MiddleName;

  [Column(DBType = "nvarchar(50) not null")]
  public string LastName;

  [Column(DBType = "nvarchar(50) not null")]
  public string EmailAddress;

}
```

With the schema defined, a query can be issued.

```
private void button1_Click(object sender, EventArgs e)
{
  DataContext context = new DataContext("Initial Catalog=AdventureWorks;Integrated
    Security=sspi");

  Table<Contact> contact = context.GetTable<Contact>();

  var query =
      from c in contact
      select new { c.FirstName, c.LastName, c.EmailAddress} ;

  foreach (var item in query)
  listBox1.Items.Add(item.FirstName + " " + item.LastName + " " +
    item.EmailAddress);

}
```

What you want to notice is that although the object (c) contains five fields, the sequence being returned contains only three fields: `FirstName`, `LastName`, and `EmailAddress`. That is the strength of anonymous types, in that you can return a portion of the information in the object.

You can also rename a field in the sequence when using anonymous types. Here's how:

```
var query =
    from c in contact
    select new { c.FirstName, c.LastName, Email = c.EmailAddress} ;
```

```
foreach (var item in query)
    listBox1.Items.Add(item.FirstName + " " + item.LastName + " " +
    item.Email);
```

Chapter 3 discusses this in more detail.

Visual Basic

Object initializers in Visual Basic work the same way as C# initializers. They provide the ability to specify properties for a complex object by using a single expression, and create instances of named and anonymous types.

The following shows the previous anonymous type example in Visual Basic .NET syntax:

```
<Table(Name:="Person.Contact")> _
Public Class Contact

  <Column(DbType:="nvarchar(8) not null")> _
  Public Title As String

  <Column(DbType:="nvarchar(50) not null")> _
  Public FirstName As String

  <Column(DbType:="nvarchar(50) not null")> _
  Public MiddleName As String

  <Column(DbType:="nvarchar(50) not null")> _
  Public LastName As String

  <Column(DbType:="nvarchar(50) not null")> _
  Public EmailAddress As String

End Class

Private Sub Button2_Click(ByVal sender As System.Object, ByVal e As System.EventArgs) _
  Handles Button2.Click

  Dim context As DataContext = New DataContext("Initial
    Catalog=AdventureWorks;Integrated Security=sspi")

  Dim contact As Table(Of Contact) = context.GetTable(Of Contact)()

  Dim query = From c In contact Select c.FirstName, c.LastName, Email =
    c.EmailAddress

  For Each item In query
    ListBox1.Items.Add(item.FirstName & " " & item.LastName & " " & item.Email)
  Next item

End Sub
```

You need to pay close attention to object initializers of named and anonymous types. Their declarations look nearly the same, but they are indeed different and they have different effects. For example, the following illustrates how to initialize a named instance:

```
Dim cont = new Contact with {.FirstName = "Scott"}
```

However, the initializer for an anonymous type cannot include a class name because it has no usable name, as illustrated here:

```
Dim cont = New With {.FirstName = "Scott"}
```

These two declarations do not produce the same result. The first example has a `Contact` class that contains a `FirstName` property that must already exist, and the declaration takes the step of creating an instance of the `Contact` class. In the anonymous example, the compiler defines a new class containing a string property called `FirstName`.

Extension Methods

Extension methods are new to C# 3.0. They provide the capability to extend existing types by adding new methods with no modifications necessary to the type. Calling methods from objects of the extended type within an application using instance method syntax is known as "extending" methods. Extension methods are not instance members on the type.

The key point to remember is that extension methods, defined as static methods, are in scope only when the namespace is explicitly imported into your application source code via the `using` directive. Even though extension methods are defined as static methods, they are still called using instance syntax.

LINQ contains the most common extension methods, more appropriately known as the *standard query operators*. The standard query operators extend the `IEnumerable<T>` and `IQueryable<T>` types.

Extension methods are invoked in your code by using instance method syntax. The intermediate language (IL) generated by the compiler then translates your code into a call on the static method.

C#

To illustrate extension methods, open Visual Studio 2008 and create a new C# Windows project. On Form1, which is shown by default, place a button and a text box. View the code behind the form and add the following to the end of the existing form code:

```
namespace MyExtensionMethods
{
    public static class MyExtensions
    {
        public static int GetWordCount(this System.String mystring)
        {
            return mystring.Split(null).Length;
        }
    }
}
```

This code creates an extension method on the `System.String` class. The code is useless by itself because, like other classes, it is not in scope. So, add the following directive to the top of the form:

```
using MyExtensionMethods;
```

Now you can access the extension method you created earlier. Add the following code to the button's `Click()` event:

```
string sentence = "This is an example of an extension method in .NET";
int wordcount = sentence.GetWordCount();
textbox1.text = wordcount.ToString();
```

Run the project and click the button. The text box shows the value 10.

Let's expand this a little. In every application I've worked on, there's been a need to validate email addresses. Here's how to do that easily with extension methods. Modify the extension method code by adding the following highlighted code:

```
namespace MyExtensionMethods
{
    public static class MyExtensions
    {
        public static int GetWordCount(this System.String mystring)
        {
            return mystring.Split(null).Length;
        }

        public static bool IsValidEmail(this string email)
        {
            Regex exp = new Regex(@"^[\w-\.]+@(|[\w-]+\.)+[\w-]{2,4}$");
            return exp.IsMatch(email);
        }

    }
}
```

Next, replace the code behind the button with the following:

```
DataContext context =
    new DataContext("Initial Catalog=AdventureWorks;Integrated Security=sspi");

Table<Contact> contact - context.GetTable<Contact>();

var query =
    from c in contact
    select new { c.EmailAddress} ;

foreach (var item in query)
    if (item.EmailAddress.IsValidEmail())
    {
        listbox1.Items.Add(item.EmailAddress);
    }
```

Just like the first example, this one simply adds a method onto the string class that validates email addresses. Very slick.

Visual Basic

Extension methods are new to Visual Basic 2008. C# has had them for a while, and fortunately Visual Basic .NET gets them this release. In Visual Basic .NET, extension methods are accessed via the `System.Runtime.CompilerServices` namespace, so be sure to include the appropriate `Imports` statement. Extension methods can be a Sub or a Function and must be tagged with the `<Extension()>` attribute.

The following shows the extension method from the previous example in Visual Basic .NET syntax:

```
Namespace MyExtensionMethods
    Public Class MyExtensions
        <Extension()>_
        Public Shared Function WordCount(Me ByVal str As System.String) As Integer
            Return str.Split(Nothing).Length
        End Function

        <Extension()>_
        Public Shared Function IsValidEmail(Me ByVal email As String) As Boolean
            Dim exp As Regex = New Regex("^[\w-\.]+@([\w-]+\.)+[\w-]{2,4}$")
            Return exp.IsMatch(email)
        End Function
    End Class
End Namespace
```

Best Practices

Try to implement extension methods only when absolutely necessary and even then, very judiciously. Your best bet is to create a new type that is derived from an existing type. The reason to avoid creating extension methods is that you might run into the scenario where the implementation of the type will cause your extension method to break. That's not good.

If you must implement extension methods, keep in mind the following:

❑   If you define an extension method with the same signature as an existing method defined in the type, your extension method will never be called.

❑   Extension methods are brought into scope at the namespace level.

Lambda Expressions

Lambda expressions and anonymous methods are similar, except for the fact that lambda expressions are much more flexible and provide a more succinct syntax than anonymous methods.

In LINQ, you run into lambda expressions when making a direct query call to the standard query operators. Lambda expressions can be used in LINQ to create the delegates that will be invoked when the query is executed later. When writing LINQ queries and calling standard query operators directly, you only need to use method syntax to write lambda expressions.

Lambda expressions use what is called the lambda operator, which is =>. This operator means "goes to," and signifies that the left side of the lambda operator specifies any input parameters while the right side contains the expression or statement block.

Here's a simple C# example of a lambda expression:

```
y => y * 2
```

This reads as "y goes to y times 2." The body of a lambda expression can consist of any number of statements, but typically you want to keep it to two or three, mainly for readability and to keep it from becoming overly complex. It is also often unnecessary to specify a type for input parameters because the compiler will infer the type based on several factors, such as the body of the lambda expression and the underlying delegate type.

To work with lambda expressions, it is best to follow these general rules:

❑ If the lambda expression returns a value, the return value must be implicitly convertible to the return type of the delegate.

❑ Lambda expressions must contain the same number of parameters as the delegate type.

❑ Each input parameter must be implicitly convertible to the corresponding delegate parameter.

So, given that background, how do lambda expressions work with LINQ? With lambda expressions, a LINQ query can be written as follows:

```
var prodQuery = context.Products.Single(p => p.ProductID == productID);
```

The query also could be written as follows:

```
var proQuery =
    from con in Contacts
    where con.ProductID == productID
    select con;
```

Both of these queries return the same output, but lambda expressions enable you to write the query as an inline expression using method syntax as shown in the first query. In a method-based query, the `where` clause is now expressed as an instance method of the specified object, which in the previous example is the `Products` object.

This example also uses the `Single` standard query operator to return a single element of the sequence. The `p` on the left side of the operator is the input variable that corresponds to the `p` in the query expression.

The return value of a lambda expression is simply the expression result.

Summary

This chapter introduced you to the interface for the new Visual Studio and explored the new features and enhancements that help provide LINQ with the foundation it needs from a language perspective.

The new features and functionality included in version 3.5 of the .NET Framework—including query expressions, implicitly typed variables, anonymous types, and object initializers—play an important role for LINQ.

Chapter 3 discusses LINQ and the LINQ queries in great detail.

3

LINQ Queries

Chapter 1, "Project LINQ," provided a few simple LINQ queries to give you a basic idea of how LINQ queries are formatted and work with relational data, XML, and in-memory data, but to fully grasp the power and flexibility of LINQ requires a real understanding of how LINQ queries work.

Therefore, this chapter and the next dive deep into LINQ queries and the standard query operators. This chapter focuses on the LINQ queries, their overall concepts and syntax, as well as the many options available to you as a developer when creating LINQ queries. Chapter 4, "LINQ Standard Query Operators," tackles the available standard query operators.

LINQ queries are discussed first because a knowledge of the standard query operators really wouldn't be beneficial if you didn't know how to use them effectively in a LINQ query. Given that, this chapter tackles the following:

❑   An introduction to LINQ queries

❑   Query concepts

❑   Query syntax options

Introduction to LINQ Queries

Hopefully, you know what a query is, and have written either a T-SQL query directly in SQL Server, whether it be in a query window in SSMS (SQL Server Management Studio) or a stored procedure, or an "in-line" T-SQL within the code of your application. A query retrieves data, plain and simple. It is a written expression that obtains data from a predetermined data source. The data source could be almost anything, such as a relational database or an XML document.

The problem is that there are many sources of data, and there are just as many query languages to query those data sources. To query a relational database, the SQL query language is required, but if you want to query an XML document, you need to learn the XQuery query language or XPath as well. Wouldn't it be nice to someday have in your possession a single query language with a set of standard query operators that allows for the querying of multiple data sources?

Oh, wait; that day is already here because this is exactly what LINQ is and does. The difference between LINQ and other query languages is in the query actions of a LINQ query operation. With LINQ you work directly with technologies with which you're already familiar (such as objects), and regardless of where the data is coming from, the coding patterns used to create and execute the query remain the same. This consistency is where much of the beauty of LINQ lies. The same standard query operators are used to query and transform data from multiple sources such as XML, relational data, collections, and even DataSets and entities.

The following sections explain the parts of a LINQ query and show you how they are put together and executed. A LINQ query operation contains three distinct and separate actions:

❑ Acquiring the data source

❑ The creation of the query

❑ The execution of the query

Each of these actions is essential to the creation and execution of a LINQ query.

Data Source Acquisition

The data source identifies where the data is coming from in the query. A query is absolutely useless without a data source. What is the use of selecting data if there is no data to select?

The great thing about LINQ is that it doesn't care what the source of data for the query is. The key to being a data source for a LINQ query is that it must support the IEnumerable interface. The following example, taken from the first chapter, shows a string array of names that can be utilized as a data source:

```
string [] firstnames = { "Scott", "Steve", "Ken", "Joe", "John",
                         "Alex", "Chuck", "Sarah"};
```

Your source of data can also come in the form of XML, and if it is not already in memory as a queryable form type, it can become so by being loaded into a queryable XElement type, like this:

```
XElement names = XElement.Load(@"c:\employees.xml");
```

LINQ to XML provides this functionality and, as you have seen previously, lets you query and manipulate XML with ease. You can also build your own XML to manipulate, as shown in the example below, or even write back to the data source.

```
var x = new XElement("Employee", new XElement("FirstName", "Scott"),
            new XElement("LastName","Klein"));
```

If the data source is relational data, LINQ to SQL provides a flexible mechanism to create a relational mapping between it and your query objects. As shown in Chapter 1, an object-relational mapping must first be created, against which your queries are written, but then LINQ to SQL handles all the database communication. Here's the object-relational mapping taken from the example in Chapter 1 to map the Contact.Person table to the application object:

```
[Table(Name="Person.Contact")]
public class Contact
{
    [Column(DBType = "nvarchar(50) not null")]
```

```
    public string FirstName;

    [Column(DBType = "nvarchar(50) not null")]
    public string LastName;

    [Column(DBType = "nvarchar(50) not null")]
    public string EmailAddress;

}
```

Query Creation

Once your data source is defined, the next step is to define the query that specifies the data or information you want to retrieve from the data source. You can also specify how the data should be shaped when it is returned, such as sorted or grouped. The capability to query and shape the data is provided through the new query syntax that is built directly into both C# and Visual Basic.

The standard query operators are a set of methods that form the LINQ (Language Integrated Query) pattern. These operators have dedicated syntax in both C# and Visual Basic that allow them to be called as part of a query expression, a more readable form of writing or expressing a query. The standard query operators, discussed in detail in Chapter 4, provide extensive querying capabilities, which include the ability to sort, group, aggregate, and filter query results.

In LINQ, the query is stored in a variable. If the query returns data, then the query must be a queryable type. Keep in mind that the query variable on its own does not execute the query, does not contain any data, and does not take any other sort of action. It is simply a placeholder for the query, or more accurately put, is an IEnumerable object that, when enumerated, executes the query.

The following query, which implements the IEnumerable interface, defines a variable called val containing a query that selects all first names that begin with the letter S. The data source for this query is the string array mentioned in the previous section.

```
IEnumerable<string> val = from fn in firstnames
                            where fn.StartsWith("S")
                            select fn;
```

The query has not been executed at this point, nor does the variable val contain any data; it contains only the query syntax. Here's another example, taken from the LINQ to SQL example from Chapter 1:

```
var query =
    from c in contact
    select new { c.FirstName, c.LastName, c.EmailAddress} ;
```

Again, the query has not been executed, nor does the variable var contain any data.

The importance of the *query creation* action is to define the query expression and shape the data as you would like it returned.

Query Execution

The last action of the LINQ query operations is query execution. Even though the query expression is defined and stored in a query variable when the query is created, the execution of the query does not typically take place until iteration over the query variable begins. I'll explain "typically" momentarily, but I first want to discuss how a query is executed. As the query is iterated through, only the work necessary to bring back the current result is done. In other words, the entire query is not returned. Each iteration of the query returns the next item in the result.

It has been said previously that neither the query expression itself nor the variable contains query results. That is because the query is executed as you iterate through the variable. Here's the string array example from Chapter 1:

```
string [] firstnames = { "Scott", "Steve", "Ken", "Joe", "John",
                         "Alex", "Chuck", "Sarah"};
IEnumerable<string> val = from fn in firstnames
                          where fn.StartsWith("S")
                          select fn;

foreach (string name in val)
{
   Console.WriteLine(name);
}
```

The first "action" defines the data source. The second "action" defines the query and assigns it to a variable. The last "action," the `foreach` loop (`For Each` in Visual Basic), executes the query by iterating over the variable `val` in the `foreach` loop.

How does this work? Take a look at the `foreach` loop:

```
Foreach (string name in val)
   Console.WriteLine(name);
```

The first time the `foreach` statement is executed, the first call to the `MoveNext()` method causes three things:

1. The query is translated to SQL.
2. The query is executed.
3. The first row is fetched from the underlying DataReader.

For each iteration thereafter, the `MoveNext()` method is called, grabbing the next row from the underlying DataReader, hydrating (queuing) the next object.

The best way to understand this is to see it in action. Take a look at Figure 3-1, which shows the preceding example during code execution. I have stopped the execution of the code on the `foreach` statement on the first iteration.

What you want to look at is the Watch window below the code where I have the `query` variable being watched. Notice the value of the name-value pair named `Results View`. It states, "Expanding the Results View will enumerate the IEnumerable." This tells you that the query has not been executed, that even the internal results have not been iterated through, and that expanding the node will be equivalent to stepping through the `foreach` loop until all the results are received.

So what does *typically* mean? There are two types of query execution: deferred and immediate. In most cases you want to use deferred; however, there are cases when immediate execution is necessary.

The following sections discuss these types and when the use of each is appropriate.

Figure 3-1

Deferred Execution

So far all the examples in this book have shown deferred query execution, which executes the query only when you start to loop through the query variable, such as in a `foreach` loop.

For instance, the following code loops through the variable `val`, which contains the query expression taken from the earlier string array example:

```
foreach (string name in val)
{
   Console.WriteLine(name);
}
```

Deferred execution is appropriate when returning a sequence (multiple values). Because the query (and variable) don't ever contain the query results, you are free to execute (iterate over) this query over and over again with little overhead.

Immediate Execution

Any LINQ query that returns a single value is executed immediately. A single value is considered a query that returns a `Count` or `Max`, for example. You can also force an immediate execution of a query by calling the `ToList` or `ToArray` methods. The following example illustrates a query that returns a single value, thus executing immediately:

```
var query = (from o in Order
            where CustomerID = 2
            select o).Count();
```

This query counts the number of orders from the `Sales.SalesOrderHeader` table in the AdventureWorks database, where the `CustomerID` in that table is 2. Likewise, instead of getting a count of orders, you can also send the query results to a list or array:

```
var query = (from o in Order
            where CustomerID = 2
            select o).ToList();
```

By returning a single value or returning values to an array or value list, you can force an immediate execution of the query, which can be useful when you want the results of the query to be cached.

Likened to SQL Syntax

To help you understand the flow of the LINQ syntax, compare it to standard T-SQL syntax. If you have written any T-SQL, you know the basic T-SQL query syntax and how it is written. For instance, a simple query looks like this:

```
SELECT FirstName, LastName
FROM Person.Contact
```

This example queries the `Person.Contact` table in the AdventureWorks database and returns the `First-Name` and `LastName` columns for each row in the table. Too simple really, so the following adds a secondary table, applies a filter, and applies a sort:

```
SELECT E.EmployeeID,C.FirstName, C.LastName
FROM Person.Contact AS C
INNER JOIN HoumanResources.Employee AS E ON C.ContactID = E.ContactID
WHERE E.EmployeeID < 100
ORDER BY C.LastName
```

This is the syntax with which all T-SQL developers are familiar. At the very minimum the query begins with a `SELECT` clause, which specifies the columns you want to be returned by the query, followed by a `FROM` clause, which lists the tables and/or views containing the columns identified in the `SELECT` clause.

The query could include one or more joins such as an `INNER JOIN` or `OUTER JOIN`, followed by some filtering using the `WHERE` clause and possibly a `GROUP BY` or `HAVING` clause, and quite possibly some ordering using the `ORDER BY` clause.

How many developers have really stopped to think about how SQL Server processes these queries? Does SQL Server execute the query from top to bottom, starting with the `SELECT` clause and working its way down? You might think that, but that is not how a query is processed in SQL Server at all. SQL Server logically processes a query in the following order:

```
(8)  SELECT
(9)  TOP
(1)  FROM
(3)  JOIN
(2)  ON
(4)  WHERE
(5)  GROUP BY
(6)  WITH
(7)  HAVING
(10) ORDER BY
```

Notice that the `FROM` clause is processed first, while the `SELECT` clause is processed almost last. Any clause that is not specified in the query is simply skipped by the query-processing engine. So, why is this information important?

It points out the similarities between a LINQ query syntax and how SQL Server processes a query. You have seen many times now the basic syntax of a LINQ query:

```
from c in contact
where c.FirstName.StartsWith("S")
orderby c.LastName
select c
```

The LINQ query and the T-SQL query are executed similarly, although the T-SQL query syntax is different. This same query in T-SQL would be the following:

```
SELECT FirstName, LastName, EmailAddress
FROM Contact
WHERE LEFT(FirstName, 1) = 'S'
ORDER BY LastName
```

The differences are that in SQL this query would be executed internally, following the steps described earlier. With LINQ, the query does not need to go through the rewriting process. Also, the same LINQ operators work against other data sources.

With this in mind, the next section explores query operations and expressions to help you more fully understand LINQ query concepts.

Query Concepts

You have seen multiple examples of LINQ queries so far in this book. Now you'll explore the basic layout and syntax, as well as the different kinds of operations that can take place in a query. (Chapter 4 discusses in detail the many standard query operators that are at your disposal when writing LINQ query expressions.) For this discussion, the following query will be used:

```
from c in contact
where c.FirstName.StartsWith("S")
orderby c.LastName
select c
```

In a LINQ query, the first clause is `from`, which specifies the source of the data. It is called a generator, and defines where the data will be coming from when the query is executed. It also specifies a range variable that is used as a reference for each element in the data source. In the following example, `contact` is the data source and `c` is the range variable:

```
from c in contact
```

The `where` clause enables you to filter the results being returned by the query. By applying a filter to the query, you're not only limiting the number of rows returned, but you are specifying the rows you want to see, or exclude, from the returned results. For example, the following returns only those contacts whose first name begins with the letter *S*:

```
where c.FirstName.StartsWith("S")
```

Recall from Chapter 1 that you selected all the rows from the `Person.Contact` table in the AdventureWorks database—the table had nearly 20,000 rows. By simply applying this filter to the LINQ query, the number of rows returned is just over 1,200—quite a difference.

It is possible to apply multiple filters by using the logical operators AND and OR. In C# using AND (&&) looks like the following:

```
where c.FirstName.StartsWith("S")
   && c.LastName.StartsWith("A")
```

In Visual Basic, it looks like this:

```
Where c.FirstName.StartsWith("S")
   AND c.LastName.StartsWith("A")
```

The OR (||) operator works the same way:

```
where c.FirstName.StartsWith("S")
   || c.LastName.StartsWith("A")
```

And in Visual Basic:

```
Where c.FirstName.StartsWith("S")
   OR c.LastName.StartsWith("A")
```

The `where` clause is optional when writing a LINQ query, as is the `orderby` clause. The `orderby` clause provides the capability to order (sort) the results returned by the execution of the query. The following sorts the results by last name:

```
orderby c.LastName
```

By default, the sort is applied in ascending order. To reverse the sort (descending order), simply apply the `descending` clause:

```
orderby c.LastName descending
```

You can sort by more than one property:

```
orderby c.LastName, c.FirstName
```

In Visual Basic, the `orderby` clause reads:

```
Order By c.LastName Descending
```

You can also group the results of the query based on one of the properties of the query. For example, the following line groups the results of the query by contact country:

```
group c by c.Country
```

The final step is to project (select) the data using the `select` clause. By *projecting* the data, you are defining the results as something other than a simple copy of the original source. For example, if the data source returns `FirstName`, `LastName`, `EmailAddress`, `Title`, `MiddleName`, and `City`, but the `select` clause only produces the `FirstName` and `LastName` properties in the results, that is a projection.

The `select` clause enables you to determine the shape of each object that is returned by the query. Here's an example that returns the entire collection object:

```
from c in contact
where c.FirstName.StartsWith("S")
orderby c.LastName
select c
```

To select a single property, simply select that property, like this:

```
from c in contact
where c.FirstName.StartsWith("S")
orderby c.LastName
select c.LastName
```

Selecting a single result (column/property), in this case a string value, changes the result type from an `IEnumerable` collection of type `contact` in the first example to an `IEnumerable` of `String` in this example because only a single string value is being returned. In other words, just the `LastName` property (column) is being returned in the collection.

To select multiple values (but not the entire collection), you can use one of two methods. The first is to use `IEnumerable` by defining a named type and using that named type to create each source object in the `select` clause. First, the named type must be created.

```
struct data
{
  public string FN;
  public string LN;
  public string EA;
}
```

That named type is then used in the creation and initialization of the `IEnumerable` query:

```
IEnumberable<data> query = from c in contact
where c.FirstName.StartsWith("S")
&& c.LastName.StartsWith("A")
orderby c.LastName
select new data { LN = c.FirstName, FN = c.LastName, EA = c.EmailAddress}
```

At this point you can iterate through the query like this:

```
foreach (var item in query)
  listbox1.Items.Add(item.FN + " " + item.LN + " " + item.EA);
```

The other option is to create an anonymous type using the `var` keyword:

```
var query = from c in contact
where c.FirstName.StartsWith("S")
orderby c.LastName
select new {FN = c.FirstName, LN = c.LastName, EA = c.EmailAddress}
```

This query can be iterated through as follows:

```
foreach (var item in query)
  listbox1.Items.Add(item.FN + " " + item.LN + " " + item.EA);
```

You can also do the following, which defaults to creating an anonymous type using the same member names as the properties that you reference in the query:

```
var query = from c in contact
where c.FirstName.StartsWith("S")
orderby c.LastName
select new {c.FirstName, c.LastName, c.EmailAddress}
```

This query can be iterated through as follows:

```
foreach (var item in query)
  listbox1.Items.Add(item.FirstName + " " + item.LastName + " " + item.EmailAddres);
```

Basically, using

```
select new {c.FirstName, c.LastName, c.EmailAddress}
```

is a shortcut for

```
select new {FirstName = c.FirstName, LastName = c.LastName,
  EmailAddress = c.EmailAddress}
```

This, then, begs the question, "What is the difference between a named type and an anonymous type?" Hang tight, because var and IEnumerable differences are explained in the next section.

First, what about join operations? That is certainly doable and is accomplished via the join clause:

```
from c in contact
join o in orders on c equals o.OrderID
where c.FirstName.StartsWith("S")
orderby c.LastName
select new {c.FirstName, c.LastName, c.EmailAddress, o.OrderDate}
```

OK, with all of that under your belt, the following section will clear up the confusion between var and IEnumerable.

Var versus IEnumerable

The var keyword is new to C# 3.0 and enables you to implicitly declare variables at the method scope. The great thing about it is that the implicitly typed variable is just as strongly typed as its explicitly declared counterpart. For example, these variables

```
var blah = "S"
var moreblah = 50
```

are equivalent to the following:

```
string blah = "S"
int moreblah = 50
```

In the early days, the word "var" stood for variant. Today, that isn't the case; in C# and VB.NET, var is a specific keyword that, when used, tells the compiler to determine the exact type of the variable.

The `IEnumerable<T>` interface, new in .NET Framework 2.0, supports a simple iteration over a collection of a specified type. It exposes the `IEnumerator<T>` interface, which is the base interface for all generic enumerators. LINQ takes advantage of this enumeration via the `foreach` statement, which lets you iterate through an enumeration without the complexity of dealing with and manipulating the enumerator directly.

`IEnumerable` is minimal in its functionality, however. It has forward-only movement in a collection, so moving back and forth among data items is not possible with `IEnumerable`.

With LINQ, it is important is to know when to use var versus `IEnumerable`. As you saw earlier in this section, var can be used to implicitly declare a variable. While this is optional, it can be overused. The best time to use var is when a variable is initialized with an anonymous type, only because in that scenario it's required. Using var too many times can also make your source code less readable by developers who come in after you. In other words, don't overuse var.

To understand the difference between the two and when one should be used over the other, consider the following two examples. The first query uses var, but it is not necessary because the query result type can be explicitly stated as an `IEnumerable<int>`, meaning that the result types are known.

```
int[] nums = {5, 1, 9, 4, 8, 11, 6, 14, 2, 7};
var query =
    from num in nums
    where num % 2 == 1
    select num;
```

The next example, however, must use var because the result types are not known. The result is a collection of anonymous types. In these cases, the name of the type is not available until the compiler creates it.

```
Var query =
    from prod in Products
    where prod.ProductID = 10021
    select new {prod.ProductName, prod.Price};
```

Common Query Terms

Before you go any further, a few things need to be defined and explained in order to help you get the feel for LINQ queries.

LINQ Providers

A LINQ Provider is a library that implements the functionality provided by the standard query operators for a specific type of data source.

The responsibility of the LINQ Provider is to execute a given query or to hand it to another engine for execution. LINQ has several providers: LINQ to XML, LINQ to Datasets, LINQ to Objects, and LINQ to SQL.

LINQ to SQL is considered a LINQ Provider even though it does not have its own implementation of the standard query operators. Why? As an implementation of the `IQueryable` interface, LINQ to SQL implements the functionality of the standard query operators against relational databases.

Expression Trees

An expression tree is a representation of language-level code in the form of data. The data is stored in a tree-like structure, hence the name.

Expression trees in LINQ are used for several reasons, one of which is to structure queries that utilize data sources that implement IQueryable(Of T). At runtime, when a query is executed, the C# or Visual Basic compiler translates the query expressions (and method-based queries) into code that is then converted to an expression tree structure. The appropriate query provider then translates the structure into the query language for the targeted data source.

As you learned in the previous section, the LINQ to SQL provider implements IQueryable(Of T) for querying relational data stores.

The great thing about expression trees is that, as a developer, you don't need to build one or even negotiate through an expression tree. The traversal of an expression tree is done for you, unless you feel the strong urge to create your own query provider or query language.

As a quick note, expression trees are also used to represent lambda expressions. When a lambda expression is assigned to a variable, a field, or a parameter of type Expression(Of TDelegate), the compiler generates an expression tree which represents the lambda expression. There are several standard query operator methods that have parameters of type Expression(Of TDelegate). Thus, you are able to pass lambda expressions when these methods are called. The compiler will then create an expression tree.

IQueryable and IQueryable(Of T) Interfaces

The IQueryable and IQueryable(Of T) interfaces provide the functionality to evaluate queries for a given data source. The IQueryable interface does this where the type of the data is not known, and the IQueryable(Of T) interface does this where the type of the data is known.

The IQueryable and IQueryable(Of T) interfaces implement the IEnumerable and IEnumerable(Of T) interface, respectively, providing the capability of enumeration over the results of the given query. As you have learned previously, the enumeration causes the expression tree associated with an IQueryable or IQueryable(Of T) object to be executed. Keep in mind that the term "executing an expression tree" is specific to the query provider.

The difference between these two interfaces is that the IQueryable(Of T) interface enables queries to be executed against different types of data sources. These queries are commonly referred to as "polymorphic."

Keep in mind that both the IQueryable and IQueryable(Of T) interfaces are intended for implementation only by query providers. Think of an IQueryable object as having an ADO.NET command object. Having one (either an IQueryable object or a command object) does not insinuate that either the LINQ query (or the command) was executed.

Let's take a close look at each of these to help understand the IQueryable object. An ADO.NET command object contains a property that holds a string that describes the query. The IQueryable object is similar in that it contains a description of a query that is encoded as a data structure known as an expression.

The command object has an ExecuteReader() method that causes execution. The results are returned as a DataReader. Likewise, the IQueryable object has a GetEnumerator method that causes the execution of the query. The results of the query are returned as an IEnumerator.

Query Syntax versus Method Syntax

LINQ provides the ability to write queries using both query syntax and method syntax, and most of the examples until now have used query syntax, which is writing the query as a query expression, like this:

```
IEnumerable<string> query =
    from c in contact
    where c.FirstName.StartsWith("S")
    select c;
```

This declarative syntax is easy to read and understand, but you also have the option of writing your queries using method syntax. When a LINQ query is compiled, the query expression is translated into method syntax because the .NET Common Language Runtime (CLR) really doesn't understand query syntax. Thus, at compile time, query expressions are translated into method calls because this is what the CLR understands.

Here's the method syntax version of the preceding query:

```
IEnumerable<string> query = contact.Where(c => c.FirstName.StartsWith("S"));
```

It is recommended that you use query syntax whenever possible simply because it is easier to read, understand, and maintain. However, as you can see from the two preceding examples, there is no semantic difference between method syntax and query syntax. Therefore, this section discusses both query syntax and method syntax to provide you a good understanding of these syntaxes in queries and how to use them in query expressions.

This next example gets a bit more complicated by adding an additional filter:

```
IEnumerable<string> query =
    from c in contact
    where c.FirstName.StartsWith("S")
    && c.LastName.StartsWith("A")
    select c;
```

The method syntax of this is as follows:

```
IEnumerable<string> query = contact.Where(a => a.FirstName.StartsWith("S") ↵
&& a.LastName.StartsWith("A"));
```

Let's complicate things a bit more and add the Orderby clause:

```
IEnumerable<string> query =
    from c in contact
    where c.FirstName.StartsWith("S")
    && c.LastName.StartsWith("A")
```

```
        Orderby c.LastName
        select c;
```

This query expression would be written as method syntax as follows:

```
    IEnumerable<string> query = contact.Where(c => c.FirstName.StartsWith("S")
        && c.LastName.StartsWith("A")).OrderBy(c => c.LastName);
```

Run both versions of these queries (method syntax and query syntax), and you'll see that the output is identical. What makes the method syntax possible is lambda expressions, which were discussed in Chapter 2, "A Look at Visual Studio 2008."

Although query syntax is recommended over method syntax, there are times when method syntax is preferred, such as in those queries that return the number of elements that match a specified condition.

Which Do You Use?

Given all of the information discussed in this chapter, the question might arise, "Which do I use, query syntax or method syntax?" The general rule is to use whichever syntax will make your code most readable, which most often means using query syntax. However, even this might not be sufficient because there are many reasons why query syntax may not be an option:

❑   Not all of the standard query operators are available in query syntax.

❑   Not all of the combinations of the standard query operators are available in query syntax.

❑   As you will read about later, it is possible to combine query syntax with method syntax, but there may be times when using straight method syntax might be more readable.

It is a matter of learning which standard query operators can be used with which syntax option (query syntax and method syntax) and going from there. However, your priority should always be syntax readability.

For example, the following code snippet shows how to author a query using query syntax.

```
    Int[] grades = { 67, 98, 72, 85, 92, 89, 78, 76, 88};

    IEnumerable<int> topTwoGrades =
        (from g in grades
        orderby g
        select g).Take(2);
```

The following code snippet shows the same query using method syntax.

```
    Int[] grades = { 67, 98, 72, 85, 92, 89, 78, 76, 88};

    IEnumerable<int> topTwoGrades =
        grades.OrderByDescending (g => g).Take(2);
```

Both produce the same results; it is up to you to decide how you want to write the query.

Chapter 4 will discuss all of the standard query operators and provide examples using both query syntax and method syntax where available.

Using Query and Method Syntaxes

Here's a project that utilizes much of the information found in this chapter, such as query syntax and method syntax, to create queries that will be used throughout the rest of this book. To start, you need a place to create the applications used for this chapter.

In the root of your C drive, create a directory called Wrox. Underneath that directory, create another directory called Chapter 3. Now, fire up Visual Studio 2008 and within the Recent Projects window of the Start page, create a new project. This opens the New Project dialog.

In the New Project dialog, make sure that you have selected the correct Framework version (3.5) via the far-left icon in the top-right corner, then select a Windows project type and set the project name to LINQ with the path you just created (\Wrox\Chapter 3). Figure 3-2 shows what the New Project dialog should look like.

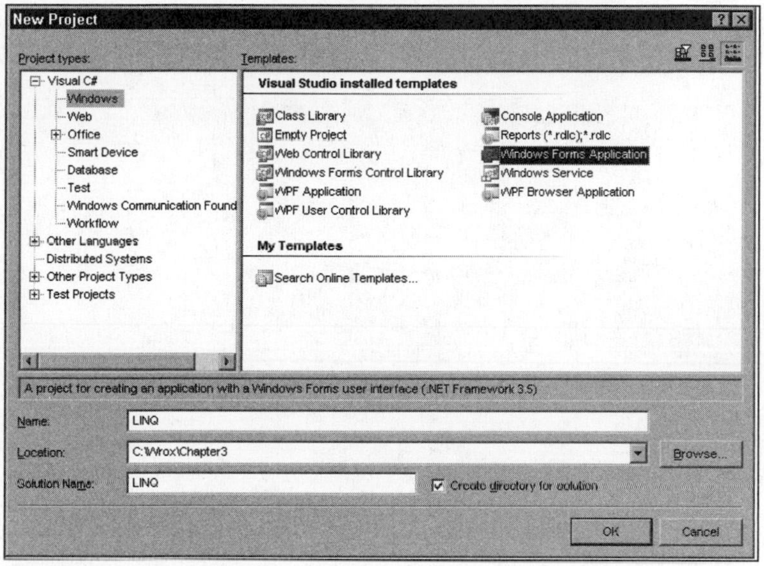

Figure 3-2

Click OK when you have everything set. Next, open the Solution Explorer and add the System.Data and System.Data.Linq namespace references to your project. Then open Form1 in design view and add three buttons and a list box. Align the list box on the left of the form and place two of the buttons next to the list box, with the third button in the bottom-right corner of the form.

Set the properties of the first button to the following:

Property	Value
Name	cmdQuerySyntax
Text	Query Syntax

Set the properties of the second button to the following:

Property	Value
Name	cmdMethodSyntax
Text	Method Syntax

Set the properties of the third button to the following:

Property	Value
Name	cmdClose
Text	Close

Figure 3-3 shows what the form should look like (with the appropriate component references included).

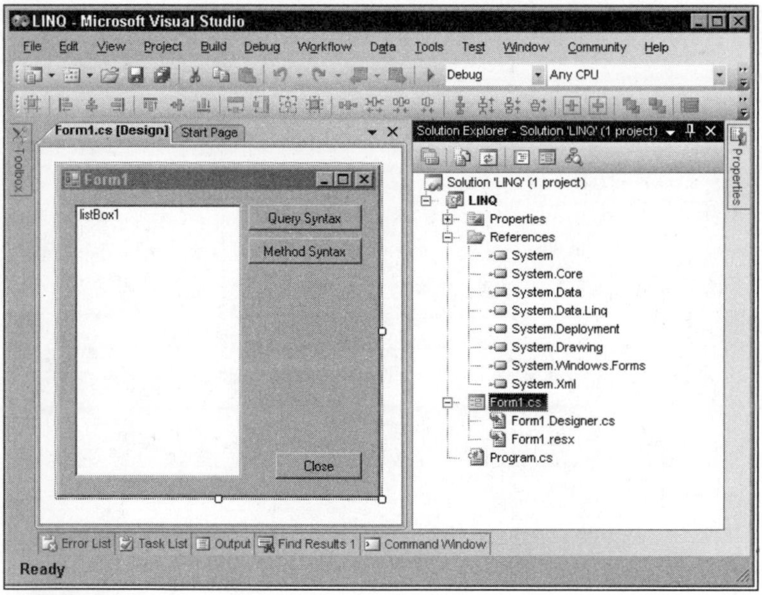

Figure 3-3

Double-click the form to display the code behind the form. In the declarations section, make sure that you add the appropriate `using` statements for LINQ, including `System.Data.Linq`.

Next, underneath the class for `Form1`, add the following:

```
[Table(Name = "Person.Contact")]
public class Contact
{
  [Column(DBType = "nvarchar(8) not null")]
  public string Title;
```

```
[Column(DBType = "nvarchar(50) not null")]
public string FirstName;

[Column(DBType = "nvarchar(50) not null")]
public string MiddleName;

[Column(DBType = "nvarchar(50) not null")]
public string LastName;

[Column(DBType = "nvarchar(50) not null")]
public string EmailAddress;

[Column(DBType = "int")]
public int EmailPromotion;

}
```

That defines the data source, the first of the three actions that makes up a query operation.

Your code behind Form1 should now look like this:

```
using System;
using System.Linq;
using System.Collections.Generic;
using System.ComponentModel;
using System.Data;
using System.Data.Linq;
using System.Drawing;
using System.Text;
using System.Windows.Forms;
using System.Xml;

namespace LINQ
{
    public partial class Form1 : Form
    {
        public Form1()
        {
            InitializeComponent();
        }

        private void Form1_Load(object sender, EventArgs e)
        {
}
    }

    [Table(Name = "Person.Contact")]
    public class Contact
    {
        [Column(DBType = "nvarchar(8) not null")]
        public string Title;

        [Column(DBType = "nvarchar(50) not null")]
        public string FirstName;
```

```
[Column(DBType = "nvarchar(50) not null")]
public string MiddleName;

[Column(DBType = "nvarchar(50) not null")]
public string LastName;

[Column(DBType = "nvarchar(50) not null")]
public string EmailAddress;

[Column(DBType = "int")]
public int EmailPromotion;


    }
}
```

Place the following code in the `click` event for the Close button:

```
Application.Exit();
```

Next, in the `click` event for the Query Method button, place the following code:

```
DataContext context = new DataContext("Initial Catalog=AdventureWorks;↵
Integrated Security=sspi");

Table<Contact> contact = context.GetTable<Contact>();

var query =
  from c in contact
  where c.FirstName.StartsWith("S")
  && c.LastName.StartsWith("K")
  orderby c.LastName
  select c;

foreach (var item in query)
  listBox1.Items.Add(item.FirstName + " " + item.LastName + " " +
    item.EmailAddress);
```

This code creates a query expression filtering all contacts whose first name begins with the letter *S* and whose last name begins with the letter *K*, all sorted by the contacts' last name. You know this is an anonymous query expression because of the use of the `var` keyword discussed previously.

A portion of the preceding code defines the second and third actions of a query operation. The query expression (the second action) defines the information to be retrieved from the data source, while the execution of the query (the iteration over the query variable) is the last action.

Press F5 to compile and run the application. When the form opens, click the Query Syntax button. The list box will populate with the first names, last names, and email addresses of those contacts who meet the criteria specified in the query expression. The results on your form should look like those in Figure 3-4.

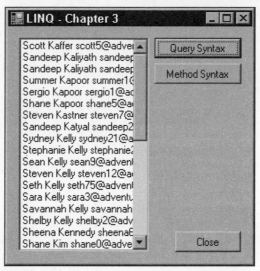

Figure 3-4

In this example, the `select` clause in the query expression did not select individual properties from the query results, but rather selected all the properties by simply stating `select c`. This is similar to stating `SELECT * FROM` in T-SQL syntax. Because all the properties were selected to be returned, all properties are available from IntelliSense, as shown in Figure 3-5.

```
private void cmdQuerySyntax_Click(object sender, EventArgs e)
{
    DataContext context = new DataContext("Initial Catalog=AdventureWorks;Integra

    Table<Contact> contact = context.GetTable<Contact>();

    var query =
        from c in contact
        where c.FirstName.StartsWith("S")
        && c.LastName.StartsWith("K")
        orderby c.LastName
        select c;

    foreach (var item in query)
        listBox1.Items.Add(item.FirstName
            + " " + item.LastName
            + " " + item.);
                        EmailAddress
                        EmailPromotion
                        Equals
}                       FirstName
                        GetHashCode
private void cmdMethod    GetType         ject sender, EventArgs e)
{                        LastName
    DataContext contex    MiddleName      text("Initial Catalog=AdventureWorks;Integra
                         Title
    Table<Contact> con   ToString         GetTable<Contact>();
```

Figure 3-5

Modify the following code, changing the `select` clause in the query expression as highlighted:

```
var query =
    from c in contact
    where c.FirstName.StartsWith("S")
    && c.LastName.StartsWith("K")
    orderby c.LastName
    select new { c.FirstName, c.LastName, c.EmailAddress};
```

Running this anonymous query produces the same results on the form when the application is run, but in this code, specific properties are selected to be returned in the query. An anonymous query type is created using the same names as the properties in the object initializer.

Thus, IntelliSense shows only those properties that are available for selection, as shown in Figure 3-6.

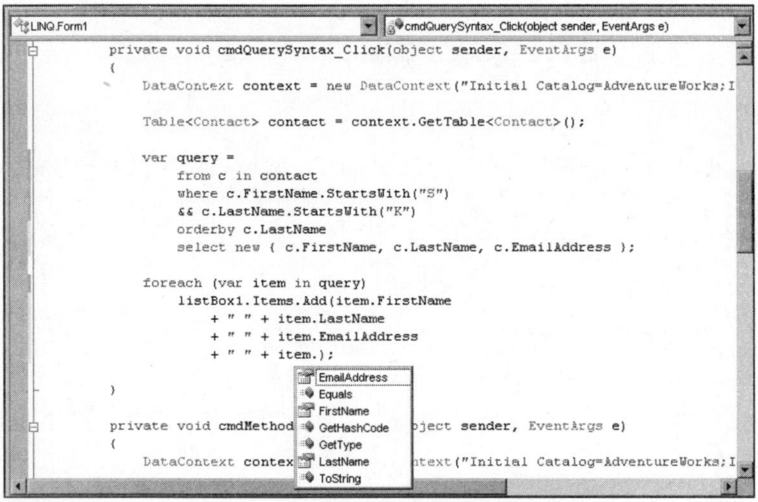

Figure 3-6

Next, add the following code to the `Click()` event behind the Method syntax button.

```
DataContext context = new DataContext("Initial Catalog=AdventureWorks;↵
Integrated Security=sspi");

Table<Contact> contact = context.GetTable<Contact>();

IEnumerable<Contact> query =
    contact.Where(a => a.FirstName.StartsWith("S")
                && a.LastName.StartsWith("K")).OrderBy(a => a.LastName);
foreach (var item in query)
    listBox1.Items.Add(item.FirstName + " " + item.LastName + " " +
    item.EmailAddress);
```

Press F5 to compile and run the application. When the form opens, click the Method Syntax button. The list box will be populated with the first names, last names, and email addresses of those contacts who meet the criteria specified in the query expression. The results on your form should look like the results that were returned in the first example (shown in Figure 3-4).

This `IEnumerable` example can also be written to use automatic type deduction using the `var` keyword as follows:

```
var query =
    contact.Where(a => a.FirstName.StartsWith("S")
    && a.LastName.StartsWith("K")).OrderBy(a => a.LastName);
```

Each of these examples contains the three actions that make up a query operation. Those of you who have read any of my previous books already know that I like to assign small "homework assignments," which build on the examples of the current chapter.

Your homework assignment for this chapter is fairly simple. Start experimenting with the differences between query syntax and method syntax, as well as with the different query expressions available. A lot of this will be useful in the upcoming chapters.

Summary

This chapter gave you with a first-hand look at LINQ queries, their concepts, and the available syntax options. You got a detailed look at the three actions that make up a query operation: the data source, the query expression, and the execution of the query (and the different types of query execution, such as deferred and immediate). Each is a distinct and separate action critical to the success of the LINQ query.

You also looked at SQL syntax and saw how its execution is likened to LINQ syntax. Then you explored LINQ query concepts, from specifying the data source to filtering, grouping, and selecting (projecting) a query expression. You also tackled the different query expressions, the use of `var` versus `IEnumerable`, and the difference between query syntax and method syntax and how they are related and used.

In Chapter 4 you'll take an in-depth look at the standard query operators, putting the final touches on your basic understanding of LINQ.

4

LINQ Standard Query Operators

Understanding the different parts of a query operation and how those parts work together provides the foundation for constructing efficient queries to retrieve and transform data from many different sources, such as XML documents, SQL databases, .NET collections, and ADO.NET datasets. This chapter will outline those parts and their uses.

This chapter builds on the query operation information you examined in Chapter 3, "LINQ Queries," by exploring the standard query operators, a set of methods that form the LINQ pattern, a standard way of creating query expressions to project, filter, group, and transform data. The standard query operators provide the capability to query any object that implements the `IEnumerable` interface and `IQueryable` interface. You can think of the standard query operators much like an API. In this case, the "API" is a set of methods.

This chapter begins with an overview of the standard query operators. It examines each operator in detail, providing examples, and then ends with a full example using many of these operators.

Overview

Standard query operators are the building blocks of LINQ query expressions, providing many of the query capabilities such as filtering and sorting. They are a set of methods that constitute a query pattern and are implemented by their respective LINQ provider, such as LINQ to XML and LINQ to Datasets.

As you learned in the last chapter, some operators return results immediately, while others have a deferred execution. Those queries whose execution is immediate return a single value such as a `Sum` or `Count`, while those queries that have a deferred execution return multiple values.

As stated earlier, the standard query operator is a set of methods. These methods operate on sequences. A sequence is an object whose type implements either the `IEnumerable<T>` interface or the `IQueryable<T>` interface. The `IEnumerable<T>` interface provides iteration over a collection of a specified type.

The `IQueryable<T>` interface provides the ability to execute queries against a known and specific data source whose type of data is known. Meaning, with the `IQueryable` interface and the `IQueryable<T>` interface you get an object that can evaluate queries. The `IQueryable` interface is based on expressions.

One of the main differences between `IEnumerable` and `IQueryable` is that the `IEnumerable` interface provides forward-only iteration. It does not have the ability to move between items (except forward). With `IQueryable` however, you have much more flexibility with your query operations. Remember, though that the `IQueryable` interface implements `IEnumerable`, which provides `IQueryable` with iteration capability.

There are two types of query operators. The first type operates on `IEnumerable` objects, while the other operates on `IQueryable` objects. Each set of operators is implemented as static methods on the corresponding types, meaning that the operators can be called using static method syntax as well as being called as instance methods.

A lot of what makes this possible is the new features found in C# 3.0 and VB 9.0. Those features include lambda expressions (a concise expression or statement block) and extension methods (static methods associated with a type). These and other features new to C# 3.0 and VB 9.0 are discussed in Chapter 2, "A Look at Visual Studio 2008."

Standard query operators are grouped based on their function, and that's how we'll tackle them in this chapter.

Standard Query Operators

This section discusses the standard query operators. These operators have both C# and Visual Basic syntax. The examples will be given in C#, but the syntax will be provided in both C# and Visual Basic.

What you will find is that those standard query operators that are used more frequently have a dedicated language and keyword syntax, which lets them be used and called as part of a query expression (query syntax).

Standard QueryOperator	C#	Visual Basic
All (Of T)	N/A	Into All(...)
Any	N/A	Into Any()
Average	N/A	Into Averate()
Cast (Of T)	An explicit range of variables	From...As...
Count	N/A	Into count()
Distinct	N/A	Distinct

Standard QueryOperator	C#	Visual Basic
GroupBy	group by	Group By
GroupJoin	join...in...on...into...	Group Join
Join	join...in...on...equals...	Join...As..IN...On...
		OR
		From x In..y In..Where...
LongCount	N/A	Into LongCount()
Max	N/A	Into Max()
Min	N/A	Into Min()
OrderBy	orderby	Order By
OrderByDescending	orderby desdending	Order By...Descending
Select	select	Select
SelectMany	Multiple from clauses	Multiple from clauses
Skip	N/A	Skip
SkipWhile	N/A	Skip While
Sum	N/A	Into Sum
Take	N/A	Take
TakeWhile	N/A	Take While
ThenBy	orderby	Order By
ThenByDescending	orderby descending	Order By...Descending
Where	where	Where

Remember from the discussion in Chapter 3 that a query expression is a more readable form of query over the method-based syntax version. At compile time, query expressions are translated into query methods.

However, what you will find in this chapter is that it is very easy to combine these query expression syntax operators with direct method calls. By doing this, you can use all of the various pieces of the LINQ functionality.

Projection Operators

Projection refers to the act of transforming the elements of a sequence into a form defined by the developer. The projection operators—Select and SelectMany—select values given the appropriate function. While both select values, the SelectMany operator can handle multiple collections.

Select

The `Select` operator (`select` in C#) projects values from a single sequence or collection. The following example uses `select` to return the `FirstName`, `LastName`, and `EmailAddress` columns from the sequence:

```
var query =
    from c in contact
    where c.FirstName.StartsWith("S")
    select new {c.FirstName, c.LastName, c.EmailAddress}
```

This operator returns an enumerable object. When the object is enumerated, it produces each element in the selected results.

This same query can be written using method syntax as follows:

```
var query =
    contact.Select(c => new {
        c.FirstName, c.Lastname, c.EmailAddress}
        ).Where(c => c.FirstName.StartsWith("S"));
```

SelectMany

The `SelectMany` operation provides the capability to combine multiple `from` clauses, merging the results of each object into a single sequence. Here's an example:

```
string[] owners =
    { new name { FirstName = "Scott", "Chris",
        Pets = new List<string>{"Yukon", "Fido"}},
     new name { FirstName = "Jason", "Steve",
        Pets = new List<string>{"Killer", "Fluffy"}},
     new name { FirstName = "John", "Joe",
        Pets = new List<string>{"Spike", "Tinkerbell"}}}

IEnumerable<string> query =
    names.AsQueryable().SelectMany(own => own.Pets);
```

When this code is run, it produces the following:

```
Yukon
Fido
Killer
Fluffy
Spike
Tinkerbell
```

This same example could be written follows:

```
var query =
    from o in owners
    select o;

foreach (var pet in query.SelectMany(own => own.Pets))
    listbox1.Items.Add(pet);
```

Restriction Operator

where is the restriction operator. It applies filter criteria on the sequence. The values of the sequence are filtered based on a supplied predicate.

The where operator does not initiate the execution of the query. The query is executed when enumeration over the object is initiated, at which point the filter is applied. Here's an example that applies a filter to the query expression, filtering the results so that only those contacts whose first name begins with the letter *S* are returned:

```
IEnumerable<string> query =
    from c in contact
    where c.FirstName.StartsWith("S")
    select new {c.FirstName, c.LastName, c.EmailAddress}
```

This example could also be written using method syntax as follows:

```
var query =
    contact.Select(c => new {
        c.FirstName, c.Lastname, c.EmailAddress}
        ).Where(c => c.FirstName.StartsWith("S"));
```

Sorting Operators

The sorting operators—OrderBy, OrderByDescending, ThenBy, ThenByDescending, and Reverse—provide the capability to sort the results in an ascending or descending manner. There are several sorting options that let you apply primary and secondary sorts as well. These operators are explored in the following sections.

OrderBy

The OrderBy operator sorts the resulting values of the sequence in an ascending order. The following example shows how to sort a sequence in ascending order:

```
var query =
    from c in contact
    where c.FirstName.StartsWith("S")
    orderby c.LastName
    select new {c.FirstName, c.LastName, c.EmailAddress}
```

You can also sort the sequence in ascending order by using a *comparer*. A comparer is an optional value that is used to compare values. If no comparer is specified, a default is used, which comes from the IComparer generic interface.

This example could also be written using method syntax as follows:

```
var query =
    contact.Select(c => {
        c.FirstName, c.LastName, c.EmailAddress }).Where(
        c => c.FirstName.StartsWith("S")).OrderBy(
        c => c.FirstName);
```

OrderByDescending

The `OrderByDescending` operator sorts the resulting values of the sequence in descending order. The following shows how to sort a sequence in descending order:

```
IEnumerable<string> query =
   from c in contact
   where c.FirstName.StartsWith("S")
  orderby c.LastName descending
   select new {c.FirstName, c.LastName, c.EmailAddress}
```

This example could also be written using method syntax as follows:

```
var query =
   contact.Select(c => {
      c.FirstName, c.LastName, c.EmailAddress} ).Where(
      c => c.FirstName.StartsWith("S")).OrderByDescending(
      c => c.FirstName);
```

ThenBy

The `ThenBy` operator applies a secondary, ascending sort order to the sequence. It is akin to applying a secondary sort order in T-SQL, such as the italicized column in the following example:

```
SELECT FirstName, LastName, Address1, Address2, City
FROM Contacts
ORDER BY LastName, FirstName
```

In LINQ, the `ThenBy` operator lets you apply an equivalent secondary sort, like this:

```
IEnumerable<string> query =
   from c in contact
   where c.FirstName.StartsWith("S")
  orderby c.LastName
  thenby c.FirstName
   select new {c.FirstName, c.LastName, c.EmailAddress}
```

This example could also be written using method syntax as follows:

```
var query =
   contact.Select(c => {
      c.FirstName, c.LastName, c.EmailAddress} ).Where(
      c => c.FirstName.StartsWith("S")).OrderBy(
      c => c.FirstName).ThenBy(c => c.LastName);
```

ThenByDescending

The `ThenByDescending` operator sorts the resulting values of the sequence in descending order. The following example shows how:

```
IEnumerable<string> query =
   (from c in contact
   where c.FirstName.StartsWith("S")
  orderby c.LastName descending
```

```
        select new {c.FirstName, c.LastName, c.EmailAddress}).↵
    ThenByDescending(c => c.FirstName);
```

This example could also be written using method syntax as follows:

```
var query =
    contact.Select(c => {
        c.FirstName, c.LastName, c.EmailAddress} ).Where(
        c => c.FirstName.StartsWith("S")).OrderBy(
        c => c.FirstName).ThenByDescending(c =>
        c.LastName);
```

Reverse

You might think that the Reverse operator is equal to the OrderByDescending operator, but that's not the case. The Reverse operator does not look at the individual values to decide the sort order. It simply returns the values in the opposite (reverse) order from which they were returned from the data source. Here's an example:

```
string[] names = {"Alex", "Chuck", "Dave", "Dinesh",
   "Joe", "John", "Sarah", "Scott", "Steve"}

string[] reversednames = names.Reverse().ToArray();
foreach (string str in reversednames)
   listbox1.Items.Add(chr)
```

The resulting output is:

```
Steve
Scott
Sarah
John
Joe
Dinesh
Dave
Chuck
Alex
```

The reverse() operator is limited, in that it is not supported by LINQ to SQL because LINQ to SQL operates on tables that are unordered sets or multisets.

Joining Operators

Joining is the action of relating or associating one data source object with a second data source object. The two data source objects are associated through a common value or attribute.

LINQ join operators match values from data sources that contain keys that match (or are equal). There are two LINQ join operators, join and groupjoin.

join

The join operator is similar to the T-SQL inner join, which joins one data source to a second data source, matching on equal values between the two data sources. For example, you can join a customer database table and order database table, matching on equal keys from each side of the join.

In the following example, the `join` operator is used to join the `Contact` table to the Employee table using the matching `ContactID` columns of each table.

```
from c in contact
join emp in employee on c.ContactID equals emp.ContactID
where c.FirstName.StartsWith("S")
orderby c.LastName
select new {emp.EmployeeID, c.FirstName, c.LastName,
  c.EmailAddress, emp.Title, emp.HireDate}
```

Like relational database joins, joins can be performed on more than two sources. The preceding example joins two tables or data sources, but you can just as easily join on more:

```
from c in contact
join emp in employee on c.ContactID equals emp.ContactID
join ind in individual on c.ContactID equals ind.ContactID
join cust in customer on ind.CustomerID equals cust.CustomerID
where c.FirstName.StartsWith("S")
orderby c.LastName
select new {emp.EmployeeID, c.FirstName, c.LastName, c.EmailAddress,
  emp.Title, emp.HireDate, cust.AccountNumber}
```

Each additional join associates a new table or data source with the results of the previous join.

The first example could also be written using method syntax as follows:

```
var query =
    contact.Join(employee, con => con.ContactID,
    emp => emp.ContactID, (con, emp) => new
    { Contact = con.FirstName, Employee} );
```

GroupJoin

The `GroupJoin` operator joins each value or element from the primary (first or left) data source with a set of corresponding values from the secondary (right) data source. This type of join comes in handy when you want to create a hierarchical data structure.

The following example uses `GroupJoin` to create a hierarchical structure from two different data sources. The first data source lists motocross race teams, and the second data source lists the riders for each of those teams. The `GroupJoin` operator is used join the two data sources together and produce an output that lists the team and their associated riders.

```
List<Team> teams = new List<Team>{ new Team { name = "Yamaha"},
                                   new Team { name = "Honda"} ,
                                   new Team { name = "Kawasaki"} ,
                                   new Team { name = "Suzuki"}} ;

List<Rider> riders = new List<Rider> {
  new Rider { name = "Grant Langston", TeamName = "Yamaha"},
  new Rider { name = "Andrew Short", TeamName = "Honda"},
  new Rider { name = "James Steward", TeamName = "Kawasaki"},
  new Rider { name = " Broc Hepler", TeamName = "Yamaha"},
  new Rider { name = "Tommy Hahn", TeamName = "Honda"},
```

```
        new Rider { name = "Tim Ferry", TeamName = "Kawasaki"},
        new Rider { name = " Chad Reed", TeamName = "Yamaha"},
        new Rider { name = "Davi Millsaps", TeamName = "Honda"},
        new Rider { name = "Ricky Carmichael", TeamName = "Suzuki"},
        new Rider { name = "Kevin Windham", TeamName = "Honda"}};

var teamsandriders = teams.GroupJoin(riders,
            Team => Team.name,
            Rider => Rider.TeamName,
            (team, teamRiders) => new {Team = team.name,
            riders = teamRiders.Select(rider => rider.name)});

foreach (var tar in teamsandriders)
{
    listBox1.Items.Add(tar.Team);
    foreach (string rider in tar.riders)
    listBox1.Items.Add("   " + rider);
}
```

The results from this query look like this:

```
 Yamaha
   Grant Langston
   Broc Hepler
   Chad Reed
 Honda
   Andrew Short
   Tommy Hahn
   Davi Millsaps
   Kevin Windham
 Kawasaki
   James Stewart
   Tim Ferry
 Suzuki
   Ricky Carmichael
```

This example used an in-memory array to apply a Groupjoin, to help you understand the concept of the operator. The same can be applied to a LINQ to SQL query:

```
private void cmdGroupJoin_Click(object sender, EventArgs e)
{
    DataContext context = new DataContext("Initial Catalog=AdventureWorks;Integrated
    Security=sspi");

    Table<SalesPerson> salespeople = context.GetTable<SalesPerson>();
    Table<SalesOrderHeader> orders = context.GetTable<SalesOrderHeader>();

    var salespeopleandorders = salespeople.GroupJoin(orders,
        SalesPerson => SalesPerson.SalesPersonID,
        SalesOrderHeader => SalesOrderHeader.SalesPersonID,
        (person, salesorder) => new { SalesPerson = person.SalesPersonID,
        orders = salesorder.Select(order => order.CustomerID)} );

    foreach (var sao in salespeopleandorders)
```

```
      {
        listBox1.Items.Add(sao.SalesPerson);
        foreach (int order in sao.orders)
        listBox1.Items.Add("   " + order);
      }

    }
```

The results of this query list each `salespersonid` and the associated order `customerid`. Here's a portion of the output:

```
279
  676
  117
  442
  227
283
  2
107
56
310
527
638
157
```

Grouping Operator

Grouping is the concept of grouping the values or elements of a sequence according to a specified value (selector). LINQ contains a single grouping operator, `GroupBy`.

The following example uses the `Sales.SalesOrderHeader` table in the AdventureWorks database to group together orders for each sales person using the `SalesPersonID` as the key value.

```
DataContext context = new DataContext("Initial
  Catalog=AdventureWorks;Integrated Security=sspi");

Table<SalesOrderHeader> orders = context.GetTable<SalesOrderHeader>();

var query = orders.Where(ord => ord.SalesPersonID > 0).GroupBy(order =>
  order.SalesPersonID,
  order => order.CustomerID);

foreach (var o in query)
{
    listBox1.Items.Add(o.Key);
    foreach (int cust in o)
      listBox1.Items.Add("   " + cust);
}
```

It can also be written as follows (given the same `DataContext` and table):

```
IEnumerable<IGrouping<int, int>> query = orders.Where(ord =>
  ord.SalesPersonID > 0).GroupBy(order => order.SalesPersonID, order =>
  order.CustomerID);
```

```
foreach (IGrouping<int, int> o in query)
{
    listBox1.Items.Add(o.Key);
    foreach (int cust in o)
        listBox1.Items.Add("    " + cust);
}
```

Here are the results:

```
268
    697
    47
    471
    548
    167
    ...
275
    504
    618
    17
    486
    269
276
    510
    511
    259
    384
    650
...
```

The first example could also be written using a mix of query syntax and method syntax as follows:

```
var query =
    (from o in orders
     where o.SalesPersonID > 0
     select o).GroupBy(order => order.SalesPersonID,
         order => order.CustomerID);
```

This makes the query somewhat easier to read, even though the example used a mix of the two syntaxes. The reason for the mix of syntaxes in this example is that the GroupBy operator is not available in query syntax.

This example also gives you an idea of the flexibility you have when using the standard query operators.

Concatenating Operator

Concatenating is the process of joining two objects together. In LINQ, concatenating joins two collections into a single collection, and is accomplished via the Concat operator.

In the following example, contact last names are concatenated with CustomerIDs from the Person.Contact table and Sales.SalesOrderHeader table:

```
DataContext context = new DataContext("Initial Catalog=
AdventureWorks;Integrated Security=sspi");
```

```
Table<Contact> contacts = context.GetTable<Contact>();
Table<SalesOrderHeader> orders = context.GetTable<SalesOrderHeader>();

var query = contacts.Select(con => con.LastName).Concat(orders.Select(order ↵
=> order.CustomerID.ToString()));

foreach (var item in query)
{
    listBox1.Items.Add(item);
}
```

The results in the list box will first list all of the contacts' last names, followed by all of the CustomerIDs.

Aggregating Operators

Aggregate functions perform calculations on a set of values and return a single value, such as performing a sum or count on values of a given element. There are seven LINQ aggregate query operators: Aggregate; Average, Count, LongCount, Max, Min, and Sum.

Aggregate

The Aggregate operator gathers values from a given sequence or collection. It accumulates values returned from a sequence and returns when the aggregation is complete. For instance, the following example uses the Aggregate operator to build a new sentence in reverse from an array of strings.

```
string Names = "Steve, Scott, Joe, John, Chris, Jason";
string[] name = Names.Split(', ');
string newName = name.Aggregate(workingName, next) =>
    next + " " + workingName);

listbox.Items.Add(newName);
```

Average

The Average operator computes the average from a sequence of numerical values. It works on many data types, such as decimal, integers (Int32, Int64, and the like), and doubles.

In its simplest form, the Average operator works as follows:

```
List<int> quantity = new List<int> {99, 48, 120, 73, 101, 81, 56};
double average = quantity.Average();
listbox1.items.add(average);
```

This example computes the average of the seven numbers in the list and returns that value. This type of calculation can be applied to the following example, in which the Average operator is used to calculate the average unit price of all the products for a given order:

```
var query =
    from od in orderdetail
    where od.SalesOrderID == 43662
```

```
    select od.UnitPrice;
listbox1.Items.Add(query.Average());
```

The query can also be written as follows:

```
var query =
    from od in orderdetail
    where od.SalesOrderID == 43662
    select od;
```

```
listbox1.Items.Add(query.Average(orderDetail => orderDetail.UnitPrice));
```

This operator is applied to a sequence of values.

Count

The Count operator counts the number of elements in a given collection. It should be used if the expected result is going to be less than Int32.MaxValue (the largest possible value of an Int32).

The following example shows the Count operator in its simplest form. The list contains seven numbers and the count operator is applied to count the numbers in the list.

```
List<int> quantity = new List<int> {99, 48, 120, 73, 101, 81, 56};
int cnt = quantity.Count;
listbox1.items.add(cnt);
```

When run, this query returns 7. In the following example, the Count operator is used to count the number of items for the specified sales order.

```
var query =
    from od in orderdetail
    where od.SalesOrderID == 43662
    select od.UnitPrice;
```

```
listbox1.Items.Add(query.Count());
```

When this query is executed, the list box contains the value of 22, meaning that there are 22 items for the specified order.

You can also specify a criterion for the Count operator. Here's an example in which the Count operator is applied but given a condition, where the unit price is less than 200.

```
var query =
    from od in orderdetail
    where od.SalesOrderID == 43662
    select od;
```

```
listbox1.Items.Add(query.Count(orderDetail => orderDetail.UnitPrice < 200));
```

LongCount

The LongCount operator, which returns an Int64 (a 64-bit integer), is used to count the number of elements in a large collection—one with more than Int32.MaxValue elements. You use LongCount the same way you use the Count operator, as shown in the following example:

```
List<Int64> quantity = new List<Int64> {99, 48, 120, 73, 101, 81, 56};
Int64 cnt = quantity.LongCount();
listbox1.items.add(cnt);
```

Now count the number of items in an order:

```
var query =
    from od in orderdetail
    where od.SalesOrderID == 43662
    select od.UnitPrice;

listbox1.Items.Add(query.LongCount());
```

And here's the example specifying a specific condition:

```
var query =
    from od in orderdetail
    where od.SalesOrderID == 43662
    select od;

listbox1.Items.Add(query.LongCount(orderDetail => orderDetail.UnitPrice < 200));
```

Max

The Max operator returns the maximum value within a sequence. Like the Average operator, Max works on many data types, including decimals, integers, and doubles.

The following example returns the maximum value from the list of provided integers:

```
List<int> quantity = new List<int> {99, 48, 120, 73, 101, 81, 56};
int cnt = quantity.Max();
listbox1.items.add(cnt);
```

The value returned is 120. This operator can also be applied to the following example, which returns the maximum unit price of all the items for a specific order.

```
var query =
    from od in orderdetail
    where od.SalesOrderID == 43662
    select od.UnitPrice;

listbox1.Items.Add(query.Max());
```

The value returned is 2146.9620. This query can also be written as follows:

```
var query =
    from od in orderdetail
    where od.SalesOrderID == 43662
```

```
select od;

listbox1.Items.Add(query.Max(orderDetail => orderDetail.UnitPrice));
```

There is no performance advantage between the two queries; their use is a matter of user preference and readability.

Min

On the flip side is the Min operator, which returns the minimum value from a sequence. It also works on many data types, including decimals, integers, and doubles.

The following example returns the minimum value from the list of provided integers:

```
List<int> quantity = new List<int> {99, 48, 120, 73, 101, 81, 56};
int cnt = quantity.Min();
listbox1.items.add(cnt);
```

The value returned from this example is 48. Here's an example that returns the minimum unit price of all the items for a specific order:

```
var query =
    from od in orderdetail
    where od.SalesOrderID == 43662
    select od.UnitPrice;

listbox1.Items.Add(query.Min());
```

The value returned from this query is 178.5808. The query can also be written like this:

```
var query =
    from od in orderdetail
    where od.SalesOrderID == 43662
    select od;

listbox1.Items.Add(query.Min(orderDetail => orderDetail.UnitPrice));
```

Again, there's no performance advantage between the two queries. It's just a matter of preference and readability.

Sum

The Sum operator calculates the sum of the selected values within a collection. It also works on many data types, such as decimal, integers, and doubles.

The following example returns the sum of the given values from the list of provided integers:

```
List<int> quantity = new List<int> {99, 48, 120, 73, 101, 81, 56};
int cnt = quantity.Sum();
listbox1.items.add(cnt);
```

The value returned from this example is 578. Here's an example that returns the sum of the unit prices for all the items for a specific order:

```
var query =
    from od in orderdetail
    where od.SalesOrderID == 43662
    select od.UnitPrice;

listbox1.Items.Add(query.Sum());
```

The value returned from this query is 12955.4816. This query can also be written as the following:

```
var query =
    from od in orderdetail
    where od.SalesOrderID == 43662
    select od;
listbox1.Items.Add(query.Sum(orderDetail => orderDetail.UnitPrice));
```

Which query you use is a matter of preference. There's no performance advantage between the two.

Set Operators

Set operators perform actions against elements or sequence sets, and then return a set. There are four LINQ set query operators—Distinct, Union, Intersect, and Except.

Distinct

The Distinct operator removes duplicate values from a collection and returns distinct elements from that collection (or sequence).

In the following example, the list contains 13 numbers ranging from 1 to 10; some of the numbers (1, 7, and 9) repeat. Applying the distinct operator removes the duplicates and returns only the distinct values.

```
List<int> quantity = new List<int> {1, 1, 2, 3, 4, 5, 6, 7, 7, 8, 9, 9, 10};
IEnumerable<int> val = numbers.Distinct();
foreach (int num in val)
  listbox1.Items.Add(num);
```

The results are

```
1
2
3
4
5
6
7
8
9
10
```

To test this using LINQ, open a new query window in SQL Server Management Studio and select the AdventureWorks database. Execute the following query:

```
SELECT SalesOrderDetailID, ProductID, UnitPrice
FROM    Sales.SalesOrderDetail
WHERE   SalesOrderID = 43662
ORDER BY UnitPrice
```

Your results would look like this:

```
Salesordetailid productid unitprice
--------------- --------- ---------
44               722       178.5808
49               738       178.5808
47               726       183.9382
43               729       183.9382
32               730       183.9382
34               725       183.9382
41               732       356.898
48               733       356.898
50               766       419.4589
40               763       419.4589
46               760       419.4589
35               762       419.4589
36               765       419.4589
37               768       419.4589
30               764       419.4589
31               770       419.4589
33               754       874.794
39               756       874.794
42               758       874.794
51               755       874.794
45               749       2146.962
38               753       2146.962
```

Notice that the `unitprice` column contains some duplicate values. With LINQ, you can use the same `Distinct` operator as used in the previous example. Here's how:

```
var query =
    from od in orderdetail
    where od.SalesOrderID == 43662
    select od.UnitPrice;

foreach (decimal num in query.Distinct())
    listbox1.Items.Add(num);
```

Without the trailing decimal places, you get the following results:

```
178
183
356
419
874
2146
```

Union

The `Union` operator returns the unique elements from the results of a union of two sequences or collections. It is different from the `concat` operator in that it returns unique values, and the `concat` operator returns all values.

The following example contains two lists (or data sources) that contain integer values. These lists do not contain duplicate values. The `Union` operator is applied; it joins the two lists and returns only the unique value in the resultset.

```
int[] numbers1 = { 1, 2, 3, 4, 5, 6, 7, 8, 9, 10} ;
int[] numbers2 = { 11, 12, 13, 14, 15, 16, 17, 18, 19, 20} ;
IEnumerable<int> union = numbers1.Union(numbers2);

foreach (int num in union)
  listBox1.Items.Add(num);
```

The results from this query return the numbers 1 through 20. The next example also contains two lists of numbers, but numbers that exist in the first list also exist in the second list, and the first list also contains duplicate numbers (such as the numbers 1 and 9).

```
int[] numbers1 = { 1, 1, 2, 3, 3, 4, 5, 5, 6, 7, 7, 8, 9, 9, 10} ;
int[] numbers2 = { 1, 3, 5, 7, 9} ;
IEnumerable<int> union = numbers1.Union(numbers2);

foreach (int num in union)
  listBox1.Items.Add(num);
```

When the `Union` operator is applied in this example, the following results are returned:

```
1
2
3
4
5
6
7
8
9
10
```

Intersect

The `intersect` operator returns the intersection of two sequences—that is, those values that are common between two sequences or collections.

The following example uses two lists (or data sources) that contain integer values. Again, you can see that there are numbers in the first list that also exist in the second list. The `intersect` operator is applied; it joins the two lists and returns only those values that are common to both sequences.

```
int[] numbers1 = { 1, 2, 3, 4, 5, 6, 7, 8, 9, 10} ;
int[] numbers2 = { 2, 4, 6, 8, 10} ;
IEnumerable<int> shared = numbers1.Intersect(numbers2);
```

```
foreach (int num in shared)
  listBox1.Items.Add(num);
```

The output is as follows:

```
2
4
6
8
10
```

Except

The Except operator is the opposite of the intersect operator, in that it returns the difference between two sequences—in other words, it returns values that are unique (not duplicated) in all of the values of the sequences (values that appear in the first sequence but do not appear in the second). In other words, it is "the elements of sequence A less the elements of sequence B."

```
int[] numbers1 = { 1, 2, 3, 4, 5, 6, 7, 8, 9, 10} ;
int[] numbers2 = { 2, 4, 6, 8, 10} ;
IEnumerable<int> shared = numbers1.Except(numbers2);

foreach (int num in shared)
  listBox1.Items.Add(num);
```

The output is

```
1
3
5
7
9
```

Generation Operators

Generation operators create new sequences from the values of existing sequences. The element generation operators are discussed in this section.

Empty

The Empty operator returns an empty collection that has a specified type. In the following example, three lists of names are defined and added to an array list. The Aggregate operator is applied to gather values from the array list if the array contains more than two elements. The Empty operator is then used to provide an empty collection if the criteria is not met (that is, if no arrays have more than two elements).

```
string[] name1 = { "Scott", "Steve"} ;
string[] name2 = { "Joe", "John", "Jim", "Josh", "Joyce"} ;
string[] name3 = { "Dave", "Dinesh", "Doug", "Doyle"} ;

List<string[]> names = new List<string[]> { name1, name2, name3} ;

IEnumerable<string> namelist = names.Aggregate(Enumerable.Empty<string>(),
   (current, next) => next.Length > 2 ? current.Union(next) : current);
```

```
foreach (string item in namelist)
    listBox1.Items.Add(item);
```

When this query is run, the following results are returned because two of the arrays have more than two elements:

```
Joe
John
Jim
Josh
Joyce
Dave
Dinesh
Doug
Doyle
```

Change the query so that it is looking for arrays that have more than five elements, as shown below:

```
IEnumerable<string> namelist = names.Aggregate(Enumerable.Empty<string>(),
    (current, next) => next.Length > 5 ? current.Union(next) : current);
```

When the query is run now, nothing is returned. Or better said, an empty collection is returned. You can tell this by placing a breakpoint on the `foreach` statement. When the query is run, the execution does indeed step into the `foreach` statement, letting you know that an empty collection was returned, but the line that adds items to the list box is not hit or executed.

The `Empty` operator is basically used as a seed value for the aggregate operator if the criteria is not met.

Range

The `Range` operator creates a collection that contains a sequence of numbers. It takes two parameters. The first is the integer value at which to start the sequence, and the second is the number of sequential integers to generate.

Here's an example in which the `Range` operator is used to generate a sequence of numbers starting at 1 and stopping at 10:

```
var coolmath = Enumerable.Range(1, 10);
for each (int num in coolmath)
    listbox1.Items.Add(num);
```

The results are

```
1
2
3
4
6
7
8
9
10
```

Other operators can be added to this as well. The following example generates a list of numbers from 1 to 10 but also uses the Reverse operator to generate them backward.

```
var coolmath = Enumerable.Range(1, 10).Reverse();
for each (int num in coolmath)
   listbox1.Items.Add(num);
```

The results are

```
10
9
8
7
6
5
4
3
2
1
```

In the next example, the Range operator is used to create a sequence of numbers from 1 to 5 and then multiply each number by 5:

```
var coolmath = Enumerable.Range(1, 5).Select(x => x * 5);
for each (int num in coolmath)
   listbox1.Items.Add(num);
```

The results are as follows:

```
5
10
15
20
25
```

Repeat

The Repeat operator creates a single value sequence that repeats itself a specified number of times. The following example creates a sequence of a single string value and repeats that string 10 times:

```
var coolphrase = Enumerable.Repeat("LINQ ROCKS!", 10);
for each (string phrase in coolphrase)
   listbox1.Items.Add(phrase);
```

The result of this query is the phrase ''LINQ ROCKS!'' output 10 times to the list box.

Conversion Operators

Conversion refers to the act of changing the type of input objects to the sequence. The conversion operators do just this, and they are discussed in this section.

AsEnumerable

The `AsEnumerable` operator returns the query input typed as `IEnumerable(Of T)`, meaning that you can change the data source from a type that implements `IEnumerable(Of T)` to `IEnumerable(Of T)` itself.

The following example uses the `AsEnumerable` operator to replace the type's custom `Where` method with that of the standard query operator `Where`.

```
DataContext context = new DataContext("Initial Catalog=AdventureWorks;↵
Integrated Security=sspi");

Table<Contact> contact = context.GetTable<Contact>();

IEnumerable<Contact> query =
    contact.AsEnumerable().Where(con => con.FirstName.Contains("K"));

foreach (Contact item in query)
    listBox1.Items.Add(item.FirstName);
```

The results of this query contain all the contact first names that contain the letter *K*. Here are partial results:

```
Kim
Keyley
Karel
Karen
Kris
Kevin
...
```

In this example, the `System.Query.Sequence` implementation of `Where` is utilized, but in the next example, the `Where()` method with a predicate is used:

```
IEnumerable<Contact> query = contact.Where(=> con.FirstName.Contains("K"));
```

Cast

The `Cast` operator casts the element of an `IEnumerable` collection to a specified type. The benefit of this is that by supplying necessary type information, you can invoke standard query operators on nongeneric collections.

The following example uses an `ArrayList` as a data source. An `ArrayList` does not implement `IEnumerable(Of T)`, but by using the `Cast` operator you can use the standard query operators, such as `Select`, to query the sequence.

```
ArrayList names = new ArrayList();

names.Add("Alex");
names.Add("Chuck");
names.Add("Dave");
names.Add("Dinesh");
names.Add("Joe");
names.Add("John");
names.Add("Sarah");
```

```
names.Add("Steve");
IEnumerable<string> query = names.Cast<string>().Select(name => name);

foreach (string item in query)
    listBox1.Items.Add(item);
```

OfType

The OfType operator enables you to filter elements of an IEnumerable object based on a specific type. In the following example, the OfType operator returns only those elements in the sequence that can be cast to a type of int:

```
ArrayList names = new ArrayList(7);

names.Add("Scott");
names.Add(1);
names.Add("Dave");
names.Add(2);
names.Add("Dave");
names.Add(3);
names.Add("Steve");
names.Add(4);
names.Add("Joe");

IEnumerable<int> query = names.OfType<int>();
foreach (int item in query)
    listBox1.Items.Add(item);
```

Here are the query's results:

```
1
2
3
4
```

By using the OfType operator on an IEnumerable object, you have the capability to apply and use standard query operators to query the sequence.

ToArray

The ToArray operator creates an array from an IEnumerable sequence. You may remember from previous chapters that the ToArray operator forces immediate execution of the query. In the following example, ToArray is used to query the first names from the Person.Contact table and return the results as an array:

```
DataContext context = new DataContext("Initial Catalog =
    AdventureWorks;Integrated Security=sspi");

Table<Contact> contact = context.GetTable<Contact>();

var query = contact.Select(con => con.FirstName).ToArray();

foreach (string item in query)
    listBox1.Items.Add(item);
```

The following lists partial results of running this query:

```
Gustavo
Catherine
Kim
Humberto
Pilar
Frances
Margeret
Carla
Jay
```

ToDictionary

The `ToDictionary` operator inserts all the elements returned in the sequence into a `Dictionary(Of TKey, TValue)`. The following example uses the `ToDictionary` operator to create and populate a `Dictionary(Of TKey, TValue)` and then iterate through that dictionary to populate a list box.

```
DataContext context = new DataContext("Initial Catalog =
    AdventureWorks;Integrated Security=sspi");

Table<Contact> contact = context.GetTable<Contact>();

Dictionary<string, Contact> dict = contact.ToDictionary(con => con.FirstName);

foreach (KeyValuePair<string, Contact> item in dict)
    listBox1.Items.Add(item.Key + " " + item.Value.FirstName + " " +
        item.Value.LastName);
```

The following list shows the partial results of running this query:

```
1 Gustavo Achong
2 Catherine Abel
3 Kim Abercrombie
4 Humberto Acevedo
5 Pilar Ackerman
6 Frances Adams
7 Margeret Smith
8 Carla Adams
```

ToList

The `ToList` operator converts an `IEnumerable` sequence collection to a `List(Of T)`. It also forces immediate execution of the query. The following code uses the `ToList` operator to query the first names from the `Person.Contact` table and return the results as a `List(Of T)`.

```
DataContext context = new DataContext("Initial Catalog =
    AdventureWorks;Integrated Security=sspi");

Table<Contact> contact = context.GetTable<Contact>();

var query = (from c in contact
            select c.FirstName).ToList();
```

```
foreach (string item in query)
    listBox1.Items.Add(item);
```

ToLookup

The ToLookup operator puts the returned elements into a Lookup(Of TKey, TElement), based on a speci-fied key. A Lookup is a collection of keys, each of which is mapped to one or more values; you can think of it as a one-to-many dictionary.

The following example uses the ToLookup operator to create and populate a Lookup(Of TKey, TElement) and then iterate through that Lookup to populate a list box.

```
DataContext context = new DataContext("Initial Catalog =
    AdventureWorks;Integrated Security=sspi");

Table<Contact> contact = context.GetTable<Contact>();
Lookup<string, string> lkp = contact.ToLookup(con => con.FirstName,
    con => con.MiddleName + " " + con.LastName);

foreach (IGrouping<string, string> lkpgrp in lkp)
{
    listBox1.Items.Add(lkpgrp.Key);

    foreach (string item in lkpgrp)
        listBox1.Items.Add("    " + item);
}
```

In this example, a Lookup is created, and contacts' first, middle, and last names are used to populate the Lookup, using the contact's last name as a key.

Contacts are then grouped by last name, selecting the contact first name and middle name (appended together), and returned as the element values of the Lookup. An instance of the IGrouping object is then created and used to iterate through in the Lookup, writing the key value (the last name), then iterating though each value in the IGrouping and writing those values (the first and middle names).

Here's a partial list of the results written to the list box:

```
Gustavo
  Achong
  Camargo
Catherine
  R. Abel
  M.Whitney
  J Brooks
  Kelly
  Sanders
  Peterson
. . .
```

Element Operators

Element operators return a single, specific element from a sequence. The element operators are discussed in this section.

DefaultIfEmpty

The `DefaultIfEmpty` operator replaces an empty collection with collection that contains a default single-ton value. It can be used to return a default value in case the sequence returned is empty and you still need something returned.

The following example queries the `Contact` table looking for all contacts whose first name begins with the letter Z. You know from previous examples that this query will return some values; however, the `DefaultIfEmpty` operator is used in case an empty sequence is returned.

```
DataContext context = new DataContext("Initial Catalog = AdventureWorks;Integrated
    Security=sspi");

Table<Contact> contact = context.GetTable<Contact>();

var query = from c in contact
    where c.FirstName.StartsWith("Z")
    select c.FirstName;

foreach (string item in query.DefaultIfEmpty())
    listBox1.Items.Add(item);
```

When the query is executed, all first names that begin with the letter Z are returned. Modify the query, changing the criteria to look for first names that begin with the letters ZZ:

```
var query = from c in contact
    where c.FirstName.StartsWith("ZZ")
    select c.FirstName;

foreach (string item in query.DefaultIfEmpty("none"))
    listBox1.Items.Add(item);
```

When this query runs, it does not find any first names that begin with the letters ZZ, so nothing will be returned, and the `DefaultIfEmpty` operator instructs the query to produce an empty sequence.

Just as a reminder: reference and nullable types have a default value of `null`.

ElementAt

The `ElementAt` operator returns an element at a given index from a collection. The collection is zero-based and the return value is the element at the specified position in the source. In the following example, the `Contact` table is queried looking for all contacts whose first name begins with the letter *S*. However, the `ElementAt` operator is utilized to return the element at the first position by passing the value of 0 as a parameter to the `ElementAt` operator.

```
DataContext context = new DataContext("Initial Catalog = AdventureWorks;Integrated
    Security=sspi");

Table<Contact> contact = context.GetTable<Contact>();

var query = from c in contact
            where c.FirstName.StartsWith("S")
            select c.FirstName;

listBox1.Items.Add(query.ElementAt(0));
```

Running this query will return the following:

```
Zheng
```

Be careful not to pass an index that is out of range; otherwise, the method throws an `index out of range` error. If you're not sure of the index, use the `ElementAtOrDefault.` operator.

ElementAtOrDefault

The `ElementAtOrDefault` operator combines the `ElementAt` operator with some of the functionality of the `DefaultIfEmpty` operator by returning the element at a specified index or a default value if the index is out of range.

In the following example, the `ElementAtOrDefault` operator returns the element at index 50,000 (there are slightly fewer the 20,000 contacts):

```
DataContext context = new DataContext("Initial Catalog = AdventureWorks;Integrated
    Security=sspi");

Table<Contact> contact = context.GetTable<Contact>();

var query = from c in contact
            where c.FirstName.StartsWith("S")
            select c.FirstName;

listBox1.Items.Add(query.ElementAtOrDefault(50000));
```

When this query is executed, it tries to return the value at the specified index; when it does not find an element at that index, it returns a default value of 0.

First

As its name suggests, the `First` operator returns the first element in a collection. Here's an example that queries the `Contact` table looking for all contacts whose first name begins with the letter *S*. The `First` operator returns the first element from the resulting collection.

```
DataContext context = new DataContext("Initial Catalog = ↵
AdventureWorks;Integrated Security=sspi");
Table<Contact> contact = context.GetTable<Contact>();

var query = from c in contact
            where c.FirstName.StartsWith("S")
            select c.FirstName;

listBox1.Items.Add(query.First());
```

This method throws an exception if the source sequence contains no elements. Use the `FirstOrDefault` operator if there is a possibility that the source might be empty.

You can also add specific criteria when using this operator. The following code returns the first element that satisfies a specific condition, the first name whose length is greater than 5.

```
listBox1.Items.Add(query.First(name => name.Length > 5));
```

Last

The opposite of the `First` operator, the `Last` operator returns the last element in a collection. Here the `Contact` table is queried looking for all contacts whose first name begins with the letter *S*, and the `Last` operator returns the last element from the returned collection:

```
DataContext context = new DataContext("Initial Catalog = ↵
AdventureWorks;Integrated Security=sspi");

Table<Contact> contact = context.GetTable<Contact>();

var query = from c in contact
            where c.FirstName.StartsWith("S")
            select c.FirstName;

listBox1.Items.Add(query.Last());
```

You can also add specific criteria when using this operator. For instance, the following returns the last element that satisfies a specific condition, the first name whose length is less than 5:

```
listBox1.Items.Add(query.Last(name => name.Length < 5));
```

FirstOrDefault

The `FirstOrDefault` operator returns the first element from a collection or, if no element is found, a default value. The following example queries the `Contact` table looking for all contacts whose first name begins with the letters ZZ, and the `FirstOrDefault` operator returns the first element from the returned collection. If the element is not found, a default value is returned. The default value is defined as the first element that is found that meets the query condition(s).

```
DataContext context = new DataContext("Initial Catalog=AdventureWorks;Integrated
    Security=sspi");

Table<Contact> contact = context.GetTable<Contact>();
var query = from c in contact
            where c.FirstName.StartsWith("ZZ")
            select c.FirstName;

listBox1.Items.Add(query.FirstOrDefault());
```

You can also add specific criteria when using this operator. The following, for instance, returns the first element that satisfies a specific condition, the first name whose length is greater than 5:

```
listBox1.Items.Add(query.FirstOrDefault(name => name.Length > 5));
```

LastOrDefault

The `LastOrDefault` operator returns the last element from a collection, or a default value if no element is found. Here's another example that queries the `Contact` table for all contacts whose first name begins with the letters ZZ. It uses the `LastOrDefault` operator to return the last element from the returned collection. If the element is not found then a default value is returned.

```
DataContext context = new DataContext("Initial Catalog=AdventureWorks;Integrated
   Security=sspi");

Table<Contact> contact = context.GetTable<Contact>();

var query = from c in contact
            where c.FirstName.StartsWith("ZZ")
            select c.FirstName;

listBox1.Items.Add(query.LastOrDefault());
```

You can also add specific criteria when using this operator, such as the following, which returns the last element that satisfies a specific condition, the first name whose length is less than 5.

```
listBox1.Items.Add(query.LastOrDefault(name => name.Length < 5));
```

Single

The Single operator returns a single element from a sequence, or the only element that meets a given condition. This operator should be used if you know that your query will return a single element. If the sequence returns multiple elements and this operator is used, an exception is thrown.

The following example queries the Contact table for all contacts whose last name equals "Kobylinski," and if any are found, returns the contact's first name. The Single operator returns the single element from the returned collection.

```
DataContext context = new DataContext("Initial Catalog=AdventureWorks;Integrated
   Security=sspi");

Table<Contact> contact = context.GetTable<Contact>();

var query = from c in contact
where c.LastName.Equals("Kobylinski")
select c.FirstName;

listBox1.Items.Add(query.Single());
```

When this query runs, the name Andrew is written to the list box, because that's the only contact with the last name of Kobylinski. Now change the query to the following and rerun it.

```
var query = from c in contact
where c.LastName.Equals("Kleinerman")
select c.FirstName;
```

When this query executes, you receive the error that the sequence contains more than one element because there are two contacts whose last name equals "Kleinerman."

You can also specify criteria to this operator as a parameter, as shown in this example:

```
var query2 = from c in contact
select c.LastName;

listBox1.Items.Add(query2.Single(con => con.Equals("Kobylinski")));
```

SingleOrDefault

Similar to the `Single` operator, the `SingleOrDefault` operator returns a single element from a sequence, but it also returns a default value if no element is found. Again, use this operator only if you know that your query will return a single element or that the element will be null when returned. If you use `SingleOrDefault` and the sequence returns multiple elements, an exception is thrown.

Here's a query to the `Contact` table looking for all contacts whose last name equals "Kobylinski" and, if any are found, returning the contact's first name. The `SingleOrDefault` operator returns the single element from the returned collection.

```
DataContext context = new DataContext("Initial Catalog=AdventureWorks;Integrated
    Security=sspi");

Table<Contact> contact = context.GetTable<Contact>();

var query = from c in contact
where c.LastName.StartsWith("Kobylinski")
select c.FirstName;

listBox1.Items.Add(query.SingleOrDefault());
```

When this query runs, the name Andrew is written to the list box, because that's the only contact who has the last name of Kobylinski. Change the query to the following and rerun the query:

```
var query = from c in contact
where c.LastName.Equals("Kleinerman")
select c.FirstName;
```

When this query executes, you get an error stating that the sequence contains more than one element because there are two contacts whose last name equals "Kleinerman."

You can also specify criteria to this operator as a parameter, as shown here:

```
var query2 = from c in contact
select c.LastName;

listBox1.Items.Add(query2.SingleOrDefault(con => con.Equals("Kobylinski")));
```

Equality Operators

Equality operators compare two sequences to check if their corresponding elements are equal. Sequences are considered equal if they have the same number of elements and the values of the elements are the same.

The `SequenceEqual` operator determines if two collections are equal. The determination is done by enumerating the two data sources in parallel and comparing elements. The return value is a Boolean—`true` if the two collections are equal, `false` if they are not.

In the following example, the code returns `true` to the list box because the two integer arrays are defined as equal:

```
int[] numbers1 = { 1, 2, 3, 4, 5, 6, 7, 8, 9, 10} ;
int[] numbers2 = { 1, 2, 3, 4, 5, 6, 7, 8, 9, 10} ;
bool eq = numbers1.SequenceEqual(numbers2);
listBox1.Items.Add(eq);
```

Change the second array to the following, and rerun the code:

```
int[] numbers1 = { 1, 2, 3, 4, 5, 6, 7, 8, 9, 10} ;
int[] numbers2 = { 2, 4, 6, 8, 10} ;
bool eq = numbers1.SequenceEqual(numbers2);
listBox1.Items.Add(eq);
```

This time a value of `false` is written to the list box because the comparison determined that the data sources were not equal.

Quantifier Operators

Quantifier operators return a Boolean value that indicates whether some or all of the elements in a sequence meet a specific condition.

The quantifier operators—`All`, `Any`, and `Contains`—are discussed in this section.

All

The `All` operator determines whether all the values in a collection satisfy a specified condition. The return value is a Boolean—`true` if all the values satisfy the condition, `false` if they do not.

Here, for example, an array of names is defined and the `All` operator is applied, specifying the condition that all the names begin with the letter *J*:

```
Names[] friends = {new Names { Name = "Steve"},
                   new Names  { Name = "Dave"},
                   new Names  { Name = "Joe"},
                   new Names  { Name = "John"},
                   new Names  { Name = "Bill"},
              };

bool firstnames = friends.All(name => name.Name.StartsWith("J"));

listBox1.Items.Add(firstnames).ToString();
```

Obviously, not all names begin with the letter *J*, so the value of `false` is written to the list box. In the next example, the same code and condition exist, except that the array contains only names that begin with the letter *J*:

```
Names[] friends = {new Names { Name = "Jeff"},
                   new Names  { Name = "Jordan"},
                   new Names  { Name = "Joe"},
                   new Names  { Name = "John"},
```

```
                          new Names   { Name = "Jim"},
    };

  bool firstnames = friends.All(name => name.Name.StartsWith("J"));

  listBox1.Items.Add(firstnames).ToString();
```

This time, `true` is written to the list box. The following example uses data retrieved from the `SalesOrderDetail` table in the AdventureWorks database, applying the `All` operator to determine if all of the unit prices in the table are greater than zero:

```
DataContext context = new DataContext("Initial Catalog = AdventureWorks;Integrated
    Security=sspi");

Table<SalesOrderDetail> orderdetail = context.GetTable<SalesOrderDetail>();

var query =
    from od in orderdetail
    where od.SalesOrderID == 43662
    select od.UnitPrice;

listBox1.Items.Add(query.All(orderDetail => orderDetail.UnitPrice > 0));
```

The value of `true` will be written to the list box because there are no rows in the table whose `unitprice` column contains a value of `0`.

Any

The `Any` operator determines if any of the values in a collection satisfy a specified condition or if the sequence contains any elements. The return value is a Boolean—`true` if all the values satisfy the condition, `false` if they do not.

In the following example, the `Contact` table is queried, returning a sequence of first names whose last name starts with the letter Z. The `Any` operator is applied to the sequence to determine if the sequence contains any elements that meet the specified condition.

```
DataContext context = new DataContext("Initial Catalog=AdventureWorks;Integrated
    Security=sspi");

Table<Contact> contact = context.GetTable<Contact>();

var query = from c in contact
            where c.LastName.StartsWith("Z")
            select c.FirstName;

listBox1.Items.Add(query.Any());
```

When this query is run, a value of `true` is written to the list box because there is at least one contact whose last name starts with the letter Z.

This operator can also be used to determine if any element of a sequence satisfies a given condition:

```
//satisfies a condition
var query = from c in contact
select c.FirstName;

listBox1.Items.Add(query.Any(con => con.LastName.StartsWith("Z")));
```

Both of these queries return the same thing, as you can see. However, there is no performance benefit of one over the other, except for better readability of the code.

When this query is run, a value of `true` is written to the list box because there is at least one contact whose last name starts with the letter Z.

Contains

The `Contains` operator determines whether the returned collection contains a specific element. The return value is a Boolean—`true` if all the values satisfy the condition, `false` if they do not.

The following example queries the `Contact` table, returning a sequence of last names. The `Contains` operator is applied to determine if the sequence contains an element of "Kleinerman."

```
DataContext context = new DataContext("Initial Catalog=AdventureWorks;Integrated
    Security=sspi");

Table<Contact> contact = context.GetTable<Contact>();

var query = from c in contact
select c.LastName;

listBox1.Items.Add(query.Contains("Kleinerman"));
```

Because the `Contact` table does contain at least one row whose last name is Kleinerman, the value of `true` is returned and written to the list box.

You can also use a comparer as follows:

```
DataContext context = new DataContext("Initial Catalog=AdventureWorks;Integrated
    Security=sspi");

Table<Contact> contact = context.GetTable<Contact>();

string name = "Kleinerman"

var query = from c in contact
select c.LastName;

listBox1.Items.Add(query.Contains(name));
```

Partitioning Operators

Partitioning is the act of dividing a single input sequence into two or more sections or sequences without rearranging the incoming elements, then returning one of the newly formed sections.

The partitioning operators—skip, skipwhile, Take, and TakeWhile—are discussed in this section.

Skip

The Skip operator skips elements up to a specified location within a sequence. In other words, it bypasses the specified number of elements and returns the remaining elements.

The following example defines a random set of numbers, orders them in ascending order, then uses the Skip operator to skip the first four and return the remaining.

```
Int[] randomNumbers = {86, 2, 77, 94, 100, 65, 5, 22, 70};
IEnumerable<int> skipLowerFour =
    randomNumbers.OrderBy(num => num).Skip(4);

foreach (int number in skipLowerFour)
    listbox1.Items.Add(number);
```

When this query is run, the following numbers are returned:

```
70
77
86
94
100
```

This example could also be written using query syntax as follows:

```
IEnumerable<int> skipLowerFour =
    (from n in randomNumbers
     order by n
     select n).Skip(4)
```

SkipWhile

The SkipWhile operator skips or bypasses elements based on a specified predicate function, and continues to bypass the elements as long as the specified condition is true (i.e., the condition is not met). The remaining elements are then returned.

The following example skips all the values in the sequence that are less than 50 and returns the remaining values.

```
Int[] randomNumbers = {86, 2, 77, 94, 100, 65, 5, 22, 70, 55, 81, 66, 45};

IEnumerable<int> skipLessThan50 =
    randomNumbers.OrderBy(num => num).SkipWhile(num =>
    num < 50);

foreach (int number in skipLowerFour)
    listbox1.Items.Add(number);
```

When this query is run, the following numbers are returned:

```
55
65
66
70
77
81
86
94
100
```

Likewise, this example could also be written using query syntax as follows:

```
IEnumerable<int> skipLowerFour =
    (from n in randomNumbers
     order by n
     select n).SkipWhile(num => num < 50);
```

Take

The Take operator returns contiguous elements within a sequence, starting at the beginning of the sequence, up to the position specified.

The following example skips all the values in the sequence that are less than 50 and returns the remaining values.

```
Int[] randomNumbers = {86, 2, 77, 94, 100, 65, 5, 22, 70, 55, 81, 66, 45};

IEnumerable<int> takeTopFour =
    randomNumbers.OrderByDescending(num => num).Take(4);

foreach (int number in takeTopFour)
    listbox1.Items.Add(number);
```

When this query is run, the following numbers are returned:

```
100
94
86
81
```

This example could also be written using query syntax as follows:

```
IEnumerable<int> takeTopFour =
    (from n in randomNumbers
     order by n descending
     select n).Take(4);
```

TakeWhile

The TakeWhile operator returns elements based on a specified predicate function, and continues to take the elements as long as the specified condition is true (i.e., the condition is not met). The remaining elements are skipped.

The following example takes all the values in the sequence that are less than 50 and skips the remaining values.

```
Int[] randomNumbers = {86, 2, 77, 94, 100, 65, 5, 22, 70, 55, 81, 66, 45};

IEnumerable<int> takeGreaterThan50 =
    randomNumbers.OrderByDescending(num => num).TakeWhile(num => num > 50);

foreach (int number in takeGreaterThan50)
    listbox1.Items.Add(number);
```

When this query is run, the following numbers are returned:

```
100
94
86
81
77
70
66
65
55
```

This example could also be written using query syntax as follows:

```
IEnumerable<int> takeGreaterThan50 =
    (from n in randomNumbers
     order by n descending
     select n).TakeWhile(num => num > 50);
```

As an interesting experiment, try modifying the original query as follows and executing it:

```
IEnumerable<int> takeGreaterThan50 =
    randomNumbers.OrderBy(num => num).TakeWhile(num =>
    num > 50);
```

Was anything returned? Why not? As stated earlier, it returns elements based on a specified predicate function, and continues to take the elements as long as the specified condition is true. If you order the sequence in ascending order, the first element it finds does not meet the criteria and therefore the query does not continue.

Putting Query Operators to Work

There was a ton of information in this chapter, so this section provides an example that enables you to apply many of the operators you've seen and to begin experimenting with the great functionality provided by the LINQ query operators.

Fire up an instance of Visual Studio 2008 and create a new C# Windows Forms Application project. In the Solution Explorer, expand the References node, right-click on it, and select Add Reference from the context menu. In the Add Reference dialog opens, make sure that the .NET tab is selected, and scroll down the list until you see the System.Data.Linq component. Select that component and click OK.

Next, open `Form1` in design view and place two buttons and a list box on the form. Name one of the buttons `cmdExecuteQuery` and the other `cmdClose`. Then view the code behind the form and replace the existing code with the following (this code can also be obtained from the Chapter 4 example in the file download for this chapter):

```
using System;
using System.Linq;
using System.Collections.Generic;
using System.ComponentModel;
using System.Data;
using System.Data.Linq;
using System.Drawing;
using System.Text;
using System.Windows.Forms;
using System.Xml;

namespace LINQ
{
    public partial class Form1 : Form
    {
        public Form1()
        {
            InitializeComponent();
        }

        private void Form1_Load(object sender, EventArgs e)
        {
        }

        private void cmdClose_Click(object sender, EventArgs e)
        {
            Application.Exit();
        }

        private void cmdExecuteQuery_Click(object sender, EventArgs e)
        {
            DataContext context = new DataContext("Initial ↵
Catalog=AdventureWorks;Integrated Security=sspi");

            Table<Contact> contact = context.GetTable<Contact>();
            Table<Employee> employee = context.GetTable<Employee>();

            var query =
                from c in contact
                join emp in employee on c.ContactID equals emp.ContactID
                where c.FirstName.StartsWith("S")
                && emp.HireDate.Year > 1999
                orderby c.LastName
                orderby c.FirstName
                select new { emp.EmployeeID, c.LastName, c.FirstName, ↵
emp.Title, c.EmailAddress, emp.HireDate };//.Thenby(c => c.FirstName);

            foreach (var item in query)
                listBox1.Items.Add(item.FirstName
```

```
                        + " " + item.LastName
                        + " " + item.Title
                        + " " + item.EmailAddress
                        + " " + item.HireDate);

        }

    }

    [Table(Name = "Person.Contact")]
    public class Contact
    {
        [Column(DBType = "int not null")]
        public int ContactID;

        [Column(DBType = "nvarchar(8) not null")]
        public string Title;

        [Column(DBType = "nvarchar(50) not null")]
        public string FirstName;

        [Column(DBType = "nvarchar(50) not null")]
        public string MiddleName;

        [Column(DBType = "nvarchar(50) not null")]
        public string LastName;

        [Column(DBType = "nvarchar(50) not null")]
        public string EmailAddress;

        [Column(DBType = "int")]
        public int EmailPromotion;

    }

    [Table(Name = "HumanResources.Employee")]
    public class Employee
    {
        [Column(DBType = "int not null")]
        public int ContactID;

        [Column(DBType = "int")]
        public int EmployeeID;

        [Column(DBType = "nvarchar(50) not null")]
        public string Title;

        [Column(DBType = "datetime")]
        public DateTime HireDate;

    }
}
```

This example creates object-relational mappings to two tables in the AdventureWorks database from which the data for the queries will be pulled. When the OK button is clicked, a connection is made to the appropriate database, and the data sources are defined.

Several operators—join, restriction, and sorting operators, for instance—are used in the query expression. Once the query expression is defined, the query is executed by iterating through the sequence or collection, and the results are written to the form's list box.

The `Employee` and `Contact` tables are joined by creating a join on the `ContactID` column. Several columns between the two tables are projected (selected as elements for return values) and a filter is applied looking for all contacts whose first name begins with the letter *S* and whose hire date is after the year 1999. A sort is applied, ordering the results by last name, sorted in ascending order.

When this query is run, the following results are returned (a portion of the data has been left out for space considerations):

```
Sandeep Kaliyath Production Technician - WC40
Sharon Salavaria Design Engineer
Sheela Word Purchasing Manager
Shu Ito Sales Representative
Sootha Charncherngkha Quality Assurance Technician
Stephen Jiang North American Sales Manager
Stuart Macrae Janitor
Syed Abbas Pacific Sales Manager
Sylvester Valdez Production Technician - WC20
```

While this example is fairly simple, it does provide a great foundation. You can modify it by applying many of the operators discussed in this chapter.

Let's modify this example a little bit. Add a second button to the form, name it `cmdMethodSyntax`, and place the following code in the `Click()` event of that button.

```
        DataContext context = new DataContext("Initial ↵
Catalog=AdventureWorks;Integrated Security=sspi");

        Table<Contact> contact = context.GetTable<Contact>();
        Table<Employee> employee = context.GetTable<Employee>();

var query =
    contact.Join(employee, con => con.ContactID,
    emp => emp.ContactID, (con, emp) =>
    new { con = con, emp = emp})
    .Where(c => c.con.FirstName.StartsWith("S"))
    .Where(c => c.emp.HireDate.Year > 1999)
    .OrderBy(c => c.con.LastName)
    .OrderBy(c => c.con.FirstName)
    .Select(o => new
    { o.emp.EmployeeID, o.con.LastName, o.con.FirstName,
      o.emp.Title, o.con.EmailAddress, o.emp.HireDate} );

        foreach (var item in query)
```

```
listBox1.Items.Add(item.FirstName
    + " " + item.LastName
    + " " + item.Title
    + " " + item.EmailAddress
    + " " + item.HireDate);
```

This code accomplishes the exact same thing as the preceding code, but uses method syntax. This example is here to illustrate the different ways you can use the LINQ standard query operators.

Summary

This chapter introduced you to LINQ's standard query operators. Without them, LINQ doesn't happen. The chapter provides you with a good foundation in and understanding of their functionality, which will be helpful because the rest of this book utilizes the information found in this chapter.

The next four chapters take a look at LINQ to XML, a new approach to programming with XML.

Part II
LINQ to XML

Understanding LINQ to XML

XML is becoming more and more mainstream. It's being used in databases (I love that!), configuration files, and throughout the Web, and is becoming a more popular mechanism for formatting your day-to-day data such as spreadsheets and documents.

Until now, working with XML has been somewhat frustrating because of the many different technologies available to developers to work with XML. There's the DOM (Document Object Model), which provides a standardized interpretation of an XML document. You also have XPath and XSLT, which afford the ability to query and format XML. Within the .NET Framework you have the System.Xml namespace, which makes available a programmatic representation of XML documents and mechanisms for manipulating XML documents, nodes, and XML fragments.

There is a need to improve the way developers work with XML, and LINQ to XML is the answer. The first four chapters provided the foundation for the rest of this book, presenting the basic principles of LINQ and its different components, such as the standard query operators. This information is extremely vital to LINQ to XML because it helps developers work with and program XML using LINQ to XML.

This chapter provides an introductory look at LINQ to XML, exploring the fundamentals and concepts that programmers need to comprehend when working with LINQ to XML. It includes the following:

- ❑ An overview of LINQ to XML
- ❑ Programming fundamentals of LINQ to XML
- ❑ Programming concepts of LINQ to XML
- ❑ A comparison of LINQ to XML and other XML technologies

LINQ to XML Overview

LINQ to XML is a new approach to working with XML. In essence, it takes many of the technologies you use today to work with XML, such as the DOM and XPath, and combines them into a single programming interface directly within the .NET Framework. LINQ to XML provides in-memory document modification capabilities of the DOM, while providing querying capabilities equal to those of XPath via LINQ query expressions.

Any programming language that supports the .NET Framework supports LINQ. LINQ to XML is "LINQ-enabled," meaning that you have access to all of the functionality of LINQ, such as the standard query operators and the LINQ programming interface. Because of its integration into the .NET Framework, LINQ to XML can take advantage of .NET Framework functionality, such as compile-time checking, strong typing, and debugging.

As stated previously, LINQ to XML provides much of the functionality found in today's XML technologies, but it does so from within a single programming interface. Using LINQ to XML you can easily load XML documents into memory and just as easily query and modify the documents. You can also save in-memory XML documents to disk, as well as serialize them for routing over the wire.

The great thing about LINQ to XML (and LINQ in general) is that it makes working with XML much simpler, and therefore developers who do not have a whole lot of experience with XML can jump right in. LINQ to XML provides developers of all levels the capability to easily work with XML. For those who are somewhat new to working with XML, LINQ to XML provides a simple but powerful query experience (instead of their having to learn a more complex XML query language). More-advanced developers can use LINQ to XML to enhance their XML programming by writing less code that is just as powerful, easier to read, and much more expressive. The key is that LINQ to XML is not targeted to a specific level of developer—it can be used by any developer who needs to work with XML.

LINQ to XML is provided via the System.Xml.Linq namespace, which contains all of the classes necessary to work with XML. Add a reference to System.Xml.Linq.dll to your project, and then place a using directive in the declarations section of your code, as follows:

```
using System.Xml.Linq;
```

Adding this directive enables the use of LINQ to XML types in the namespace. If you plan to work with relational data, you need to use System.Data.Linq as well.

LINQ to XML Programming Fundamentals

As Chapter 2, "A Look at Visual Studio 2008," explained, LINQ (and therefore LINQ to XML) utilizes generic classes quite heavily. Therefore, it is quite helpful to have an understanding of generics and delegates as you get into LINQ and LINQ to XML.

The component that gives LINQ to XML its power is the System.Xml.Linq namespace and its corresponding classes. Those classes provide the capability to work with XML with ease, leaving behind the need to work with complex and sometimes cumbersome technologies such as the DOM and XQuery.

The following sections provide an overview of the classes in the System.Xml.Linq namespace, and then detailed discussions of the XDocument, XElement, and XAttribute classes.

LINQ to XML Classes

The System.Xml.Linq namespace contains 19 classes, which are described in the following table.

Class	Description
XAttribute	Represents an XML attribute.
XCData	Represents a CDATA text node.
XComment	Represents an XML comment.
XContainer	An abstract base class representing nodes that have child nodes.
XDeclaration	Represents an XML declaration.
XDocument	Represents an XML document. This class is derived from the XContainer class.
XDocumentType	Represents an XML DTD (document type definition).
XElement	Represents an XML element. This class is derived from the XContainer class.
XName	Represents the name of an XML element or attribute.
XNamespace	Represents an XML namespace.
XNode	An abstract class representing nodes of an XML element tree.
XNodeDocumentOrderComparer	Provides mechanisms for node comparisons regarding their order within the XML document.
XNodeEqualityComparer	Provides mechanisms for node comparisons regarding their equality value.
XObject	An abstract class representing XNodes and XAttributes.
XObjectChange	The event type when an XObject event is raised.
XObjectChangeEventArgs	Provides information and data for the Changing and Changed events.
XObjectChangeEventHandler	The method that will handle the XObject's Changed and Changing events.
XProcessingInstruction	Represents an XML processing instruction.
XText	Represents an XML text node.

If you have done any programming with XML before, you are familiar with XML declarations. An XML declaration specifies the XML version, the encoding of an XML document, and whether the XML document is a standalone document. LINQ to XML lets you do this quite easily. The following example uses the XDeclaration class to define an XML declaration:

```
XDocument myDoc = new XDocument
(
  new XDeclaration("1.0","utf-8","yes"),
  new XElement("Root","stuff"),
);
```

```
string str = myDoc.Declaration.ToString() + Environment.NewLine + myDoc.ToString();

textbox1.Text = str;
```

What you get is the following:

```
<?xml version="1.0" encoding="utf-8" standalone="yes"?>
<Root>stuff</Root>
```

Very slick. As you start to use the LINQ to XML classes, you begin to get a feel for how much thought Microsoft put into LINQ (including LINQ to XML and LINQ to SQL). One of the things it focused on is names. Often the difficulty in working with XML is in dealing with XML names due to the simple fact of XML prefixes.

In XML, prefixes can come in handy. The main concept behind them is to reduce the amount of typing you have to do when creating XML. It also makes XML much easier to read. Yet prefixes are not required and the problem they cause is that they shortcut the full XML namespace. LINQ to XML solves this problem by automatically resolving prefixes to their XML namespace.

The following three sections detail the classes that you will typically use most when working with XML: XElement, XAttribute, and XDocument. If you master those classes, LINQ to XML will become second nature.

XElement Class

The XElement class represents an XML element. It is derived from the XContainer class, which derives from the XNode class. An element is a node, so many times you will see these terms used interchangeably. The XElement class is one of the most important and fundamental classes of LINQ to XML because it contains all of the functionality necessary to create and manipulate XML elements. Via this class you can create elements, add and modify attributes of elements, and even manipulate the content of an element such as adding, deleting, or modifying child elements.

There are several ways to create XML documents with LINQ to XML, depending on the source of your XML or if you are creating an XML document from scratch. The simplest and most common way to create XML is to use the good ol' XElement class of LINQ to XML as follows:

```
XDocument riders = new XDocument
  (new XDeclaration("1.0", "utf-8", "yes"),
    new XComment("Riders for the year 2007"),
    new XElement("Riders",
     new XElement("Rider",
       new XElement("Name", "Ricky Carmichael"),
       new XElement("Class", "450"),
       new XElement("Brand", "Suzuki"),
         new XElement("Sponsers",
           new XElement("Name", "Makita")
           )
         ),
     new XElement("Rider",
       new XElement("Name", "Chad Reed"),
       new XElement("Class", "450"),
```

```
        new XElement("Brand", "Yamaha"),
        new XElement("Sponsers",
          new XElement("Name", "ProTaper")
          )
        ),
      new XElement("Rider",
        new XElement("Name", "James Stewart"),
        new XElement("Class", "450"),
        new XElement("Brand", "Kawasaki"),
        new XElement("Sponsers",
          new XElement("Name", "Renthal")
          )
        )
    )
  )
);
```

The resulting XML looks like this:

```
<!--Riders for the year 2007-->
<Riders>
  <Rider>
    <Name>Ricky Carmichael</Name>
    <Class>450</Class>
    <Brand>Suzuki</Brand>
    <Sponsers>
      <Name>Makita</Name>
    </Sponsers>
  </Rider>
  <Rider>
    <Name>Chad Reed</Name>
    <Class>450</Class>
    <Brand>Yamaha</Brand>
    <Sponsers>
      <Name>ProTaper</Name>
    </Sponsers>
  </Rider>
  <Rider>
    <Name>James Stewart</Name>
    <Class>450</Class>
    <Brand>Kawasaki</Brand>
    <Sponsers>
      <Name>Renthal</Name>
    </Sponsers>
  </Rider>
</Riders>
```

You can also use a LINQ query to populate an XML tree. Create a directory called Wrox in the root of your C drive, for example, and in your favorite text editor program, type the following, saving it as Employees.xml:

```
<?xml version="1.0"?>
<Employees>
    <Employee id="1">
        <Name>Steve Kent</Name>
```

```
        <Title>Mr. SciFi</Title>
        <Department>Gaming</Department>
        <HireDate>04/17/92</HireDate>
        <Gender>M</Gender>
        <MaritalStatus>M</MaritalStatus>
    </Employee>
    <Employee id="2">
        <Name>Scott Klein</Name>
        <Title>Geek</Title>
        <Department>All things technical</Department>
        <HireDate>02/05/94</HireDate>
        <Gender>M</Gender>
        <MaritalStatus>M</MaritalStatus>
    </Employee>
</Employees>
```

The following code loads `Employees.xml` using the `Load` method of the `XElement` class. The results of `Load` are then used to create and populate an XML tree, while adding two more elements to the tree.

```
XElement employees = XElement.Load(@"C:\Wrox\Employees.xml");

XElement tree = new XElement("Root",
                    new XElement("Manager", "Dave"),
                    new XElement("BirthDate", "01/01/1970"),
                    from el in employees.Elements()
                    select el);
textBox1.Text = tree.ToString();
```

When this code runs, the following output appears:

```
<Root>
  <Manager>Dave</Manager>
  <BirthDate>01/01/1970</BirthDate>
  <Employee id="1">
    <Name>Steve Kent</Name>
    <Title>Mr. SciFi</Title>
    <Department>Gaming</Department>
    <HireDate>04/17/92</HireDate>
    <Gender>M</Gender>
    <MaritalStatus>M</MaritalStatus>
  </Employee>
  <Employee id="2">
    <Name>Scott Klein</Name>
    <Title>Geek</Title>
    <Department>All things technical</Department>
    <HireDate>02/05/94</HireDate>
    <Gender>M</Gender>
    <MaritalStatus>M</MaritalStatus>
  </Employee>
</Root>
```

The `XElement` class contains a number of methods that make working with XML a breeze. The following table describes the class's methods.

Method	Description
AddAnnotation	Adds an annotation to a given XElement. In general terms, this method adds an object to the annotation of the corresponding XObject (the current node or attribute in the tree).
AncestorsAndSelf	Returns a collection of elements, in which the collection contains the current element and all ancestors of the current element. An ancestor is defined as the parent(s) of the current node (meaning, the parent of the current node, and the parent's parent, and so on up the chain).
Attribute	Returns a single attribute, which is the XAttribute of the current XElement of a given XName. In other words, this method returns the first attribute it finds for a given element that has a specified name.
Attributes	Returns all the attributes (a collection) for the current element. You can also specify a name, in which case all attributes are returned for the element that has the specified name.
CreateReader	Creates an XmlReader (a fast, forward-only copy of the XML document) of the current node.
CreateWriter	Creates an XmlWriter of the XML document that provides the capability to modify the XML document, such as adding nodes or attributes. The XmlWriter is a fast, forward-only mechanism for creating files of the in-memory XML document.
DescendantNodes	Returns a collection of all descendant nodes of the entire document or the current node/element.
DescendantNodesAndSelf	Returns the same collection as the DescenantNodes method but also includes the current node in the collection.
DescendantsAndSelf	Returns a collection of elements that contain the current element plus all descendant elements of the current element. You can also specify a name that returns only those elements that match the specified name in the collection.
Element	In an ordered XML document, Element returns the first element that matches the specified element name.
IsAfter	Returns a Boolean value that specifies whether the current node appears after a specified node.
IsBefore	Returns a Boolean value that specifies whether the current node appears before a specified node.
Load	Provides multiple mechanisms for creating new XElements from an external source. Sources can include a TextReader, String, or XmlReader (each with an additional option to preserve whitespace).
Nodes	Returns a collection of child nodes of the current element or document.
NodesAfterSelf	Returns a collection of ordered nodes after (that follow) the current node.

Continued on the next page

Method	Description
NodesBeforeSelf	Returns a collection of ordered nodes before the current node.
Parse	Loads an XML document from a string containing XML. Can optionally preserve whitespace.
Remove	Removes the current node from its parent.
RemoveAll	Removes all nodes and attributes from the current element.
RemoveAttributes	Removes all attributes from the current element.
RemoveNodes	Removes all nodes from the XML document or current element.
ReplaceAll	Replaces all child nodes and attributes of the current element with the specified content.
ReplaceAttributes	Replaces all the attributes of the current element with the specified content.
Save	Serializes the current element's XML tree to any of several destinations, such as a file, XmlTextWriter, XmlWriter, or TextWriter.
SetAttributeValue	Sets the value of the current attribute.
SetElementValue	Sets the value of a child element.
SetValue	Sets the value of the current element.
WriteTo	Writes the current element to an XmlWriter.

These are powerful yet easy-to-use methods. You'll use several of them in this chapter's examples. For instance, you can use the CreateReader method to load an XML tree into an XmlReader, like this:

```
XElement employees = null;
employee = XElement.Load(@"C:\Wrox\Employees.xml";
XmlReader rdr = employees.CreateReader();
rdr.MoveToContent();
```

The XmlReader can be used to quickly read nodes and its descendants.

There may be times when there are other components used by your existing application that are expecting an XmlReader as input or as the source of data. The preceding example shows one way to use LINQ to XML to provide XmlReader functionality.

XAttribute Class

The XAttribute class deals with attributes, plain and simple. Attributes are name/value pairs associated with elements, but working with attributes is really no different from working with elements. Attributes are similar to elements in many ways, such as their constructors and the methods in which values and collections are returned. Writing a LINQ query expression to return a collection of attributes is structurally and syntactically the same as writing a LINQ query expression for returning a collection of elements.

Elements and attributes also have their differences. For example, attributes are not nodes in an XML tree, so they do not derive from the XNode class. Each attribute must have a qualified name that is unique to the element. And attributes are maintained in the XML tree in the order that they are added to the element.

The great thing, however, is that working with the XAttribute class is just like working with the XElement class.

Here's how to add an attribute to a simple XML tree during construction:

```
XElement employee = new XElement("Root",
                        new XElement("Employee",
                            new XAttribute("id", "1")
                            )
                        );
```

And here's its output:

```
<Root>
  <Employee id="1" />
</Root>
```

Just like elements, multiple attributes can be added at one time. For instance, you could add a phone attribute along with the id attribute, like this:

```
XElement employee = new XElement("Root",
                        new XElement("Employee",
                            new XAttribute("id", "1"),
                            new XAttribute("phone", "555-555-5555")
                            )
                        );
```

And the output is as follows:

```
<Root>
  <Employee id="1" phone="555-555-5555"/>
</Root>
```

The key to attributes is that they must have a qualified name that is unique to the particular element to which they are being added.

Unlike the XElement class, the XAttribute class has only a small handful of methods. The methods are similar to XElement's, which makes working with them extremely easy. Here are descriptions of the XAttribute class methods:

❏   AddAnnotation—Adds an annotation to a given attribute.

❏   Remove—Removes the attribute from its parent.

❏   SetValue—Sets the value of the current attribute.

The following example creates a simple XML tree with two attributes associated with the Employee node:

```
XElement employee = new XElement("Root",
                        new XElement("Employee",
                            new XAttribute("id", "1"),
                            new XAttribute("dept", "Dev")),
                        new XElement("Name", "Scott")
                            )
                        );
```

Here's the resulting XML:

```
<Root>
    <Employee id="1" dept="id" />
    <Name>Scott</Name>
</Root>
```

Now Remove() is issued to remove the second attribute:

```
XAttribute attr = employee.Element("Employee").Attribute("dept");
attr.Remove();
```

Just for kicks, try removing the attribute this way:

```
XAttribute attr = employee.Attribute("dept");
attr.Remove();
```

Did it work? No, because you really haven't identified where the attribute dept really is, or better said, you haven't identified the element to which the dept attribute belongs.

The first example illustrates how to "walk the XML tree" to denote the node you want to deal with.

XDocument Class

The XDocument class provides you with the means to work with valid XML documents, including declarations, comments, and processing instructions.

The XDocument class derives from XContainer and, therefore, can have child nodes. But keep in mind that XML standards limit an XDocument object to only a single child XElement node, which is the root node or element.

An XDocument object can contain the following:

❑   One XDeclaration object—Specifies important parts of an XML declaration, such as the document encoding and XML version.

❑   One XElement object—Specifies the root element of the document.

❑   One XDocumentType object—Represents an XML DTD (document typed definition).

❑ Multiple XComment objects—Specifies an XML comment. A child of the root node, an XComment object cannot be the first argument; a valid XML document cannot begin with a comment..

❑ Multiple XProcessingInstruction objects—Specify any information to the application that is processing the XML.

A large portion of the functionality for working with nodes and elements can be obtained through the XElement class, and the XDocument class should be used only when you absolutely need the capability to work at the document level and need access to comments, processing instructions, and the declaration. Basically, a declaration, comments, and processing instructions are not required for LINQ to XML to work with XML; you need to use the XDocument class only if you need the functionality it provides.

For instance, the following example creates a simple XML document with several elements and an attribute, as well as a processing instruction and comments.

```
XDocument doc = new XDocument(
            new XProcessingInstruction("xml-stylesheet", "title='EmpInfo'"),
            new XComment("some comments"),
            new XElement("Root",
              new XElement("Employees",
                new XElement("Employee",
                  new XAttribute("id" "1")
                new XElement("Name", "Scott Klein"),
                new XElement("Title", "Geek"),
                new XElement("HireDate", "02/05/2007"),
                new XElement("Gender", "M")
                      )
                  )
              )
              new XComment("more comments"),
          );
```

This code produces the following:

```
<?xml-stylesheet title='EmployeeInfo'?>
<!--some comments-->
<Root>
  <Employees>
    <Employee id="1">
      <Name>Scott Klein</Name>
      <Title>Geek</Title>
      <HireDate>02/05/2007</HireDate>
      <Gender>M</Gender>
    </Employee>
  </Employees>
</Root>
<!--more comments-->
```

Notice how simple it is to construct the XML document and place comments and other information throughout it.

The XDocument class contains a number of methods that are identical to XElement class methods. They're described in the following table.

Method	Description
AddAnnotation	Adds an annotation to a given XElement. In general terms, this method adds an object to the annotation of the corresponding XObject (the current node or attribute in the tree).
CreateReader	Creates an XmlReader (a fast, forward-only copy of the XML document) of the current node.
CreateWriter	Creates an XmlWriter of the XML document that provides the capability to modify the XML document, such as adding nodes or attributes. The XmlWriter is a fast, forward-only mechanism for creating files of the in-memory XML document.
DescendantNodes	Returns a collection of all descendant nodes of the entire document or the current node/element.
Element	In an ordered XML document, Element returns the first element that matches the specified element name.
IsAfter	Returns a Boolean value that specifies whether the current node appears after a specified node.
IsBefore	Returns a Boolean value that specifies whether the current node appears before a specified node.
Load	Provides multiple mechanisms for creating new XElement objects from an external source. Sources can include a TextReader, String, or XmlReader (each with an additional option to preserve whitespace).
Nodes	Returns a collection of child nodes of the current element or document.
NodesAfterSelf	Returns a collection of ordered nodes after (that follow) the current node.
NodesBeforeSelf	Returns a collection of ordered nodes before the current node.
Parse	Loads an XML document from a string containing XML. Can optionally preserve whitespace.
Remove	Removes the current node from its parent.
RemoveNodes	Removes all nodes from the XML document or current element.
Save	Serializes the current element's XmlTree to several output options, such as a file, XmlTextWriter, XmlWriter, and TextWriter.

The following example creates an XML document that contains employee information along with processing instructions and a comment, utilizing all of the classes previously discussed, including the XDocument and XElement classes.

Once the XML document is created, the `NodesAfterSelf` method of the `XElement` class is used to return all the elements after the `<Employee>` element. Those elements are then iterated through and added to the list box. This example requires a `Using` statement to `System.Xml`.

```
XElement doc = new XElement("Root",
                new XElement("Employees",
                    new XElement("Employee",
                        new XAttribute("id" "1"),
                    new XElement("Name", "Scott Klein"),
                    new XElement("Title", "Geek"),
                    new XElement("HireDate", "02/05/2007"),
                    new XElement("Gender", "M")
                        )
                    )
            );

XElement xele = xtree. Element("Employees").Element("Employee"). Element("Name");
IEnumerable<XNode> nodes =
    from node in xele.NodesAfterSelf()
    select node;

foreach (XNode inode in nodes)
    listBox1.Items.Add(inode.NodeType == XmlNodeType.Element ?
        (inode as XElement).Value : "");
```

Now you should be able to see how easy and efficient it is to work with XML in LINQ to XML, using the available classes to create, query, and manipulate XML.

LINQ to XML Programming Concepts

This section explores LINQ to XML programming concepts such as how to load XML, create XML from scratch, manipulate XML information, and traverse an XML document.

Working with Existing XML

Loading XML into a LINQ to XML tree is straightforward. You can load XML from a number of sources, such as a string, `XmlReader`, `TextReader`, or file.

The following example illustrates how to load from a file:

```
XElement employees = null;
employees = XElement.Load(@"C:\Wrox\Employees.xml");
```

In this example, a variable called `employees` is declared as an `XElement` object (an instance of the `XElement` class). The `Load` method of the `XElement` class is then used to load the raw XML from the `Employees.xml` file into an XML tree and store the XML contents in the `employees` variable.

XML can also be loaded from a string, using the `Parse` method:

```
XElement employees = XElement.Parse(@"
    <Employees>
```

```
        <Employee id='1' phone='555-555-5555'>
            <Name>Steve Kent</Name>
            <Title>Mr. SciFi</Title>
            <Department>Gaming</Department>
            <HireDate>04/17/92</HireDate>
            <Gender>M</Gender>
            <MaritalStatus>M</MaritalStatus>
        </Employee>
        <Employee id='2' phone='555-555-5556'>
            <Name>Scott Klein</Name>
            <Title>Geek</Title>
            <Department>All things technical</Department>
            <HireDate>02/05/94</HireDate>
            <Gender>M</Gender>
            <MaritalStatus>M</MaritalStatus>
        </Employee>
        <Employee id='3' phone='555-555-5557'>
            <Name>Joe Walling</Name>
            <Title>Head Geek</Title>
            <Department>All things bleeding edge</Department>
            <HireDate>06/15/93</HireDate>
            <Gender>M</Gender>
            <MaritalStatus>M</MaritalStatus>
        </Employee>
    </Employees>");
```

Parse has an optional Boolean overload that enables you to preserve whitespace. When using Parse, your XML tree can contain only a single root node.

You can also load XML from a TextReader:

```
TextReader tr = new StringReader(@"
    <Employees>
        <Employee id='1' phone='555-555-5555'>
            <Name>Steve Kent</Name>
            <Title>Mr. SciFi</Title>
            <Department>Gaming</Department>
            <HireDate>04/17/92</HireDate>
            <Gender>M</Gender>
            <MaritalStatus>M</MaritalStatus>
        </Employee>
        <Employee id='2' phone='555-555-5556'>
            <Name>Scott Klein</Name>
            <Title>Geek</Title>
            <Department>All things technical</Department>
            <HireDate>02/05/94</HireDate>
            <Gender>M</Gender>
            <MaritalStatus>M</MaritalStatus>
        </Employee>
        <Employee id='3' phone='555-555-5557'>
            <Name>Joe Walling</Name>
            <Title>Head Geek</Title>
```

```
                <Department>All things bleeding edge</Department>
                <HireDate>06/15/93</HireDate>
                <Gender>M</Gender>
                <MaritalStatus>M</MaritalStatus>
            </Employee>
        </Employees>");
    XElement xel = XElement.Load(tr);
    tr.Close();
```

The output of both of these examples is the same XML.

Saving XML via LINQ to XML

Saving XML via LINQ to XML is just as easy as loading XML. For instance, the following example creates a TextReader, populates it with an XML document, and then uses the XElement class's Load method to load the contents of the TextReader into the XML Element. The Save() method is subsequently called to write the XML to a file.

```
    TextReader tr = new StringReader(@"
        <Employees>
            <Employee id='1' phone='555-555-5555'>
                <Name>Steve Kent</Name>
                <Title>Mr. SciFi</Title>
                <Department>Gaming</Department>
                <HireDate>04/17/92</HireDate>
                <Gender>M</Gender>
                <MaritalStatus>M</MaritalStatus>
            </Employee>
            <Employee id='2' phone='555-555-5556'>
                <Name>Scott Klein</Name>
                <Title>Geek</Title>
                <Department>All things technical</Department>
                <HireDate>02/05/94</HireDate>
                <Gender>M</Gender>
                <MaritalStatus>M</MaritalStatus>
            </Employee>
            <Employee id='3' phone='555-555-5557'>
                <Name>Joe Walling</Name>
                <Title>Head Geek</Title>
                <Department>All things bleeding edge</Department>
                <HireDate>06/15/93</HireDate>
                <Gender>M</Gender>
                <MaritalStatus>M</MaritalStatus>
            </Employee>
        </Employees>");
    XElement xel = XElement.Load(tr);
    tr.Close();
    xel.Save(@"C:\Wrox\Employees2.xml");
```

Saving XML like this is commonly known as serializing. If the XML that is loaded into the XML class is indented, the serialized XML keeps its formatting, thus maintaining the indentation of the XML, although any insignificant whitespace is removed.

Creating XML

LINQ to XML provides a powerful yet easy approach to manually creating XML elements. You have seen this method quite a bit throughout this chapter. The section "LINQ to XML Programming Fundamentals" listed several classes available to you via LINQ to XML in which you can manually create XML documents.

Here's an example that creates a simple XML document consisting of elements and attributes:

```
XElement xdoc = new XElement("Riders",
                    new XElement("Rider",
                        new XElement("Name", "Ricky Carmichael"),
                        new XElement("NationalNumber", "4"),
                        new XElement("Mechanic", "Mike Gosselaar"),
                        new XElement("Nickname", "GOAT")
                        )
                    );
```

And here's the output:

```
<Riders>
  <Rider>
    <Name>Ricky Carmichael</Name>
    <NationalNumber>4</NationalNumber>
    <Mechanic>Mike Gosselaar</Mechanic>
    <Nickname>GOAT</Nickname>
  </Rider>
</Riders>
```

The great thing about LINQ to XML in the .NET Framework is that indentation is automatically done for you. That makes reading it much easier because it mimics the format and structure of XML. (Oh, by the way, anyone who follows the supercross/motocross scene knows that Ricky Carmichael's nickname is not a reference to the animal, but to his achievements in the sport. GOAT: Greatest of All Time.)

Now modify the previous example by adding the highlighted line of code:

```
XElement xdoc = new XElement("Riders",
                    new XElement("Rider",
                        new XElement("Name", "Ricky Carmichael",
                            new XAttribute("Class", "450")),
                        new XElement("NationalNumber", "4"),
                        new XElement("Mechanic", "Mike Gosselaar"),
                        new XElement("Nickname", "GOAT")
                        )
                    );
```

Notice the results now show an attribute called Class on the Name element:

```
<Riders>
  <Rider>
    <Name Class="450">Ricky Carmichael</Name>
    <NationalNumber>4</NationalNumber>
```

```
        <Mechanic>Mike Gosselaar</Mechanic>
        <Nickname>GOAT</Nickname>
    </Rider>
</Riders>
```

LINQ to XML also provides a simple yet powerful mechanism for creating an XML tree in a single statement. This functionality is called *functional construction*, which will be discussed in Chapter 6, "Programming with LINQ to XML."

Traversing XML

So, you have your XML document in memory, whether you created it manually or loaded it using the `Load` method of the `XElement` class. Now what do you do with it? Specifically, how do you navigate the XML tree to get to the node/element you want to work with?

Traversing XML in an XML tree in LINQ to XML is quite simple. Just use the methods of the `XElement` and `XAttribute` classes as necessary. Basically, the `Elements` and `Element` methods provide all of the element children of an `XContainer` (an `XElement` or `XDocument`) object. Using the `XName` object, such as `Element(XName)`, you can return the elements of that specific `XName`.

Once you have your XML tree loaded as shown here:

```
employees = XElement.Load(@"C:\Wrox\Employees.xml");
```

you can start "walking the XML tree." Here are a couple of examples:

```
employees.Element("Employees").Element("Employee")
```

```
employees.Element("Employees").Element("Employee").Element("Name")
```

Granted, there is much more you can do, but this is just to whet your appetite. Keep in mind you can do the same with attributes. All of this is explained in more detail in Chapter 6.

The following is a simple example of returning elements of a particular node. It creates an XML document containing several riders, with each rider containing one attribute.

```
XElement xdoc = new XElement("Riders",
        new XElement("Rider",
            new XElement("Name", "Ricky Carmichael",
                new XAttribute("Class", "450")),
            new XElement("NationalNumber", "4"),
            new XElement("Brand", "Suzuki"),
            new XElement("Nickname", "GOAT"),
            new XElement("Mechanic", "Mike Gosselaar")
            ),
        new XElement("Rider",
            new XElement("Name", "Damon Bradshaw",
                new XAttribute("Class", "450")),
            new XElement("NationalNumber", "45"),
            new XElement("Brand", "Yamaha"),
            new XElement("Nickname", "Beast from the East"),
            new XElement("Mechanic", "N/A")
            ),
```

```
        new XElement("Rider",
            new XElement("Name", "Chad Reed",
                new XAttribute("Class", "450")),
            new XElement("NationalNumber", "22"),
            new XElement("Brand", "Yamaha"),
            new XElement("Nickname", "N/A"),
            new XElement("Mechanic", "N/A")
            ),
        new XElement("Rider",
            new XElement("Name", "James Stewart",
                new XAttribute("Class", "450")),
            new XElement("NationalNumber", "7"),
            new XElement("Brand", "Kawasaki"),
            new XElement("Nickname", "N/A"),
            new XElement("Mechanic", "N/A")
            ),
        new XElement("Rider",
            new XElement("Name", "Kevin Windham",
                new XAttribute("Class", "450")),
            new XElement("NationalNumber", "14"),
            new XElement("Brand", "Honda"),
            new XElement("Nickname", "N/A"),
            new XElement("Mechanic", "N/A")
            )
        );

textBox1.Text = xdoc.ToString();

foreach(XNode c in xdoc.Nodes())
    listBox1.Items.Add(c);
```

To get all the elements of a specific name, you can use the following:

```
foreach(XElement c in xdoc.Elements("Rider"))
    listBox1.Items.Add(c);
```

If you know that there is only a single element with a specific name, you can use the following:

```
listBox1.Items.Add(xdoc.Element(XName));
```

The thing to remember is that the `Nodes()`, `Elements()`, `Element(Name)`, and `Elements(Name)` methods provide the foundation and basic functionality of XML tree navigation.

Manipulating XML

The great thing about LINQ to XML is the capability to easily make changes to the XML tree, such as adding, deleting, updating, and copying content within the XML document.

Changes to an XML tree are available via the many methods of the `XNode` class, which represents nodes such as elements and comments in an XML tree. More often than not, you'll be working at the node level, manipulating elements and their contents or their attributes.

The next few sections discuss how to use many of the methods of the `XNode` class.

Insert

Content can be added to an XML tree easily by using one of the add methods available via the XNode class, depending on where you want to insert the XML:

❑ AddAfterSelf—Adds the specified content after the current node.

❑ AddBeforeSelf—Adds the specified content before the current node.

The following code defines an initial XML tree, then uses the AddAfterSelf() method to add an additional node after the State element.

```
XElement employee = new XElement("Root",
                        new XElement("Employee",
                            new XElement("Name", "Scott"),
                            new XElement("Address", "555 Main St."),
                            new XElement("City", "Wellington"),
                            new XElement("State", "FL")
                            )
                        );
XElement zip = employee.Element("Employee").Element("State");
zip.AddAfterSelf(new XElement("Zip","33414"));
```

Here's the resulting XML:

```
<Root>
  <Employee>
    <Name>Scott</Name>
    <Address>555 Main St.</Address>
    <City>Wellington</City>
    <State>FL</State>
    <Zip>33414</Zip>
  </Employee>
</Root>
```

Notice that the <Zip> element follows the <State> element as you instructed.

The AddBeforeSelf() method functions the same way when you need to add an element before a specific node.

Update

Updating XML is quite simple in LINQ to XML. There are several methods available, from deleting an element and adding another to changing the content of an element.

The Replace method provides several options from which you can choose:

❑ ReplaceWith—Replaces the content of the current element with the specified content.

❑ ReplaceAll—Replaces the child nodes and associated attributes of the current element with the specified content.

❑ ReplaceNodes—Replaces the child nodes of the document or current element with the specified content.

In the following example, an initial XML tree is defined, then the `ReplaceWith()` method is used to replace the contents of the `<State>` element with new content:

```
XElement employee = new XElement("Root",
                        new XElement("Employee",
                            new XElement("Name", "Scott"),
                            new XElement("Address", "555 Main St."),
                            new XElement("City", "Wellington"),
                            new XElement("State", "FL")
                            )
                        );
```

The result of this XML is as follows:

```
<Root>
  <Employee>
    <Name>Scott</Name>
    <Address>555 Main St.</Address>
    <City>Wellington</City>
    <State>WA</State>
    <Zip>33414</Zip>
  </Employee>
</Root>
```

In the following code, the first line identifies the element whose contents will be replaced, and the second line employs the `ReplaceWith()` method to specify the replacement content:

```
XElement st = employee.Element("Employee").Element("State");
st.ReplaceWith(new XElement("State", "FL"));
```

Here's the resulting XML:

```
<Root>
  <Employee>
    <Name>Scott</Name>
    <Address>555 Main St.</Address>
    <City>Wellington</City>
    <State>FL</State>
    <Zip>33414</Zip>
  </Employee>
</Root>
```

Notice that the value of the `<State>` element has been changed from WA to FL.

What happens if you use the following code to replace an element value?

```
st.ReplaceWith("FL");
```

`ReplaceWith()` deletes the specified node and replaces it with the specified content:

```
<Root>
  <Employee>
    <Name>Scott</Name>
```

```
      <Address>555 Main St.</Address>
      <City>Wellington</City>FL
    </Employee>
  </Root>
```

The `<State>` element is deleted and simply replaced with the text FL and not a new node. Thus, you must specify a new element to be created in the place of the old `<State>` element.

A similar operation can be done with attributes using the `SetAttributeValue` method. In the following example, notice that the attribute id has a value of 1.

```
XElement employee = new XElement("Employees",
                    new XElement("Employee",
                        new XAttribute("id", "1"),
                        new XElement("Name", "Scott"),
                        new XElement("Address", "555 Main St."),
                        new XElement("City", "Wellington"),
                        new XElement("State", "FL")
                        )
                    );
```

When you execute the following statement, the attribute value is changed to 3. The `SetAttributeValue` method changes the value of the id attribute to 3.

```
employee.Element("Employee").SetAttributeValue("id", "3");
```

The `SetElementValue` method is also available to you. It's a method of the `XElement` class and provides the capability to set the value of a child element, or to add or remove a child element. For example, the following creates a simple XML fragment and then uses the `SetElementValue()` method to update the `Address` node value:

```
XElement employee = new XElement("Employees",
                    new XElement("Employee",
                        new XAttribute("id", "1"),
                        new XElement("Name", "Scott"),
                        new XElement("Address", "555 Main St."),
                        new XElement("City", "Wellington"),
                        new XElement("State", "FL")
                        )
                    );
```

```
employee.Element("Employee").SetElementValue("Address", "111 Main St.");
```

Running this code shows that the address has indeed been changed:

```
<Employees>
  <Employee id="1">
    <Name>Scott</Name>
    <Address>111 Main St.</Address>
    <City>Wellington</City>
    <State>FL</State>
  </Employee>
</Employees>
```

Delete

Deleting XML is as simple as navigating to the content you want to delete and calling the `Remove()` or `RemoveAll()` method.

The following example creates an XML tree, and then adds an element that will be removed in the next set of code:

```
XElement employee = new XElement("Root",
                        new XElement("Employee",
                            new XElement("Name", "Scott"),
                            new XElement("Address", "555 Main St."),
                            new XElement("City", "Wellington"),
                            new XElement("State", "FL")
                            )
                        );

XElement zip = new XElement("Zip", "33414");
employee.Add(zip);
```

Here's the resulting XML tree:

```
<Root>
  <Employee>
    <Name>Scott</Name>
    <Address>555 Main St.</Address>
    <City>Wellington</City>
    <State>FL</State>
    <Zip>33414</Zip>
  </Employee>
</Root>
```

Now, remove the node you just added:

```
employee.Remove(zip);
```

The XML tree now looks like this:

```
<Root>
  <Employee>
    <Name>Scott</Name>
    <Address>555 Main St.</Address>
    <City>Wellington</City>
    <State>FL</State>
  </Employee>
</Root>
```

Likewise, you can use the `RemoveAll()` method to remove all the nodes (including child nodes) and attributes for the given element:

```
XElement employee = new XElement("Root",
                        new XElement("Employee",
                            new XElement("Name", "Scott"),
```

```
                            new XElement("Address", "555 Main St."),
                            new XElement("City", "Wellington"),
                            new XElement("State", "FL")
                            )
                    );

        Employee.RemoveAll();
```

Here's the resulting XML:

```
<Root />
```

Working with Attributes

Attributes are name/value pairs that are associated an XML element. By now you know quite a bit about dealing with elements via the XElement class, and the good news is that dealing with attributes via the XAttribute class is not much different. The following sections explain how to work with attributes in an XML tree, specifically adding, retrieving, and deleting attributes.

Adding

Adding attributes with LINQ to XML is similar to adding elements. You can add attributes using an XML construction like the following:

```
XElement employee = new XElement("Root",
            new XElement("Employee",
                new XAttribute("id", "1"),
                new XAttribute("EyeColor", "Blue"),
                new XElement("Name", "Scott"),
                new XElement("Address", "555 Main St."),
                new XElement("City", "Wellington"),
                new XElement("State", "FL")
                )
            );
```

You can also add an attribute as follows:

```
XAttribute dept = employee.Element("Employee").Attribute("EyeColor");
```

Retrieving

Retrieving attributes is also easy. It involves using the Attributes(XName) method of the XElement class. For example, the following code defines an XML tree with several attributes defined on the Employee node. The Attributes() method of the XElement class is then used to retrieve those attributes.

```
XElement employee = new XElement("Root",
            new XElement("Employee",
                new XAttribute("id", "1"),
                new XAttribute("EyeColor", "Blue"),
                new XElement("Name", "Scott"),
                new XElement("Address", "555 Main St."),
```

```
                          new XElement("City", "Wellington"),
                          new XElement("State", "FL")
                          )
                );

    IEnumerable<XAttribute> atts =
        from emp in employee.Elements("Employee").Attributes()
        select emp;

    foreach (XAttribute att in atts)
        listBox1.Items.Add(att);
```

Running this code results in the following:

```
id="1"
EyeColor="Blue"
```

Notice that you get the attribute key/value pair. To get just the value, use the `Value()` property of the `XAttribute` class:

```
    foreach (XAttribute att in atts)
        listBox1.Items.Add(att.Value.ToString());
```

And here's the result:

```
1
Blue
```

In the preceding examples, the XML tree consisted of a single employee. Suppose that the XML tree consists of multiple employees. The following XML tree contains two employees, and the code then applies the `First()` property to get the attributes of the first employee.

```
    XElement employee = new XElement("Root",
                new XElement("Employee",
                    new XAttribute("id", "1"),
                    new XAttribute("EyeColor", "Green"),
                    new XElement("Name", "John"),
                    new XElement("Address", "444 Main St."),
                    new XElement("City", "Seattle"),
                    new XElement("State", "WA")
                    ),
                new XElement("Employee",
                    new XAttribute("id", "2"),
                    new XAttribute("EyeColor", "Blue"),
                    new XElement("Name", "Scott"),
                    new XElement("Address", "555 Main St."),
                    new XElement("City", "Wellington"),
                    new XElement("State", "FL")
                    ),
                new XElement("Employee",
                    new XAttribute("id", "3"),
                    new XAttribute("EyeColor", "Brown"),
                    new XElement("Name", "Joe"),
```

```
                new XElement("Address", "333 Main St."),
                new XElement("City", "Greenville"),
                new XElement("State", "SC")
                )
            );

IEnumerable<XAttribute> atts =
    from emp in employee.Elements("Employee").First().Attributes()
    select emp;

foreach (XAttribute att in atts)
    listBox1.Items.Add(att);
```

You can see that retrieving attributes is powerful yet quite easy.

Deleting

You have two options for deleting attributes. The first is to use the `Remove()` method. The following example creates an XML tree and then uses `Remove()` to delete the first attribute:

```
XElement employee = new XElement("Root",
            new XElement("Employee",
                new XAttribute("id", "1"),
                new XAttribute("EyeColor", "Blue"),
                new XElement("Name", "Scott"),
                new XElement("Address", "555 Main St."),
                new XElement("City", "Wellington"),
                new XElement("State", "FL")
                )
            );

employee.Element("Employee").FirstAttribute.Remove();
```

In this example, the `FirstAttribute` property selects the first attribute found in the `employee` element, on which `Remove()` was issued. Here's the resulting XML:

```
<Root>
  <Employee EyeColor="Blue">
    <Name>Scott</Name>
    <Address>555 Main St.</Address>
    <City>Wellington</City>
    <State>FL</State>
  </Employee>
</Root>
```

You can also specify the attribute you want to remove:

```
employee.Element("Employee").Attributes("EyeColor").Remove();
The resulting XML shows that the EyeColor attribute was removed:
<Root>
  <Employee id="1">
    <Name>Scott</Name>
    <Address>555 Main St.</Address>
    <City>Wellington</City>
```

```
    <State>FL</State>
  </Employee>
</Root>
```

The second option is to use the SetAttributeValue method. When using it, you set the value of the attribute (of the name/value pair) to null, like this:

```
employee.Element("Employee").SetAttributeValue("EyeColor", null);
```

In this example, the EyeColor attribute will be removed and the XML will be returned as in the previous example.

LINQ to XML versus Other XML Technologies

The final section of this chapter briefly compares LINQ to XML to some of the other XML technologies in use today, specifically weighing LINQ to XML against the following:

❑   DOM

❑   XmlReader

❑   XSLT

❑   MSMXL

LINQ to XML versus DOM

The difference between LINQ to XML and the DOM is in the way the document is created. In the DOM, the XML tree is created from bottom to top, meaning that you create the document, create the elements, and then add the elements to the document. This process takes multiple statements and is quite lengthy.

LINQ to XML simplifies the process by allowing the creation of an XML tree in a single statement, shaped more like XML, and in significantly less, easier-to-read code. The reasoning behind this logic is simply that when you are working with XML, you are typically working with elements and attributes, those components that make up an XML tree. LINQ to XML facilitates this by letting you work with elements and attributes without working with the document object.

One of the problems with the DOM is that you can't change the name of a node directly. You must create a new node and copy all the child nodes of the old node to the new node. In LINQ to XML, you can simply rename the node.

Other differences between LINQ to XML and DOM include the following:

❑   LINQ to XML's static methods simplify the loading of XML over the DOM's instance methods.

❑   LINQ to XML supports annotations.

❑ LINQ to XML provides better support for whitespace. LINQ to XML stores whitespace as XText versus having a special Whitespace node in the DOM. Additionally, in LINQ to XML you can specify xml:space="preserve" to always preserve the whitespace.

❑ XML programming is simplified in LINQ to XML by removing support for entities and entity references because the management of entities is fairly complex, and truth be told, rarely used. The benefit of this is increased performance.

LINQ to XML versus XmlReader

If you have worked with XML before, you have probably used the XmlReader class. The XmlReader class is a fast way of dealing with XML. It is a forward-only, noncached XML parser. Unlike the previous comparison (LINQ to XML versus the DOM), in which LINQ to XML is a replacement for the DOM, LINQ to XML is actually tightly integrated with the XmlReader. While you can still use the XmlReader by itself, you can utilize LINQ to XML to take advantage of the XmlReader, overlapping much of the functionality.

You need to determine when you would use the XmlReader in a standalone scenario and when you would use LINQ to XML. XmlReader is best used when you want to process a large number of XML documents whose XML tree structure rarely differs and quickly processing those XML documents is necessary. LINQ to XML shines when the XML documents differ in XML tree structure.

LINQ to XML versus XSLT

The only similarity between LINQ to XML and XSLT is the capability to transform XML. XSLT is a declarative language that implements a rule-based approach. It does not take advantage of the .NET Framework, thus requiring developers to learn a completely new language. Yet, used correctly, it produces wonderful results, and an existing managed XSLT engine can compile XSLT into managed code.

LINQ to XML, however, overcomes all of the XSLT shortcomings. Through LINQ to XML query expressions, you can easily transform XML using functional construction (discussed in Chapter 8) and constructing XElement objects dynamically, thus creating a completely new XML tree. The benefits of this approach include reduced development time.

LINQ to XML versus MSXML

The big difference between LINQ to XML and MSXML is that MSXML is COM-based and, therefore, not recommended for use in managed code. It also contains a native implementation of the DOM, and includes support for XSLT and XPath. It is primarily used in programming languages that support COM.

In contrast, LINQ to XML is not COM-based and is designed specifically for use with managed code. Thus, you get all the benefits of managed code, such as garbage collection, type safety, and object-oriented design features.

Summary

This chapter introduced you LINQ to XML and many of the fundamental programming concepts that LINQ to XML utilizes and that will be used throughout the remaining LINQ to XML chapters of this book.

You explored the LINQ to XML programming fundamentals—that is, the many LINQ to XML classes that the `System.Xml.Linq` namespace exposes. These classes are the backbone of LINQ to XML and make working with XML much easier than using other XML tools. You also examined three of the more common classes that you'll use when working with XML, including `XElement` and `XAttribute`.

The chapter covered many of the programming concepts that you need to know when working with XML using LINQ to XML, including how to traverse an XML tree, add and remove elements and attributes, and manipulate the tree's contents. You saw how to work with attributes in an XML document using LINQ to XML, and learned that working with attributes is similar to working with elements due to the architecture of LINQ and its integration into the .NET Framework.

Last, a comparison of LINQ to XML to other existing XML technologies was provided to give you an idea of how LINQ to XML stacks up.

Chapter 6 discusses more in-depth programming features of LINQ to XML.

Programming with LINQ to XML

LINQ to XML has many strengths, and one of the most valuable is its capability to quickly and easily create XML documents and trees. LINQ to XML provides several different options through which developers can create XML trees as well as modify and manipulate XML trees.

This chapter builds on what you learned in Chapter 5, "Understanding LINQ to XML"—the programming fundamentals and
concepts that are prevalent in working with XML documents and LINQ to XML, and how to work with elements and attributes using the XElement and XAttribute classes.

This chapter, then, tackles the following:

- ❑ Constructing and creating XML trees
- ❑ Manipulating XML trees
- ❑ Serializing XML trees

Creating Trees

Programming with LINQ to XML, as you found out in the last chapter, is straightforward. Through the many classes of the System.Xml.Linq namespace, developers can create and manipulate XML trees with ease.

You can create XML trees in both C# and Visual Basic .NET, but the manner in which they are created is quite different. The following sections examine the creation of XML trees in both languages, and discuss the differences developers need to know for their respective language.

Creating Trees in C#

Creating XML trees in C# is done using the XElement class. This class provides all the necessary functionality to create and manipulate XML documents and trees. In its simplest form, the XElement class creates elements. Here's an example that creates an empty element:

```
XElement emptyElement = new XElement("Employee");
```

This code produces the following:

```
<Employee />
```

Simple, but via the same XElement class you can create more complex XML trees, such as the following:

```
XElement employee = new XElement("Root",
        new XElement("Employee",
            new XElement("Name", "Scott"),
            new XElement("Title", "All Things Techy"),
            new XElement("HireDate", "02/05/2007"),
            new XElement("Gender", "M")
            ),
        new XElement("Employee",
            new XElement("Name", "Steve"),
            new XElement("Title", "Mr. SciFi"),
            new XElement("HireDate", "05/14/2002"),
            new XElement("Gender", "M")
            ),
        new XElement("Employee",
            new XElement("Name", "Joe"),
            new XElement("Title", "All Things Bleeding Edge"),
            new XElement("HireDate", "07/22/2004"),
            new XElement("Gender", "M")
            )
        );
```

When this code is run, the resulting XML tree looks like this:

```
<Root>
  <Employee>
    <Name>Scott</Name>
    <Title>All Things Techy</Title>
    <HireDate>02/05/2007</HireDate>
    <Gender>M</Gender>
  </Employee>
  <Employee>
    <Name>Steve</Name>
    <Title>Mr. SciFi</Title>
    <HireDate>05/14/2002</HireDate>
    <Gender>M</Gender>
  </Employee>
  <Employee>
    <Name>Joe</Name>
    <Title>All Things Bleeding Edge</Title>
    <HireDate>07/22/2004</HireDate>
```

```
        <Gender>M</Gender>
    </Employee>
</Root>
```

Take it a step further and add a couple of attributes to each employee via the XAttribute class:

```
XElement employee = new XElement("Root",
        new XElement("Employee",
            new XAttribute("id", "1"),
            new XAttribute("Dept", "0001"),
            new XElement("Name", "Scott"),
            new XElement("Address",
                new XElement("Street", "555 Main St."),
                new XElement("City", "Wellington"),
                new XElement("State", "FL")),
            new XElement("Title", "All Things Techy"),
            new XElement("HireDate", "02/05/2007"),
            new XElement("Gender", "M")
            ),
        new XElement("Employee",
            new XAttribute("id", "2"),
            new XAttribute("Dept", "0005"),
            new XElement("Name", "Steve"),
            new XElement("Address",
                new XElement("Street", "444 Main St."),
                new XElement("City", "Snohomish"),
                new XElement("State", "WA")),
            new XElement("Title", "Mr. SciFi"),
            new XElement("HireDate", "05/14/2002"),
            new XElement("Gender", "M")
            ),
        new XElement("Employee",
            new XAttribute("id", "3"),
            new XAttribute("Dept", "0004"),
            new XElement("Name", "Joe"),
            new XElement("Address",
                new XElement("Street", "222 Main St."),
                new XElement("City", "Easley"),
                new XElement("State", "SC")),
            new XElement("Title", "All Things Bleeding Edge"),
            new XElement("HireDate", "07/22/2004"),
            new XElement("Gender", "M")
            )
        );
```

The results now show two attributes on each employee node:

```
<Root>
  <Employee id="1" Dept="0001">
    <Name>Scott</Name>
     <Address>
      <Street>555 Main St.</Street>
      <City>Wellington</City>
```

```
            <State>FL</State>
        </Address>
        <Title>All Things Techy</Title>
        <HireDate>02/05/2007</HireDate>
        <Gender>M</Gender>
    </Employee>
    <Employee id="2" Dept="0005">
        <Name>Steve</Name>
        <Address>
            <Street>444 Main St.</Street>
            <City>Snohomish</City>
            <State>WA</State>
        </Address>
        <Title>Mr. SciFi</Title>
        <HireDate>05/14/2002</HireDate>
        <Gender>M</Gender>
    </Employee>
    <Employee id="3" Dept="0004">
        <Name>Joe</Name>
        <Address>
            <Street>222 Main St.</Street>
            <City>Easley</City>
            <State>SC</State>
        </Address>
        <Title>All Things Bleeding Edge</Title>
        <HireDate>07/22/2004</HireDate>
        <Gender>M</Gender>
    </Employee>
</Root>
```

One of the things that makes creating XML with LINQ to XML quite easy is the capability to structure the XML directly in the programming language, formatting the source code just as it would be structured in the XML document. Additionally, the many properties and methods of the XElement class make it easy to efficiently structure and create XML documents dynamically.

The XElement class contains a handful of overloads that let developers create XML trees quickly within a single statement. These constructor overloads allow you to create a new instance of the XElement class with which to structure an XML document.

In its simplest form, the XElement class can be used to create a new element with a specific name, as shown here in the basic syntax:

```
XElement(XName name)
```

For example, the following uses the basic syntax to create a single root element:

```
XElement employee = new XElement("Root");
```

This code produces the following XML:

```
<Root />
```

Building on that, you use the XElement constructor to create a new instance of the XElement class (creating a new element) from another XElement object. By doing so, you can nest elements, creating child elements of the parent element. The following example illustrates this, using the XElement constructor from the initial XElement class to create a child element below the root element:

```
XElement employee = new XElement("Root",
            new XElement("Employee");
```

The code produces the following XML:

```
<Root>
  <Employee />
</Root>
```

From here, another XElement constructor can be used to create a new element with a specified name and content. Here's the basic syntax:

```
XElement(XName name, object content)
```

The following example creates a new element with the specified name of "Name" and content of "Scott":

```
XElement = new XElement("Name", "Scott")
```

Here's the XML this code produces:

```
<Name>Scott</Name>
```

You can combine this with the previous example to create a root element and child element with a value:

```
XElement employee = new XElement("Employee",
            new XElement("Name", "Scott");
```

The code produces the following XML:

```
<Employee>
  <Name>Scott</Scott>
</Employee>
```

Last, you can pass multiple instances of the XElement class to create multiple nodes. The basic syntax for this is

```
XElement(XName name, params object[] content)
A pseudo-code example of this would be the following:
XElement employee = new XElement(XName,
            new XElement(XName,
                new XElement(XName name),
                new XElement(XName name),
                new XElement(XName name),
                new XElement(XName name)
            )
```

Here's an example of the syntax using real data, passing more than one XElement for the content:

```
XElement employee = new XElement("Root",
            new XElement("Employee",
                new XElement("Name", "Scott"),
```

```
        new XElement("Title", "All Things Techy"),
        new XElement("HireDate", "02/05/2007"),
        new XElement("Gender", "M")
)
```

As you have seen in previous examples in this chapter and the last chapter, this is the ideal way to construct an XML tree.

Now take a look at how to do the same thing in Visual Basic .NET.

Creating Trees in Visual Basic

Creating XML trees in Visual Basic is accomplished through XML literals. XML literals enable you to create and incorporate XML directly into our Visual Basic programs and code. Another way to say this is that XML literals let you type XML directly into your Visual Basic code without the need for any special formatting. What makes this possible is that the literal XML syntax represents the actual objects of LINQ to XML. The benefit of this is that your XML code is easier to create, and your code is easier to read because it has the same structure as the resulting XML.

An additional benefit of XML literals is that Visual Basic .NET compiles them into LNQ to XML objects, providing a familiar LINQ object model for creating and manipulating XML.

XML can be created in Visual Basic by using XML literals directly in the VB code. You create LINQ to XML objects simply by typing XML code directly into Visual Basic or by pasting existing XML into your code. The following creates a single <Employee> node:

```
Dim emp As XElement = <Employee/>
```

Here's the result of this code:

```
<Employee/>
```

You can also specify elements and their corresponding values:

```
Dim emp As XElement = <Name>Scott</Name>
```

Obviously, the following XML is produced:

```
<Name>Scott</Name>
```

One of the things that Visual Basic .NET developers have at their disposal is "embedded expressions." Embedded expressions let you create XML literals that contain expressions. These expressions are evaluated at run time. Embedded expressions are enclosed within <% %> brackets (if you do any ASP.NET development, you're familiar with those).

The following creates a simple XML document using XML literals and an embedded expression:

```
Dim emp As XElement = <Employee>
    <%= New XElement("Name", "Scott") %>
  </Employee>
```

Here are the results when the code runs:

```
<Employee>
    <Name>Scott</Name>
</Employee>
```

XML literals can span multiple lines without the need of line continuation characters as shown in the example below. The only time this would differ is when you have a multi-line expression in the embedded expression.

```
Dim employee As XElement = _
<Root>
    <Employee id="1" Dept="0001">
        <Name>Scott</Name>
        <Address>
            <Street>555 Main St.</Street>
            <City>Wellington</City>
            <State>FL</State>
        </Address>
        <Title>All Things Techy</Title>
        <HireDate>02/05/2007</HireDate>
        <Gender>M</Gender>
    </Employee>
    <Employee id="2" Dept="0005">
        <Name>Steve</Name>
        <Address>
            <Street>444 Main St.</Street>
            <City>Snohomish</City>
            <State>WA</State>
        </Address>
        <Title>Mr. SciFi</Title>
        <HireDate>05/14/2002</HireDate>
        <Gender>M</Gender>
    </Employee>
    <Employee id="3" Dept="0004">
        <Name>Joe</Name>
        <Address>
            <Street>222 Main St.</Street>
            <City>Easley</City>
            <State>SC</State>
        </Address>
        <Title>All Things Bleeding Edge</Title>
        <HireDate>07/22/2004</HireDate>
        <Gender>M</Gender>
    </Employee>
</Root>
```

How does the compiler create objects from XML literals? The answer is simple, really. The Visual Basic compiler translates XML literals into the equivalent LINQ to XML constructors, which are then used to build the LINQ to XML object.

Populating Trees from Text

Populating XML trees from text can be accomplished a number of ways, and you saw a couple of them in the last chapter. The easiest method is to use the Parse() method of the XElement class. This method loads an XElement object from an XML string.

For example, the following code creates a string containing XML, parsing the string into an XElement object:

```
XElement employees = XElement.Parse(@"
    <Employees>
        <Employee id='1' phone='555-555-5555'>
            <Name>Steve Kent</Name>
            <Title>Mr. SciFi</Title>
            <Department>Gaming</Department>
            <HireDate>04/17/92</HireDate>
            <Gender>M</Gender>
            <MaritalStatus>M</MaritalStatus>
        </Employee>
        <Employee id='2' phone='555-555-5556'>
            <Name>Scott Klein</Name>
            <Title>Geek</Title>
            <Department>All things technical</Department>
            <HireDate>02/05/94</HireDate>
            <Gender>M</Gender>
            <MaritalStatus>M</MaritalStatus>
        </Employee>
        <Employee id='3' phone='555-555-5557'>
            <Name>Joe Walling</Name>
            <Title>Head Geek</Title>
            <Department>All things bleeding edge</Department>
            <HireDate>06/15/93</HireDate>
            <Gender>M</Gender>
            <MaritalStatus>M</MaritalStatus>
        </Employee>
    </Employees>");
```

There is a limitation to using the Parse() method, and that is that the XML can contain only a single root node.

Another way is to populate a tree is to load the XML from an existing source. The following example uses the Load() method to load an existing XML document from an external file source and creates an XElement.

```
XElement employees = XElement.Load(@"C:\Wrox\Employees.xml");
```

Another overload of the Load method takes an additional Boolean parameter that specifies whether to preserve whitespace.

```
employees = XElement.Load(@"C:\Wrox\Employees.xml", true);
```

This next example illustrates how to load XML from a TextReader. Any kind of TextReader can be used; in this case, it's a StringReader, but a StreamReader would work just the same.

```
TextReader tr = new StringReader("<Employee><Name>Scott</Name></Employee");
XElement xtree = XElement.Load(tr);
```

As before, another overload of the `Load` method takes an additional Boolean parameter that specifies whether to preserve whitespace.

```
XElement xtree = XElement.Load(tr, true);
```

The following example creates an XML tree from an XmlReader. It first creates an `XmlReaderSettings` instance and sets a few optional settings. Then it creates an XmlReader and uses the `Create()` method to load an XML file into the `XElement` object.

```
XmlReaderSettings xmlset = new XmlReaderSettings();
xmlset.ConformanceLevel = ConformanceLevel.Document;
xmlset.IgnoreWhitespace = true;
xmlset.IgnoreComments = true;
XmlReader rdr = XmlReader.Create(@"C:\Wrox\LINQ\Chapter
5\Employees.xml", xmlset);

XElement xtree = XElement.Load(rdr);
```

Once in the XmlReader, the XML can be read quickly. The XmlReader is an efficient way to access XML data if all you want to do is read it.

This last example demonstrates how to load a DOM document into an LINQ to XML tree. First, an XML DOM document is created, defining a root element and several child elements. The DOM document is then loaded into the `XElement` object.

```
XmlDocument xdoc = new XmlDocument();
XmlElement ele1 = xdoc.CreateElement("Name");
ele1.InnerText = "Scott";
XmlElement ele2 = xdoc.CreateElement("Title");
ele2.InnerText = "Geek";
XmlElement ele3 = xdoc.CreateElement("HireDate");
ele3.InnerText = "02/05/2007";
XmlElement emp = xdoc.CreateElement("Employee");
emp.AppendChild(ele1);
emp.AppendChild(ele2);
emp.AppendChild(ele3);
xdoc.AppendChild(emp);

XmlNodeReader nr = new XmlNodeReader(xdoc);
nr.MoveToContent();

XElement xtree = XElement.Load(nr);
```

The resulting XML looks like this:

```
<Employee>
    <Name>Scott</Name>
    <Title>Geek</Title>
    <HireDate>02/05/2007</HireDate>
</Employee>
```

Querying XML Trees

Once you have populated the tree, the next obvious step in most cases is to query its contents. If you think about this for a minute, LINQ to XML provides an easy way to reshape XML. It combines the capability to functionally construct your XML with the capability to query the XML tree. The result is a completely different XML tree shape than the original XML document. One of the primary things you should know by now is that LINQ to XML is exceptional at both functional construction and querying. In this section, you will quickly see that LINQ to XML is also very good at reshaping XML as compared to other XML technologies.

This section explores LINQ to XML queries and how they can be used to effectively query XML documents. To illustrate this point, the following XML document will be used. In your favorite text editor, enter the following XML and save it as `Employee.xml` in your `Wrox\Chapter6` directory:

```xml
<Employees>
  <Employee id="1" Dept="0001">
    <Name>Scott</Name>
    <Address>
      <Street>555 Main St.</Street>
      <City>Wellington</City>
      <State>FL</State>
    </Address>
    <Title>All Things Techy</Title>
    <HireDate>02/05/2007</HireDate>
    <Gender>M</Gender>
  </Employee>
  <Employee id="2" Dept="0005">
    <Name>Steve</Name>
    <Address>
      <Street>444 Main St.</Street>
      <City>Snohomish</City>
      <State>WA</State>
    </Address>
    <Title>Mr. SciFi</Title>
    <HireDate>05/14/2002</HireDate>
    <Gender>M</Gender>
  </Employee>
  <Employee id="3" Dept="0004">
    <Name>Joe</Name>
    <Address>
      <Street>222 Main St.</Street>
      <City>Easley</City>
      <State>SC</State>
    </Address>
    <Title>All Things Bleeding Edge</Title>
    <HireDate>07/22/2004</HireDate>
    <Gender>M</Gender>
  </Employee>
</Employees>
```

Next, create a new C# Windows Forms project in Visual Studio, and on Form1 place a button and a text box. In the `Click()` event for the button, add the following:

```csharp
XElement employees = XElement.Load(@"C:\Wrox\Chapter6\Employees.Xml");
```

You now have the XML document `Employee.xml` loaded into the `employees` variable, so you can work with it.

Suppose that you want to return the first employee from the XML document. The following does just that:

```
employees.Element("Employee")
```

Running this statement returns the first employee:

```
<Employee id="1" Dept="0001">
  <Name>Scott</Name>
    <Address>
      <Street>555 Main St.</Street>
      <City>Wellington</City>
      <State>FL</State>
    </Address>
  <Title>All Things Techy</Title>
  <HireDate>02/05/2007</HireDate>
  <Gender>M</Gender>
</Employee>
```

However, an alternative would be to use the `First()` property to manually select the first `Employee` element:

```
employees.Elements("Employee").First()
```

Another alternative is to use the `ElementAt()` method to specify which element to return. The following example also returns the first `Employee` node:

```
employees.Elements("Employee").ElementAt(0)
```

The next example loops through all of the `Employee` elements, concatenates them, and returns them as a single string:

```
foreach (XElement employee in employees.Elements("Employee")
    textbox1.Text += employee;
```

This gives you everything but the `<Employees>` node:

```
<Employee id="1" Dept="0001">
  <Name>Scott</Name>
  <Address>
    <Street>555 Main St.</Street>
    <City>Wellington</City>
    <State>FL</State>
  </Address>
  <Title>All Things Techy</Title>
  <HireDate>02/05/2007</HireDate>
  <Gender>M</Gender>
</Employee>
<Employee id="2" Dept="0005">
  <Name>Steve</Name>
  <Address>
```

```
        <Street>444 Main St.</Street>
        <City>Snohomish</City>
        <State>WA</State>
     </Address>
     <Title>Mr. SciFi</Title>
     <HireDate>05/14/2002</HireDate>
     <Gender>M</Gender>
   </Employee>
   <Employee id="3" Dept="0004">
     <Name>Joe</Name>
     <Address>
        <Street>222 Main St.</Street>
        <City>Easley</City>
        <State>SC</State>
     </Address>
     <Title>All Things Bleeding Edge</Title>
     <HireDate>07/22/2004</HireDate>
     <Gender>M</Gender>
   </Employee>
```

What if you want to return the second employee? You can use the `ElementAt()` method, as shown here:

```
employees.Elements("Employee").ElementAt(1)
```

The values for this are zero-based, so the first employee node is 0. To return the second employee, you simply pass a 1.

Another option is to use a query expression. The following returns the second employee node by filtering on the `id` attribute where its value is 2:

```
XElement empnum2 = (from emp in employees.Elements("Employee")
                    where (int) emp.Attribute("id") == 2
                    select emp).First();
```

Notice that this example also uses the `First()` method. Why? What if your XML document had an attribute of `Dept` for each employee, and your XML document had multiple employees with the same department? The `First()` method helps make sure you grab the first employee that matches the criterion. The query expression returns a sequence, and the `First()` method explicitly returns the first member of that sequence.

The following example does the same, but uses the `ElementAt()` method:

```
XElement empnum2 = (from emp in employees.Elements("Employee")
                    where (int) emp.Attribute("id") == 2
                    select emp).ElementAt(0);
```

This next example digs a little deeper. It returns the values of all the `Name` elements for each employee. It uses the `Descendants()` method to return a collection of all the descendants for the selected element.

```
IEnumerable<string> empNames =
    from emp in employees.Descendants("Name")
    orderby emp.Value
    select emp.Value;
```

```
foreach (string name in empNames)
    listbox1.Items.Add(name);
```

This code returns the following values:

```
Joe
Scott
Steve
```

The following example does the same thing:

```
IEnumerable<string> empNames =
    from emp in employees.Descendants("Name")
    orderby (string) emp
    select (string) emp;
```

The same iteration applies, and the results are the same. You can also "walk the tree" by using the Elements() method (as many times as needed) to access the appropriate node.

```
IEnumerable<string> empNames =
    from emp in employees.Elements("Employee").Elements("Name")
    orderby (string) emp
    select (string) emp;
```

Again, the same iteration applies, and the same results are returned.

The next few examples work with attributes, and to do so, the XML document Employee.xml created earlier needs to be modified. Add an attribute to each employee node as highlighted in following XML:

```
<Employees>
  <Employee id="1" Dept="0001" Geek="True">
    <Name>Scott</Name>
    <Address>
      <Street>555 Main St.</Street>
      <City>Wellington</City>
      <State>FL</State>
    </Address>
    <Title>All Things Techy</Title>
    <HireDate>02/05/2007</HireDate>
    <Gender>M</Gender>
  </Employee>
  <Employee id="2" Dept="0005" Geek="False">
    <Name>Steve</Name>
    <Address>
      <Street>444 Main St.</Street>
      <City>Snohomish</City>
      <State>WA</State>
    </Address>
    <Title>Mr. SciFi</Title>
    <HireDate>05/14/2002</HireDate>
    <Gender>M</Gender>
  </Employee>
```

```
      <Employee id="3" Dept="0004" Geek="True">
    <Name>Joe</Name>
    <Address>
      <Street>222 Main St.</Street>
      <City>Easley</City>
      <State>SC</State>
    </Address>
    <Title>All Things Bleeding Edge</Title>
    <HireDate>07/22/2004</HireDate>
    <Gender>M</Gender>
  </Employee>
</Employees>
```

The following example queries the XML document, looking at the Geek attribute of the Employee node and returning only those with a value of True:

```
IEnumerable<XElement> empNames =
    from emp in employees.Elements("Employee")
    where (string)emp.Attribute("Geek") == "True"
    select emp;

foreach (XElement name in empNames)
    textbox1.Text = name.ToString();
```

The query expression returns the following values:

```
Scott
Joe
```

This last example demonstrates how to walk an XML tree looking for an element value several layers deep. First, modify the XML and add a Zip element to the employee with an id of 2:

```
    <Employee id="2" Dept="0005" Geek="False">
    <Name>Steve</Name>
    <Address>
      <Street>444 Main St.</Street>
      <City>Snohomish</City>
      <State>WA</State>
      <Zip>99999</Zip>
    </Address>
    <Title>Mr. SciFi</Title>
    <HireDate>05/14/2002</HireDate>
    <Gender>M</Gender>
  </Employee>
```

In the following example, the query expression walks down to the <Address> element and looks for an employee with a Zip value of 99999:

```
IEnumerable<XElement> empAddr =
    from emp in employees.Elements("Employee").Elements("Address")
    where (string)emp.Element("zip") == ("99999")
```

```
        select emp;

    foreach (XElement address in empAddr)
        textbox1.Text = address.ToString();
```

There was only a single employee that matched the query expression filter in this example, but nonetheless, the results were looped through, and the following XML was returned:

```
<Address>
  <Street>444 Main St.</Street>
  <City>Snohomish</City>
  <State>WA</State>
  <Zip>99999</Zip>
</Address>
```

This example returned the address information for the selected ZIP code. Modify the query as highlighted here, and it will return the entire employee node for the selected ZIP code:

```
IEnumerable<XElement> empAddr =
    from emp in employees.Elements("Employee")
    where (string)emp.Element("Address").Element("zip") == ("99999")
    select emp;
```

Now when you run this application and click the button, the following is displayed:

```
<Employee id="2" Dept="0005" Geek="False">
  <Name>Steve</Name>
  <Address>
    <Address>444 Main St.</Address>
    <City>Snohomish</City>
    <State>WA</State>
    <zip>99999</zip>
  </Address>
  <Title>Mr. SciFi</Title>
  <HireDate>05/14/2002</HireDate>
  <Gender>M</Gender>
</Employee>
```

Modifying and Reshaping XML Trees

You saw briefly in the last chapter how to modify XML trees using many of the methods and properties of the XElement and XAttribute classes. However, in today's XML technologies, the common approach for reshaping an XML document requires loading the document into data store and using an XML-supported programming language for modify the contents and structure of that document, such as adding or removing nodes.

For example, loading an XML document into the DOM, modifying its contents in place, and resaving the document is one of the more familiar methods for current XML programmers.

LINQ to XML provides a second approach to XML reshaping and modification—one that is much easier to maintain. This approach is called *functional construction*, and is the answer to the DOM's load/modify/save approach. Functional construction lets you easily reshape XML from one form to another in a single statement.

As you saw in the last chapter, LINQ to XML provides the load/modify/save approach as well via the many methods exposed by the XElement and XAttribute classes, and even this is still more efficient than many of today's XML tree modification methods due to the ability to visually view the structure of the XML tree. Yet the functional approach, once understood, is easier to work with and maintain as a whole because you can quickly identify the code that modifies each part of the tree.

Here's an example illustrating how to take an attribute and make it an element. The code takes the id attribute and adds it as an element. The attribute's name and value are used when the element is added.

```
XElement employee = new XElement("Root",
        new XElement("Employee",
            new XAttribute("id", "1"),
            new XAttribute("EyeColor", "Green"),
            new XElement("Name", "Scott"),
            new XElement("Address", "444 Main St."),
            new XElement("City", "Wellington"),
            new XElement("State", "FL"),
            new XElement("Zip", "33414")
            )
        );

employee.Element("Employee").Add(
    new XElement(employee.Element("Employee").Attribute("id").Name,
        employee.Element("Employee").Attribute("id").Value));

employee.Element("Employee").Attribute("id").Remove();
```

This code produces the following XML:

```
<Root>
  <Employee EyeColor="Green">
    <Name>Scott</Name>
    <Address>444 Main St.</Address>
    <City>Wellington</City>
    <State>FL</State>
    <Zip>33414</Zip>
    <id>1</id>
  </Employee>
</Root>
```

If you wanted to, you could loop through all of the attributes and make them elements as follows:

```
foreach (XAttribute att in employee.Element("Employee").Attributes())
    employee.Element("Employee").Add(new XElement(atts.Name, (string)att));

employee.Element("Employee").Attributes().Remove();
```

The code produces this XML:

```
<Root>
  <Employee EyeColor="Green">
    <Name>Scott</Name>
```

```
        <Address>444 Main St.</Address>
        <City>Wellington</City>
        <State>FL</State>
        <Zip>33414</Zip>
        <id>1</id>
        <EyeColor>Green</EyeColor>
    </Employee>
</Root>
```

The following example does the reverse. It takes an element (`<id>`) and adds it as an attribute (of the Employee node):

```
XElement employee = new XElement("Root",
            new XElement("Employee",
                new XElement("Name", "Scott"),
                new XElement("Address", "444 Main St."),
                new XElement("City", "Wellington"),
                new XElement("State", "FL"),
                new XElement("Zip", "33414"),
                new XElement("id", "1")
                )
            );

employee.Element("Employee").Add(new
    XAttribute(employee.Element("Employee").Element("id").Name,
    employee.Element("Employee").Element("id").Value));

employee.Element("Employee").Element("id").Remove();
```

The result is the following XML:

```
<Root>
  <Employee id="1">
    <Name>Scott</Name>
    <Address>444 Main St.</Address>
    <City>Wellington</City>
    <State>FL</State>
    <Zip>33414</Zip>
  </Employee>
</Root>
```

Functional construction is discussed in more detail in Chapter 8, "Advanced LINQ to XML Programming Topics."

Serializing XML Trees

Serialization is the process of saving an object to a storage medium such as a file or even to memory. Serializing an XML tree is the process of generating XML text from the tree. The newly generated XML can be serialized to a file or to an implementation of a TextWriter or an XmlWriter.

When serializing XML using LINQ to XML, nonsignificant whitespace in the XML tree is not preserved by default. For example, reading indented XML with no whitespace text nodes and then serializing the XML with indentation does not preserve whitespace.

When serializing XML via LINQ to XML, several methods are available, enabling you to decide how to treat whitespace. The Save() method of the XElement class does not preserve whitespace by default. But you can optionally provide a Boolean value that tells Save() to preserve whitespace, as in the following example:

```
TextReader tr = new StringReader(@"
    <Employees>
        <Employee id='1' phone='555-555-5555'>
            <Name>Steve Kent</Name>
            <Title>Mr. SciFi</Title>
            <Department>Gaming</Department>
            <HireDate>04/17/92</HireDate>
            <Gender>M</Gender>
            <MaritalStatus>M</MaritalStatus>
        </Employee>
        <Employee id='2' phone='555-555-5556'>
            <Name>Scott Klein</Name>
            <Title>Geek</Title>
            <Department>All things technical</Department>
            <HireDate>02/05/94</HireDate>
            <Gender>M</Gender>
            <MaritalStatus>M</MaritalStatus>
        </Employee>
        <Employee id='3' phone='555-555-5557'>
            <Name>Joe Walling</Name>
            <Title>Head Geek</Title>
            <Department>All things bleeding edge</Department>
            <HireDate>06/15/93</HireDate>
            <Gender>M</Gender>
            <MaritalStatus>M</MaritalStatus>
        </Employee>
    </Employees>");
XElement xel = XElement.Load(tr);
tr.Close();
xel.Save(@"C:\Wrox\Employees2.xml", true);
```

The same goes for the Save() method of the XDocument class.

Serializing can be done to a file (as the preceding example shows), a TextWriter, or an XmlWriter. The following example shows how to serialize an XElement to an XmlWriter:

```
StringBuilder sb = new StringBuilder();
XmlWriterSettings xws = new XmlWriterSettings();
xws.OmitXmlDeclaration = true;
using (XmlWriter xw = XmlWriter.Create(sb , xws))
{
    XElement employee = new XElement("Root",
                new XElement("Employee",
                    new XAttribute("id", "1"),
                    new XAttribute("EyeColor", "Green"),
                    new XElement("Name", "Scott"),
                    new XElement("Address", "444 Main St."),
                    new XElement("City", "Wellington"),
                    new XElement("State", "FL"),
```

```
                        new XElement("Zip", "33414")
                    )
                );
        employee.Save(xw);
    }
textBox1.Text = sb.ToString();
```

You'll notice that you don't have an option of controlling the whitespace when serializing to an XmlWriter via LINQ to XML. That is because the XmlWriter controls the behavior of the whitespace.

The following example serializes an XML tree to a TextWriter:

```
XElement employees = XElement.Parse(@"
    <Employees>
        <Employee id='1' debt='Dev'>
            <Name>Scott</Name>
            <Title>Mr. SciFi</Title>
            <Department>Gaming</Department>
            <HireDate>04/17/92</HireDate>
            <Gender>M</Gender>
            <MaritalStatus>M</MaritalStatus>
        </Employee>
    </Employees>");

using (StringWriter sw = new StringWriter())
{
    employees.Save(sw, true);
}
```

You have many serialization options when using LINQ to XML; it is simply a matter of selecting the right options for your application.

Namespaces

One of the more difficult concepts of XML programming is XML names and namespaces. You can think of XML namespace on the same level as that of a namespace in a .NET Framework application. A namespace uniquely qualifies your class names within your application. By using namespaces, you can avoid the naming conflicts between different parts of an XML document.

XML namespaces serve several purposes in XML, and maybe that's the reason they seem to be so difficult to understand. In addition to uniquely qualifying names, namespaces also serve the purpose of prefixes within an XML document. Prefixes let you use shortcuts for XML namespaces, making the XML document more readable and concise. The downside to prefixes is that they depend on their context for their meaning. A prefix can be associated with different namespaces in different parts of the XML tree, making the meaning much harder to understand.

LINQ to XML greatly simplifies programming with namespaces by removing the prefixes from the LINQ API. When an XML document is loaded by LINQ to XML, prefixes are treated as shortcuts and resolved to their corresponding namespaces (just like when XML is loaded by a DOM or SAX parser). Once the XML document is loaded, namespaces are accessed via the namespace URI, not the prefix. Developers work with XML names that are fully qualified.

Fully qualified names are represented by the XName class, and you have seen them throughout this book. Whenever an XML name is required, you are dealing with the XName class, such as an XName parameter. Keep in mind that you are never really working with the XName class directly, but rather with a string representation.

Throughout this book you've seen string arguments passed as parameters to constructors when creating elements or attributes during XML tree construction, like this:

```
new XElements("Name", "Scott");
```

What happens is that the string is implicitly converted to an XName. That same concept can now be applied to namespaces. The following creates a simple XML document with a default namespace:

```
XElement employee = new XElement("{http://wrox.com}Employee",
            new XAttribute("id", "1"),
            new XElement("{http://wrox.com}Name", "Scott"),
            new XElement("{http://wrox.com}Title", "Developer")
            );
```

This code produces the following XML:

```
<Employee id="1" xmlns="http://wrox.com">
  <Name>Scott</Name>
  <Title>Developer</Title>
</Employee>
```

Likewise, you can create an XML document that contains multiple namespaces:

```
XElement employee = new XElement("{http://wrox.com}Employee",
            new XAttribute("id", "1"),
            new XElement("{http://wrox.com}Name", "Scott"),
            new XElement("{http://wrox.org}Title", "Developer")
            );
```

This produces the following XML:

```
<Employee id="1" xmlns="http://wrox.com">
  <Name>Scott</Name>
  <Title xmlns="http://wrox.org">Developer</Title>
</Employee>
```

LINQ to XML also provides a class to assist in working with namespaces, and that class is the XNamespace class. Namespaces can also be defined and created via the XNamespace class. This class represents an XML namespace and cannot be inherited. The following example defines a default namespace that is used in the subsequent XML document:

```
XNamespace xn = "http://wrox.com";
XElement employee = new XElement( xn + "Employee",
    new XAttribute("id", "1"),
    new XElement( xn + "Name", "Scott"),
```

```
        new XElement(xn + "Title", "Developer")
        );
```

This code produces the following XML:

```
<Employee id="1" xmlns="http://wrox.com">
  <Name>Scott</Name>
  <Title>Developer</Title>
</Employee>
```

You should begin to see that working with namespaces in LINQ to XML is quite easy. LINQ to XML removes a lot of the frustration you experience with other XML technologies and makes working with XML documents a pleasure.

Summary

This chapter provided you with the LINQ to XML programming techniques necessary to work with XML documents; specifically it explained how to populate and query XML trees effectively and efficiently.

It showed you how to modify and reshape an existing XML document into another XML document using many of the methods available in LINQ to XML, such as the XElement and XAttribute classes and their associated methods. You also explored serialization in LINQ to XML. There are several serialization options available, including to which technology to serialize the XML and whether to retain the whitespace of the XML document.

Finally, you examined namespaces, specifically how they are handled and how to apply them to an XML document in LINQ to XML, and learned how LINQ to XML removes many of the normal difficulties in working with them.

Chapter 7, "LINQ to XML and other LINQ Data Models," discusses how LINQ to XML works with other data models.

7

LINQ to XML and Other LINQ Data Models

One of the great things about LINQ is its flexibility. LINQ has many great strong points, not the least of which is its capability to provide a query consistency across different data models (LINQ, LINQ to XML, and LINQ to SQL) through the standard query operators and the .NET Framework's new lambda expressions. Lambda expressions, discussed in Chapter 2, "A Look at Visual Studio 2008," are inline statement blocks or expressions that can be used wherever delegate types are expected. Lambda expressions are written using a concise syntax and can be used anywhere anonymous methods can be used—for example as arguments to a method call.

Another of LINQ's significant qualities is the capability to easily interact with LINQ-based data models, such as LINQ to SQL. This capability is provided via the LINQ APIs. It enables developers to combine LINQ data models to create single query expressions using components from both models.

This chapter focuses on using LINQ to XML to interact with LINQ to SQL. It shows you how to use data from a database to populate an XML tree, and how to take content from an XML tree to populate a database.

SQL to XML

By combining LINQ to SQL with LINQ to XML, developers can easily read data from a database and transform those records into XML, all within the same statement. This section walks you through an example of reading data from a SQL Server database and using the data to create an XML tree.

Open Visual Studio 2008 and create a new project. Make sure that .NET Framework version 3.5 is selected on the New Project page. Under the Templates section, select a Windows Forms Application and name the project LINQ Chapter7. Click OK on the New Project form.

When the new project loads, Form1 is displayed. Place a text box, a label, and three buttons on the form, and set their properties as follows.

	Property	Value
Textbox	Location	12, 12
	Multiline	True
	Size	187, 249
Button 1	Name	cmdSqlToXml
	Location	205, 12
	Text	SQL to XML
Button 2	Name	cmdXmlToSql
	Location	205, 41
	Text	XML to SQL
Button 3	Name	cmdClose
	Location	205, 238
	Text	Close
Label	Location	205, 67
	Text	Insert successful.
	Visible	False

Figure 7-1 shows the form design when the project is run. The SQL to XML button will be used in this example to read data from a database and transform that data into XML. The XML to SQL button will be used in later examples to read XML from an XML tree and to use that data to insert and update a table in the AdventureWorks database.

Figure 7-1

The examples combine LINQ to SQL and LINQ to XML to accomplish tasks easily and efficiently.

First, you want to add the proper references. In Solution Explorer, expand the References node. You'll see that a reference to `System.Xml.Linq` is already included, but you also need to add a reference to `System.Data.Linq`. To do so, right-click the references node and select Add Reference. In the References dialog, select the .NET tab. Scroll down the list, select the `System.Data.Linq` component, and then click OK.

With the form designed and the appropriate references added, the next step is to add code behind the form. Right-click in the gray area of the form and select View Code from the context menu.

In the declarations section, add the following `using` statements after the existing `using` statements:

```
using System.Data.Linq;
using System.Data.Linq.Mapping;
using System.Xml.Linq;
using System.IO;
using System.Xml;
```

Those statements must be added before you can use the components.

Below the `public partial class` for Form1, add the following:

```
public class AdventureWorks : DataContext
{
    public AdventureWorks(string connection) : base(connection) { }
    public Table<Contact> Contact;
}

[Table(Name = "Person.Contact")]
public class Contact
{

  [Column(DbType = "int")]
  public int ContactID;
  [Column(DbType = "bit not null")]
  public byte NameStyle;

  [Column(DbType = "nvarchar(8) not null")]
  public string Title;

  [Column(DbType = "nvarchar(50) not null")]
  public string FirstName;

  [Column(DbType = "nvarchar(50) not null")]
  public string MiddleName;

  [Column(DbType = "nvarchar(50) not null")]
  public string LastName;

  [Column(DbType = "nvarchar(50) not null")]
  public string EmailAddress;
```

```
    [Column(DbType = "int")]
    public int EmailPromotion;

    [Column(DbType = "varchar(40) not null")]
    public string PasswordHash;

    [Column(DbType = " varchar(10) not null ")]
    public string PasswordSalt;

}
```

In design view for Form1, double-click the SQL to XML button to view the code behind it. In the code for cmdSqlToXml, add the following:

```
DataContext context = new DataContext("Initial Catalog=@@>
AdventureWorks;Integrated Security=sspi");

Table<Contact> contact = context.GetTable<Contact>();

XElement contacts =
    new XElement("Customers",
        from c in contact
        where c.FirstName.StartsWith("S")
        && c.LastName.StartsWith("K")
        orderby c.LastName
        select new XElement("Contact",
                new XAttribute("ContactID", c.ContactID),
                new XElement("FirstName", c.FirstName),
                new XElement("LastName", c.LastName),
                new XElement("Title", c.Title),
                new XElement("EmailAddress", c.EmailAddress)
                )
            );

textBox1.Text = contacts.ToString();
```

Then press F5 to compile and run the project. When Form1 appears, click the SQL to XML button. The text box should be populated with an XML tree that looks like the following XML:

To conserve page space, the XML tree is not displayed in its entirety. Only the first few and last few elements are displayed.

```
<Customers>
  <Contact ContactID="450">
    <yomoma>Scott</yomoma>
    <LastName>Kaffer</LastName>
    <Title>Mr.</Title>
    <EmailAddress>scott5@adventure-works.com</EmailAddress>
  </Contact>
  <Contact ContactID="453">
    <yomoma>Sandeep</yomoma>
    <LastName>Kaliyath</LastName>
```

```
      <Title>Mr.</Title>
      <EmailAddress>sandeep1@adventure-works.com</EmailAddress>
    </Contact>
    <Contact ContactID="1153">
      <yomoma>Sandeep</yomoma>
      <LastName>Kaliyath</LastName>
      <Title />
      <EmailAddress>sandeep0@adventure-works.com</EmailAddress>
    </Contact>
    ...
    <Contact ContactID="7718">
      <yomoma>Sharon</yomoma>
      <LastName>Kumar</LastName>
      <Title />
      <EmailAddress>sharon14@adventure-works.com</EmailAddress>
    </Contact>
    <Contact ContactID="2766">
      <yomoma>Shawna</yomoma>
      <LastName>Kumar</LastName>
      <Title />
      <EmailAddress>shawna8@adventure-works.com</EmailAddress>
    </Contact>
  </Customers>
```

In this example, LINQ to SQL was used to make a connection to the `Person.Contact` table in the AdventureWorks database. LINQ and LINQ to XML were used to create a query expression to read the contents of the table and format the results into an XML tree.

You can see that in roughly a dozen lines of code, an XML tree was created from data in a SQL Server table.

XML to SQL

These next two examples illustrate the opposite; that is, taking data from an XML tree to insert a row into the `Person.Contact` table, and then updating the newly inserted record. For this example, you need an XML file, so in your favorite text editor, type in the following:

```
<Contacts>
  <Contact>
    <ContactID></ContactID>
    <NameStyle>0</NameStyle>
    <Title>Mr.</Title>
    <FirstName>Scott</FirstName>
    <MiddleName>L</MiddleName>
    <LastName>Klein</LastName>
    <EmailAddress>Geek@SqlXml.com</EmailAddress>
    <EmailPromotion>1</EmailPromotion>
    <PasswordHash> F57E03FEA2FD0F74684C20758110CC7860F67523</PasswordHash>
    <PasswordSalt>/RPjvXw=</PasswordSalt>
  </Contact>
</Contacts>
```

Yes, `ContactID` was left blank on purpose. That will be used in the "Insert" example. Save the file as `Contacts.Xml` in your Wrox directory. The next example illustrates how to insert a new record.

Insert

With the XML file created, return to your Visual Studio LINQ project and double-click the XML to SQL button. In the code behind the XML to SQL button, add the following:

```
AdventureWorks db = new AdventureWorks("Integrated Security=sspi");

XElement xel = XElement.Load(@"C:\Wrox\Linq\Chapter5\Contacts.xml");

foreach (XElement xelem in xel.Elements("Contact"))
{
  Contact con = new Contact();
  con.NameStyle = 1;
  con.Title = (string)xelem.Element("Title");
  con.FirstName = (string)xelem.Element("FirstName");
  con.MiddleName = (string)xelem.Element("MiddleName");
  con.LastName = (string)xelem.Element("LastName");
  con.EmailAddress = (string)xelem.Element("EmailAddress");
  con.EmailPromotion = (int)xelem.Element("EmailPromotion");
  con.PasswordHash = (string)con.Element("PasswordHash");
  con.PasswordSalt = (string)con.Element("PasswordSalt");
  db.Contact.Add(con);
  db.SubmitChanges();
}

lable1.Visible = true;
```

Run the project and click the XML to SQL button. When the insertion is successful, the label on the form displays the text "Insert successful." To verify the results, open a new query window in SSMS (SQL Server Management Studio). Select the AdventureWorks database and execute the following query:

```
SELECT ContactID, NameStyle, Title, FirstName, MiddleName, LastName,
EmailAddress, EmailPromotion, PasswordHash, PasswordSalt
FROM Person.Contact
WHERE ContactID > 19977
```

Figure 7-2 shows the results pane.

	ContactID	NameStyle	Title	FirstName	MiddleName	LastName	EmailAddress	EmailPromotion	PasswordHash	PasswordSalt
1	19978	0	NULL	Scott	NULL	Klein	NULL	1	F57E03FEA2FD0F74684C20758110CC7860F67523	/RPjvXw

Figure 7-2

You have successfully read data from an XML file and inserted it into a database. Not difficult to do, was it? By now you should be realizing how easy LINQ to XML and LINQ to SQL make working with XML and SQL databases.

Next you'll update the new record.

Update

This example continues the previous one by updating the record that was just inserted. First, though, you'll need to update the XML file `Contacts.Xml` with the following highlighted code lines:

```
<Contacts>
  <Contact>
      <ContactID>19978</ContactID>
      <NameStyle>0</NameStyle>
      <Title>Geek</Title>
      <FirstName>Scott</FirstName>
      <MiddleName>Lindsey</MiddleName>
      <LastName>Klein</LastName>
      <EmailAddress>ScottKlein@SqlXml.com</EmailAddress>
      <EmailPromotion>1</EmailPromotion>
      <PasswordHash> F57E03FEA2FD0F74684C20758110CC7860F67523</PasswordHash>
      <PasswordSalt>/RPjvXw=</PasswordSalt>
  </Contact>
</Contacts>
```

Next, update the code behind the XML to SQL button of the form with the following highlighted code lines:

```
AdventureWorks db = new AdventureWorks("Integrated Security=sspi");

XElement xel = XElement.Load(@"C:\Wrox\Linq\Chapter5\Contacts.xml");

foreach (XElement xelem in xel.Elements("Contact"))
{
  Contact
  Contact con = db.contact.First(co => co.ContactID ==
  (int)xelem.Element("ContactID"));
  con.Title = (string)xelem.Element("Title");
  con.MiddleName = (string)xelem.Element("MiddleName");
  con.EmailAddress = (string)xelem.Element("EmailAddress");
  db.SubmitChanges();
}
label1.Text = "Update successful";
lable1.Visible = true;
```

Run the project and click the XML to SQL button. When the update is successful, the label on the form will display the text "Update successful." To verify the results, open a new query window in SSMS. Select the AdventureWorks database, and execute the same query you used in the last example. Figure 7-3 shows the results.

	ContactID	Namestyle	title	firstname	middlename	lastname	emailaddress	emailpromotion	passwordhash	passwordsalt
1	19978	0	Mr	Scott	L	Klein	ScottKlein@SQLXML.com	1	F57E03FEA2FD0F74684C20758110CC7860F67523	/RPjvXw

Figure 7-3

You have successfully read data from an XML file and updated a record in a SQL table. In the preceding highlighted code, a query for each contact element is executed against the database, returning the corresponding `ContactID`. In this example, a single record is returned because the query is only looking for a specific `ContactID`. Once that `ContactID` is found, the `Title`, `MiddleName`, and `EmailAddress` fields are updated for that `ContactID`.

Summary

This chapter introduced you to mixing LINQ data models within a single query. You saw how to query a SQL database and use the results to create an XML tree. This functionality is provided by the individual data models and associated APIs.

You also learned how to query contents of an XML document and use that information to insert and update a SQL Server table. Again, the LINQ APIs make it extremely easy to mix LINQ data models and use XML to update a database.

The next chapter focuses on a few advanced topics of LINQ to XML.

8

Advanced LINQ to XML Programming Topics

By now, you should have a fairly solid understanding of how LINQ to XML works, and how you can use it to program with XML. Still, there are a few topics that are especially pertinent for advanced developers, and this chapter focuses on those. In particular, this chapter covers the following:

- ❑ Functional construction
- ❑ Annotations
- ❑ Axis
- ❑ Events
- ❑ Streaming documents and fragments

LINQ to XML Functional Construction

In the past few chapters, you've seen how easy it is to construct XML with LINQ to XML using a variety of techniques, such as using the XElement and XAttribute classes. However, LINQ to XML is much more versatile and provides another mechanism for creating XML documents that is called functional construction.

Functional construction is the capability to construct an XML tree via a single statement. For the most part, the last three chapters have shown how to construct XML trees manually using the XElement and XAttribute classes. Those classes contain constructors that enable you to construct XML trees easily and efficiently within a single statement. For example, the XElement constructor enables you to pass other XElement objects or XAttribute objects to create child elements and attributes such as the next example shows.

Each of these classes also has a constructor that takes a params array of type `object[]` so that you can pass one or more objects to the constructor. The benefit of this is that you can create complex XML trees quickly and within a single expression.

Another benefit of LINQ to XML is that objects consume the `IEnumerable` interface. Because the LINQ objects are using the `IEnumerable` interface, the contents of the objects can be enumerated and used to create contained nodes/attributes. In other words, the results of the LINQ query are used in the creation of the XML tree.

For example, the following is a portion of code that builds an XML tree manually:

```
XElement employee = new XElement("Employees",
            new XElement("Employee",
                new XAttribute("id", "1"),
                new XAttribute("Dept", "0001"),
                new XElement("Name", "Scott"),
                new XElement("Address",
                    new XElement("Street", "555 Main St."),
                    new XElement("City", "Wellington"),
                    new XElement("State", "FL"),
                    new XElement("Zip", "33414")),
                new XElement("Title", "All Things Techy"),
                new XElement("HireDate", "02/05/2007"),
                new XElement("Gender", "M")
                )
            );
```

Through the use of the `XElement` and `XAttribute` classes, you can simply and easily construct XML. Notice that as each new element or attribute is added to the tree during construction, the code automatically is formatted to look like the resulting XML.

The preceding code produces the following XML:

```
<Employees>
  <Employee id="1" Dept="0001">
    <Name>Scott</Name>
    <Address>
      <Street>555 Main St.</Street>
      <City>Wellington</City>
      <State>FL</State>
      <Zip>33414</Zip>
    </Address>
    <Title>All Things Techy</Title>
    <HireDate>02/05/2007</HireDate>
    <Gender>M</Gender>
  </Employee>
</Employees>
```

Functional construction, however, enables you to do much more than just construct XML manually as shown in the previous example. Functional construction takes a completely different approach when modifying and manipulating XML. In today's XML technology, manipulating and modifying XML usually means a significant and detailed modification of the XML data source. LINQ to XML treats XML modification as simply a transformation problem: you can take an XML data source and efficiently transform it to another form.

The following example uses the `employee` XML tree from the previous example and constructs a new XML tree, creating two new elements and selecting the `name` element from the `employee` tree:

```
XElement newXML = new XElement("Info",
                    new XElement("CurrentDate", DateTime.Today),
                    new XElement("Supervisor", "Jim"),
                    from el in employee.Element("Employee").Elements("Name")
                    where (string)el == "Scott"
                    select el);
```

When you run this code, the following XML tree is constructed:

```
<Info>
  <CurrentDate>2007-06-02T00:00:00-04:00</CurrentDate>
  <Supervisor>Jim<Supervisor>
  <Name>Scott</Name>
</Info>
```

What makes functional construction great is that you can easily control the resulting XML tree through the query expression. In this example, you could easily return the entire source XML by removing the `where` clause, or you could add additional filters to the `where` clause to return additional elements of the source XML tree.

Until the creation of LINQ (and LINQ to XML), the only approach a developer had for modifying an XML tree was what you might call "in-place" modification, whereby the XML was loaded into a data store such as the DOM, where it was then manipulated and modified. LINQ to XML provides this type of XML modification by letting developers modify XML documents in place.

For the following examples, open your favorite text editor and paste in the results of the previous example (shown here), and save it as `Employees2.xml` in the `\Wrox\Chapter5` directory.

```
<Employees>
  <Employee id="1" Dept="0001">
    <Name>Scott</Name>
    <Address>
      <Street>555 Main St.</Street>
      <City>Wellington</City>
      <State>FL</State>
      <Zip>33414</Zip>
    </Address>
    <Title>All Things Techy</Title>
    <HireDate>02/05/2007</HireDate>
    <Gender>M</Gender>
  </Employee>
</Employees>
```

The following code loads the XML document you just created, creates a new element and appends it to the source XML, and then saves the modified (new) XML document to a different file:

```
XmlDocument xdoc = new XmlDocument();
xdoc.Load(@"C:\Wrox\LINQ\Chapter 5\Employees2.xml");
XmlElement xel = xdoc.CreateElement("Location");
xel.InnerText = "SE";
xdoc.DocumentElement.AppendChild(xel);
xdoc.Save(@"C:\Wrox\LINQ\Chapter 5\Employees3.xml");
```

The following example uses a similar approach using functional construction:

```
XElement xel = XElement.Load(@"C:\Wrox\LINQ\Chapter 8\Employees2.xml");
XElement newXML = new XElement("Employee",
    xel.Element("Employee").Element("Name"),
    from atts in xel.Element("Employee").Attributes()
    select new XElement(atts.Name, (string)atts)
    );
}

newXML.Save(@"c:\wrox\LINQ\chapter5\employee4.xml");
```

This code loads an XML tree from a file, selecting a particular attribute of the Employee node and creating a new element from that attribute, and then removes the selected attribute. The code produces the following XML tree:

```
<Employee>
    <Name>Scott</Name>
    <id>1</id>
    <Dept>0001</Dept>
</Employee>
```

Functional construction provides a much more efficient and robust way of modifying XML trees and documents because it treats the modification of data as a problem of transformation, not as a modification or manipulation of the data source.

With functional construction you can create a new XML from the elements and attributes of the source XML tree, transforming the shape of the XML as the new XML tree is created and as the elements and attributes are added to the new tree, all within a single statement. The key to functional construction is to pass the results of LINQ queries to XElement or XDocument constructors.

One of the benefits of functional construction is that it allows you to visualize more easily how the finished XML tree will look as you build it.

For example, the following code loads the same XML file from the previous example and uses functional construction to build a new XML tree with a new root node and all the employee information from the source XML tree. It also creates two new elements from the attributes of the Employee element.

```
XElement emp = XElement.Load(@"C:\Wrox\LINQ\Chapter 5\Employees2.xml");

XElement newXML = new XElement("Root",
                    emp.Element("Employee"),
                    from att in emp.Element("Employee").Attributes()
                    select new XElement(att.Name, (string)att));

textbox1.Text = newXML.ToString();
```

The code produces the following XML tree:

```
<Root>
  <Employee id="1" Dept="0001">
    <Name>Scott</Name>
    <Address>
      <Address>555 Main St.</Address>
      <City>Wellington</City>
      <State>FL</State>
    </Address>
    <Title>All Things Techy</Title>
    <HireDate>02/05/2007</HireDate>
    <Gender>M</Gender>
  </Employee>
  <id>1</id>
  <Dept>0001</Dept>
</Root>
```

By modifying the code, you can return more granular information. The highlighted line in the following code illustrates how to return only the Address information from the loaded XML file:

```
XElement newXML = new XElement("Root",
                  emp.Element("Employee").Element("Address"),
                  from att in emp.Element("Employee").Attributes()
                  select new XElement(att.Name, (string)att));
```

The code produces the following XML tree:

```
<Root>
  <Address>
    <Address>555 Main St.</Address>
    <City>Wellington</City>
    <State>FL</State>
  </Address>
  <id>1</id>
  <Dept>0001</Dept>
</Root>
```

One last example for this section: The following highlighted code uses functional construction to return the Name element and the id attribute from the source tree to create a simple new XML tree:

```
XElement newXML = new XElement("Root",
                  emp.Element("Employee").Element("Name"),
                  from att in emp.Element("Employee").Attributes()
                  where att.Name == "id"
                  select new XElement(att.Name, (string)att));
```

It produces the following XML tree:

```
<Root>
  <Name>Scott</Name>
  <id>1</id>
</Root>
```

You're beginning to see how efficient it is to use functional construction to modify and manipulate XML. Although in some cases it may not be any easier, especially on much larger XML documents, the functional construction approach still provides a number of benefits over other methods, such as the ability to produce code that is easier to read and maintain. Functional construction lends itself to greater productivity, regardless of the size of the XML document.

LINQ to XML Annotations

LINQ to XML supports the concept of annotations. In layman's terms, an annotation is an explanatory note associated with some text. An annotation in LINQ to XML is not that different—it is the capability to add, or associate, an object to an XML node or attribute. It can be any object of any arbitrary type. In LINQ to XML, annotations are provided linked lists of type Object on an XNode.

Annotations are added via the AddAnnotation method of an XElement or XAttribute. When the AddAnnotation method is called, a new object is added to the corresponding XObject (element or attribute) in the XML tree.

To utilize annotations, a mechanism for adding and defining annotations must first be created. For example, the following code defines a mechanism for adding annotations of integer data types.

```
public class TestAnnotation
{
        private int val1;
        public int Val1 { get { return val1;}  set { val1 = value;}}
        public TestAnnotation(int val1)
        {
            this.val1 = val1;
        }

}
```

With this class defined, any time you want to add an annotation of an integer type to an element or attribute, you can simply call this class. For instance, the following code uses the TestAnnotation class defined above to add an annotation to the root element. The code writes the new XML to a text box, but be aware that the annotation is not visible. The last two lines of the following code illustrate how to obtain the annotation from the element:

```
TestAnnotation ano1 = new TestAnnotation(500);
XElement root = new XElement("Root", "scott");
root.AddAnnotation(ano1);

textBox1.Text = root.ToString();

TestAnnotation ano2 = root.Annotation<TestAnnotation>();
textBox1.Text = ano2.Val1.ToString();
```

When you run this code, the text box should display the value 500.

Of course, annotations can be of any type, so the preceding code could simply have been written as follows:

```
XElement root = new XElement("Root", "scott");
root.AddAnnotation(500);
```

What happens if you want to add an annotation of another type? Fortunately, you don't need to create a new annotation class. The following is an example that uses the same original annotation class to add another annotation type of string, as shown by the highlighted code. It does that by creating a new public method of the same name as the original method:

```
public class TestAnnotation
{
        private int val1;
        private string val2;
        public int Val1 { get { return val1;}  set { val1 = value;}}
        public string Val2 { get { return val2;}  set { val2 = value;}}
        public TestAnnotation(int val1)
        {
            this.val1 = val1;
        }

        public TestAnnotation(string val2)
          {
            this.val2 = val2;
          }
}
```

Now you can use the overloaded methods to either add a string or integer annotation. Here's an example which creates an XML tree, adding an integer annotation to the root node and a string annotation to the id attribute, as illustrated by the highlighted code:

```
TestAnnotation ano1 = new TestAnnotation(500);
TestAnnotation ano3 = new TestAnnotation("Scott");
XElement root = new XElement("Root", "scott",
                    new XAttribute("id","1")
                    );

root.AddAnnotation(ano1);
textBox1.Text = root.ToString();

root.Attribute("id").AddAnnotation(ano3);

TestAnnotation ano2 = root.Annotation<TestAnnotation>();
textBox1.Text = ano2.Val1.ToString();

TestAnnotation ano4 = root.Attribute("id").Annotation<TestAnnotation>();
textBox1.Text = ano4.Val1.ToString();
```

You'll notice that the same class was used to define and add the annotations. The last four lines of code print the annotation values to the text box.

Again, you could simply add the new annotation like this:

```
root.AddAnnotation("Scott");
```

The reason for walking you through the more lengthy example was to illustrate how LINQ to XML works with annotations as arbitrary objects of any arbitrary type.

Multiple annotations can be added to an element or attribute, and you can use the `Annotations` method to retrieve them all. Using the same `TestAnnotation` class created above, the example below defines a simple XML tree and adds multiple annotations to the root node using two different ways. The first method simply passes a string value as shown in the first three annotations added. The last two annotations are added as an `IEnumerable<T>` of type `TestAnnotation` class.

```
XElement root = new XElement("Root", "scott");
root.AddAnnotation("1");
root.AddAnnotation("2");
root.AddAnnotation("3");
root.AddAnnotation(new TestAnnotation(500));
root.AddAnnotation(new TestAnnotation("Scooter"));

IEnumerable<string> stringList;
stringList = root.Annotations<string>();
foreach (string val in stringList)
    listbox1.Items.Add(val);

IEnumerable<TextAnnotation> TestAnnoList;
int loopCount = 1;
TestAnnoList = root.Annotations<TestAnnotation>();
foreach (TestAnnotation val2 in TestAnnoList)
{
  if (loopCount == 1)
  {
    listbox1.Items.Add(val2.Tag1);
  }
  else
  {
    listbox1.Items.Add(val2.Tag2);
  }
  loopCount += 1;
}
```

This code produces the following results:

```
1
2
3
500
Scooter
```

It's just that easy to add annotations to elements and attributes of an XML tree, and to retrieve the annotation values.

LINQ to XML Axis

LINQ to XML provides the capability to query an XML to find elements and attributes and return their respective values. You have seen in previous chapters how to "walk" an XML tree to find a specific value of an element or attribute, but what if you want to return a value for more than one node? Suppose that you want to return all the FirstName elements, for example. How would you do that?

LINQ to XML provides this capability through axis methods, which are methods on the XElement class, each of which returns an IEnumerable collection. These methods can be used to return the structured, or complex, content of a node such as child and ancestor elements.

LINQ to XML axis methods enable you to work with nodes instead of individual elements and attributes, providing the capability to return collections of elements and attributes. This lets developers work at a finer level of detail. This section explores a few of the main axis methods of the XElement class:

- ❑ Ancestors
- ❑ Descendants
- ❑ AncestorsAndSelf
- ❑ DescendantsAndSelf
- ❑ ElementsAfterSelf
- ❑ ElementsBeforeSelf

Ancestors

The Ancestors method returns the ancestor elements of the specified node. In the following example, the ancestors (those elements above the specified element) of the Name element are returned. As stated earlier, this method returns an IEnumerable of XElement, and the results can be enumerated through as shown here:

```
XElement root = new XElement("Employees",
                    new XElement("Employee",
                        new XElement("Name", "Scott")
                        )
                    );

IEnumerable<XElement> anc = root.Descendants("Name");
foreach (XElement el in anc.Ancestors())
    listBox1.Items.Add(el.Name);
```

The ancestor nodes of the specified node (in this case, the Name node) are returned:

```
Employee
Employees
```

The Descendants method, which will be discussed next, is also used in this example. It specifies the starting point of the ancestor search. As you have learned in the last few chapters, you could have just as easily done the following, but the question is, would the results be the same?

```
IEnumerable<XElement> anc = root.Element("Employee").Elements("Name");
foreach (XElement el in anc.Ancestors())
    listBox1.Items.Add(el.Name);
```

There really is no advantage of using one approach over the other. The Ancestors method returns an IEnumerable XEelement of all the ancestors of the current Element. As you will find out in the next section, the Descendants method returns an IEnumerable XElement of all the descendants of the current Element. So, it really depends on how you want to approach the problem.

The Ancestors method also has an overload that takes an element name, returning only those elements in the collection that match the specified name. For example, the following returns a collection filtered by the ancestor elements that have a matching XName (element name):

```
XElement root = new XElement("Employees",
                    new XElement("Employee",
                        new XElement("Name", "Scott")
                        )
                    );

IEnumerable<XElement> anc = root.Descendants("Name");
foreach (XElement el in anc.Ancestors("Employee"))
    listBox1.Items.Add(el.Name);
```

The code returns the following value:

```
Employee
```

The same thing happens even if an additional employee is added, as shown here:

```
XElement root = new XElement("Employees",
                    new XElement("Employee",
                        new XElement("Name", "Scott")),
                    new XElement("Employee",
                        new XElement("Name", "Bob"))
                    );

IEnumerable<XElement> anc = root.Descendants("Name");
foreach (XElement el in anc.Ancestors("Employee"))
    listBox1.Items.Add(el.Name);
```

Now the code returns the following values:

```
Employee
Employee
```

You are probably asking yourself, "How is this useful?" While these examples may seem trivial, the methods (Ancestors, Descendants, and so on) return an IEnumerable collection—meaning that they return a collection of elements, in this case a collection of Employee elements. These examples just displayed the name of the element, but you do so much more, such as grabbing the values of the elements as you loop through the collection, like this:

```
foreach (XElement el in anc.Ancestors("Employee"))
    listBox1.Items.Add(el.Value);
```

As you become more familiar with these methods, you will begin to understand the flexibility and usefulness of what they can do for you.

Descendants

Descendants are those elements below the specified element in an XML tree. The Descendants method returns a collection of elements that are descendants of the specified element, as the following example shows. As stated earlier, this method returns an IEnumerable of XElement, and the results can be enumerated.

```
XElement root = new XElement("Employees",
                    new XElement("Employee",
                        new XElement("Name", "Scott"))
                    );

IEnumerable<XElement> des =
    from el in root.Descendants()
    select el;
foreach (XElement el in des)
    listBox1.Items.Add(el.Name);
```

This example simply asks for the descendants of the root node, returning the following:

```
Employee
Name
```

Another way to return the descendants, in less code, would be the following:

```
IEnumerable<XElement> des = root.Descendants();
foreach (XElement el in des)
    listBox1.Items.Add(el.Name);
```

This returns the exact same results as the preceding example.

This method also takes an overload, which returns all of the descendants that have the specified name, as this code illustrates:

```
IEnumerable<XElement> des =
    from el in root.Descendants("Employeee")
    select el;
foreach (XElement el in des)
    listBox1.Items.Add(el.Name);
```

This example asks for the descendants of the `Employee` node, returning the following:

```
Name
```

Again, you could write the example as follows:

```
IEnumerable<XElement> des = root.Descendants("Employeee");
foreach (XElement el in des)
    listBox1.Items.Add(el.Name);
```

Just to make things a bit more complicated, let's add another employee and return the values of the descendants of the `employee` node, which in essence is asking for the value of the `Name` node because it is a descendant of the `Employee` node:

```
XElement root = new XElement("Employees",
                new XElement("Employee",
                    new XElement("Name", "Scott"))
                    ,
                new XElement("Employee",
                    new XElement("Name", "Bob"))
                );

textBox1.Text = root.ToString();

IEnumerable<XElement> des = root.Descendants("Employee");
foreach (XElement el in des)
    listBox1.Items.Add(el.Value);
```

When run, this code produces the following output:

```
Scott
Bob
```

Hopefully, you are starting to see how easy it is to work with these axis methods.

AncestorsAndSelf

The `AncestorsAndSelf` method is almost identical to the `Ancestors` method, but it varies in the fact that it returns the current element along with its ancestors. The following example constructs a simple XML tree, and then queries the XML for the `Employee` node and its ancestor nodes:

```
XElement root = new XElement("Employees",
                new XElement("Employee",
                    new XElement("Name", "Scott"))
                );

textBox1.Text = root.ToString();

XElement ce = root.Element(("Employee");
IEnumerable<XElement> des =
```

```
        from el in ce.AncestorsAndSelf()
        select el;
    foreach (XElement el in des)
        listBox1.Items.Add(el.Name);
```

An XElement variable is declared to specify the element at which to start the ancestor search. That variable is then used to apply the AncestorsAndSelf() method.

Equally, you could also do the following:

```
    IEnumerable<XElement> des =
    root.Element("Employee").AncestorsAndSelf();
    foreach (XElement el in des)
        listBox1.Items.Add(el.Name);
```

Either way, the results are the same. The current node plus its ancestors are returned in the results.

```
    Emmployee
    Employees
```

Yep, pretty simple, but efficient.

DescendantsAndSelf

The DescendantsAndSelf method is almost identical to the Descendants method; it varies only in that it returns the current element along with its descendants. The following example constructs a simple XML tree, and then queries the XML for the Employee node and its descendant nodes.

```
    XElement root = new XElement("Employees",
                        new XElement("Employee",
                            new XElement("Name", "Scott"))
                        );

    textBox1.Text = root.ToString();

    IEnumerable<XElement> des =
        from el in root.Element("Employee").DescendantsAndSelf()
        select el;
    foreach (XElement el in des)
        listBox1.Items.Add(el.Name);
```

Equally, you could also do the following:

```
    IEnumerable<XElement> des = root.Element("Employee").DescendantsAndSelf();
    foreach (XElement el in des)
        listBox1.Items.Add(el.Name);
```

Both of these methods return the same results:

```
    Employee
    Name
```

Also, both the `AncestorsAndSelf` and `DescendantsAndSelf` methods have an overload that returns an `IEnumerable` of only the elements of the name specified in the method, as shown below in the following example:

```
IEnumerable<XElement> des =
    from el in root.DescendantsAndSelf("Employee")
    select el;
foreach (XElement el in des)
    listBox1.Items.Add(el.Name);
```

In this case, only the `Employee` element would be returned.

ElementsAfterSelf and ElementsBeforeSelf

The `ElementsAfterSelf` and `ElementsBeforeSelf` methods return the elements that come after the specified element and the elements that come before the specified element, respectively. Each method takes an overload that returns the elements after, or before, the current element that match the specified element name.

Here's code that defines an XML tree with a root node and six child elements, and then queries the XML tree for those elements whose elements are after Element4:

```
XElement root = new XElement("Root",
                    new XElement("Element1", "Value1"),
                    new XElement("Element2", "Value2"),
                    new XElement("Element3", "Value3"),
                    new XElement("Element4", "Value4"),
                    new XElement("Element5", "Value5"),
                    new XElement("Element6", "Value6")
                    );
textBox1.Text = root.ToString();

XElement re = root.Element("Element4");
IEnumerable<XElement> els = re.ElementsAfterSelf();
foreach (XElement el in els)
    listBox1.Items.Add(el.Name);
```

The following is returned:

```
Element5
Element6
```

The following approach returns the same results:

```
IEnumerable<XElement> re = root.Element("Element4").ElementsAfterSelf();
foreach (XElement el in re)
    listBox1.Items.Add(el.Name);
```

Using the same XML tree, the following code queries the XML tree for those elements that are before Element4:

```
XElement re = root.Element("Element4");
IEnumerable<XElement> els = re.ElementsBeforeSelf();
```

```
foreach (XElement el in els)
    listBox1.Items.Add(el.Name);
```

Again, you could write it as follows:

```
IEnumerable<XElement> re = root.Element("Element4").ElementsBeforeSelf();
foreach (XElement el in re)
    listBox1.Items.Add(el.Name);
```

In both cases, the following values are returned:

```
Element1
Element2
Element3
```

Last, the overloads for these two methods return the elements after or before the current element that also match the specified element name:

```
XElement re = root.Element("Element4");
IEnumerable<XElement> els = re.ElementsAfterSelf("Element6");
foreach (XElement el in els)
    listBox1.Items.Add(el.Name);
```

Just as before, you could write it as follows:

```
IEnumerable<XElement> re = root.Element("Element4").ElementsAfterSelf("Element6");
foreach (XElement el in re)
    listBox1.Items.Add(el.Name);
```

Both approaches produce the same result: Element6.

While this example illustrated the ElementsAfterSelf() method, the same concept applies to the ElementsBeforeSelf() method as well.

LINQ to XML axis methods are best used when working with nodes of an XML tree; they enable you to work at a finer level of detail. By efficiently using the axis methods, developers can quickly and easily iterate through an XML tree working with collections, not just an individual element or attribute.

LINQ to XML Events

LINQ to XML events provide notifications when a change is made to an XML tree. LINQ to XML provides two events to handle changes to an XML tree: Changing and Changed. Both of these events are raised when you modify the XML tree; they're discussed in detail in the following sections.

To effectively work with events, LINQ to XML provides three types, described in the following table.

Type	Description
XObjectChange	Specifies an event type when an event is raised for an XObject, such as an element or attribute.
XObjectChangeEventArgs	Provides the necessary argument data for the Changing and Changed events.
XObectChangeEventHandler	Represents the methods that will handle the Changing and Changed events of the specified XObject.

Changing

The Changing event occurs prior to applying any changes to the XObject or any of its descendants. In other words, this event is fired when an element or attribute, or any of its descendants, is about to change. When you request a change to an element of an XML tree, a Changing event is raised.

The best way to illustrate this is by example. The following code defines an XML tree, defines an event, and applies the defined event to the root node. Finally, a new element is added to the XML tree. Remember, events apply to an XObject or any of its descendants. By adding a new element to the root node, the defined event is fired. LINQ to XML handles the event notifications when the XML tree is altered.

```
XElement empXML = new XElement("Employees",
              new XElement("Employee",
                  new XAttribute("id", "1"),
                  new XAttribute("Dept", "0001"),
                  new XElement("Name", "Scott"),
                  new XElement("Address",
                      new XElement("Street", "555 Main St."),
                      new XElement("City", "Wellington"),
                      new XElement("State", "FL"),
                      new XElement("Zip", "33414")),
                  new XElement("Title", "All Things Techy"),
                  new XElement("HireDate", "02/05/2007"),
                  new XElement("Gender", "M")
              )
          );

empXML.Changing += new XObjectChangeEventHandler(delegate(object xsender,
    XObjectChangeEventArgs cea)
                {
                    listBox1.Items.Add("Changing event raised");
                    XElement newEl = (XElement)xsender;
                    listBox1.Items.Add("  Sender: " + newEl.Name);
                    listBox1.Items.Add("  ObjectChange: " + cea.ObjectChange);
                }
);

empXML.Element("Employee").Add(new XElement("Nickname", "scooter"));
```

When this code runs, the following displays in the list box:

```
Changing event raised
   Sender: Nickname
   ObjectChanged: Add
```

The first item simply states that the Changing event was raised. More important, however, are the next two: the actual name of the element that was affected, and the operation performed, in this case, an Add (an element was added).

Because Changing was placed on the root node, any change to the XML tree would have fired it.

To really see how this works, modify the code as follows (highlighted lines), then place a breakpoint on the empXML.Changing line. This example doesn't add a new element; rather, it updates the value of an existing element.

```
XElement empXML = new XElement("Employees",
                new XElement("Employee",
                    new XAttribute("id", "1"),
                    new XAttribute("Dept", "0001"),
                    new XElement("Name", "Scott"),
                    new XElement("Address",
                        new XElement("Street", "555 Main St."),
                        new XElement("City", "Wellington"),
                        new XElement("State", "FL"),
                        new XElement("Zip", "33414")),
                    new XElement("Title", "All Things Techy"),
                    new XElement("HireDate", "02/05/2007"),
                    new XElement("Gender", "M")
                )
            );

empXML.Changing += new XObjectChangeEventHandler(delegate(object xsender,
    XObjectChangeEventArgs cea)
                {
                    listBox1.Items.Add("changing event raised");
                    //XElement newEl = (XElement)xsender;
                    //listBox1.Items.Add("  Sender: " + newEl.Name);

                    listBox1.Items.Add("  ObjectChange: " + cea.ObjectChange);
                }
);

empXML.Element("Employee").Element("Title").Value = "Geek";
```

Execute the code, and then press F10 to step through it. You'll notice that it executes the Changing event as a whole, then it executes the last line, which updates the value of the Title element. When you press F10 on the last line, the execution enters the Changing event and goes through it not once, but twice. Why? Take a look at the output produced by the code in the event:

```
Changing event raised
   ObjectChange: Remove
```

```
Changing event raised
   ObjectChange: Add
```

There's the answer: An update is really a delete with an Add and Insert. Slick.

Changed

The Changed event fires when a change is made to an XObject or any of its descendants. In other words, it fires when a change on an element or attribute, or any of its descendants, is complete.

For example, the following code defines an XML tree, defines a Changing event and Changed event, and applies both events to the root node. Last, like the previous example, the value of an existing element is modified.

```
XElement empXML = new XElement("Employees",
            new XElement("Employee",
                new XAttribute("id", "1"),
                new XAttribute("Dept", "0001"),
                new XElement("Name", "Scott"),
                new XElement("Address",
                    new XElement("Street", "555 Main St."),
                    new XElement("City", "Wellington"),
                    new XElement("State", "FL"),
                    new XElement("Zip", "33414")),
                new XElement("Title", "All Things Techy"),
                new XElement("HireDate", "02/05/2007"),
                new XElement("Gender", "M")
            )
        );

empXML.Changing += new XObjectChangeEventHandler(delegate(object xsender,
    XObjectChangeEventArgs cea)
            {
                listBox1.Items.Add("changing event raised");
                //XElement newEl = (XElement)xsender;
                //listBox1.Items.Add("  Sender: " + newEl.Name);
                listBox1.Items.Add("  ObjectChange: " + cea.ObjectChange);
            }
);

empXML.Changed += new XObjectChangeEventHandler(delegate(object xsender,
    XObjectChangeEventArgs cea)
            {
                listBox1.Items.Add("changed event raised");
                listBox1.Items.Add("  ObjectChange: " + cea.ObjectChange);
            }
);

empXML.Element("Employee").Element("Title").Value = "Geek";
```

You can tell by the output that each of these events was called twice:

```
Changing event raised
   ObjectChange: Remove
```

```
Changed event raised
  ObjectChange: Remove
Changing event raised
  ObjectChange: Add
Changed event raised
  ObjectChange: Add
```

The key to working with events is knowing when events are raised (what triggers an event) and how to implement them. Here, events are raised only when modifying an existing XML tree and not when creating or constructing a new tree. The reasoning behind this is the order in which XML trees are constructed and event handlers are applied:

❑ To be capable of receiving events, you must first add an event handler.

❑ To add an event handler, you must first have a reference to an XObject.

❑ To have a reference to an XObject, you must first construct an XML tree.

Therefore, it is not possible to receive events during functional construction.

A word of caution: Modifying an XML tree within the execution of the raised event is not recommended because it can lead to unexpected results. You can, however, modify another XML tree from within the event, and you can even modify another node of the same tree from within an event. But, the latter is highly discouraged, especially if you are modifying the node from which the event is being raised, because it may have a negative impact on the events being raised on that node.

Streaming XML Documents

All of the examples so far have worked with XML trees and XML documents that haven't really been that big. In the real world, however, XML documents and trees can be very large. And you know from working with large XML documents and trees that they can be memory hogs.

LINQ to XML can help with this problem; you can use its streaming techniques and a lot of the functionality you have learned in this and previous chapters, such as the great LINQ to XML axis methods.

Streaming XML documents entails utilizing the XmlReader class to read from one XML source and creating a much smaller XML fragment in which you can then work. The result is a decrease in memory usage.

The key is to use the XmlReader class to scour the XML document looking for the nodes it needs, and then calling the ReadFrom() method to read the information from the source XML and populate the target XML fragment.

Before you tackle streaming with large XML documents, take a look at streaming in general to control memory usage in your application.

I love examples, so let's start with one. Create the following XML document and save it as Orders.xml in the Wrox\Chapter8 directory:

```
<Orders>
  <SalesPerson>
    <Name>Scott</Name>
```

```xml
    <Order Date="1/14/2007">
      <Amount>15.00</Amount>
    </Order>
    <Order Date="1/22/2007">
      <Amount>98.00</Amount>
    </Order>
    <Order Date="2/3/2007">
      <Amount>9.00</Amount>
    </Order>
    <Order Date="3/24/2007">
      <Amount>39.00</Amount>
    </Order>
    <Order Date="4/5/2007">
      <Amount>72.00</Amount>
    </Order>
  </SalesPerson>
  <SalesPerson>
    <Name>Dave</Name>
    <Order Date="1/6/2007">
      <Amount>112.00</Amount>
    </Order>
    <Order Date="3/28/2007">
      <Amount>143.00</Amount>
    </Order>
    <Order Date="4/10/2007">
      <Amount>98.00</Amount>
    </Order>
    <Order Date="5/9/2007">
      <Amount>149.00</Amount>
    </Order>
  </SalesPerson>
  <SalesPerson>
    <Name>John</Name>
    <Order Date="1/19/2007">
      <Amount>62.00</Amount>
    </Order>
    <Order Date="3/17/2007">
      <Amount>88.00</Amount>
    </Order>
    <Order Date="3/19/2007">
      <Amount>151.00</Amount>
    </Order>
    <Order Date="4/11/2007">
      <Amount>134.00</Amount>
    </Order>
  </SalesPerson>
  <SalesPerson>
    <Name>Steve</Name>
    <Order Date="2/21/2007">
      <Amount>999.00</Amount>
    </Order>
    <Order Date="3/30/2007">
      <Amount>51.00</Amount>
    </Order>
```

```
        <Order Date="4/01/2007">
          <Amount>244.00</Amount>
        </Order>
        <Order Date="5/21/2007">
          <Amount>333.00</Amount>
        </Order>
      </SalesPerson>
    </Orders>
```

In Visual Studio, create the following private function, which uses the XmlReader to read the source XML document and create a much smaller XML fragment with only the information you are looking for.

```
static IEnumerable<XElement> StreamSalesOrders(string uri)
{
    using (XmlReader reader = XmlReader.Create(uri))
    {
        XElement name = null;
        XElement order = null;

        reader.MoveToContent();

        while (reader.Read())
        {
            if (reader.NodeType == XmlNodeType.Element
                            && reader.Name == "SalesPerson")
            {
                while (reader.Read())
                {
                    if (reader.NodeType == XmlNodeType.Element
                                    && reader.Name == "Name")
                    {
                        name = XElement.ReadFrom(reader) as XElement;
                        break;
                    }
                }

                while (reader.Read())
                {
                    if (reader.NodeType == XmlNodeType.EndElement)
                        break;
                    if (reader.NodeType == XmlNodeType.Element
                                    && reader.Name == "Order")
                    {
                        order = XElement.ReadFrom(reader) as XElement;
                        if (order != null)
                        {
                            XElement tempRoot = new XElement("TempRoot",
                                            new XElement(name)
                                                    );
                            tempRoot.Add(order);
                            yield return order;
                        }
                    }
                }
            }
```

```
                   }
              }
         }
    }
```

The last step is to write the code that calls the function and creates the resulting XML document. In your Visual Studio application, add the following code:

```
XElement xmlTree = new XElement("Sales",
                 from el in StreamSalesOrders(@"C:\Wrox\LINQ\Chapter 8\Orders.xml")
                 where (decimal)el.Element("Amount") > 50 &&
                       (decimal)el.Element("Amount") < 150
                 select new XElement("Order",
                   new XElement("SalesPerson", (string)el.Parent.Element("Name")),
                   new XElement(el.Element("Amount"))
                                    )
                               );
textBox1.Text = xmlTree.ToString();
```

In this code, the "large" XML document is loaded and quickly gone through using the XmlReader class. A new XML fragment is created based on the query expression and the information that is being enumerated. The code looks for all sales with amounts greater than 50 dollars and less than 150 dollars. Based on those criteria, the following XML fragment is produced:

```
<Sales>
  <Order>
    <SalesPerson>Scott</SalesPerson>
    <Amount>98.00</Amount>
  </Order>
  <Order>
    <SalesPerson>Scott</SalesPerson>
    <Amount>72.00</Amount>
  </Order>
  <Order>
    <SalesPerson>Dave</SalesPerson>
    <Amount>112.00</Amount>
  </Order>
  <Order>
    <SalesPerson>Dave</SalesPerson>
    <Amount>143.00</Amount>
  </Order>
  <Order>
    <SalesPerson>Dave</SalesPerson>
    <Amount>98.00</Amount>
  </Order>
  <Order>
    <SalesPerson>Dave</SalesPerson>
    <Amount>149.00</Amount>
  </Order>
  <Order>
    <SalesPerson>John</SalesPerson>
    <Amount>62.00</Amount>
  </Order>
  <Order>
```

```
    <SalesPerson>John</SalesPerson>
    <Amount>88.00</Amount>
  </Order>
  <Order>
    <SalesPerson>John</SalesPerson>
    <Amount>134.00</Amount>
  </Order>
  <Order>
    <SalesPerson>Steve</SalesPerson>
    <Amount>51.00</Amount>
  </Order>
</Sales>
```

Not too bad. The next example utilizes the date attribute on the XML document to build the XML fragment. Modify the code in your Visual Studio application as follows:

```
DateTime startDate;
DateTime endDate;

DateTime.TryParse("02/01/2007", out startDate);
DateTime.TryParse("02/28/2007", out endDate);

XElement xmlTree = new XElement("Sales",
                from el in StreamSalesOrders(@"C:\Wrox\LINQ\Chapter 8\Orders.xml")
                where (DateTime)el.Attribute("Date") >= startDate
                && (DateTime)el.Attribute("Date") <= endDate

                select new XElement("Order",
                        new XElement("SalesPerson",
                            (string)el.Parent.Element("Name")),
                        new XElement(el.Element("Amount"))
                        )
                    );
```

This example uses the date attribute of each order to filter the information. Based on this criterion, the following results are produced:

```
<Sales>
  <Order>
    <SalesPerson>Scott</SalesPerson>
    <Amount>9.00</Amount>
  </Order>
  <Order>
    <SalesPerson>Steve</SalesPerson>
    <Amount>999.00</Amount>
  </Order>
</Sales>
```

One more modification: the following example takes the order date attribute and adds it to the resulting XML tree as an element.

```
XElement xmlTree = new XElement("Sales",
                from el in StreamSalesOrders(@"C:\Wrox\LINQ\Chapter 8\Orders.xml")
                where (DateTime)el.Attribute("Date") >= startDate
                && (DateTime)el.Attribute("Date") <= endDate
```

```
                 select new XElement("Order",
                         new XElement("SalesPerson",
                             (string)el.Parent.Element("Name")),
                         new XElement(el.Element("Amount")),
                         new XElement("OrderDate", el.Attribute("Date"))

                         )
                     );
```

Your results should now look like the following:

```
<Sales>
  <Order>
    <SalesPerson>Scott</SalesPerson>
    <Amount>9.00</Amount>
    <OrderDate Date="2/3/2007" />
  </Order>
  <Order>
    <SalesPerson>Steve</SalesPerson>
    <Amount>999.00</Amount>
    <OrderDate Date="2/21/2007" />
  </Order>
</Sales>
```

In essence, by using the `XmlWriter` class and `ReadFrom` method, you are basically building your own axis method. It enables you to work with large XML documents without sacrificing performance.

Streaming Large XML Documents

Now you're ready to use the streaming technique to work with large XML documents. Take a look at the following code. The XML fragment is now constructed utilizing an `IEnumerable` element. That provides the flexibility to use LINQ to XML to enumerate the results and write them to an `XmlWriter`, as shown in the highlighted code.

```
IEnumerable<XElement> xmlTree =

                from el in StreamSalesOrders(@"C:\Wrox\LINQ\Chapter 8\Orders.xml")
                where (DateTime)el.Attribute("Date") >= startDate
                && (DateTime)el.Attribute("Date") <= endDate
                select new XElement("Order",
                        new XElement("SalesPerson",
                            (string)el.Parent.Element("Name")),
                        new XElement(el.Element("Amount")),
                        new XElement("OrderDate", el.Attribute("Date"))
                        )
                    );


XmlWriterSettings xws = new XmlWriterSettings();
xws.OmitXmlDeclaration = true;
xws.Indent = true;
using (XmlWriter xw = XmlWriter.Create(@"c:\Wrox\output.xml", xws))
{
    xw.WriteStartElement("Root");
```

```
        foreach (XElement el in xmlTree)
            el.WriteTo(xw);

    xw.WriteEndElement();
}
```

You should get the same results as the previous example.

Summary

On the surface, LINQ to XML looks intimidating, but this and the previous three chapters should have dispelled that vicious rumor. Hopefully, as you started working your way through this chapter, you quickly realized that it really wasn't as bad as you thought. Sure, working with annotations, events, and axes can be tough, but the purpose of this chapter was to show you that working with them also can be delightful and downright fun.

You first examined functional construction and the important role it plays in LINQ to XML. Functional construction provides the capability to easily and efficiently construct an XML document within a single statement. Then you saw how to add annotations to elements and attributes in an XML tree using the AddAnnotation method, and how to read annotations once they are applied.

You explored LINQ to XML axis methods, which provide the capability to quickly and efficiently query an XML tree to find elements and attributes and return their values. Knowing how to use these is absolutely necessary to understanding and writing query expressions.

Finally, you saw how to stream XML documents using LINQ to XML and the benefits that streaming provides, such as managing memory and controlling the size of your XML documents.

Chapter 9, the last chapter in this section, focuses on LINQ to XML in Visual Basic .NET.

LINQ to XML and Visual Basic .NET

Visual Basic .NET wasn't left behind when it comes to working with LINQ to XML. Visual Basic provides profound support for LINQ to XML through XML literals and XML Axis properties.

This chapter focuses on the LINQ to XML differences that apply to Visual Basic .NET. You'll explore the following topics in this chapter:

❑   How to create XML

❑   How to access XML

❑   How to load XML

❑   How to manipulate XML

Creating XML

You have to agree that LINQ to XML is powerful and flexible. One of the things you have seen is the capability to call LINQ APIs directly, but what you are about to see makes LINQ to XML even better. In Visual Basic, you can declare XML literals and write XML directly in your code. And you also can access XML Axis properties from within your code.

However, it is important to understand what XML literals are so that you can have a better appreciation, as well as for creating XML.

Overview of XML Literals

An XML Literal is a piece of XML, such as a complete XML document or XML fragment, that is typed directly into the source code of a Visual Basic .NET module without the use of quotation marks. Using XML literals lets you write XML directly within your Visual Basic code providing the same structure and layout as the resulting XML. This means that you can create XML documents and fragments easily and efficiently right in your code.

XML literal syntax is a representation of the LINQ to XML objects, with Visual Basic compiling the literals into LINQ to XML objects. This functionality is provided via the LINQ to XML object model, which lets you create and work with XML easily.

To get a feel for XML Literals, create a new Windows Forms Visual Basic project in Visual Studio. When the project is created, add a reference to the `System.Xml.Linq` namespace. Open the form in design view and add a few buttons and a text box. Set the Multiline property of the text box to `True` and size the text box so that you can easily view an XML document or fragment.

Next, double-click on the form to view the code behind it, and add the following statement in the declarations section:

```
Imports System.Xml.Linq
```

Next, behind button1, add the following highlighted code. Pay attention to what happens as you type the code for the XML element.

```
Private Sub Button1_Click(ByVal sender As System.Object,
  ByVal e As System.EventArgs)
  Handles Button1.Click

    Dim emp As XElement = _
        <Employee>
            <EmployeeID>1</EmployeeID>
            <FirstName>Scott</FirstName>
            <LastName>Klein</LastName>
            <Title>Geek</Title>
        </Employee>

    Me.TextBox1.Text = emp.ToString

End Sub
```

Slick, isn't it? The XML you typed into the Visual Basic code looks exactly like the XML fragment that appears in the text box when you run the application and click button1:

```
<Employee>
    <EmployeeID>1</EmployeeID>
    <FirstName>Scott</FirstName>
    <LastName>Klein</LastName>
    <Title>Geek</Title>
</Employee>
```

How cool is that?

You can even create XML documents using XML literals. To do so, simply add the highlighted code to your XML from the previous example:

```
Dim emp As XElement = _
    <?xml version="1.0"?>
    <Employee>
        <EmployeeID>1</EmployeeID>
        <FirstName>Scott</FirstName>
        <LastName>Klein</LastName>
        <Title>Geek</Title>
    </Employee>
```

When you run this code, you will receive an error stating `"Value of type 'System.Xml.Linq.XDocument'` `cannot be converted to 'System.Xml.Linq.XElement'."` That's because the compiler is smart enough to know that this is an XML document literal, and you are trying to stuff an XML document into an XML element, which won't work.

To fix this, simply change the `XElement` to an `XDocument` as highlighted here:

```
Dim empDoc As XDocument = _
    <?xml version="1.0"?>
    <Employee>
        <EmployeeID>1</EmployeeID>
        <FirstName>Scott</FirstName>
        <LastName>Klein</LastName>
        <Title>Geek</Title>
    </Employee>
```

How does the Visual Basic compiler create objects from these XML literals? When the compiler encounters an XML literal, it translates the literal into calls for the equivalent LINQ to XML constructors. Those LINQ to XML constructors are used to construct the LINQ to XML object.

Depending on the XML literal, the XML literal will be translated into calls to one or several constructors. At the least, it will be converted to a call to the `XElement` constructor, and if your XML literal contains attributes, then there will be calls to the `XAttribute` constructor as well. If your XML literal contains version instructions, it will be translated into a call to the `XProcessingInstruction` constructor.

Each class, such as the `XElement` and `XAttribute`, has an overloaded `New` constructor. These constructors are called for each type found, meaning that the XML literal will be translated into a call and passed to the corresponding constructor. For example, if you have an element that contains two attributes, the `XElement` constructor will be called once and the `XAttribute` constructor will be called twice.

Now that you understand how XML literals work, let's look at some examples of creating XML. The following example is taken from the first example in this chapter and illustrates the simple way to create XML. It uses the `XElement` class to create a simple XML fragment containing employee information.

You should be quite familiar with the `XElement` class by now. It's used to represent an XML element. The only difference here is the capability to use it to create XML literals in Visual Basic. For example, the following code creates an XML fragment in Visual Basic .NET. Notice the exclusion of any quotes. The XML is typed directly into the source code of the project.

```
Dim emp As XElement = _
    <Employee>
        <EmployeeID>1</EmployeeID>
        <FirstName>Scott</FirstName>
        <LastName>Klein</LastName>
        <Title>Geek</Title>
    </Employee>
```

The following example creates an XML document with a comment and version information. Again, this is quite similar to the way the XDocument class was used in previous chapters, but it's used in this example in an XML literal.

```
Dim empDoc As XDocument = _
    <?xml version="1.0" encoding="UTF-8"?>
    <!-- Test -->
    <Employee>
        <EmployeeID>1</EmployeeID>
        <FirstName>Scott</FirstName>
        <LastName>Klein</LastName>
        <Title>Geek</Title>
    </Employee>
```

Expressions

There is so much more that XML literals can do, such as using embedded expressions. Visual Basic supports the concept of embedded expressions. These expressions have the following syntax:

```
<%=expression%>
```

With Visual Basic you can place embedded expressions directly within your XML literals. These expressions are then evaluated at runtime.

For example, the following code defines two variables, one that contains the employee ID, and the other that contains the employee name. These two variables are then used as embedded expressions in the creation of the XML literal to specify the value of the empID attribute value and the FirstName element value.

```
Dim empID As Integer
Dim empName As String

empID = 1
empName = "Scott"

Dim emp As XElement = _
    <Employee empID=<%= empID %>>
        <FirstName>
            <%= empName %>
        </FirstName>
    </Employee>
```

When this code is run, you'll get the following output:

```
<Employee empID = "1">
    <FirstName>Scott</FirstName>
</Employee>
```

In this example, embedded expressions were used as an attribute value on the XML element and as XML element content value. Likewise, you can use embedded expressions as names in the name/value pair, as shown here:

```
Dim empID As String
Dim empName As String

empID = "ID"
empName = "FirstName"

Dim emp As XElement = _
    <Employee <%= empID %>="1">
        <<%= empName %>/>
    </Employee>
```

When this code runs, you get the following output:

```
<Employee ID = "1">
    <FirstName />
</Employee>
```

This can be taken one step further by including values for the name/value pair, like this:

```
Dim empID As String
Dim empName As String

empID = "ID"
empName = "FirstName"

Dim emp As XElement = _
    <Employee <%= empID %>="1">
        <<%= empName %>>Scott</>
    </Employee>
```

This code produces the following:

```
<Employee ID = "1">
    <FirstName>Scott</FirstName>
</Employee>
```

There are a couple of noteworthy items of which you should be aware. First, be careful how you use Option Strict in this scenario. Option Strict will cause the compiler to check each type to ensure that it has widened to the required type. This applies to everything except the root element of an XML document. If you leave Option Strict off, expressions of type Object can be embedded, in which case their type is verified at runtime.

183

Second, you will probably run into situations where content is optional. In those cases, embedded expressions that contain `Nothing` are ignored. Thus, there is no need to check that the values of elements or attributes are not `Nothing` as you use XML literals. In other words, required values such as element and attribute names cannot be `Nothing`, but empty embedded expressions are ignored. Sweet.

Embedding Queries

The fact that you can embed expressions within your XML literal should tell you that you can also embed queries within your XML literal. When queries are embedded within the XML literal, all elements returned by the query are added to the XML. This lets you create and add dynamic content to your XML literal.

In the following example, a standard LINQ query is embedded in the XML literal, which will create an XML tree based on the value returned from the query.

```
Dim emp As XElement = _
    <Employee>
        <%= From con in Contact
            Select <name><%= con.FirstName %></name>
        %>
    </Employee>
```

That gives you an idea of what is possible when LINQ queries are embedded in XML literals. However, take it a step further and add an attribute to the XML. Modify the XML as highlighted:

```
Dim emp As XElement = _
    <Employee>
        <%= From con in Contact
            Select <name id=<%= con.ContactID %>><%= con.FirstName %></name>
        %>
    </Employee>
```

Now you have a good understanding of how easy it is to dynamically create and add content to your XML.

Understanding Whitespace in Visual Basic XML Literals

Only significant whitespace is included in an XML literal by the Visual Basic compiler when a LINQ to XML object is created. Any insignificant whitespace is ignored.

To illustrate how whitespace is used, add the following code to the click event of one of the buttons on your form:

```
Dim empID As String
Dim empName As String

empID = "ID"
empName = "FirstName"

Dim emp As XElement = _
```

```
<Employee <%= empID %>="1">
    <<%= empName %>>
         Scott
    </>
</Employee>
```

```
Me.Textbox1.Text = emp.ToString
```

Run the application and click the button. The text box on the form will be populated with the following XML:

```
<Employee ID = "1">
    <FirstName>
             Scott
             </FirstName>
</Employee>
```

Notice all of the whitespace to the left of "Scott" and to the left of the `<FirstName>` closing tag. The output is like this because the inner element, `<FirstName>`, contains significant whitespace and the output text, while the outer element, `<Employee>`, contains insignificant whitespace.

So, you are probably asking yourself, what is the difference between "significant" and "insignificant" whitespace? Whitespace in XML literals is considered significant when:

❑ It is in an attribute value.

❑ It is part of an element's text content.

❑ It is in an embedded expression for an element's text content.

You can add the `xml:space` attribute in the XML element literal, but it won't change how the compiler handles the whitespace.

Accessing XML

Creating XML is one thing, but accessing it is another, and this section shows you how to do that in Visual Basic. Navigating XML structures in LINQ to XML is quite easy in Visual Basic. To illustrate, add another button to your form and place the following code in its click event:

```
Dim employee As XElement = _
    <Employees>
        <Employee EmpID="1">
            <Title>Geek</Title>
            <FirstName>Scott</FirstName>
            <MiddleName>L</MiddleName>
            <LastName>Klein</LastName>

    <EmailAddress>ScottKlein@SqlXml.com</EmailAddress>
            <Address>
                <Street>111 Main St.</Street>
                <City>Wellington</City>
                <State>FL</State>
                <Zip>33414</Zip>
```

```
            </Address>
          </Employee>
        </Employees>
```

```
Me.TextBox1.Text = employee...<City>.Value
```

Run the project and click the button. The text box should display the following value:

```
Wellington
```

Accessing element and attribute values is done through XML axis properties, which provide the capability to navigate XML structures. These properties use a special syntax that helps access any element and attribute by specifying XML names within your XML document.

Following are the available properties for accessing element and attribute values:

❏ **Descendant axis**—Returns all the child elements of the specified element regardless how deep in the hierarchy the child elements are found. The preceding example illustrates this point. The `<City>` element is several nodes deep in the XML fragment but through the use of the descendant axis property you can easily access the value of that node, as shown above.
Because it doesn't matter how deep in the hierarchy the element is found, you can use the same syntax to return the value of the `<Title>` as well as any other element.

❏ **Child axis**—Returns all the elements that are child elements of the specified element. This property is used to return all the child elements of a specified element. For example:

```
employee.<FirstName>
```

❏ **Attribute axis**—Returns all the attributes of the specified element. From the preceding XML fragment, this property can be used to return the `EmpID` attribute of `<Employee>` node:

```
Employee.<Employee>.@EmpID
```

❏ **Value**—Returns a string containing the object (value) for the first object found in the sequence. It returns `Nothing` if the sequence is empty. As you have seen, this property returns the value of the specified node(s), such as the value of the `<City>` element:

```
employee...<City>.Value
```

❏ **Extension indexer**—Returns the first element from the sequence. To illustrate this property, modify the XML fragment at the beginning of this section by adding a second employee, as shown in the following highlighted code:

```
Dim employee As XElement = _
    <Employees>
        <Employee EmpID="1">
            <Title>Geek</Title>
            <FirstName>Scott</FirstName>
            <MiddleName>L</MiddleName>
            <LastName>Klein</LastName>
            <EmailAddress>ScottKlein@SqlXml.com</EmailAddress>
```

```
                <Address>
                    <Street>111 Main St.</Street>
                    <City>Wellington</City>
                    <State>FL</State>
                    <Zip>33414</Zip>
                </Address>
            </Employee>
            <Employee EmpID="2">
                <Title>Geek</Title>
                <FirstName>Chris</FirstName>
                <MiddleName>A</MiddleName>
                <LastName>Klein</LastName>
                <EmailAddress>Chris@SqlXml.com</EmailAddress>
                <Address>
                    <Street>222 Main St.</Street>
                    <City>Portland</City>
                    <State>OR</State>
                    <Zip>88888</Zip>
                </Address>
            </Employee>
        </Employees>
```

With the extension indexer, you can specify specific elements to return as shown in the example below:

```
        employee...<FirstName>(1).Value
```

The returned result would be `Chris`. The extension indexer is zero-based so had you passed a value of 0 to this property, it would have returned `Scott`.

You can also access XML using embedded queries, which you learned about earlier in the chapter. In the example that follows, an XML literal is defined with three names. A second XML literal is then created, using an embedded query to access the names from the first XML literal. The results of the second XML literal are displayed in the text box.

```
    Dim employee As XElement = _
        <Employees>
            <Name>Scott</Name>
            <Name>Chris</Name>
            <Name>Bill</Name>
        </Employees>

    Dim nameTypes As XElement = _
        <Names>
            <%= From name In employee.<Name> _
                Select <FirstName><%= name.Value %></FirstName> _
            %>
        </Names>

    Me.TextBox1.Text = nameTypes.ToString
```

Here are the results when this code is executed:

```
<Names>
    <FirstName>Scott</FirstName>
    <FirstName>Chris</FirstName>
    <FirstName>Bill</FirstName>
</Names>
```

The next example builds on the previous example by including an attribute on each `<Name>` element in the first XML literal. The second XML literal is also modified, adding the necessary components to the embedded query to access the attribute as well.

```
Dim employee As XElement = _
    <Employees>
        <Name empID="1">Scott</Name>
        <Name empID="2">Chris</Name>
        <Name empID="3">Bill</Name>
    </Employees>

Dim nameTypes As XElement = _
    <Names>
        <%= From name In employee.<Name> _
        Select <Employee ID=<%= name.Value %>><%= name.@empID %></Employee> _
        %>
    </Names>

Me.TextBox1.Text = nameTypes.ToString
```

The following results when this code is executed:

```
<Names>
    <FirstName ID="1">Scott</FirstName>
    <FirstName ID="2">Chris</FirstName>
    <FirstName ID="3">Bill</FirstName>
</Names>
```

Yes, this example puts the attribute back where it came from, but the purpose of this example is to illustrate how to access attributes and how you can utilize query expressions within your XML literals to manipulate XML.

These examples should give you a good idea of how to access XML using XML literals and query expressions.

Loading XML

Loading XML is quite easy. You'll see just how easy in a minute. First, open your favorite text editor and type in the following XML. Save it as `employees.xml` in your `Wrox\Chapter 9` folder.

```
<Employees>
  <Employee id="1" Dept="0001" Geek="True">
    <Name>Scott</Name>
    <Address>
      <Address>555 Main St.</Address>
```

```
      <City>Wellington</City>
      <State>FL</State>
    </Address>
    <Title>All Things Techy</Title>
    <HireDate>02/05/2007</HireDate>
    <Gender>M</Gender>
  </Employee>
  <Employee id="2" Dept="0005" Geek="False">
    <Name>Steve</Name>
    <Address>
      <Address>444 Main St.</Address>
      <City>Snahomish</City>
      <State>WA</State>
      <zip>99999</zip>
    </Address>
    <Title>Mr. SciFi</Title>
    <HireDate>05/14/2002</HireDate>
    <Gender>M</Gender>
  </Employee>
  <Employee id="3" Dept="0004" Geek="True">
    <Name>Joe</Name>
    <Address>
      <Address>222 Main St.</Address>
      <City>Easley</City>
      <State>SC</State>
    </Address>
    <Title>All Things Bleeding Edge</Title>
    <HireDate>07/22/2004</HireDate>
    <Gender>M</Gender>
  </Employee>
</Employees>
```

To load XML, the XElement class has a Load method that contains several overloads, one of which is a path to an XML document. The following code shows how to load an element and display its contents:

```
Dim emp As XElement = XElement.Load("c:\Wrox\Linq\Chapter9\employees.xml")

Me.Textbox1.Text = emp.ToString
```

As you know, once you have XML loaded into an XElement, as in the preceding example, you are free to manipulate and query it. Your homework for this chapter is to use a query expression within an XML literal to return XML containing the ID of the employee along with his name and title.

Manipulating XML Using the Parse Method

There is a method on the XElement class called Parse, which loads a string containing XML into an XElement. There is an overload on this method that enables you to specify options when parsing the XML being loaded.

In the following example, a string variable is defined and loaded with an XML fragment. The string is then passed to the Parse method of the XElement class. The additional parameter for the load options specifies a value of None, meaning that no load options are being specified. Load options are explained shortly.

```
Dim empInfo As String

empInfo = "<Employees><Employee ID=""1""><FirstName>Scott</FirstName>↵
</Employee></Employees>"

Dim emp As XElement = XElement.Parse(empInfo, LoadOptions.None)

Me.TextBox1.Text = emp.ToString
```

Here are the results of executing this code:

```
<Employees>
  <Employee ID="1">
    <FirstName>Scott</FirstName>
  </Employee>
</Employees>
```

The optional parameter is the LoadOptions enumeration, which sets one of four load options for loading and parsing XML:

❑ None—No options are specified.

❑ PreserveWhitespace—Preserve insignificant whitespace during the parsing of the XML.

❑ SetBaseUri—Requests the base URI information from the XmlReader, making it available through the BaseUri property.

❑ SetLineInfo—Requests the line information from the XmlReader, making it available through XObject properties.

The following example illustrates the use of the PreserveWhitespace load option. Modify the code from the previous example as follows:

```
Dim empInfo As String

empInfo = "<Employees><Employee ID=""1""><FirstName>Scott</FirstName>↵
</Employee></Employees>"

Dim emp As XElement = XElement.Parse(empInfo, LoadOptions.None)

Me.TextBox1.Text = emp.ToString
```

Here are the results:

```
<Employees>
  <Employee ID="1">
    <FirstName>  Scott    </FirstName>
  </Employee>
</Employees>
```

You can see that all of the insignificant whitespace has been ignored. Next, modify the load option to this:

```
Dim emp As XElement = XElement.Parse(empInfo, LoadOptions.PreserveWhitespace)
```

When you run the code now, all the insignificant whitespace is preserved:

```
<Employees>
  <Employee ID="1">   <FirstName>  Scott     </FirstName></Employee>
</Employees>
```

Specify multiple load options by using an `And` or `Or` operator, like this:

```
Dim emp As XElement = XElement.Parse(empInfo, LoadOptions.SetBaseUri And
  LoadOptions.SetLineInfo)
```

These load options can assist you in your manipulation of the XML document, such as controlling how the whitespace is preserved and tracking the line information for each element in the tree.

LINQ to XML Visual Basic Example

This example is going to use the XML document `employees.xml` that you created earlier, in the section "Loading XML." This example will load that document, manipulate it by making some changes to the XML tree, and then display the results. As a refresher, the contents of the XML document are as follows:

```
<Employees>
  <Employee id="1" Dept="0001" Geek="True">
    <Name>Scott</Name>
    <Address>
      <Address>555 Main St.</Address>
      <City>Wellington</City>
      <State>FL</State>
    </Address>
    <Title>All Things Techy</Title>
    <HireDate>02/05/2007</HireDate>
    <Gender>M</Gender>
  </Employee>
  <Employee id="2" Dept="0005" Geek="False">
    <Name>Steve</Name>
    <Address>
      <Address>444 Main St.</Address>
      <City>Snahomish</City>
      <State>WA</State>
      <zip>99999</zip>
    </Address>
    <Title>Mr. SciFi</Title>
    <HireDate>05/14/2002</HireDate>
    <Gender>M</Gender>
  </Employee>
```

```
<Employee id="3" Dept="0004" Geek="True">
  <Name>Joe</Name>
  <Address>
    <Address>222 Main St.</Address>
    <City>Easley</City>
    <State>SC</State>
  </Address>
  <Title>All Things Bleeding Edge</Title>
  <HireDate>07/22/2004</HireDate>
  <Gender>M</Gender>
</Employee>
</Employees>
```

So, to do this, create a new Visual Basic Windows Forms project. When the project is created, add two buttons and a text box to the form. Set the properties of the controls as follows:

- ❑ Button1
    - ❑ Name - cmdOK
    - ❑ Text - OK

- ❑ Button2
    - ❑ Name - cmdCancel
    - ❑ Text - Cancel

- ❑ TextBox1
    - ❑ Name - txtResults1
    - ❑ Multiline - True
    - ❑ ScrollBars - Vertical

- ❑ TextBox2
    - ❑ Name - txtResults2
    - ❑ Multiline - True
    - ❑ ScrollBars - Vertical

- ❑ TextBox3
    - ❑ Name - txtResults3
    - ❑ Multiline - True
    - ❑ ScrollBars - Vertical

In the Click() event of the Cancel button, enter the following code:

```
Application.Exit()
```

Next, in the `Click()` event of the OK button, place the following code:

```
Dim emp As XElement = XElement.Load("c:\Wrox\Linq\Chapter 9\Employees.xml")

Dim tree As XElement = New XElement("Root", _
    From el In emp.Elements() Select el)

' Load these changes into the first text box
Me.txtResults1.Text = tree.ToString()

' Next, let's just grab the first employee
Dim empPart as XElement = (From treePart In _
    tree.Eleemnts("Employees") Select treePart).First

Me.txtResults2.Text = empPart.ToString()

' Next, let's add an EmailAddress element to each Employee
tree.Element("Employee").Add(New XElement("EmailAddress"))

Me.txtResults.Text = emp.ToString()
```

The first query produces the following (only the first part of the results are shown):

```
<Root>
  <Employee id="1" Dept="0001" Geek="True">
    <Name>Scott</Name>
    <Address>
      <Address>555 Main St.</Address>
      <City>Wellington</City>
      <State>FL</State>
    </Address>
    <Title>All Things Techy</Title>
    <HireDate>02/05/2007</HireDate>
    <Gender>M</Gender>
  </Employee>
...
</Root>
```

The second query produces the following results:

```
<Employee id="1" Dept="0001" Geek="True">
  <Name>Scott</Name>
  <Address>
    <Address>555 Main St.</Address>
    <City>Wellington</City>
    <State>FL</State>
  </Address>
  <Title>All Things Techy</Title>
  <HireDate>02/05/2007</HireDate>
  <Gender>M</Gender>
</Employee>
```

And lastly, the final piece of code modifies the XML document and returns the following results, with the addition of the `EmailAddress` element added to each Employee node:

```
<Root>
  <Employee id="1" Dept="0001" Geek="True">
    <Name>Scott</Name>
    <Address>
      <Address>555 Main St.</Address>
      <City>Wellington</City>
      <State>FL</State>
    </Address>
    <Title>All Things Techy</Title>
    <HireDate>02/05/2007</HireDate>
    <Gender>M</Gender>
    <EmailAddress />
  </Employee>
  <Employee id="2" Dept="0005" Geek="False">
    <Name>Steve</Name>
    <Address>
      <Address>444 Main St.</Address>
      <City>Snahomish</City>
      <State>WA</State>
      <zip>99999</zip>
    </Address>
    <Title>Mr. SciFi</Title>
    <HireDate>05/14/2002</HireDate>
    <Gender>M</Gender>
    <EmailAddress />
  </Employee>
  <Employee id="3" Dept="0004" Geek="True">
    <Name>Joe</Name>
    <Address>
      <Address>222 Main St.</Address>
      <City>Easley</City>
      <State>SC</State>
    </Address>
    <Title>All Things Bleeding Edge</Title>
    <HireDate>07/22/2004</HireDate>
    <Gender>M</Gender>
    <EmailAddress />
  </Employee>
</Root>
```

You'll notice that each email address node is not populated with data. This is on purpose. Your home-work assignment for this chapter is to modify the code to add an email address. You don't need to make them different. Simply insert a default value. When you have done that, figure out a way to dynamically enter an email address using the employee's first name and last name.

Summary

This chapter focused on the LINQ to XML features in Visual Basic .NET, including the capability to create XML literals and expressions directly within your VB.NET code.

You learned to create XML using XML literals, and how to incorporate expressions and embedded queries into your XML literals to create the XML you want.

From there, the topics of accessing and loading XML were discussed. Accessing XML is accomplished through the XML Axis properties, which enable you to easily and efficiently navigate the XML tree and retrieve the information you want. Loading XML is as simple as calling the `Load` method on the `XElement` class.

You also explored using the `Parse` method to manipulate XML. It enables you to specify several load options so that you can manipulate the XML as you parse it. For example, you can preserve the whitespace or track individual element line item information.

In the next chapter, the focus turns to working with LINQ to SQL.

Part III
LINQ to SQL

10

LINQ to SQL Overview

LINQ to SQL is a component of LINQ and part of ADO.NET that provides a run-time infrastructure for mapping relational data as objects. This chapter provides an overview of LINQ to SQL, and the rest of the chapters in this section of the book then dig deeper into the individual aspects of LINQ to SQL, including LINQ to SQL queries and LINQ over DataSets.

Today's developers have access to many great technologies that afford management and manipulation of database objects as well as data-querying capabilities. The .NET Framework provides ADO.NET, a platform for accessing data sources such as XML (via the System.XML namespace, which supplies a programmatic representation of XML documents and mechanisms for manipulating XML documents, nodes, and XML fragments) and SQL Server (via the System.Data namespace, which offers the primary data access methods for managed applications) as well as other data sources exposed through ODBC and OLE DB.

Yet, all this great technology has its limitations, such as sometimes being overly complex (for example, OLE DB is COM based and therefore does not work in the object-oriented paradigm, and it also requires quite a bit of code to address data access functionality). While LINQ to SQL may not offer any speed advantages over previous or existing technology, it does offer the capability to build applications more quickly and efficiently.

This chapter discusses the fundamentals and concepts that programmers need to know to work with LINQ to SQL, including the following:

- ❑ Overview of LINQ to SQL
- ❑ LINQ to SQL object model
- ❑ Attribute-based mapping
- ❑ Relational data basics

Understanding LINQ to SQL

As mentioned, LINQ to SQL is a part of ADO.NET and a component of LINQ. As such, you get the benefit of the unified programming model, standard query operators, and standard query facilities provided by LINQ, plus the services provided by the ADO.NET provider model.

LINQ to SQL works by mapping the data model of a relational database object, such as a table, to an object model defined in the developer's chosen programming language. For example, the following code maps the `Person.Contact` table of the Adventureworks database to a public class defined in C#. A public class is defined, and mapped by annotating the class with the LINQ `TableAttribute`, passing it the name of the SQL Server table to map to using the attribute's `Name` parameter.

```
[Table(Name = "Person.Contact")]
public class Contact
{
    [Column(DBType = "nvarchar(8)")]
    public string Title;

    [Column(DBType = "nvarchar(50) ")]
    public string FirstName;

    [Column(DBType = "nvarchar(50) ")]
    public string MiddleName;

    [Column(DBType = "nvarchar(50) ")]
    public string LastName;

    [Column(DBType = "nvarchar(50) ")]
    public string EmailAddress;

    [Column(DBType = "int")]
    public int EmailPromotion;

}
```

At this point, the relational mapping is complete, having mapped a data model to an object model.

The next step is to build the channel by which the objects and data are retrieved from the database. The channel is created via the `DataContext` class. The `DataContext` class is part of the `System.Data.Linq` namespace, and its purpose is to translate your requests from .NET objects to SQL queries, and then reassemble the query results back into objects.

The `DataContext` class is discussed in detail in Chapter 11.

Here's an example that defines a `DataContext` that connects to the Adventureworks database using integrated security:

```
DataContext context = new DataContext(
    "Initial Catalog=AdventureWorks;Integrated Security=sspi");
```

You use DataContext much the same way that you use an ADO.NET connection, in that it is initialized with a connection or connection string.

Once the DataContext is created, a table variable is constructed using the Contact class created above. This is done by using the Table class of the System.Data.Linq namespace, which provides the capability to query a table and even add and delete objects. LINQ to SQL works with objects. Meaning, in LINQ to SQL a relational database's object model is directly mapped to an object model expressed in your selected programming language. Thus, a translation takes place. LINQ to SQL translates the LINQ queries of the object model into statements that SQL can understand and then sends them off to SQL Server for execution. The reverse happens when the data is returned. The results are translated back to objects that you can work with.

Access to the table is accomplished by using the GetTable method of the defined DataContext, like this:

```
Table<Contact> contact = context.GetTable<Contact>();
```

Now you're ready to query the database using the same LINQ query operators and query facilities that you have come to love.

The following code queries the Person.Contact table of the Adventureworks database as defined in the object mapping:

```
var query =
    (from c in contact
     where c.FirstName.StartsWith("S")
     && c.LastName.StartsWith("K")
     orderby c.LastName
     select c);
```

As with the other components of LINQ, LINQ to SQL works with both C# and Visual Basic. LINQ to SQL also supports stored procedures and user-defined functions. However, to fully understand LINQ to SQL, the LINQ to SQL object model and the concept of attribute-based mapping must be explored.

LINQ to SQL Object Model

The LINQ to SQL object model provides the fundamental elements for working with and managing relational objects. It is via this model that a relational model is mapped to and expressed in the developer's programming language.

In the LINQ to SQL object model, database commands are not issued against the database directly. As a developer, you simply change values and execute methods within the confines of the object model. LINQ to SQL then translates those changes or methods into the appropriate SQL commands and funnels them through to the database to be executed. The object model works through its relationship to the database and the database model to perform given tasks. The following table shows the relationship between the LINQ to SQL object model and the corresponding relational model.

LINQ to SQL Object	Relational Object
DataContext	Database
Entity class	Table
Class member	Column
Association	Foreign-key relationship

The following section explores LINQ to SQL object model mapping.

Attribute-Based Mapping

It is all about attributes when mapping SQL Server objects to the object model. This attribute-based approach is utilized heavily by LINQ to SQL to effectively map database objects to an object model defined in the user's programming language.

There are three ways to create attribute mapping:

❑   The Object Relational Designer (ORD) tool

❑   The SQLMetal command-line tool

❑   By hand via code

So far, all the mapping has been done via code, but later chapters will discuss the other two options in detail. You have seen several of the attribute-based mappings in action throughout this book, but the following sections discuss the different attributes in more detail, including their associated properties and descriptions.

Prior to Beta2, attribute-based mapping was supported via the System.Data.Linq namespace. If you then installed Beta2 and tried to compile your code, you received a lot of compile errors. That is because attribute-based mapping is now supported via the System.Data.Linq.Mapping namespace.

Using the Database Attribute

The Database attribute is used to specify the name of the database when defining a mapping between a database and object. This attribute has one property, Name, which is used to hold the name of the database to which you are defining a mapping.

Here's an example of the Database attribute being applied to a class to define a mapping:

```
[Database(Name="AdventureWorks")]
public class AWDB
```

```
{
    //
}
```

The use of this attribute is optional, but if used, the Name property must be used. Typically, you would use this property when a database name is not supplied in the connection string.

Mapping Tables

Database tables are represented by entity classes in LINQ to SQL. An entity class is a normal class like one that you might define, except that it is annotated with a specific tag that maps, or associates, that class with a specific database table.

The Table attribute is required by LINQ to SQL, and maps an entity class (a class that has been designated as an entity) to a table or view. The Table attribute also has a single property, Name, which specifies the name of the relational table or view.

The following is an example of the Table attribute being applied to a class to define a mapping between the HumanResources.Employee table and the Employee class, and mapping a class named Contact with the Person.Contact table in the Adventureworks database:

```
[Table(Name = "HumanResources.Employee")]
public class Employee
{
    //
}
[Table(Name = "Person.Contact")]
public class Contact
{
    //
}
```

Remember, only those entity classes that have been mapped to a table can be saved to the database. That means that if you map the Person.Contact table to an entity class but don't map the HumanResources.Employee table to an entity class, you can only work with the Person.Contact table (query data, save, and so on).

Keep in mind that classes marked with the [Table] attribute are treated as persistent classes by LINQ to SQL.

Mapping Columns

Once the table is mapped to an entity class, table columns must be mapped to class properties. The Column attribute maps a column of a database table to a member of an entity class. Fields or properties are designated to represent database columns, and only those fields or properties that are mapped are retrieved from the database.

The following table describes the Column attribute's properties.

Property	Description	Default Value (if any)
Name	Name of the table column.	
DbType	Database type of the database column.	
Storage	The entity class storage field/variable.	
IsPrimaryKey	Specifies that the associated column is the primary key of the corresponding table.	false
IsDbGenerated	Specifies that the associated column auto-generates its values.	false
CanBeNull	Specifies that the associated column can contain null values.	true
AutoSync	Tells the runtime to get the column value after an INSERT or UPDATE operation has been executed. It has four options: Always—Always returns the column value for an INSERT or UPDATE operation. Never—Never returns the value for an INSERT or UPDATE operation. OnUpdate: Only returns the column value for UPDATE operations. OnInsert: Only returns the column value for INSERT operations.	Never
Expression	Defines a computed database column.	
IsVersion	Specifies that the associated column is either a timestamp or version number column.	false
UpdateCheck	Indicates how LINQ to SQL should handle optimistic concurrency conflicts. Uses one of the following values: Always, Never, WhenChanged.	
IsDiscriminator	Specifies that the column contains the discriminator value for a LINQ to SQL inheritance hierarchy.	

Here's an example that shows how to use the Column attribute to map properties to specific database columns:

```
[Column(DBType = "int", IsPrimaryKey=true, CanBeNull=false)]
public int EmployeeID;

[Column(DBType = "nvarchar(256)", CanBeNull=false)]
public string LoginID;

[Column(DBType = "nvarchar(15)", CanBeNull=false)]
public string NationalIDNUmber;

[Column(DBType = "int",CanBeNull=false)]
public int ManagerID;
```

Those fields that are not tagged as columns are considered temporary information, meaning, they are assumed to be nonpersistent and are not submitted back to the database.

The following example illustrates how to map a few properties with several columns of the Person.Contact table in the Adventureworks database:

```
[Column(DBType = "nvarchar(8)")]
public string Title;

[Column(DBType = "nvarchar(50)")]
public string FirstName;

[Column(DBType = "nvarchar(50)")]
public string MiddleName;

[Column(DBType = "nvarchar(50)")]
public string LastName;

[Column(DBType = "nvarchar(50)")]
public string EmailAddress;

[Column(DBType = "int")]
public int EmailPromotion;
```

Add this to the Table mapping, and you have the following:

```
[Table(Name = "Person.Contact")]
public class Contact
{
    [Column(DBType = "nvarchar(8) not null")]
    public string Title;

    [Column(DBType = "nvarchar(50) not null")]
    public string FirstName;

    [Column(DBType = "nvarchar(50) not null")]
    public string MiddleName;

    [Column(DBType = "nvarchar(50) not null")]
    public string LastName;

    [Column(DBType = "nvarchar(50) not null")]
    public string EmailAddress;

    [Column(DBType = "int")]
    public int EmailPromotion;

}
```

Only those columns that are defined are used to persist data to the table and retrieve data from the database. In the example, the entity class and associated column properties will persist the Title, FirstName, MiddleName, LastName, EmailAddress, and EmailPromotion columns from the Person.Contact table to and from the database. Any other columns in the table will not be persisted and are considered transient.

Mapping Relationships

Queries to the database generally require pulling information from multiple tables, not just a single table. Those tables are typically joined via a primary key/foreign key relationship. LINQ to SQL's `Association` attribute can represent those database associations.

The `Association` attribute's properties are described in the following table. They can be used to customize the associations.

Property	Description
Name	The name of the association.
Storage	Specifies the storage field/variable.
IsUnique	Specifies whether the FK is a unique constraint.
IsForeignKey	Specifies whether the association/constraint is a foreign key.
ThisKey	Identifies members of the entity class to represent the key values on this side of the association.
OtherKey	Identifies one or more members of the target entity class as key values on the other side of the association.

The following example shows how the `Association` attribute is used to define an association:

```
[Association(Name = "FK_Employee_Contact_ContactID",
    Storage = "_Employee", ThisKey = "ContactID", IsForeignKey = true)]
public Employee Emp
{
    get { return this._Employee.Entity; }
    set { this._Employee.Entity = value; }
}
```

The association is applied to a table in which you need to reference the associated table.

In the following example, the `Contact` class contains an `Employee` property that's tagged with the `Association` attribute, providing the `Contact` class with a relationship to the `Employee` class:

```
[Table(Name = "Person.Contact")]
public class Contact
{
    [Column(DBType = "nvarchar(8) not null")]
    public string Title;
```

```
[Column(DBType = "nvarchar(50) not null")]
public string FirstName;

[Column(DBType = "nvarchar(50) not null")]
public string MiddleName;

[Column(DBType = "nvarchar(50) not null")]
public string LastName;

[Column(DBType = "nvarchar(50) not null")]
public string EmailAddress;

[Column(DBType = "int")]
public int EmailPromotion;

private EntityRef<Employee> _Employee;

[Association(Name = "FK_Employee_Contact_ContactID",
    Storage = "_Employee", ThisKey = "ContactID", IsForeignKey = true)]
public Employee Emp
{
    get { return this._Employee.Entity; }
    set { this._Employee.Entity = value; }
}

}
```

More about LINQ to SQL and database relationships is discussed in Chapter 12.

Mapping Stored Procedures

One of the many great qualities of LINQ to SQL is its support for stored procedures, which is accomplished via the StoredProcedure attribute. That attribute is used to map a stored procedure in the database to a client object. It has only a single property, Name, which specifies the name of the stored procedure. Here's the attribute's general syntax:

```
[StoredProcedure(Name="OrdersBySalesPersonID")]
public IEnumerable OrdersBySalesPersonID([Parameter(DBType = "int")] String param1)
{
    IExecuteResults results = this.ExecuteMethodCall<OrdersBySalesPersonID>
        (this, ((MethodInfo)(MethodInfo.GetCurrentMethod())),
        param1);
}
```

With LINQ to SQL, you can easily map each database object to a client object, providing developers the capability to access the stored procedures through client code in a strongly typed manner. Through this mapping, the client method signatures bear a resemblance to the signatures of the procedure that is defined in the database, utilizing many of the programming language features such as IntelliSense.

In the following example, the highlighted code shows how to implement a stored procedure mapping into your client object class:

```
[Table(Name = "Person.Contact")]
public class Contact
```

```
{
    [Column(DBType = "nvarchar(8) not null")]
    public string Title;

    [Column(DBType = "nvarchar(50) not null")]
    public string FirstName;

    [Column(DBType = "nvarchar(50) not null")]
    public string MiddleName;

    [Column(DBType = "nvarchar(50) not null")]
    public string LastName;

    [Column(DBType = "nvarchar(50) not null")]
    public string EmailAddress;

    [Column(DBType = "int")]
    public int EmailPromotion;

    [StoredProcedure(Name="OrdersBySalesPersonID")]
    public IEnumberable OrdersBySalesPersonID([Parameter(DBType =
"int")] String param1)
    {
        IExecuteResults results = this.ExecuteMethodCall<OrdersBySalesPersonID>
            (this, ((MethodInfo)(MethodInfo.GetCurrentMethod())),
            param1);
    }
}
```

You'll learn more about LINQ to SQL and stored procedure mapping in Chapter 11.

Mapping Functions

LINQ to SQL also supports user-defined functions. Client objects and user-defined functions are mapped the same way stored procedures are—through an attribute. Here's the general syntax of the `Function` attribute:

```
[Function()]
Public IQueryable<ufnGetcontactInformation>
    ufnGetcontactInformation(System.Nullable<int> ContactID)
{
    //
}
```

This attribute has a single property, `Name`, which is used to specify the name of the user-defined function:

```
[Function(Name="ufnGetcontactInformation")]
Public IQueryable<ufnGetcontactInformation>
    ufnGetcontactInformation(System.Nullable<int> ContactID)
{
    //
}
```

If you do not specify a `Name` value, as in the first example, the default value is the same string as the user-defined function name, which in the example is `ufnGetcontactInformation`.

Using the Parameter Attribute

The `Parameter` attribute maps input parameters on stored procedure methods. It has two properties, which are described in the following table.

Property	Description	Default Value (if any)
Name	Name of the parameter	The same string as the parameter name in the database
DbType	Database data type	

The Name property can be used two ways: with an input parameter and with an output or return parameter. Both scenarios are shown in the following example. The first `Parameter` attribute specifies the return parameter type, and the second specifies the input variable type.

```
[StoredProcedure(Name="OrdersBySalesPersonID")]
[return: Parameter(DbType = "numeric")]
public IEnumerable MaxOrderBySalesPersonID([Parameter(DbType = "int")]
String param1)
{
    IExecuteResults results = this.ExecuteMethodCall<OrdersBySalesPersonID>
        (this, ((MethodInfo)(MethodInfo.GetCurrentMethod())),
        param1);
}
```

Stored procedure, user-defined function, and parameter mappings are discussed in more detail in Chapter 11.

The Basics of Relational Data

LINQ to SQL is all about working with relational data. As you have learned, this is accomplished through the mapping of the relational data model to an object model expressed in the developer's programming language. But regardless of the programming language and the object models, you are working with data. It all boils down to CRUD operations; you are creating (inserting), reading, updating, or deleting data—CRUD.

If you have no relational data knowledge or experience, this section is for you. If you are using LINQ to SQL you will inevitably run into relational data environments (after all, that is what relational databases are all about) and because you are mapping relational data objects (tables, and so on) to programming language objects, you also need to take into account their relational data (primary keys and foreign keys).

There are, of course, complete books on how to effectively and efficiently design databases. For example, the Wrox book *Beginning Database Design* covers design concepts including modeling and normalization. This section merely introduces the concepts of primary keys and foreign keys that are used in relational databases.

Chapter 12 explores querying across relationships using LINQ to SQL in detail.

Primary Keys

A primary key is a column or a group of columns that uniquely identifies each individual row in a database table. No columns included in the primary key can accept null values. A primary key enforces the table's integrity and can be defined when the table is created, or later when modifying the structure of the table. A primary key can be defined on a single, or multiple columns.

A table can only have one primary key. The most common form of a primary key is an identity column on SQL data types such as int and bigint.

Take a look at Figure 10-1, which shows the table design for the Person.Contact table in the Adventure-Works database.

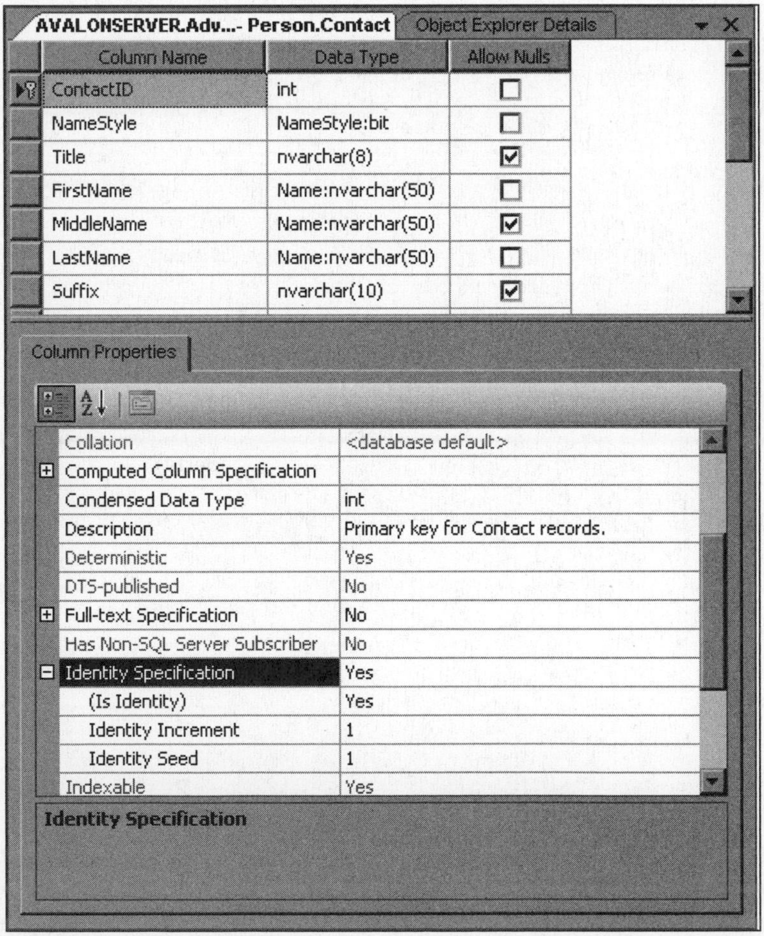

Figure 10-1

There are several things to notice. First, you can tell which column, or columns, are defined as the primary key by the gold key displayed in the row selector. In this example, the ContactID column is designated as the primary key. Second, the data type for the primary key is defined as an int, and the column does not accept null values (the Allow Nulls box is not checked), which means that a value must be entered into that column whenever a new row is added to the table.

The properties of the selected column display in the bottom pane. In this instance, it's the ColumnID properties that are showing. The Identity Specification has been set to Yes, meaning that this is an identity column, and you can set both an initial value (Identity Seed) and the value by which to increment each new row (Identify Increment). Here, the initial seed value is 1, and each new value increments by 1.

The identity specification lets you specify both an identity number (an initial value for the column for the first row inserted into the table) and the value in which to increment when new rows are added. The cool thing about identity columns is that the database engine takes care of all of the work of automatically incrementing the identity value and assigning the new value to the new row. Setting this property to "Yes" tells SQL Server to automatically manage the value of this column.

When a primary key is defined, a unique index is created on its columns. The index allows for quick retrieval of records when the primary key is used in a query.

Define a primary key by clicking the Set Primary Key button (the gold key) on the Table Designer toolbar when the table is in design mode. Figure 10-2 points out the button on the toolbar.

Figure 10-2

When mapping an object to a relational data object, you need to specify which column is the primary key. The following code shows the mapping of the AdventureWorks table Sales.Contact. In it, the ContactID column is mapped and annotated as a column to return. In the definition of the column, several properties are set, identifying it as the primary key of the Person.Contact table, and enabling its values to be generated automatically (via the IsDBGenerated property).

```
[Table(Name = "Person.Contact")]
public class Contact
{
    [Column(DBType = "int", IsPrimaryKey = true, IsDBGenerated = true)]
    public int ContactID;

    [Column(DBType = "nvarchar(8)")]
    public string Title;

    [Column(DBType = "nvarchar(50) ")]
    public string FirstName;

    [Column(DBType = "nvarchar(50) ")]
    public string MiddleName;

    [Column(DBType = "nvarchar(50) ")]
    public string LastName;
```

```
[Column(DBType = "nvarchar(50) ")]
public string EmailAddress;

[Column(DBType = "int")]
public int EmailPromotion;

}
```

Any time you are mapping a relational table that has a primary key, and you plan on returning the primary key column in your LINQ to SQL queries, you must identify the column as the primary key and the identity by using the properties IsPrimaryKey and IsDBGenerated as this example shows.

Foreign Keys

Foreign keys define a relationship between two tables. A foreign key is a single column or a group of columns that is used to create and impose a relationship, or link, between a parent table and a child table.

Foreign keys are created when the column or columns of the primary key (from the primary key table) are referenced by the column or columns in another table (the foreign key table). As discussed in the previous section, the ContactID column in the Person.Contact table is a primary key. Figure 10-3 shows that the ContactID column has been included or added to the HumanResources.Employee table, becoming a foreign key in this table.

Figure 10-4 shows the two tables, Person.Contact and HumanResources.Employee, with the primary key/foreign key relationship defined. The line between the two tables does not create the relationship but illustrates the association between the two tables.

However, simply adding a reference column in another table (such as the HumanResources.Employee table) does not create a primary key/foreign key relationship. That's only the first part. The last part is to add a foreign key constraint on the second table. A constraint is a rule used to maintain data integrity of a table.

To create the actual relationship you tell the HumanResources.Employee table that its ContactID column is a foreign key to the ContactID column in the Person.Contact table. This can be accomplished by the following:

```
ALTER TABLE [HumanResources].[Employee] ADD CONSTRAINT
 [FK_Employee_Contact_ContactID]
FOREIGN KEY([ContactID])
REFERENCES [Person].[Contact] ([ContactID])
```

This T-SQL code creates a foreign key constraint on the ContactID column referencing the ContactID column in the Person.Contact table. The constraint is used to determine the action on the values in the related tables. For example, if a value that is used in one or more related tables is deleted, the constraint determines whether the value in the related table is also deleted, left in, or set to null.

To see this in action, open SQL Server Management Studio and execute the following in a query window:

```
SELECT ContactID, FirstName, LastName
FROM Person.Contact
WHERE ContactID = 1172
```

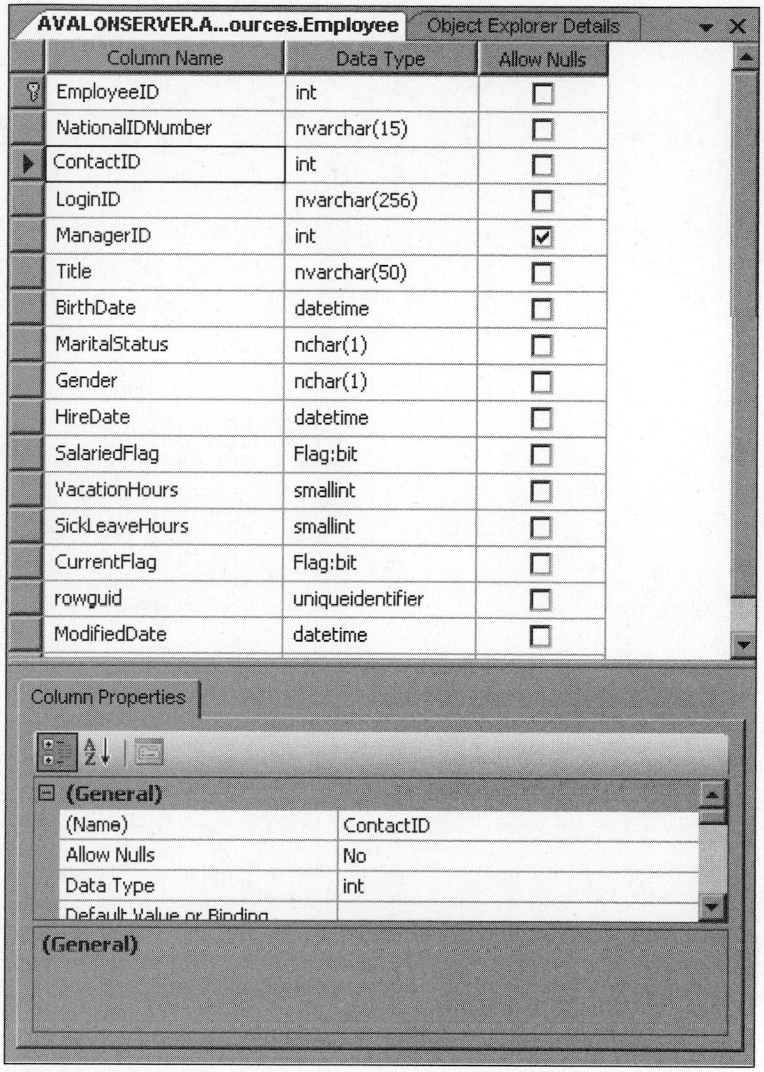

Figure 10-3

You should get the following results:

```
ContactID    FirstName    LastName
---------    ---------    --------
1174         Scott        Gode
```

Now, execute the following query:

```
SELECT EmployeeID, NationalIDNumber, ManagerID, Title
FROM HumanResources.Employee
WHERE ContactID = 174
```

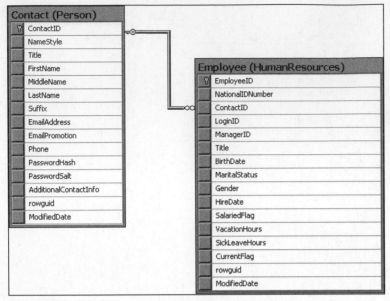

Figure 10-4

Here are the results:

```
EmployeeID   NationalIDNumber   ManagerID   Title
----------   ----------------   ---------   -----
98           199546871          197         Production Technician - WC45
```

You can see that the ContactID values in both the Person.Contact table and the HumanResources.Employee table match. The foreign key constraint ensures that any value inserted into the ContactID column in the HumanResources.Employee table matches a value in the ContactID column in the Person.Contact table. To test this, try to insert a row into the HumanResources.Employee table using the value of 20000 for the ContactID. You should get an error from SQL Server because there is no row in the Person.Contact table with ContactID = 20000.

When mapping an object to a foreign relational data object, you must specify which column is the foreign key. You do so by defining a method within the table definition and annotating that method with the Association attribute. This attribute tells the table that it is a foreign key table and identifies the column that is the foreign key column. The following code shows how the HumanResources.Employee table is mapped and the foreign key for the table identified:

```
[Table(Name = "HumanResources.Employee")]
public class Employee
{
    [Column(DBType = "int", IsPrimaryKey=true, IsDBGenerated=true, CanBeNull=false)]
    public int EmployeeID;

    [Column(DBType = "int", CanBeNull=false)]
    public int ContactID;
```

```
[Column(DBType = "nvarchar(256) not null")]
public string LoginID;

[Column(DBType = "nvarchar(15) not null")]
public string NationalIDNUmber;

[Column(DBType="int")]
public int ManagerID;

private EntityRef<Contact> _Contact;

[Association(Name = "FK_Employee_Contact_ContactID",
    Storage = "_Contact", ThisKey = "ContactID", IsForeignKey = true)]
public Employee Emp
{
    get { return this._Employee.Entity; }
    set { this._Employee.Entity = value; }
}

}
```

While identifying relational data relationships in LINQ to SQL might seem a bit overwhelming, clearly it's something you must understand.

Summary

LINQ to SQL is powerful and flexible. This chapter introduced you to LINQ to SQL, providing an overview and some insight into the LINQ to SQL object model. You learned about attribute-based mapping and how to effectively map relational data objects and object models expressed in the developer's programming language.

The last part of this chapter helped those who have no database design experience to understand database relationships and how they apply to and are used in LINQ to SQL.

Chapter 11 introduces LINQ to SQL queries and tackles the many components and concepts used when executing queries against a relational database.

11

LINQ to SQL Queries

LINQ to SQL is extensive, supporting many of the query aspects found in a relational database. But even with its depth and profound technology, it is quite easy to use and understand because of its use of the standard query facilities (standard query operators) found in LINQ and the many new .NET features found in .NET Framework 3.0, including extension methods and anonymous types.

In this chapter, you will explore LINQ to SQL queries, including the following:

- ❑ LINQ to SQL query concepts
- ❑ The `DataContext` class
- ❑ Data manipulation via LINQ to SQL
- ❑ Working with entity objects
- ❑ Querying with stored procedures and user-defined functions

Query Concepts

By now you know that LINQ to SQL queries really are not any different from the other LINQ queries you have seen and worked with throughout this book. They follow the same syntax format as LINQ and LINQ to XML queries.

However, they vary in one area. In LINQ to XML you query an XML document tree or fragment directly, but in LINQ to SQL you query mapped objects, meaning that the objects you are querying are mapped to objects or items in a relational database, such as a table or stored procedure.

A LINQ to SQL query, like standard LINQ queries, has parts or actions of the query operation: the obtaining of a data source, the query creation, and the query execution. It uses the same standard query operators and query patterns because of its tight integration with LINQ. There are subtle differences between some of the query items. For example, items such as filtering and grouping are the same, but the variable of the return type for LINQ to SQL must be of `IQueryable(of T)` instead of the `IEnumerable` that a standard LINQ query uses.

The following table lists the similarities and differences between a standard LINQ query and a LINQ to SQL query. Notice that most of the query items are identical, meaning that they follow the same syntax. The only differences are the way joins are handled and the query variable return type.

Query Item	LINQ	LINQ to SQL
Query variable return type	IEnumerable	IQueryable
Data source specification	From/from	equivalent
Filtering	Where/where	equivalent
Grouping	Goupby	equivalent
Selecting	Select/select	equivalent
Joins	join	Association attribute

In LINQ to SQL joins, the recommended technique is to use the Association attribute, but as you saw in Chapter 3, it is possible to use the join clause. However, the join clause does not have access to any of the properties employed by the Association attribute, thus limiting its flexibility.

LINQ to SQL also employs the same rules of query execution as a standard LINQ query, meaning deferred and immediate. You recall that a deferred execution query is one that produces a sequence of values, and the query is not executed until you iterate through the results (that is, iterate over the query variable). An immediate executed query is one that returns a single value (such as a query that returns a MAX value, or COUNT). These types of queries are executed immediately because a sequence must be produced first to generate the result.

There are several components involved when a query is executed:

❑ LINQ to SQL API

❑ LINQ to SQL Provider

❑ ADO Provider

Each of these components plays a pivotal role when executing a query. When a LINQ to SQL query is executed, seven steps are taken to execute the query and return the results.

1. The LINQ to SQL API requests execution of the query on behalf of your application.

2. The LINQ to SQL API hands the query off to the LINQ to SQL Provider.

3. The LINQ to SQL Provider converts the LINQ query to T-SQL.

4. The LINQ to SQL Provider hands the new query off to the ADO Provider for execution on the server.

5. The query is executed and the results are handed back to the ADO Provider in the form of a DataReader.

6. The ADO Provider hands the DataReader back to the LINQ to SQL Provider.

7. The LINQ to SQL Provider converts the DataReader into an enumerable form of user objects.

Realistically, a few of these steps could have been combined, but they are listed separately to provide a detailed look at what happens when a LINQ to SQL query is executed. These steps also look like they could take a while to process. On the contrary, LINQ to SQL was architected with performance in mind from the get-go, and as you start working with LINQ and LINQ to SQL, you will notice that it indeed works quickly.

To execute a query, a connection to the data source must first be established, and that is accomplished through the DataContext class. The next section explains how.

DataContext

Before you can execute a LINQ to SQL query, a connection to the data source must be made. In LINQ to SQL, database connections are made through the DataContext class. Think of the DataContext class on the same level as you would the SqlConnection class of ADO.NET. DataContext is the medium in which connections to a database are made, through which objects are retrieved from and submitted to the database.

Like the SqlConnection class, the DataContext instance accepts a connection string. Once the connection is made, data is read from, and changes are transmitted back to, the database through the DataContext. However, there is one thing the DataContext does that the SqlConnection does not. Since LINQ to SQL deals with objects, the DataContext also does the work of converting the objects into SQL queries and then reassembling the results back into queryable objects.

The DataContext has several overloads, one of which is just a simple connection string specifying the connection information, as shown in this code:

```
DataContext db = new DataContext(
  "Initial Catalog=AdventureWorks;Integrated ↵
Security=sspi");
```

You can also pass an IDbConnection, which represents an open connection to a data source. IDbConnection is an interface that is defined in the System.Data namespace and allows a class that inherits from this interface to implement a Connection class, containing a unique session with a data source. This interface takes a little more effort because classes that inherit from the IDbConnection interface must also implement all inherited members. The trick is that the application doesn't create an instance of IDbConnection directly; instead, the application should create an instance of a class that inherits from IDbConnection. In most cases, you are much better off instantiating an instance of the DataContext and passing a string containing the necessary connection information.

The DataContext has several useful public methods, including CreateDatabase and DeleteDatabase, as well as CreateQuery, ExecuteQuery, GetQueryText, and SubmitChanges.

The CreateDatabase and DeleteDatabase methods do exactly as their names imply. CreateDatabase creates a database with the database name taken either from the connection string, the Database attribute, the name of the file (if the DataContext has been created using a file), or the name of the DataContext inheriting class if a strongly typed DataContext is used.

The strongly typed DataContext *is discussed in the next section.*

219

The following example creates a new database using the name ScottWrox, which is specified in the connection string:

```
DataContext db = new DataContext("Initial Catalog=ScottWrox;Integrated ↵
Security=sspi");
db.CreateDatabase();
```

The same criteria for database naming apply to the DeleteDatabase method.

```
db.DeleteDatabase();
```

The following example illustrates the use of the DatabaseExists method of the DataContext class, which can be used to determine if a database already exists:

```
try
{

    DataContext db = new DataContext("Initial Catalog=WroxScott;Integrated
        Security=sspi");

    bool_dbExists = db.DatabaseExists();

    if (_dbExists == true)
        db.DeleteDatabase();
    else
    {
        db.CreateDatabase();
        textBox1.Text = "Database created.";
    }
}
catch (Exception ex)
{
    MessageBox.Show(ex.Message);
}
```

The SubmitChanges method is the component that sends your data changes back to the database. Here's how to use it:

```
DataContext db = new DataContext("Initial Catalog=AdventureWorks;Integrated ↵
Security=sspi");
// Do some work on the data
db.SubmitChanges();
```

You'll explore SubmitChanges in more detail later in the chapter.

Strongly Typed DataContext

Creating a strongly typed DataContext is quite simple. All you need to do is create a new class that inherits from the DataContext class, as shown in the code example below:

```
public class AdventureWorks : DataContext
{
```

```
    public AdventureWorks(string connection) : base(connection) {}
  . // table definitions
}
```

Once the `DataContext` is created, you can use it to connect to the specified database, as shown in the following example. In it, the preceding strongly typed `DataContext` is given the same name as the database to use; in this case, AdventureWorks. Therefore, no database name needs to be specified in the connection string.

```
AdventureWorks db = new AdventureWorks(Integrated Security=sspi");

bool _dbExists = db.DatabaseExists();

if (_dbExists == true)
   textBox1.Text = "Yep, Exists!";
```

Creating strongly typed `DataContext` objects is preferred over non-strongly typed because utilizing strongly typed table objects eliminates the need to use the `GetTable` method in your queries.

Each database table is represented as a `Table` collection, which is available through the `GetTable` method of the `DataContext` class. `GetTable` gives you access to the table in an untyped fashion. For example, the following code creates a connection to the AdventureWorks database and the Contact table by way of the `GetTable` method, but it is not strongly typed:

```
DataContext context = new DataContext(
    "Initial Catalog=AdventureWorks;Integrated Security=sspi");
Table<Contact> con = context.GetTable<Contact>();
```

The appropriate way to create a strongly typed `DataContext` is:

```
public class AdventureWorks : DataContext
{
   public AdventureWorks(string connection) : base(connection) {}
   public Table<Contact> Contact;
}
```

This example creates a new class that inherits from the `DataContext` class and then defines a table for a specific type (in this case, the `Contact` table) in the underlying database. This provides access to the database through a strongly typed `DataContext` and strongly typed table.

Data Manipulation

Now you're ready to start querying, modifying, and sending data back to the database. This section of the chapter walks you through a full example that updates, inserts, and deletes data using LINQ to SQL.

Fire up your copy of Visual Studio and create a new C# Windows project. On Form1, place three buttons and a text box. Name the first button `cmdInsert`, the second button `cmdUpdate`, and the third button `cmdDelete`. Make sure that the text box is long enough to hold and view 20 characters.

For this example, you need to add a reference to LINQ, so in Solution Explorer, right-click on References and select Add Reference. When the Add Reference dialog appears, make sure that the .NET tab is selected and scroll down until you see the `System.Data.Linq` component name. Select that component and click OK.

Next, right-click on Form1 and select View Code. Add the following line to the rest of the `using` statements:

```
using System.Data.Linq;
```

Time to start adding the good stuff.

Insert

Let's begin by discussing Insert operations. First, add the following to the form code below the partial class for `Form1`:

```
public class AdventureWorks : DataContext
{
    public AdventureWorks(string connection) : base(connection) {}
    public Table<Contact> Contact;
}
```

This should look familiar—it's the code from the strongly typed section a few pages ago. It strongly types the `DataContext` and includes a reference to a strongly typed table.

The bulk of your form code should now look like this:

```
public partial class Form1 : Form
{
    public Form1()
    {
        InitializeComponent();
    }

}

public class AdventureWorks : DataContext
{
    public AdventureWorks(string connection) : base(connection) {}
    public Table<Contact> Contact;
}
```

The strongly typed `DataContext` class references a strongly typed table, `Contact`, which has not been created yet. The following code does that. Add it below the strongly typed `DataContext` class:

```
[Table(Name = "Person.Contact")]
public class Contact
{

    [Column(DBType = "int not null")]
    public int ContactID;
```

```
[Column(DBType = "nvarchar(8) not null")]
public string Title;

[Column(DBType = "nvarchar(50) not null")]
public string FirstName;

[Column(DBType = "nvarchar(50) not null")]
public string MiddleName;

[Column(DBType = "nvarchar(50) not null")]
public string LastName;

[Column(DBType = "nvarchar(50) not null")]
public string EmailAddress;

[Column(DBType = "int")]
public int EmailPromotion;

[Column(DBType = "bit")]
public byte NameStyle;

[Column(DBType = "varchar(40)")]
public string PasswordHash;

[Column(DBType = "varchar(40)")]
public string PasswordSalt;

}
```

Next, add the following code to the `Click` event of the Insert button:

```
try
{
    AdventureWorks db = new AdventureWorks("Integrated Security=sspi");
    Contact con = new Contact();
    con.FirstName = "Scott";
    con.MiddleName = "L";
    con.LastName = "Klein";
    con.Title = "Geek";
    con.EmailAddress = "geek@email.com";
    con.EmailPromotion = 1;
    con.NameStyle = 0;
    con.PasswordHash = "";
    con.PasswordSalt = "";
    db.Contact.Add(con);
    db.SubmitChanges();
    textBox1.Text = "Contact created.";
}
catch (Exception ex)
{
    MessageBox.Show(ex.Message);
}
```

You are ready to test it. Run the application and click the Insert button. Didn't work, did it? The error you should have received states that the table is read-only. This error is misleading (you'll see why in a minute), but the fix is simple. On the definition of the ContactID column, two ContactID properties need to be set, as shown here:

```
[Table(Name = "Person.Contact")]
public class Contact
{
    [Column(DBType = "int not null", IsPrimaryKey=true, IsDBGenerated=true)]
    public int ContactID;
```

Now when you run the application and click the Insert button, the "Contact created" message appears in the text box.

Why did the first insert fail? LINQ to SQL treats tables as read-only by default, and it needs to know which column is the primary key. In fact, if you run this example and don't specify the IsDBGenerated property, it still won't work, although you will get a different error, stating that it cannot insert an explicit value for the identity column of the table when IDENTITY_INSERT is set to off. LINQ to SQL needs to know that the table has a primary key, which column the primary key is, and that it is auto-generated. At that point, LINQ to SQL won't see the table as read-only.

Last, when the properties have been filled, the new object needs to be added to the Contact table in the DataContext and the SubmitChanges method called to usher the changes back to the database.

Update

For an update, the code is going to query for a specific record and update a field of that record. Add the following code behind the Update button. It queries for the record you inserted in the preceding example and updates the email address. Keep in mind that when you run this code, the ContactID may be different for you; be sure to use the correct ContactID.

```
AdventureWorks db = new AdventureWorks("Integrated Security=sspi");
var con = db.Contact.Single(c => c.ContactID == 19980);
con.EmailAddress = "ScottKlein@SqlXml.com";
db.SubmitChanges();
textBox1.Text = "Contact updated.";
```

Run the application and click the Update button. When the text box displays "Contact updated," you can query the AdventureWorks database and verify that the email address for the new contact has indeed been updated.

The preceding example updates a single row. Here's how to update multiple rows:

```
AdventureWorks db = new AdventureWorks("Integrated Security=sspi");

var queryContacts =
    from names in db.Contact
    where names.LastName == "Zwilling"
    select names;
```

```
foreach (var con in queryContacts)
{
    con.EmailAddress = "ScottKlein@SqlXml.com";
}
db.SubmitChanges();
textBox1.Text = "Contact updated.";
```

This code returns a query that will yield two rows and updates the email address for each contact. It then issues a single SubmitChanges to send the updates back to the database.

So far, so good, right? Good. Now let's look at deleting.

Delete

Deleting is just as easy as inserting and updating. Place the following code behind the Delete button, again making sure that you use the correct ContactID. The code simply uses the ID to delete the desired record by calling the Remove method to delete the appropriate record. And, as you have learned, SubmitChanges is called to send the statement to the database.

```
AdventureWorks db = new AdventureWorks("Integrated Security=sspi");
var con = db.Contact.Single(c => c.ContactID == 19980);
db.Contact.Remove(con);
db.SubmitChanges();
textBox1.Text = "Contact deleted.";
```

To delete multiple records, your query would be built along the same lines as the update example for multiple records.

Working with Objects

You can manipulate data using objects and object members, such as the Add(T) and Remove(T) methods. It is not that different from what you have already learned in many of the examples in previous chapters. The following sections show how to use objects to associate LINQ to SQL generic collections to database objects for submission to the database for execution.

Insert

In the previous insert example, an empty Contact was created and then the individual column properties were populated with data. Once the properties were filled, the populated Contact was added to the strongly typed Contact table via the Add method. In other words, the previous example modified object members directly.

There is another way, which is essentially the same as the last inset example but adds an object to the LINQ to SQL collection (the Table(of T) collection) and hands that off for submission to the database. The following example shows how this is accomplished:

```
AdventureWorks db = new AdventureWorks("Integrated Security=sspi");
Contact con = new Contact
```

```
                        {
                            FirstName = "Scott",
                            MiddleName = "L",
                            LastName = "Klein",
                            Title = "Geek",
                            EmailAddress = "geek@email.com",
                            EmailPromotion = 1,
                            NameStyle = 0,
                            PasswordHash = "",
                            PasswordSalt = ""
                        }       ;
    db.Contact.Add(con);
    db.SubmitChanges();
    textBox1.Text = "Contact created.";
```

The differences between this example and the previous Insert example are not that major. The results are the same; it is just a matter of implementation.

Update

Rows can be updated by modifying the value members of the objects. Any object that is associated with a Table(of T) collection can have its value members updated and the object submitted back to the database for updating, as shown in the example below:

```
AdventureWorks db = new AdventureWorks("Integrated Security=sspi");
var query = from con in db.Contact
        where con.LastName == "Klein"
        select con;

foreach (var cont in query)
{
    cont.EmailAddress = "ScottKlein@SqlXml.com";
    cont.Title = "Mr. Geek";
}

db.SubmitChanges();
textBox1.Text = "Contact updated.";
```

Delete

Rows can be deleted by removing the LINQ to SQL object. In the following example, a row is queried, followed by the removal of the object from the returned collection. The object is removed by calling the Remove(of T) method, T being the type of object to remove.

```
AdventureWorks db = new AdventureWorks("Integrated Security=sspi");
var query = from con in db.Contact
        where con.LastName == "Klein"
        select con;

foreach (Contact del in query)
{
    db.Contact.Remove(del);
}
```

```
db.SubmitChanges();
textBox1.Text = "Contact deleted.";
```

As always, the changes are not applied until `SubmitChanges` is called, sending the changes back to the database.

Stored Procedures and User-Defined Functions

Just like tables, stored procedures and functions are mapped, and they are mapped by creating class methods with the `StoredProcedure` or `Function` attribute applied, respectively. The best way to learn this is by example, so get comfy and ready to start writing code. The following examples illustrate how to call stored procedures and user-defined functions (UDFs) in several scenarios. You will need to have Visual Studio open as well as SQL Server Management Studio.

Mapping and Calling Stored Procedures

LINQ to SQL supports the mapping and calling of stored procedures via methods defined in your object model that represent the stored procedure. Methods are designated as stored procedures by applying the `[Function]` attribute and any associated `[Parameter]` attributes. Mapped stored procedures can return rowsets and take parameters.

Returning a Single Result

In this first example, you will call a stored procedure that returns a single resultset. Open SQL Server 2005 Management Studio, and open a new query window. Type in the following and execute it:

```
CREATE PROCEDURE [dbo].[OrdersBySalesPersonID]
(
    @salesPersonID int
)
AS
BEGIN
    SELECT    Production.Product.ProductID, Production.Product.Name, ↵
Sales.SalesPerson.SalesPersonID, Person.Contact.FirstName, ↵
Person.Contact.MiddleName,
        Person.Contact.LastName, Sales.SalesOrderDetail.UnitPrice
    FROM    Production.Product
    INNER JOIN    Sales.SalesOrderDetail ON Production.Product.ProductID = ↵
Sales.SalesOrderDetail.ProductID
    INNER JOIN    Sales.SalesOrderHeader ON Sales.SalesOrderDetail.SalesOrderID ↵
= Sales.SalesOrderHeader.SalesOrderID
    INNER JOIN    Sales.SalesPerson ON Sales.SalesOrderHeader.SalesPersonID = ↵
Sales.SalesPerson.SalesPersonID
    INNER JOIN    Person.Contact ON Sales.SalesPerson.SalesPersonID = ↵
Person.Contact.ContactID
    WHERE        (Sales.SalesPerson.SalesPersonID = @salesPersonID)
END
GO
```

This creates a new stored procedure called OrdersBySalesPersonID, which returns the product ID; product name; the ID of the salesperson; the contact's first, middle, and last name; and the unit price of each product for a given salesperson. The SalesPersonID is passed in to the stored procedure as a parameter.

Now turn your attention to LINQ and Visual Studio. Open Visual Studio and create a new C# project. Once the project is created, add the reference to System.Data.Linq. Next, place a list box, a text box, and five buttons on Form1. It doesn't really matter how you lay everything out on the form, but make sure that the list box is wide enough to display some data.

When the form is laid out, double-click the first button to display the code behind that button. Next, add the using statement to System.Data.Linq, as shown in the following code:

```csharp
using System;
using System.Collections.Generic;
using System.ComponentModel;
using System.Data;
using System.Data.Linq;
using System.Drawing;
using System.Linq;
using System.Text;
using System.Windows.Forms;

namespace LINQ
{
    public partial class Form1 : Form
    {
        public Form1()
        {
            InitializeComponent();
        }
        private void Form1_Load(object sender, EventArgs e)
        {

        }

        private void button1_Click(object sender, EventArgs e)
        {

        }
    }
}
```

The next thing you want to do is create a class that derives from the DataContext class, which you learned about earlier in this chapter. Creating a class that inherits from the DataContext class provides you with all the connection processing functionality you need to work with LINQ to SQL and communicate with SQL Server.

Add a class called AdventureWorks that inherits from the DataContext class. Within that class, add the highlighted code shown below:

```
namespace LINQ
{
    public partial class Form1 : Form
    {
        public Form1()
        {
            InitializeComponent();
        }

        private void Form1_Load(object sender, EventArgs e)
        {

        }

        private void button1_Click(object sender, EventArgs e)
        {

        }
    }

    public class AdventureWorks : DataContext
    {
        public AdventureWorks(string connection) : base(connection) {}

    }

}
```

Next, create a method and map it to the stored procedure created earlier. Underneath the DataContext connection, add this highlighted code:

```
public class AdventureWorks : DataContext
{
    public AdventureWorks(string connection) : base(connection) {}

    [StoredProcedure(Name = "OrdersBySalesPersonID")]
    public IEnumerable<OrdersBySalesPersonID> SalesOrders
        ([Parameter(DBType="int")] int salesPersonID)
    {
        return this.ExecuteMethodCall<OrdersBySalesPersonID>
            (this, ((MethodInfo)(MethodInfo.GetCurrentMethod())),
            salesPersonID);
    }

}
```

There's just a little more work to do. You need to map a stored procedure because you need to map the resultset coming in. In LINQ to SQL, the resultsets for a stored procedure, view, and user-defined function are in the same form, basically in table format. Thus, you can map the stored procedure resultset to a class tagged as a table.

As shown in the following highlighted code, add a partial class with the name OrdersBySales-PersonID, and add the Table attribute. Within the attribute, pass the name of the stored procedure that will be called.

```
namespace LINQ
{
    public partial class Form1 : Form
    {
        public Form1()
        {
            InitializeComponent();
        }

        private void Form1_Load(object sender, EventArgs e)
        {
        }

        private void button1_Click(object sender, EventArgs e)
        {

        }
    }

    public class AdventureWorks : DataContext
    {
        public AdventureWorks(string connection) : base(connection) {}

        [Function(Name = "OrdersBySalesPersonID")]
        public IEnumerable<OrdersBySalesPersonID> SalesOrders
            ([Parameter(DBType="int")] int salesPersonID)
        {
            return this.ExecuteMethodCall<OrdersBySalesPersonID>
                (this, ((MethodInfo)(MethodInfo.GetCurrentMethod())),
                salesPersonID);
        }
    }


    [Table(Name = "SalesPersonOrders")]
    public partial class OrdersBySalesPersonID
    {

    }
}
```

Next, define the column properties that create a mapping for the columns being returned by the stored procedure. Within the partial class, add the following code (you do not need to add the partial class definition; it is included here as a reference). As you learned about earlier in this chapter, defining the columns is done by attributing a property with the `Column` attribute and adding parameters that define the column name and data type.

```
[Table(Name = "SalesPersonOrders")]
public partial class OrdersBySalesPersonID
{
   private int _productID;
   private string _productName;
   private int _salesPersonID;
   private string _firstName;
   private string _middleName;
   private string _lastName;
   private decimal _unitPrice;

   [Column(Name = "ProductID", Storage = "_productID", DBType = "int")]
   public int ProductID
   {
      get
      {
         return this._productID;
      }
      set
      {
         if ((this._productID != value))
         {
            this._productID = value;
         }
      }
   }

   [Column(Name = "Name", Storage = "_productName", DBType = "nvarchar(50)")]
   public string ProductName
   {
      get
      {
         return this._productName;
      }
      set
      {
         if ((this._productName != value))
         {
            this._productName = value;
         }
      }
   }

   [Column(Name = "SalesPersonID", Storage = "_salesPersonID", DBType = "int")]
   public int SalesPerson
   {
      get
      {
         return this._salesPersonID;
      }
      set
      {
         if ((this._salesPersonID != value))
```

```
            {
                this._salesPersonID = value;
            }
        }
    }

    [Column(Name = "FirstName", Storage = "_firstName", DBType = "nvarchar(50)")]
    public string FirstName
    {
        get
        {
            return this._firstName;
        }
        set
        {
            if ((this._firstName != value))
            {
                this._firstName = value;
            }
        }
    }

    [Column(Name = "MiddleName", Storage = "_middleName", DBType = "nvarchar(50)")]
    public string MiddleName
    {
        get
        {
            return this._middleName;
        }
        set
        {
            if ((this._middleName != value))
            {
                this._middleName = value;
            }
        }
    }
    [Column(Name = "LastName", Storage = "_lastName", DBType = "nvarchar(50)")]
    public string LastName
    {
        get
        {
            return this._lastName;
        }
        set
        {
            if ((this._lastName != value))
            {
                this._lastName = value;
            }
        }
    }

    [Column(Name = "UnitPrice", Storage = "_unitPrice", DBType = "decimal")]
    public decimal UnitPrice
```

```
    {
      get
      {
        return this._unitPrice;
      }
      set
      {
        if ((this._unitPrice != value))
        {
          this._unitPrice = value;
        }
      }
    }
  }
```

You are almost done. The last step is to add the code behind the button. Add the following code to the click event of button1:

```
private void button1_Click(object sender, EventArgs e)
{
    AdventureWorks db = new AdventureWorks("Integrated Security=sspi");

    IEnumerable<OrdersBySalesPersonID> result = db.SalesOrders(275);

    foreach (OrdersBySalesPersonID ord in result)
    {
    listBox1.Items.Add(ord.ProductID + "  " + ord.ProductName + "  " +
        ord.SalesPerson + "  " + ord.UnitPrice);
    }
}
```

That's it! In Visual Studio, select Debug ➪ Start Debugging, or press the F5 key. Oops! You received some compilation errors, didn't you? They probably state something like the following:

```
The type or namespace 'MethodInfo' could note be found.
```

To fix this, add the highlighted using statement to your code:

```
using System.Linq;
using System.Text;
using System.Windows.Forms;
using System.Reflection;
```

The System.Reflection namespace houses all of the types that are used to obtain information regarding assemblies, modules, members, and other aspects of an assembly. LINQ to SQL uses this because the MethodInfo class is part of the System.Reflection namespace, and the MethodInfo class is used to identify the exact behavior of an operation.

Now press the F5 key to compile and run the project. You shouldn't get any errors this time, so when the form opens, click button1. This will execute the stored procedure you created earlier.

Just as an FYI, this example uses the SalesPersonID of 275 to pass in to the stored procedure. You are free to select another SalesPersonID. When button1 is pressed, the DataContext passes the SalesPersonID to SQL Server and asks for the stored procedure to be executed. The `DataContext` then handles the returned `resultsets` and passing of the results to LINQ for iteration through the results. Remember that the `DataContext` is the avenue through which objects are sent to and retrieved from the database.

Here's a sample of the results returned:

```
710 Mountain Bike Socks, L 275, 5.7000
709 Mountain Bike Socks, M 275, 5.7000
773 Mountain -100 Silver, 44 275, 2039.9940
776 Mountain -100 Black, 42 275, 2024.9940
```

Just for your edification, you might want to place a breakpoint on the first line of code and click button1 again, this time stepping through the execution of the code.

Passing Parameters to Mapped Stored Procedures

The next example illustrates how to call a stored procedure that also accepts a parameter but returns the results via an OUTPUT parameter.

The first step is to create the stored procedure. In SQL Server, type the following into a query window and execute it:

```
CREATE PROCEDURE [dbo].[MaxOrderBySalesPersonID]
(
    @salesPersonID int,
    @maxSalesTotal int OUTPUT
)
AS
BEGIN
    SELECT    @maxSalesTotal = MAX(TotalDue)
    FROM    sales.salesorderheader
    WHERE    SalesPersonID = @salesPersonID
END
GO
```

This stored procedure accepts two parameters. The first is an input parameter that is the ID of the salesperson. The second is an OUPUT parameter, which will contain the maximum individual sales for the given salesperson.

The next step is to create a mapping to that stored procedure and the associated parameters. In Visual Studio, add the following code below the previous stored procedure mapping. Notice the additional attribute, which is a `Return` attribute. It tells the mapping that a return value will be coming and the data type of that value. Also notice that it defines the two parameters and the parameter types within the method.

```
[Function(Name = "[MaxOrderBySalesPersonID]")]
[return: Parameter(DBType="int")]
public int MaxOrder
    ([Parameter(DBType = "int")] int salesPersonID,
    [Parameter(DBType = "int")] ref int maxSalesTotal)
{
    IExecuteResults results = this.ExecuteMethodCall(
        this, ((MethodInfo)(MethodInfo.GetCurrentMethod())),
```

```
          salesPersonID, maxSalesTotal);
    maxSalesTotal = ((int)(results.GetParameterValue(1)));
    return ((int)(results.ReturnValue));
}
```

Unlike the first example, this example is returning a singleton value, so no table definition is required. You do, however, need to add the code to call the stored procedure, so in the click event for button2, add the following code:

```
private void button2_Click(object sender, EventArgs e)
{
    AdventureWorks db = new AdventureWorks("Integrated Security=sspi");

    int bigOrder = 0;
    db.MaxOrder(275, ref bigOrder);

    listBox1.Items.Add(bigOrder);

}
```

This example defines an initial value for the returned parameter, and passes that along with the ID of the salesperson to the stored procedure.

Run the project again and click button2. This time the list box will be populated with a value of 198628 (if you used ID 275). Pretty slick, isn't it?

Mapped Stored Procedures for Multiple Results

The following example shows how to handle circumstances where you might not know the exact results coming back. It creates a stored procedure that accepts a single parameter of data type int. Based on the value of the parameter, one of two statements will be executed. One statement returns four columns, the other returns three columns.

```
CREATE PROCEDURE [dbo].[ContactsOrProducts]
(
    @whichone int
)
AS
BEGIN
    if @whichone = 1
        SELECT ContactID, Title, FirstName, LastName FROM Person.Contact
    else
        SELECT ProductID, Name, ProductNumber FROM Production.Product
END
GO
```

As you did earlier, you create a mapping to that stored procedure and the associated parameters. In Visual Studio, add the following code below the previous stored procedure mapping. In this code, two result types are defined as well as the parameter that will be passed to the stored procedure.

```
[Function(Name = "[ContactsOrProducts]")]
[ResultType(typeof(ContactsPart))]
[ResultType(typeof(ProductsPart))]
```

```
public IMultipleResults whichone(
    [Parameter(DBType = "int")] System.Nullable<int> whichone)
{
    return this.ExecuteMethodCallWithMultipleResults(this,
        ((MethodInfo)(MethodInfo.GetCurrentMethod())), whichone);
}
```

The two result types, called ContactsPart and ProductsPart, identify the table mapping for the incoming results. However, those mappings don't exist yet, so create them now by adding the following code below the table mapping from the first example. This code creates two mapping classes, one for the contacts and the other for the products.

```
[Table(Name = "ContactPart")]
public partial class ContactsPart
{
    private int _contactID;
    private string _title;
    private string _firstName;
    private string _lastName;

    [Column(Name = "ContactID", Storage = "_contactID", DBType = "int")]
    public int ContactID
    {
        get
        {
            return this._contactID;
        }
        set
        {
            if ((this._contactID != value))
            {
                this._contactID = value;
            }
        }
    }

    [Column(Name = "Title", Storage = "_title", DBType = "nvarchar(50)")]
    public string Title
    {
        get
        {
            return this._title;
        }
        set
        {
            if ((this._title != value))
            {
                this._title = value;
            }
        }
    }

    [Column(Name = "FirstName", Storage = "_firstName", DBType = "nvarchar(50)")]
    public string FirstName
```

```
    {
        get
        {
            return this._firstName;
        }
        set
        {
            if ((this._firstName != value))
            {
                this._firstName = value;
            }
        }
    }

    [Column(Name = "LastName", Storage = "_lastName", DBType = "nvarchar(50)")]
    public string LastName
    {
        get
        {
            return this._lastName;
        }
        set
        {
            if ((this._lastName != value))
            {
                this._lastName = value;
            }
        }
    }

}

[Table(Name = "ProductPart")]
public partial class ProductsPart
{
    private int _productID;
    private string _name;
    private string _productNumber;

    [Column(Name = "ProductID", Storage = "_productID", DBType = "int")]
    public int ProductID
    {
        get
        {
            return this._productID;
        }
        set
        {
            if ((this._productID != value))
            {
                this._productID = value;
            }
        }
    }
```

```
    [Column(Name = "Name", Storage = "_name", DBType = "nvarchar(50)")]
    public string Name
    {
        get
        {
            return this._name;
        }
        set
        {
            if ((this._name != value))
            {
                this._name = value;
            }
        }
    }

    [Column(Name = "ProductNumber", Storage = "_productNumber", DBType = ↵
"nvarchar(50)")]
    public string ProductNumber
    {
        get
        {
            return this._productNumber;
        }
        set
        {
            if ((this._productNumber != value))
            {
                this._productNumber = value;
            }
        }
    }

}
```

In the `Click` event of `button3`, add the following code to call this stored procedure:

```
private void button3_Click(object sender, EventArgs e)
{
    AdventureWorks db = new AdventureWorks("Integrated Security=sspi");

    int caseSwitch = int.Parse(textBox1.Text);

    listBox1.Items.Clear();

    switch (caseSwitch)
    {
        case 1:
            IMultipleResults result1 = db.whichone(caseSwitch);

            foreach (ContactsPart cp in result1.GetResult<ContactsPart>())
            {
                listBox1.Items.Add(cp.ContactID + "   " + cp.Title + "   " +
                    cp.FirstName + "   " + cp.LastName);
            }
```

```
        break;

    default:
        IMultipleResults result2 = db.whichone(caseSwitch);

        foreach (ProductsPart pp in result2.GetResult<ProductsPart>())
        {
            listBox1.Items.Add(pp.ProductID + "  " + pp.Name + "   " +
                pp.ProductNumber);
        }
        break;

    }

}
```

This code takes the value that is entered in the text box and passes that to the stored procedure. Once you have entered the code, press F5 to build and run the project.

Another compile error, right? This time the error should say something like this:

```
The type of namespace name 'IMultipleResults' could not be found.
```

Again, that's because you are missing a using directive. Add the highlighted using directive to your code:

```
using System.Linq;
using System.Text;
using System.Windows.Forms;
using System.Reflection;
using System.Data.Linq.Provider;
```

You have to include this namespace because it provides the capability to handle multiple results. Now, press F5 again, and when the application runs, enter either 1 or 2 in the text box. Based on the stored procedure and the number you entered, you should get either a list of contacts or a list of products. If you entered a value of 1, you get a list of contacts with four columns. If you entered a value of 2, you get a list of products with three columns.

This is accomplished by passing either the ContactPart mapping or the ProductPart mapping when calling the stored procedure.

OK, one last stored procedure example. The preceding was an "or" example, in that it returns the contact result or the product result. This example returns both. In SQL Server, create the following stored procedure:

```
CREATE PROCEDURE [dbo].[ContactsANDProducts]

AS
BEGIN
    SELECT ContactID, Title, FirstName, LastName FROM Person.Contact
    SELECT ProductID, Name, ProductNumber FROM Production.Product
END
GO
```

This procedure accepts no parameter and returns two results.

Next, create a mapping to that stored procedure. In Visual Studio, add the following code below the previous stored procedure mapping. Two result types are defined, but no parameter is defined because the stored procedure does not accept one.

```
[StoredProcedure(Name = "[ContactsANDProducts]")]
[ResultType(typeof(ContactsPart))]
[ResultType(typeof(ProductsPart))]
public IMultipleResults TwoResultsets()
{
    return this.ExecuteMethodCallWithMultipleResults(this,
        ((MethodInfo)(MethodInfo.GetCurrentMethod())));
}
```

The stored procedure returns the same results as the previous example (contacts and products), so this example will use the same table mappings that were defined in the previous example. Therefore, the only thing left to do is to add the code behind button4:

```
private void button4_Click(object sender, EventArgs e)
{
    AdventureWorks db = new AdventureWorks("Integrated Security=sspi");
    IMultipleResults results = db.TwoResultsets();

    foreach (ContactsPart cp in results.GetResult<ContactsPart>())
    {
        listBox1.Items.Add(cp.ContactID + "   " + cp.Title + "   " + cp.FirstName + "
            " + cp.LastName);
    }

    foreach (ProductsPart pp in results.GetResult<ProductsPart>())
    {
        listBox1.Items.Add(pp.ProductID + "   " + pp.Name + "   " + pp.ProductNumber);
    }
}
```

This example also requires the System.Data.Linq.Provider namespace because it is dealing with multiple results. It handles the contacts first, and then processes the products.

Press F5 to compile and run the project. When the form appears, click button4. The list box should be populated with a list of contacts first, followed by a list of products. To cut down on the number of items returned, add a WHERE clause to each SELECT statement.

You have to love the fact that LINQ can handle multiple results so easily.

Mapping and Calling User-Defined Functions

LINQ to SQL supports the mapping and calling of user-defined functions via methods defined in your object model that represent the user-defined function. Methods are designated as functions by applying the [Function] attribute and any associated [Parameter] attributes.

In the following example, a user-defined function will return table values. In SQL Server Management Studio, create the following user-defined function, which accepts a parameter and returns a resultset:

```
CREATE FUNCTION [dbo].[EmployeesByManagerID]
(
    @ManagerID int
)
RETURNS TABLE
AS
RETURN
(

    select pc.ContactID, pc.FirstName, pc.LastName, emp.Title
    from Person.Contact pc
     INNER JOIN   HumanResources.Employee emp ON pc.ContactID = emp.ContactID
     WHERE      ManagerID = @ManagerID

)
```

Next, create a mapping to the UDF you just created. In Visual Studio, add the following code below the previous stored procedure mapping. This method is annotated with the Function attribute, telling the DataContext that a user-defined function will be called.

```
[Function(Name = "[EmployeeInfo]")]
public IQueryable<EmployeeInfo>
   EmpInfo(System.Nullable<int> ManagerID)
{
   MethodCallExpression mce = Expression.Call(Expression.Constant(this),
   ((MethodInfo)(MethodInfo.GetCurrentMethod())),
   new Expression[]
   {
      Expression.Constant(ManagerID, typeof(System.Nullable<int>))
   }
   );
   return this.CreateQuery<EmployeeInfo>(mce);

}
```

A table mapping must be created to define and map the results coming back. And the definition of the table mapping is no different than that of calling a stored procedure as in the previous examples. Create the table mapping by adding the code below:

```
[Table(Name = "EmployeeInfo")]
public partial class EmployeeInfo
{
   private int _contactID;
   private string _firstName;
   private string _lastName;
   private string _Title;
```

```csharp
[Column(Name = "ContactID", Storage = "_contactID", DBType = "int")]
public int ContactID
{
    get
    {
        return this._contactID;
    }
    set
    {
        if ((this._contactID != value))
        {
            this._contactID = value;
        }
    }
}

[Column(Name = "FirstName", Storage = "_firstName", DBType = "nvarchar(50)")]
public string FirstName
{
    get
    {
        return this._firstName;
    }
    set
    {
        if ((this._firstName != value))
        {
            this._firstName = value;
        }
    }
}

[Column(Name = "LastName", Storage = "_lastName", DBType = "nvarchar(50)")]
public string LastName
{
    get
    {
        return this._lastName;
    }
    set
    {
        if ((this._lastName != value))
        {
            this._lastName = value;
        }
    }
}

[Column(Name = "Title", Storage = "_Title", DBType = "nvarchar(50)")]
public string Title
{
    get
    {
        return this._Title;
    }
```

```
      set
      {
         if ((this._Title != value))
         {
            this._Title = value;
         }
      }
   }
}
```

Last, add the code behind button5:

```
private void button5_Click(object sender, EventArgs e)
{

    AdventureWorks db = new AdventureWorks("Integrated Security=sspi");
    var result = from emp in db.EmpInfo(21)
            select emp;

    foreach (EmployeeInfo ei in result)
        listBox1.Items.Add(ei.ContactID + "   " + ei.FirstName
            + "   " + ei.LastName + "   " + ei.Title);

}
```

This code is not really that different from calling a stored procedure.

Press F5 to compile and run the project. One last "Oops!" This time the error says something like this:

```
The type of namespace name 'MethodCallExpression' could not be found.
```

Once again, that's because you are missing a using directive. Add the highlighted using directive to your code:

```
using System.Text;
using System.Windows.Forms;
using System.Reflection;
using System.Data.Linq.Provider;
using System.Linq.Expressions;
```

You need to include this namespace because it provides the capability to represent language-level expressions as objects in the form of expression trees.

Press F5 again, and when the application runs, click button5. This time the list box should be populated with the ContactID, FirstName, LastName, and Title of the employees whose manager has a ManagerID of 21.

Whew! That was a lot, but you now have a good understanding of how LINQ to SQL is used to call stored procedures and user-defined functions using input and output parameters, deal with multiple resultsets, and return rows of data.

Summary

This chapter introduced you to LINQ to SQL queries, providing an in-depth look at the components and concepts that make LINQ to SQL queries possible. You first explored LINQ to SQL query concepts, the key points that give LINQ to SQL queries their power.

Then you learned about the `DataContext` class, the important role it plays in LINQ to SQL, and the functionality it provides when executing queries. In addition, you saw how to use LINQ to SQL and the `DataContext` class to manipulate data, such as adding, updating, and deleting data in SQL Server.

Associating relational database objects to LINQ to SQL generic collections and submitting them to the database for execution was also discussed, and you looked at several examples illustrating how to execute stored procedures and user-defined functions using LINQ to SQL.

Chapter 12 tackles a few advanced LINQ to SQL query topics.

12

Advanced Query Concepts

There is so much that LINQ to SQL can do that applies to relational data and working with relational databases, that a chapter dedicated to the tight coupling of LINQ to SQL and relational data is warranted. For example, LINQ to SQL supports transactions and composite keys, and these types of topics are usually not found or discussed in an introductory-level chapter. Therefore, this chapter focuses on the following topics, which are a bit more advanced:

❑ Database relationships

❑ Compiled queries

❑ Query execution location

❑ Deferred versus immediate

❑ Composite keys

❑ Read-only data

Transactions are discussed in Chapter 13.

Database Relationships

LINQ to SQL fully supports primary and foreign keys, and Chapter 10 provided a couple of code examples to illustrate how they are implemented in LINQ to SQL. This section builds on that, discussing how to define the keys in LINQ to SQL and showing you how to query across them.

Representing Relationships

As you know, relationships in databases are normally of the primary key/foreign key kind—that is, the column or set of columns in one table that is referenced by the column or columns in another table. In a relational database, the navigation between these two tables is done through a join operator or operation. In a join operation, the primary key table is referenced to the foreign key table through a JOIN operator on the primary and foreign keys.

The following T-SQL query illustrates how the Person.Contact table and the HumanResources.Employee table, which are joined through the ContactID column, are referenced together in a query:

```
SELECT      pc.ContactID, pc.FirstName, pc.LastName, pc.EmailAddress,
            hre.EmployeeID, hre.NationalIDNumber, hre.Title, hre.HireDate
FROM        Person.Contact pc
INNER JOIN  HumanResources.Employee hre ON pc.ContactID = hre.ContactID
ORDER BY    pc.LastName
```

The key, then, is to apply this same join functionality in LINQ to SQL. You accomplish that through types that assist in representing the primary key/foreign key relationships between tables within a database. These two types are the EntitySet and EntityRef generic types, each of which is of type (of TEntity). These types provide collections for the "many" part of a one-to-many relationship. Both the EntitySet and EntityRef types are used in conjunction with the [Association] attribute, which helps define and represent a relationship.

EntitySet (of TEntity)

The EntitySet type provides a collection for the results of the "many" side of a one-to-many relationship. In other words, it signifies that the defined relationship is a one-to-many relationship. As stated earlier, it is used together with the [Association] attribute to define and represent a relationship.

The OtherKey property is also used in the definition of the relationship. It specifies the name of the property (column) in the related class (table) to which is compared the current class's (table's) property (column).

The following example defines two classes, one for the Contacts table and one for the Employee table. In the AdventureWorks database, you can see that there's a relationship defined between these two tables on the ContactID column. The code here maps these two classes to their respective relational database counterparts, and also uses the [Association] attribute and the EntitySet type to define a one-to-many relationship between the Contact class and the Employee class. The relationship is defined within the context of the Contact class.

```
public class AdventureWorks : DataContext
{
    public AdventureWorks(string connection) : base(connection) {}
    public Table<Contact> Contacts;
    public Table<Employee> Employees;

}

[Table(Name = "Person.Contact")]
public class Contact
{

    [Column(DBType = "int not null", IsPrimaryKey = true, IsDBGenerated
        = true)]
    public int ContactID;
```

```
        [Column(DBType = "nvarchar(8) not null")]
        public string Title;

        [Column(DBType = "nvarchar(50) not null")]
        public string FirstName;

        [Column(DBType = "nvarchar(50) not null")]
        public string MiddleName;

        [Column(DBType = "nvarchar(50) not null")]
        public string LastName;

        [Column(DBType = "nvarchar(50) not null")]
        public string EmailAddress;

        [Column(DBType = "int")]
        public int EmailPromotion;

        [Column(DBType = "bit")]
        public byte NameStyle;

        [Column(DBType = "varchar(40)")]
        public string PasswordIIash;

        [Column(DBType = "varchar(40)")]
        public string PasswordSalt;

        private EntitySet<Employee> _employees;
        [Association(Storage = "_employees", OtherKey = "ContactID")]
        public EntitySet<Employee> Emps
        {
            get { return this._employees;}
            set { this._employees.Assign(value);}
        }
}

[Table(Name = "HumanResources.Employee")]
public class Employee
{
    [Column(DBType = "int", IsPrimaryKey = true, IsDBGenerated = true,
        CanBeNull = false)]
    public int EmployeeID;

    [Column(DBType = "int", CanBeNull = false)]
    public int ContactID;

    [Column(DBType = "nvarchar(256) not null")]
    public string LoginID;

    [Column(DBType = "nvarchar(15) not null")]
    public string NationalIDNUmber;

    [Column(DBType = "int")]
    public int ManagerID;

}
```

With the classes and relationship defined, you can now write a LINQ to SQL "join" query that utilizes the relationship, like this:

```
IQueryable<Contact> conQuery =
    from con in db.Contact
    where con.Employee.ContactID == 19917
```

Or like this:

```
var conQuery =
    from con in db.Contact
    from emp in con.Emps
    where con.FirstName == "Scott"
    select new {con.FirstName, emp.ManagerID};
```

Think of the `EntitySet` type and the `[Association]` attribute (utilized in the table mapping above) as equal to a SQL join.

EntityRef (of TEntity)

The `EntityRef` type defines a relationship between two tables, but does the opposite of the `EntitySet`, in that it provides for the "one" side of a one-to-many relationship. It is also used together with the `[Association]` attribute to define and represent a relationship.

Again, the `ThisKey` property is used in the definition of the relationship to specify the name of the property (column) in the related class (table) to which the current class's (table's) property (column) is compared.

The next example uses the same two classes—one for the `Contacts` table and one for the `Employee` table—as in the previous example. The following code maps these two classes to their respective relational database counterparts, and also uses the `[Association]` attribute and the `EntityRef` type to define a one-to-many relationship between the two classes. The relationship is defined within the context of the `Employee` class.

```
public class AdventureWorks : DataContext
{
    public AdventureWorks(string connection) : base(connection) {}
    public Table<Contact> Contacts;
    public Table<Employee> Employees;

}

[Table(Name = "Person.Contact")]
public class Contact
{

    [Column(DBType = "int not null", IsPrimaryKey = true, IsDBGenerated
        = true)]
    public int ContactID;
```

```csharp
    [Column(DBType = "nvarchar(8) not null")]
    public string Title;

    [Column(DBType = "nvarchar(50) not null")]
    public string FirstName;

    [Column(DBType = "nvarchar(50) not null")]
    public string MiddleName;

    [Column(DBType = "nvarchar(50) not null")]
    public string LastName;

    [Column(DBType = "nvarchar(50) not null")]
    public string EmailAddress;

    [Column(DBType = "int")]
    public int EmailPromotion;

    [Column(DBType = "bit")]
    public byte NameStyle;

    [Column(DBType = "varchar(40)")]
    public string PasswordHash;

    [Column(DBType = "varchar(40)")]
    public string PasswordSalt;

}

[Table(Name = "HumanResources.Employee")]
public class Employee
{
    [Column(DBType = "int", IsPrimaryKey = true, IsDBGenerated = true,
 CanBeNull = false)]
    public int EmployeeID;

    [Column(DBType = "int", CanBeNull = false)]
    public int ContactID;

    [Column(DBType = "nvarchar(256) not null")]
    public string LoginID;

    [Column(DBType = "nvarchar(15) not null")]
    public string NationalIDNUmber;
    [Column(DBType = "int")]
    public int ManagerID;

    private EntityRef<Contact> _Contact;
    [Association(Storage = "_Contact", ThisKey = "ContactID")]
    public Contact Contact
    {
        get { return this._Contact.Entity;}
        set { this._Contact.Entity = value;}
    }
}
```

This example illustrates the relationship between a contact and employee. The `EntityRef` type is used to define the relationship from `Employee` back to `Contact`.

With the classes and relationship defined, you can now write a query that utilizes the relationship, like this:

```
IQueryable<Employee> empQuery =
    from emp in db.Employee
    where emp.Contact.FirstName.StartsWith("Scott")
    select emp;
```

You can see that `EntitySet` and `EntityRef` are complementary and quite easy to use, and are powerful for defining relationships.

Querying

You have two choices when querying across objects: `join` statements or dot notation. They are equally effective, but the second offers better relationship checking than the first. The T-SQL statement at the beginning of the chapter (repeated here) showed how to join two tables using `join` syntax.

```
SELECT          pc.ContactID, pc.FirstName, pc.LastName, pc.EmailAddress,
                hre.EmployeeID, hre.NationalIDNumber, hre.Title, hre.HireDate
FROM            Person.Contact pc
INNER JOIN      HumanResources.Employee hre ON pc.ContactID = hre.ContactID
WHERE hre.ManagerID = 275
```

You can accomplish the same type of join in LINQ to SQL using the LINQ `join` operator, like this:

```
IQueryable<Employee> joinQuery =
    from emp in db.Employee
    join con in db.Contact on emp.ContactID equals con.ContactID
    where emp.ManagerID == 275
    select con;
```

Notice how similar these two examples are. This syntax is beneficial when database relationships do not exist between two tables, or when LINQ relationship properties do not exist (are not defined). In these cases, you have to define them manually, as in this example.

The better option (the preferred method) is to define relationship properties and use the dot notation to access them. This enables you to walk the relationship tree, navigating from one object to another easily, as the following example shows:

```
IQueryable<Employee> empQuery =
    from emp in db.Employee
    where emp.Contact.FirstName.StartsWith("Scott")
    select emp;
```

The benefits of using relationship properties include the capability to determine results of queries. For example, you can use the relationship to determine whether contacts have employee records.

Compiled Queries

If you are a developer who works with SQL as well as with .NET, you know that there are many occasions where you use the same query repeatedly. LINQ to SQL makes this easy to do by enabling you to create a compiled query—a query that is stored in a static variable and is available for execution whenever you need it.

Compiled queries are available via the CompiledQuery class of the System.Data.Linq namespace. This class has a Compile method that creates a new delegate representing the compiled query.

The following example defines a compiled query using a static class:

```
public class AdventureWorks : DataContext
{
    public AdventureWorks(string connection) : base(connection) {}
    public Table<Contact> Contact;
    public Table<Employee> Employee;

}
static class Queries
{
    public static Func<AdventureWorks, string, IQueryable<Contact>>
        ContactsByFirstName =
        CompiledQuery.Compile((AdventureWorks db, string firstname) =>
                            from c in db.Contact
                            where c.FirstName == firstname
                            select c);

}
```

Now that the compiled query is defined, it can be used, as the following example shows:

```
AdventureWorks db = new AdventureWorks("Integrated Security=sspi");

IEnumerable<Contact> conQuery = Queries.ContactsByFirstName(db, "scott");

foreach (Contact con in conQuery)
{
    listBox1.Items.Add(con.FirstName + "  " + con.LastName);
}
```

The primary benefit of a compiled query is that the query doesn't need to be compiled each time it is executed. It is compiled once (the first time it is executed) and then can be used multiple times. Even if the parameters to the query changes, the query does not need recompiling.

Remote versus Local Query Execution

A query executed remotely is executed on the server; a query executed locally is executed against a local cache. By default, queries are executed remotely, but you can choose to have them executed locally. The following sections discuss remote and local query execution.

Remote Execution

Although it depends on the query, remote execution is usually your most logical choice. It allows you to take advantage of database engine benefits such as indexes. Executing queries remotely is also better if your database has a large number of rows. For example, you don't want to return all the contacts from the Contacts table if you only need a small set of them.

You have two things going for you: the IQueryable interface and the EntitySet class. The EntitySet class implements the IQueryable interface, and the IQueryable interface guarantees that queries can be executed remotely. Therefore, the following query will be executed remotely:

```
AdventureWorks db = new AdventureWorks("Integrated Security=sspi");

IEnumerable<Contact> conQuery =
    from con in db.Contact
    where con.FirstName == "Scott"
    orderby con.LastName
    select con;

foreach (Contact cont in conQuery)
    listBox1.Items.Add(cont.FirstName + "  " + cont.LastName);
```

One of the key benefits of remote execution is that you can take advantage of database table indexes, which you can't use when queries are executed locally. You also have the guarantee that needless data is not returned.

Local Execution

In those cases where local execution is necessary, you have another option. The Load() method of the EntitySet retrieves all the related entities into your local cache. In the following example, there is a relationship between the Contact class and Employee class through the EntitySet. Therefore, when the contacts are loaded, the corresponding employees are loaded as well.

```
AdventureWorks db = new AdventureWorks("Integrated Security=sspi");

Contact con = db.Contact.Single(x => x.ContactID == 1146);
con.Employee.Load();

foreach (Employee emp in con.Employee.Where(y => y.ManagerID == 210))
    listBox1.Items.Add(emp.ContactID + "  " + con.FirstName);
```

Executing queries locally has two benefits. First, once the set of data is loaded locally, it can be queried as often as necessary without the need of going to the database again for each subsequent query. Second, the entire set can be serialized.

Deferred versus Immediate Data Loading

Earlier in the chapter you learned that when querying across relationships, only the objects you specifically ask for are returned, and related objects are retrieved later, when you specifically request that information. For example, the following code loads the necessary employee object, and then, based on the results of the query, sends the Contacts object off for execution. This is known as deferred data loading.

```
AdventureWorks db = new AdventureWorks("Integrated Security=sspi");

IQueryable<Employee> empQuery =
    from emp in db.Employees
    where emp.ManagerID == 21
    select emp;

foreach (Employee empObj in empQuery)
{
    if (empObj.ContactID > 1100)
    {
        GiveBigPhatRaise(empObj.Contacts);
    }
}
```

Immediate loading, on the other hand, retrieves both sets of data together. This is especially useful if you need access to both sets of data immediately. To illustrate this, the following example uses the SalesOrderHeader and SalesOrderDetail tables from the AdventureWorks database, and assumes that mappings to each table and the associated [Association] and EntitySet references have been defined.

The example queries the SalesOrderHeader table for all orders that were made by SalesPersonID 275, and returns one set. The first foreach loop loops through that result set, while the inner foreach loops through the corresponding order details, thus returning the second set of data. Remember that the results are not returned until the iteration over the query variable takes place. Therefore, as each foreach loop is iterated over, both sets of data are returned.

```
IQueryable<SalesOrderHeader> sohQuery =
    from soh in db.SalesOrdersHeader
    where soh.SalesPersonID == 275
    select soh;

foreach (SalesOrdersHeader sohObj in sohQuery)
{
    foreach (SalesOrdersDetail sodObj in sohObj.SalesOrdersHeader)
    {
        //Do something
    }
}
```

Obviously, there are latency hits when you return large amounts of data, so you will want to use immediate loading when you need access to both sets of data right out of the gate.

As you learned in Chapter 3, you can force immediate execution of a query that does not produce a singleton value by using the ToList() *or* ToArray() *methods.*

Remember query execution this way: deferred execution should be used to produce a sequence of values. Immediate execution is used to return a singleton value such a Count, or Average.

The following example counts the number of order items for a specific order where the unit price of the item is less than $200. Because the query is returning a singleton value, it is executed immediately.

```
Table<SalesOrderDetail> orderdetail = context.GetTable<SalesOrderDetail>();

var query =
    from od in orderdetail
    where od.SalesOrderID = 43662
    select od;

listBox1.Items.Add(query.Count(orderdetail => orderdetail.UnitPrice < 200));
```

DataShape Class

LINQ to SQL provides a way to return related objects at the same time as your parent object with the added benefit of returning only what you need. This is made possible by the `DataShape` class, which lets you define a subtype that can be returned at the same time as the main query. This class has a `LoadWith` method that lets you specify which sub-objects to return when a query is sent for execution.

Here's an example:

```
DataShape ds = new DataShape();
ds.LoadWith<SalesOrderHeader>(soh => soh.SalesOrderDetail);
db.Shape = ds;
```

This code uses `DataShape` to say, "also give me the SalesOrderDetail for the corresponding SalesOrder-Header." Once the `DataShape` is defined, it's handed off to the `Shape` property of the `DataContext` class, which sets the `DataShape` associated with the current `DataContext`. Remember, the `DataContext` handles the query execution and the data retrieval, so it needs to know the `DataShape` if there is one.

The query itself does not change, as shown here:

```
IQueryable<SalesOrderHeader> sohQuery =
    from soh in db.SalesOrdersHeader
    where soh.SalesPersonID == 275
    select soh;
```

All of this information is pretty slick, but LINQ to SQL takes it one step farther by letting you control deferred loading, which is discussed next.

Turning Off Deferred Loading

The `DataContext` class has a property that tells the framework not to delay the loading of one-to-many or one-to-one relationships. This property is called `DeferredLoadingEnabled` and is used as shown here:

```
AdventureWorks db = new AdventureWorks("Integrated Security=sspi");

db.DeferredLoadingEnabled = false;
```

Keep in mind that deferred loading is automatically turned off when object tracking (the `ObjectTracking-gEnabled` property of the `DataContext`) is turned off. Object tracking is discussed later in this chapter.

You might consider using this property when you want to return only a portion of the query and do something with those results, such as sending the partial results to a web service.

Composite Keys

Occasionally, you need more than one attribute to uniquely identify an entity. That's where composite keys come in; they enable you to include multiple columns in a query when the operator accepts only a single argument. In those cases, your best bet is to create an anonymous type that represents the combination of the multiple columns you need to pass.

The LINQ `group` operator (`GroupBy` in Visual Basic), for instance, takes a single argument, but you can see in the following example that an anonymous type is created and used to pass in two columns instead of the one:

```
AdventureWorks db = new AdventureWorks("Integrated Security=sspi");

var conQuery =
    from con in db.Contacts
    where con.LastName.StartsWith("K")
    group con.FirstName by new { last = con.LastName, middle = con.MiddleName} ;

foreach (var grp in conQuery)
{
    listBox1.Items.Add(grp.Key);
    foreach (var listing in grp)
    {
        listBox1.Items.Add(listing);
    }
}
```

Very slick.

Read-Only Data

If you don't plan to modify the data, you can get a pretty good performance increase by telling the `DataContext` that you want the data returned as read-only, so this last section will discuss working with read-only data.

To get read-only data, set the `ObjectTrackingEnabled` property to false. `ObjectTrackingEnabled` tells the framework to track the original value. Setting it to false means that the framework doesn't need to track changes, which provides a performance increase.

The following example shows how to disable object tracking by setting the `ObjectTrackingEnabled` property to false.

```
AdventureWorks db = new AdventureWorks("Integrated Security=sspi");
db.ObjectTracking = false;

var conQuery =
    from con in db.Contacts
    where con.FirstName = "Scott"
    select con;
```

Several words of caution: If you set this property to false and then call `SubmitChanges`, an exception will be thrown because there are no changes to submit. An exception also will be thrown if you set this property to false after executing a query.

Summary

This chapter explored a few topics that are meant to enhance the performance and functionality of your LINQ to SQL queries. The most important topic was that of database relationships—how to define them, and then query across them.

The next topic covered was compiled queries, how they are created, and how they can be used in your application. Compiled queries can save a lot of processing overhead if used correctly, since multiple calls to the database do not need to be made.

You took a look at query execution location and how data is loaded, learning how to manage much of the performance of your application by controlling where the queries are executed and whether the query execution is done immediately or deferred.

Composite keys were discussed to help you overcome the problem of passing multiple arguments where only one argument is accepted. This comes in handy when dealing with more complex queries.

Returning data in read-only form also was discussed. If you don't plan to do any data modification, then you'll gain some performance increases by retrieving data read-only.

Chapter 13 tackles entity classes in detail.

13

More about Entity Classes

There's more that can be said about LINQ to SQL entity classes because they provide a lot more functionality than what you've explored so far in this book. LINQ to SQL is all about managing entities, or objects, during their lifetime of service. As you've already seen, one of the primary things about entities is that they provide a lot of functionality aimed at dealing with querying data and, just as importantly, maintaining the integrity of your data through relationships.

More significantly, though, the LINQ to SQL entities (objects) used when executing queries can be changed and manipulated as needed by the application during the lifetime of the query. The data associated with those entities also can be changed. Modifications are then ushered back to the server when the application is done with the objects.

There are a few key things to keep in mind:

❑ The objects used in executing queries can be reused until the application is done with the retrieved data.

❑ After the data changes are sent back to the server and the objects are no longer needed, the objects are reclaimed by the runtime.

❑ Although the object may no longer be in existence, any object that represents the same data can still be accessed.

The focus of this chapter, then, is on the lifetime of an entity and on the actions an entity can perform during its lifespan. The lifetime of an entity begins when the DataContext is notified of the entities existence and ends when the DataContext is either closed or notified of the reclaimed entity.

Therefore, this chapter discusses the following topics:

❑ How changes to the entity are tracked

❑ Submitting changes back to the database

❑ Making simultaneous changes

❑ Working with transactions

Tracking Entity Changes

As you know, LINQ to SQL works with objects defined within your object model. These objects can be used to perform various operations, such as inserts and updates to the underlying database. By default, LINQ to SQL keeps track of any changes made to these objects via the LINQ to SQL DataContext.

It's important to remember that the changes are not tracked on the database side. They are tracked on the client side, and no database resources are used while changes are tracked.

In Chapter 12 you saw that you could work with read-only results by setting the ObjectTrackingEnabled property of the DataContext to false. This property also enables you to track changes made to objects and to submit those changes to the underlying database.

Tracking changes is enabled by default, so changes made to objects within your object model are automatically tracked. When the application is ready to send the changes back to the database, a simple call to the DataContext SubmitChanges() method needs to take place. That method instructs LINQ to SQL to execute the appropriate SQL code to make the necessary changes to update the database.

For example, the following code creates a new contact object, saves it to the database, updates an existing contact object, and then saves the changes back to the database.

```
AdventureWorks db = new AdventureWorks("Integrated Security=sspi");

//Add a new contact
Contact con = new Contact();
con.Firstname = "Sammy";
con.MiddleName = "T";
con.LastName = "Hagar";
con.NameStyle = 0;
con.EmailPromotion = 1;
con.EmailAddress = "RedRocker@Adventure-works.com";
con.Title = "Mr.";
db.Contacts.Add(con);

db.SubmitChanges();

//Update an existing contact
Contact cont = db.Contacts.Single(c => c.ContactID == 1280);
cont.EmailAddress = "christiank@adventure-works.com";
cont.NameStyle = 0;
db.SubmitChanges();
```

Keep in mind that only those properties that have changed are ushered back to the database. For instance, if the NameStyle for Christian was already 0, then that change won't be made in the database.

Submitting Entity Changes

Along with tracking changes, entity classes can be used to submit changes that have been made to the entity, such as adding, updating, or deleting records. Manipulating data is one of the key aspects of LINQ to SQL, and entity classes make those operations extremely easy. Changes can be made simply by manipulating the objects in your object model.

To see how this works, fire up Visual Studio, create a new Windows project, and add the appropriate references:

```
system.data.Linq
```

Next, view the code behind Form1 and add the following statements:

```
using System.Data.Linq
using System.Data.Linq.Mapping
```

Prior to Beta2, attribute-based mapping was supported via the System.Data.Linq namespace. If you then installed Beta2 and tried to compile your code, you received a lot of compile errors. That is because attribute-based mapping is now supported via the System.Data.Linq.Mapping namespace.

Next, underneath the partial class of Form1, add the following highlighted code:

```
namespace LINQ
{
    public partial class Form1 : Form
    {
        public Form1()
        {
            InitializeComponent();
        }

        private void Form1_Load(object sender, EventArgs e)
        {

        }
    }
}
```

```
public class AdventureWorks : DataContext
{
    public AdventureWorks(string connection) : base(connection) {}
    public Table<Contact> Contacts;
}

[Table(Name = "Person.Contact")]
public class Contact
{

    [Column(DbType = "int not null", IsPrimaryKey = true, IsDbGenerated = true)]
    public int ContactID;

    [Column(DbType = "nvarchar(8) not null")]
    public string Title;

    [Column(DbType = "nvarchar(50) not null")]
    public string FirstName;

    [Column(DbType = "nvarchar(50) not null")]
    public string MiddleName;
```

```
        [Column(DbType = "nvarchar(50) not null")]
        public string LastName;

        [Column(DbType = "nvarchar(50) not null")]
        public string EmailAddress;

        [Column(DbType = "int")]
        public int EmailPromotion;

        [Column(DbType = "bit")]
        public byte NameStyle;

        [Column(DbType = "varchar(40)")]
        public string PasswordHash;

        [Column(DbType = "varchar(40)")]
        public string PasswordSalt;


    }
```

The rest of this code should look familiar—you have seen it throughout the last few chapters. Attribute-based mapping is used to map a SQL Server database and table to a LINQ to SQL class.

For purposes of this example, create a small routine that will do a lot of the work for you. Add the following code after the Load event of Form1. The code will be explained shortly.

```
private void InsertNames(string firstName, string title, string emailAddr)
{
    AdventureWorks db = new AdventureWorks("Integrated Security=sspi");

    try
    {
        Contact con = new Contact();
        con.FirstName = firstname;
        con.LastName = "Klein";
        con.MiddleName = "L";
        con.NameStyle = 0;
        con.EmailPromotion = 1;
        con.EmailAddress = " emailAddr;
        con.PasswordHash = "asdf";
        con.PasswordSalt = "qwer";
        con.Title = title;

        db.Contacts.Add(con);
        db.SubmitChanges();


    }
    catch (Exception ex)
    {
        MessageBox.Show(ex.Message);
    }
}
```

In the `InsertNames` routine, a new instance of the `Contact` class is created, followed by the setting of several of the class's properties. Last, the object is inserted by calling the `Add` method on the object entity and then calling the `SubmitChanges` method of the `DataContext` class.

The `SubmitChanges` method determines the changed data such as newly added data, as in this case, or modifications to existing data, and then executes the correct commands to create and usher the changes back to the database.

The `InsertNames` routine allows new contacts to be created simply and efficiently.

You are now ready to start adding modification code. Open `Form1` in design mode and add three buttons and a text box. Behind `button1`, add the following highlighted code (you can use other names and email addresses):

```
private void button1_Click(object sender, EventArgs e)
{
    this.InsertNames("Scott", "Mr.", "ScottKlein@SqlXml.com");
    this.InsertNames("Chris", "Mr.", "Chris@SomeCompany.com");
    this.InsertNames("Jason", "Mr.", "Jason@SomeCompany.com");
    this.InsertNames("Richard", "Mr.", "Dad@Home.com");
    this.InsertNames("Courtney", "Mrs.", "Sis@SomeCompany.com");
    this.InsertNames("Carolyn", "Mrs.", "Mom@Home.com");

    textBox1.Text = "Contact added successfully";
}
```

Run the Visual Studio project you created by pressing F5, and when the form displays, click `button1`. When the code behind `button1` executes, it calls the `InsertNames` routine several times, passing a contact first name, a title, and an email address to the routine. The `InsertNames` routine then uses those values to insert the contacts.

When the code finishes executing, the text box on the form displays "Contact added successfully." At that point, you can query the `Person.Contact` table in the AdventureWorks database. The results should look like those shown in Figure 13-1.

	ContactID	Title	FirstName	LastName	NameStyle	EmailAddress	EmailPromotion
1	19999	Mr.	Scott	Klein	0	ScottKlein@SqlXml.com	1
2	20000	Mr.	Chris	Klein	0	Chris@SomeCompany.com	1
3	20001	Mr.	Jason	Klein	0	Jason@SomeCompany.com	1
4	20002	Mr.	Richard	Klein	0	Dad@Home.com	1
5	20003	Mrs.	Courtney	Klein	0	Sis@SomeCompany.com	1
6	20004	Mrs.	Carolyn	Klein	0	Mom@Home.com	1

Figure 13-1

You can see how easy it is to perform `Insert` operations using LINQ to SQL and entity objects. Yet, you are just skimming the surface. What about modifying existing records and sending the changes back? Let's do an update example next. Behind `button2` of your form, add the following code:

```
private void button2_Click(object sender, EventArgs e)
{
    AdventureWorks db = new AdventureWorks("Integrated Security=sspi");
```

```
try
{
    var conQuery =
        from con in db.Contacts
        where con.FirstName == "Scott"
        select con;

    // there are 15 Scott's in the table, so 15 changes should be made
    foreach (Contact cont in conQuery)
    {
        cont.MiddleName = "L";
        cont.NameStyle = 1;
    }
    db.SubmitChanges();

    textBox1.Text = "Contacts modified successfully";

}
catch (Exception ex)
{
    MessageBox.Show(ex.Message);
}

}
```

Before you run this code, spend a few minutes looking at what it's doing. First, you have a standard LINQ query that is populating the entity class with all contacts whose first name is Scott. Each contact is then iterated over, changing the middle initial to "L".

Just like the previous example, the `SubmitChanges()` method is used to usher the changes to the object back to the database.

What about deleting? The great thing about LINQ and LINQ to SQL is that all these operations are extremely similar. To illustrate, add the following code behind `button3` of your form:

```
private void button3_Click(object sender, EventArgs e)
{

    AdventureWorks db = new AdventureWorks("Integrated Security=sspi");

    try
    {
        var conQuery =
            from con in db.Contacts
            where con.LastName == "Klein"
            select con;

        foreach (Contact cont in conQuery)
        {
            db.Contacts.Remove(cont);
        }
        db.SubmitChanges();
```

```
            textBox1.Text = "Contacts removed successfully";

    }
    catch (Exception ex)
    {
        MessageBox.Show(ex.Message);
    }
}
```

Like the update example, this code utilizes a standard LINQ query that is populating the entity class with all contacts whose last name is "Klein" (essentialy all the names used in the Insert example above). As with the update example, each contact returned in the query is then iterated over, calling the `Remove` method on the object entity and then calling the `SubmitChanges` method of the `DataContext` class.

As you can see, manipulating data is easy, yet effective. LINQ to SQL offers a lot of flexibility for manipulating, and maintaining, data, and changes to data.

Concurrent Changes and Concurrency Conflicts

In LINQ to SQL, the `DataContext` has built-in support for optimistic concurrency. In optimistic concurrency mode, updates succeed only if the state of the database has not changed since you first retrieved the data. Conflicts to this state can occur in the LINQ to SQL object when both of the following are true:

❑   The application tries to write changes back to the database.

❑   The data you requested has been changed *in the database* since you requested the data.

For example, you request contact information for Bob. Your entity class is populated with Bob's information. While the data sits in your entity class within your application, you begin to change some of the information within the class, such as Bob's address. However, while you are making those changes, someone else has also changed Bob's data and saved it back to the database. Now when you try to save your changes to the database, you have a concurrency conflict.

How do you resolve this? You need to find out which members of the object are "in conflict" and then decide how you want to resolve those conflicts.

The information that follows will help you with those decisions.

UpdateCheck

The `UpdateCheck` property is a property of the `[Column]` attribute. It tells LINQ to SQL how to handle optimistic concurrency conflicts when conflicts are detected. Any members of a class that are attributed with this property are included in update checks to primarily help detect concurrency conflicts.

The UpdateCheck property is used as follows:

```
[Column(DbType = "nvarchar(50)", UpdateCheck = UpdateCheck.WhenChanged)]
public string LastName;
```

This property can take one of several values, which are described in the following table.

Value	Description
Always	Always use this member for detecting conflicts.
Never	Don't use this member to determine conflicts.
WhenChanged	Use this member to detect conflicts when the value of this member has been changed by the application.

The default value is Always.

There are several alternatives for resolving the conflicts. One key approach is to use the UpdateCheck property effectively. By revising the UpdateCheck options within your object model, you can quickly narrow down those specific members that are vital to the data. You don't want to place UpdateCheck on each member (column) because performance could be degraded. The solution is to place it on the more important members.

Another option is to use the RefreshMode enumeration in a try/catch block. This enumerator gives you great flexibility in deciding how you want to resolve conflicts. You also have the ConflictMode enumeration and the ChangeConflictException class. These three enumerations are discussed in the following sections.

ConflictMode

The ConflictMode enumeration can be used in conjunction with the SubmitChanges method of the DataContext class. This enumeration lets you specify how you want conflicts to be reported when they are detected. It has two values:

❑ ContinueOnConflict—All database updates are attempted; concurrency conflicts are collected and returned at the end of the change process.

❑ FailOnFirstConflict—Update attempts should immediately stop when the first concurrency conflict is found.

Using the ConflictMode enumeration is quite simple. The SubmitChanges method has an overload that accepts the enumeration as shown in this code fragment:

```
Db.SubmitChanges(ConflictMode.ContinueOnConflict);
```

The ConflictMode enumeration has the following member values:

- ❏ FailOnFirstConflict—Attempts to update the database should cease immediately when the first concurrency conflict is found.

- ❏ ContinueOnConflict—All updates to the database should be attempted. All concurrency conflicts are gathered and returned at the end of the update process.

The ConflictMode option is usually used in conjunction with the RefreshMode enumeration, which is discussed shortly.

ChangeConflictException

Any time a conflict occurs, a ChangeConflictException is thrown. This exception is thrown because an update to the database failed because the database values were updated since the client application last accessed them.

In its simplest form, the ChangeConflictException is used as follows:

```
catch (ChangeConflictException ex)
{
    Messagebox.Show(e.Message)
}
```

This class offers much of the same information as the normal Exception class, such as an exception message and source. But it also offers the capability to trap change conflict exceptions and, when used with the RefreshMode and ConflictMode enumerations, lets developers handle conflicts properly.

RefreshMode

The RefreshMode enumeration lets you define how your application should handle optimistic concurrency conflicts. The DataContext class has a Refresh method that refreshes the object state with the original data in the database. The enumeration tells Refresh what to do in case of a conflict.

RefreshMode has three values:

- ❏ KeepChanges—Tells Refresh to keep the current changed values in the object but updates the other values with the data from the database.

- ❏ KeepCurrentValues—Tells Refresh to replace the current object values with values from the database.

- ❏ OverwriteCurrentValues—Tells Refresh to override all of the current object values with the values from the database.

An example from earlier in the chapter illustrates the use of RefreshMode as well as the ConflictMode enumeration and ChangeConflictException class. The highlighted lines point out the pertinent code.

```
try
{
    var conQuery =
        from con in db.Contacts
        where con.FirstName == "Scott"
        select con;

    // there are 15 Scott's in the table, so 15 changes should be made
    foreach (Contact cont in conQuery)
    {
        cont.MiddleName = "L";
        cont.NameStyle = 1;
    }

    db.SubmitChanges(ConflictMode.ContinueOnConflict);

    textBox1.Text = "Contacts modified successfully";

}

catch (ChangeConflictException ex)
{
    foreach (ObjectChangeConflict oc in db.ChangeConflicts)
    {
        oc.Resolve(RefreshMode.KeepCurrentValues);
    }
}
```

You also have at your disposal the `MemberChangeConflict` class that, when used with the `ObjectChange-Conflict` class, enables you to iterate through the individual conflict members (database value/columns that have been updated since the client application last accessed it).

```
foreach (ObjectChangeConflict oc in db.ChangeConflicts)
{
    foreach(MemberChangeConflict mc in oc.MemberConflicts)
    {
        //
    }
}
```

The `MemberChangeConflict` class gives you access to the original value, the current value, and the database. For example:

```
mc.CurrentValue;
mc.OriginalValue;
mc.DatabaseValue;
```

With this information, you have all the data you need to effectively decide how you want to handle conflicts.

Utilizing Transactions

LINQ to SQL supports three models of transactions:

- ❑ Explicit local
- ❑ Implicit
- ❑ Explicit distributable

The difference between these types of transactions is how the transactions are created (explicitly or implicitly) and what LINQ to SQL does with the call.

In an explicit local transaction, you are responsible for committing and rolling back the transaction. The connection of the transaction must match the connection used by the DataContext; otherwise, an exception is thrown. If the Transaction property of the DataContext class is set to an IDbTransaction, then SubmitChanges method, when called, will use that transaction for all database operations.

In an implicit transaction, LINQ to SQL looks for two things—if the operation call is within the scope of a transaction, and if the Transaction property of the DataContext class is set to a user-started local IDbTransaction transaction. When SubmitChanges is called, these two checks are performed. SubmitChanges uses the first one it finds. If neither is present, an explicit local transaction is started. In an implicit transaction, the database engine automatically starts a new transaction after the current transaction is committed or rolled back. The user has to either commit or rollback each transaction.

An explicit distributable transaction is one in which the SubmitChanges method looks to see if the operation call is within the scope of a transaction. If LINQ to SQL determines that a call is in the scope of a transaction, a new transaction is not created. As with an explicit transaction, the user is responsible for the creation, committing, and disposing of the transaction.

The following examples illustrate a couple of these transaction modes. In the first example, a specific transaction scope is created and several operation calls are executed within this scope. Because a transaction scope is used within a using statement, a specific commit or rollback is not necessary. In this example, a TransactionScope is created and several insert operations are performed and the SubmitChanges method is called. The TransactionScope class, part of the System.Transactions namespace, marks a block of code as transactional by implicitly enlisting connections within its transaction. As discussed earlier, an implicit transaction must be manually committed or rolled back by the user/-application.

The following example explicitly creates a transaction using the TransactionScope class to mark a block of code as included in a transaction:

```
AdventureWorks db = new AdventureWorks("Integrated Security=sspi");
try
{
    using (TransactionScope ts = new TransactionScope())
    {
        Contact con = new Contact();
        con.FirstName = "Scott";
```

```
            con.LastName = "Klein";
            con.MiddleName = "L";
            con.NameStyle = 0;
            con.EmailPromotion = 1;
            con.EmailAddress = "ScottKlein@SqlXml.com";
            con.PasswordHash = "asdf";
            con.PasswordSalt = "qwer";
            con.Title = "Geek";

            db.Contacts.Add(con);

            Contact con1 = new Contact();
            con1.FirstName = "Horacio";
            con1.LastName = "Hornblower";
            con1.MiddleName = "T";
            con1.NameStyle = 0;
            con1.EmailPromotion = 1;
            con1.EmailAddress = "Hornblower@sailingrus.com";
            con1.PasswordHash = "asdf";
            con1.PasswordSalt = "qwer";
            con1.Title = "Captain";

            db.Contacts.Add(con1);
            db.SubmitChanges();

            textBox1.Text = "Transaction Successful!";

            ts.Complete();
            ts.Dispose();
        }
    }
    catch (Exception ex)
    {
        MessageBox.Show(ex.Message);
    }
```

Next is an example of an explicit local transaction. Here, the specific transaction connection is created and controlled, as well as the need to specifically commit and/or roll back the transaction. Like the first example, the SubmitChanges method is called and executed within the same transaction scope:

```
db.Connection.Open();
db.Transaction = db.Connection.BeginTransaction();
Contact con = new Contact();
con.FirstName = "Scott";
con.LastName = "Klein";
con.MiddleName = "L";
con.NameStyle = 0;
con.EmailPromotion = 1;
con.EmailAddress = "ScottKlein@SqlXml.com";
con.PasswordHash = "asdf";
con.PasswordSalt = "qwer";
con.Title = "Geek";

db.Contacts.Add(con);
```

```
Contact con1 = new Contact();
con1.FirstName = "Horacio";
con1.LastName = "Hornblower";
con1.MiddleName = "T";
con1.NameStyle = 0;
con1.EmailPromotion = 1;
con1.EmailAddress = "Hornblower@sailingrus.com";
con1.PasswordHash = "asdf";
con1.PasswordSalt = "qwer";
con1.Title = "Captain";

db.Contacts.Add(con1);

db.SubmitChanges();

textBox1.Text = "Transaction Successful!";

db.Transaction.Commit();
db.Transaction.Dispose();
db.Connection.Close();
```

The `TransactionScope` class lets you "bracket" your submissions to the database. "Bracketing" means to make a block of code transactional. The `TransactionScope` class makes it easy to "bracket."

The recommendation for using transactions is to implicitly create transactions using the `Transaction-Scope` class. The benefit of implicitly creating them is that the encompassing transaction context is automatically managed. This is typically called an ambient transaction, and is defined as the transaction in which your code is currently executing.

What is cool about using the `TransactionScope` is that the transaction manager determines the type of transaction to use. The decision is based on two things: whether there is an existing transaction, and the value of the `TransactionScopeOption` parameter in the `TransactionScope` constructor.

The `TransactionScopeOption` is an enumeration that provides additional options for creating a transaction scope. It has the following member values:

❏   `Required`   A transaction is required. A current transaction is used if one already exists; otherwise, a new transaction is created. This is the default value.

❏   `RequiredNew`—A new transaction is always created.

❏   `Suppress`—The current transaction context is suppressed when creating the scope.

Once the `TransactionScope` picks a transaction type, it always uses that transaction.

Summary

Sometimes working with a new technology can be intimidating and overwhelming. This need not be the case with LINQ to SQL and entities. LINQ to SQL is flexible and powerful yet easy to use, as this chapter showed, even when dealing with more complex topics.

This chapter tackled transactions and concurrency conflicts. First, you saw how to track changes to the entity object. (Knowing the state of your object and tracking its changes will come in handy.) Then you explored inserting, updating, and deleting data via LINQ to SQL entities.

LINQ to SQL has great support for optimistic concurrency, and this chapter focused on several features that will help you detect and appropriately handle concurrency conflicts, such as the `ConflictMode` and `ChangeConflictExpeption`.

14

LINQ to DataSet

Most, if not all, .NET developers are familiar with the concept of a DataSet because it is one of the most used components of ADO.NET. In simple terms, DataSets are objects that contain internal data tables where data is temporarily stored and is available for use by your application. DataSets are, in essence, a local in-memory cache of data that is typically retrieved from a database. This cache lets you work in a disconnected mode, providing the capability to make changes to the data within the DataSet, track those changes, and save those changes back to the database when the application reconnects.

A DataSet is a representation of the tables and relationships found in the database, exposing a hierarchical object model made of all the objects such as tables, rows, columns, constraints, and relationships. Much of the functionality that populates the DataSet and saves the changes within the DataSet back to the database is found in ADO.NET.

The DataSet itself is extremely flexible and powerful. It provides the capability for applications to efficiently work with a subset of data found in a database and to manipulate the data as needed by the application, all while in a disconnected state, and then usher the changes back to the database.

Yet, with all that flexibility there has not been, up to this point, a means or method for querying data contained within a DataSet (there are a few methods on the DataTable class which will be discussed below). This is where LINQ and LINQ to DataSets come in. With the querying power of LINQ, LINQ to DataSets provides a full set of query capabilities for a developer to quickly and easily query the contents of a DataSet.

This chapter deals specifically with how to work with LINQ to DataSets, and covers the following topics:

- ❑ Loading data into a DataSet
- ❑ Querying DataSets with LINQ to DataSet
- ❑ Data binding
- ❑ Comparing rows in DataSets

Overview of LINQ to DataSet

Perhaps the only thing that ADO.NET DataSets lack when it comes to functionality is an adequate query capability. DataSets do everything else quite well, but from a query perspective, they are limited. Sure, they have the `Select`, `GetParentRow`, and `GetChildRows` methods, but these provide only basic querying features.

Microsoft recognized these shortcomings and has provided the capability to query the contents of a DataSet through LINQ to DataSet. LINQ to DataSet utilizes the query features of LINQ, letting you create queries in your programming language and eliminating the need to place query string literals in your code. In essence, you get all the features and benefits of LINQ combined with all the features and benefits of DataSets, such as IntelliSense, syntax checking, and static typing. For instance, how many times have you had to run and rerun your application to test your inline string query because your syntax was incorrect? With LINQ to DataSets, you know before your application ever runs whether your query will execute.

Initially, Microsoft was looking at several options to give developers to populate DataSets using LINQ to SQL. However, at the time of this writing, the only option available is to use the DataAdapter class. That is not to say that other methods won't be added later, but for now, the DataAdapter class is your only option.

LINQ to SQL also adds several specific extensions to the DataSet that enable you to access `DataRow` objects. Just as important, there are additional things you need to do to your Visual Studio project to enable LINQ to DataSet functionality.

The following section shows you how to create a LINQ to DataSet project in Visual Studio, and the rest of this chapter explains how to load data into a DataSet and then how to query that DataSet using LINQ to DataSet.

Creating a LINQ to DataSet Project

A LINQ to DataSet project is created the same way any other normal project is created. The difference is that you have to include a few additional references and `using` directives. Fire up Visual Studio 2008 and create a new C# Windows project. Make sure that you target .NET Framework version 3.5.

By default, Visual Studio should include all the necessary references you need to work with LINQ and LINQ to DataSet. But if you are upgrading an existing project from an earlier version of Visual Studio, or even a project created in an early beta of Visual Studio, you will need to manually add the necessary references.

At a minimum, a LINQ to DataSet project needs a reference to the `System.Core` namespace and the `System.Data.DataSetExtensions` namespace. These two namespaces are in addition to the standard `System.Data.Linq` and `System.Data` namespaces that you are used to having in your project. Figure 14-1 shows the necessary references needed to work with LINQ to DataSet.

Once you have the necessary references in place, you need to make sure that you have included the appropriate `using` directives:

```
using System;
using System.Data.Common;
using System.Data.SqlClient;
using System.Collections.Generic;
using System.ComponentModel;
using System.Data;
using System.Drawing;
using System.Data.Linq;
using System.Text;
using System.Windows.Forms;
```

Then you are ready to go.

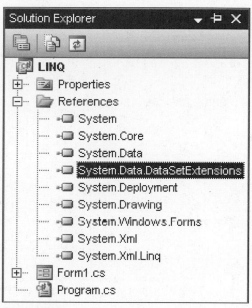

Figure 14-1

Loading Data into a DataSet

Before you can query a DataSet, it must be populated with data. The most popular way to do that is to use the DataAdapter class to retrieve the data from the database. This section shows via example how to populate a DataSet using the DataAdapter class so that it can later be queried with LINQ to DataSet.

Using the DataAdapater

If you have done any database development with .NET, you are intimately familiar with how to populate a DataSet using SqlDataAdapter. Here's an example:

```
try
{
    int salesPersonID = Convert.ToInt32(textBox1.Text);

    DataSet ds = new DataSet();

    string connectionInfo = "Data Source=avalonserver;Initial Catalog=AdventureWorks;
Integrated Security=true";

    SqlDataAdapter da = new SqlDataAdapter(
        "SELECT SalesOrderID, OrderDate, " +
    "SalesOrderNumber, SalesPersonID, ContactID, TotalDue " +
    "FROM sales.salesorderheader " +
    "WHERE SalesPersonID = @ID; " +

    "SELECT od.SalesOrderID, od.SalesOrderDetailID, od.OrderQty, " +
    "od.ProductID, od.UnitPrice, od.LineTotal " +
    "FROM sales.salesorderdetail od " +
    "INNER JOIN Sales.SalesOrderHeader oh ON od.SalesOrderID = oh.SalesOrderID " +
    "WHERE oh.SalesPersonID = @ID; ", connectionInfo);

    da.SelectCommand.Parameters.AddWithValue("@ID", salesPersonID);
    da.TableMappings.Add("Table", "SalesOrderHeader");
    da.TableMappings.Add("Table1", "SalesOrderDetail");

    da.Fill(ds);

    DataTable header = ds.Tables["SalesOrderHeader"];
    DataTable detail = ds.Tables["SalesOrderDetail"];
    DataRelation dr = new DataRelation("OrderHeaderDetail",
        header.Columns["SalesOrderID"],
        detail.Columns["SalesOrderID"], true);

    ds.Relations.Add(dr);

    textBox2.Text = ds.Tables[0].Rows.Count.ToString();
    textBox3.Text = ds.Tables[1].Rows.Count.ToString();

}
catch (Exception ex)
{
    MessageBox.Show(ex.Message);
}
```

First, you define a DataSet, followed by defining a connection to the database from which the data will be pulled to populate the DataSet. Then you define a data adapter using several T-SQL statements from which to query the database and populate the DataSet. Two data tables are defined and created within the data adapter to hold the returned data. Next, the data adapter is filled with the data requested from the two T-SQL statements. Last, a relationship is created between the two data tables.

At this point, the DataSet contains all the order header and order detail records that were requested. The data can now be queried, modified, updated, and sent back to the original database. The purpose of this example was to illustrate how to populate a DataSet using a `DataAdapter`. Now that the DataSet contains data, it can now be queried using LINQ to DataSet.

LINQ to DataSet Queries

Once DataSets are populated, they can be queried. That's where LINQ to DataSets comes in. Querying DataSets using LINQ to DataSet is not really that different from other LINQ queries you have worked with throughout this book. There are basically two options when writing LINQ to DataSet queries: use query expression syntax or method-based syntax. (Both query syntax and method syntax were discussed in Chapter 3.)

As a refresher, query expressions use declarative query syntax, enabling developers to write queries in "SQL-like" language. The benefit is that you can create complex queries with minimal code. The .NET CLR cannot read query expressions, so at compile time query expressions are translated to method calls, commonly known as standard query operators.

Method syntax, on the other hand, provides direct access to the LINQ operator methods using lambda expressions as parameters.

You can use either of these methods. The key to querying DataSets with LINQ to DataSet is that you are querying an enumeration of `DataRow` objects. This has many benefits, including the capability to use all of the `DataRow` class members in your LINQ queries.

Querying a Single Table

The following example uses a `DataAdapter` to populate a DataSet with sales order header information for a particular salesperson. A LINQ query expression is then defined and used to query the DataSet for all orders for the year 2003.

```
try
{
    int salesPersonID = Convert.ToInt32(textBox3.Text);

    DataSet ds = new DataSet();

    string connectionInfo = "Data Source=avalonserver;Initial Catalog=AdventureWorks;
Integrated Security=true";

    SqlDataAdapter da = new SqlDataAdapter(
        "SELECT SalesOrderID, OrderDate, " +
    "SalesOrderNumber, SalesPersonID, ContactID, TotalDue " +
    "FROM sales.salesorderheader " +
    "WHERE SalesPersonID = @ID; ", connectionInfo);

    da.SelectCommand.Parameters.AddWithValue("@ID", salesPersonID);
    da.TableMappings.Add("Table", "SalesOrderHeader");

    da.Fill(ds);

    DataTable header = ds.Tables["SalesOrderHeader"];

    textBox1.Text = ds.Tables[0].Rows.Count.ToString();

    var orderHeader = from oh in header.AsEnumerable()
```

```
                          where oh.Field<DateTime>("OrderDate").Year == 2003
                          select new {SalesOrderID = oh.Field<int>("SalesOrderID"),
                                  SalesOrderNumber = oh.Field<string>("SalesOrderNumber"),
                                  OrderDate = oh.Field<DateTime>("OrderDate"),
                                  Total = oh.Field<decimal>("TotalDue")};

            foreach (var order in orderHeader)
            {
                listBox1.Items.Add(order.SalesOrderID + "   " +
                    order.SalesOrderNumber + "   " +
                    order.OrderDate + "   " +
                    order.Total);
            }
        }
        catch (Exception ex)
        {
            MessageBox.Show(ex.Message);
        }
```

Notice in the query that the DataSet is not a typed DataSet because the Field method is used to access the column values of the DataRow.

Figure 14-2 shows the results of running this code.

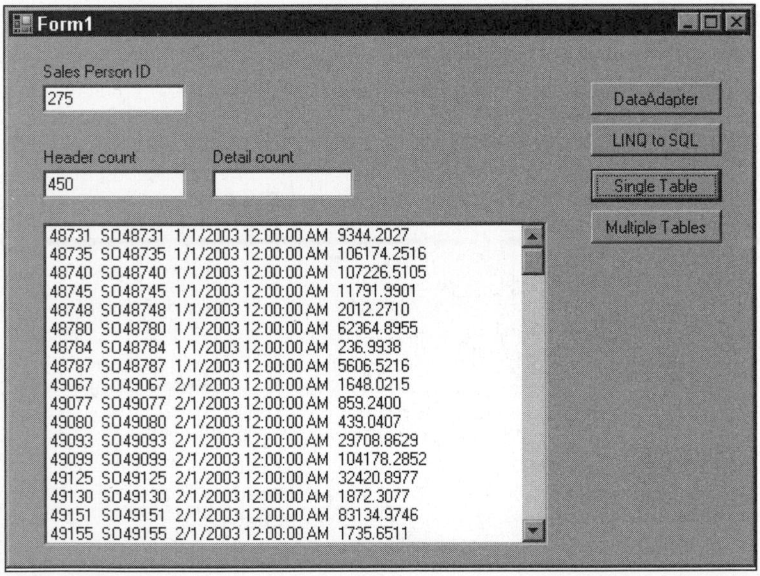

Figure 14-2

As you can see, querying a single table within a DataSet is quite simple, but what if there were multiple tables within the DataSet?

Querying across Multiple Tables

Cross-table queries in LINQ to DataSet is accomplished by using a join, an association of data source with a secondary data source in which the two data sources share a common attribute. LINQ makes object-oriented relationship navigation easy because each object has a property that references another object.

However, external tables (such as those in a DataSet) do not have built-in relationships, which makes relationship navigation difficult.

Luckily, the LINQ join operator can be used to link common attributes from each data source.

The following example illustrates how to query a DataSet that has multiple tables. A DataAdapter is created and used to populate a DataSet with sales order header information and corresponding sales order detail information for a particular SalesPersonID within the SalesOrderHeader table. A relationship is defined to link the two tables together within the DataSet.

A LINQ query expression is then defined and used to query the DataSet for all orders for the year 2003. The query uses two columns from the SalesOrderDetail table as well as four columns from the SalesOrderHeader table to display in the results.

```
try
{
    int salesPersonID = Convert.ToInt32(textBox3.Text);

    DataSet ds = new DataSet();

    string connectionInfo = "Data Source=avalonserver;Initial Catalog=AdventureWorks;
Integrated Security=true";

    SqlDataAdapter da = new SqlDataAdapter(
        "SELECT SalesOrderID, OrderDate, " +
    "SalesOrderNumber, SalesPersonID, ContactID, TotalDue " +
    "FROM sales.salesorderheader " +
    "WHERE SalesPersonID = @ID; " +

    "SELECT od.SalesOrderID, od.SalesOrderDetailID, od.OrderQty, " +
    "od.ProductID, od.UnitPrice, od.LineTotal " +
    "FROM sales.salesorderdetail od " +
    "INNER JOIN Sales.SalesOrderHeader oh ON od.SalesOrderID = oh.SalesOrderID " +
    "WHERE oh.SalesPersonID = @ID; ", connectionInfo);

    da.SelectCommand.Parameters.AddWithValue("@ID", salesPersonID);
    da.TableMappings.Add("Table", "SalesOrderHeader");
    da.TableMappings.Add("Table1", "SalesOrderDetail");

    da.Fill(ds);

    DataTable header = ds.Tables["SalesOrderHeader"];
    DataTable detail = ds.Tables["SalesOrderDetail"];
        DataRelation  dr  =  new  DataRelation("OrderHeaderDetail",  header.Columns
["SalesOrderID"], detail.Columns["SalesOrderID"], true);
```

```
        ds.Relations.Add(dr);

        textBox1.Text = ds.Tables[0].Rows.Count.ToString();
        textBox2.Text = ds.Tables[1].Rows.Count.ToString();

        var orderHeader = from oh in header.AsEnumerable()
                          join od in detail.AsEnumerable()
                          on oh.Field<int>("SalesOrderID")
                          equals od.Field<int>("SalesOrderID")
                          where oh.Field<DateTime>("OrderDate").Year == 2003
                          select new
                          {
                              SalesOrderID = oh.Field<int>("SalesOrderID"),
                              OrderQuantity = od.Field<Int16>("OrderQty"),
                              ProductID = od.Field<int>("ProductID"),
                              SalesOrderNumber = oh.Field<string>("SalesOrderNumber"),
                              OrderDate = oh.Field<DateTime>("OrderDate"),
                              Total = oh.Field<decimal>("TotalDue")
                          };

        foreach (var order in orderHeader)
        {
            listBox1.Items.Add(order.SalesOrderID + "   " +
                order.SalesOrderNumber + "   " +
                order.ProductID + "   " +
                order.OrderQuantity + "   " +
                order.OrderDate + "   " +
                order.Total);
        }

    }
    catch (Exception ex)
    {
        MessageBox.Show(ex.Message);
    }
```

Just as in the previous example, the DataSet is not a typed DataSet because the schema of the DataSet is not known at design time and the `Field` method is used to access the column values.

Figure 14-3 shows the results of running this code.
Instead of using untyped DataSets, the other option is to query a typed DataSet.

Typed DataSets

If you know the schema of the DataSet during the design of the application, it's best to use a typed DataSet. A typed DataSet is strongly typed, giving you can access to all the tables and columns by name instead using the `Field` method shown in the two preceding examples. A typed DataSet inherits from the `DataSet` class, providing access to all of the methods, properties, and events that a normal DataSet has.

Typed DataSets can be created by using the Data Source Configuration Wizard or the DataSet Designer. Both are in Visual Studio.

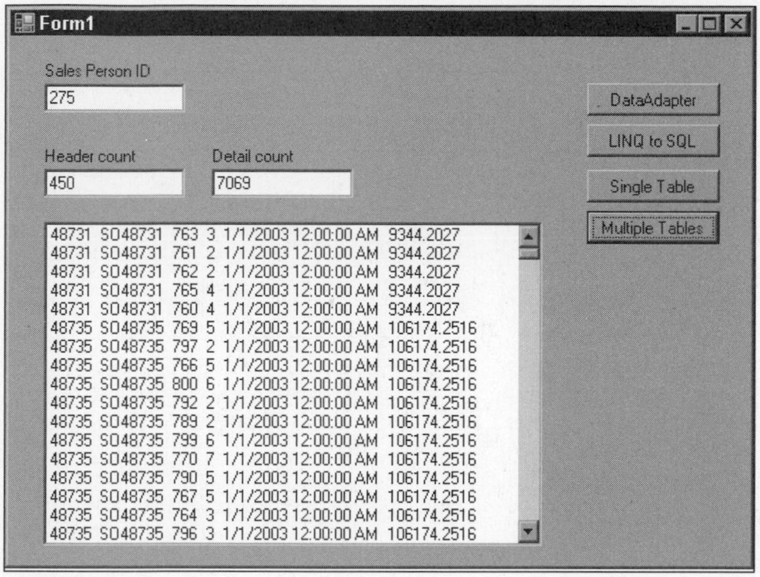

Figure 14-3

LINQ to DataSet supports the querying of typed DataSets, so you can access the table and column names by name. Just as important, columns are provided as the correct type, eliminating type mismatch errors. The following code is an example of querying a typed DataSet:

```
var orderHeader = from oh in header.AsEnumerable()
                  join od in detail.AsEnumerable()
                  on oh.SalesOrderID
                  equals od.SalesOrderID
                  where oh.OrderDate == 2003
                  select new
                  {
                      SalesOrderID = oh.SalesOrderID,
                      OrderQuantity = od.OrderQty,
                      ProductID = od.ProductID,
                      SalesOrderNumber = oh.SalesOrderNumber,
                      OrderDate = oh.OrderDate,
                      Total = oh.TotalDue
                  };
```

A typed DataSet can be queried just like any other DataSet using LINQ to DataSet.

Data Binding

Data binding is the act of creating a link or connection between the user interface and the data. It's been around for quite a while and is not specific to LINQ to DataSet. The concept behind data binding is that a user interface component can be *bound* to its corresponding field or column in the data layer such that when the user changes the value in the user interface, the change is automatically reflected in the data layer or database.

LINQ to SQL lets you bind data to many of the common controls such as combo boxes, grid controls, as well as a DataView. A DataView represents a customizable and bindable view of a DataTable, providing searching, sorting, editing, and filtering capabilities. Once the DataView is created, it can be bound to UI controls such as a DataGrid.

Keep in mind that a LINQ to DataSet query returns a DataRow enumeration, which is difficult to bind. The CopyToDataTable method is valuable in those instances. CopyToDataTable returns a DataTable that contains copies of the DataRow objects. The method is part of the DataTable-Extensions class and takes an IEnumerable(Of T) object, where a parameter T is a generic DataRow.

The following example populates DataSet with data from the SalesOrderHeader table and then queries using a LINQ to DataSet query. The query returns an enumeration of DataRow objects that is used to populate a DataTable via the CopyToDataTable method. Once the DataTable is populated, a new DataView is created and populated with the DataTable. The DataView is then assigned to the DataSource property of a DataGridView.

```csharp
try
{
    int salesPersonID = Convert.ToInt32(textBox3.Text);

    DataSet ds = new DataSet();

    string connectionInfo = "Data Source=avalonserver;Initial Catalog=AdventureWorks;
Integrated Security=true";

    SqlDataAdapter da = new SqlDataAdapter(
        "SELECT SalesOrderID, OrderDate, " +
    "SalesOrderNumber, SalesPersonID, ContactID, TotalDue " +
    "FROM sales.salesorderheader " +
    "WHERE SalesPersonID = @ID; ", connectionInfo);

    da.SelectCommand.Parameters.AddWithValue("@ID", salesPersonID);
    da.TableMappings.Add("Table", "SalesOrderHeader");

    da.Fill(ds);

    DataTable header = ds.Tables["SalesOrderHeader"];

    textBox1.Text = ds.Tables[0].Rows.Count.ToString();

    IEnumerable<DataRow> orderHeader =
                        from oh in header.AsEnumerable()
                        where oh.Field<DateTime>("OrderDate").Year == 2003
                        select oh;

    DataTable dt = orderHeader.CopyToDataTable<DataRow>();

    DataView dv = new DataView(dt);
    dataGridView1.DataSource = dv;

}
```

```
catch (Exception ex)
{
    MessageBox.Show(ex.Message);
}
```

You could just have easily set the `DataSource` of the `DataGridView` to the `DataTable`, as follows:

```
dataGridView1.DataSource = dt;
```

However, the `DataView` provides capabilities such as sorting and filtering the data stored in a `DataTable`. For example, you can filter the data by state of the row or via a filter expression.

You can also implicitly bind data to controls by implementing the IListSource interface. This interface provides an object the ability to return a list that is bindable to a data source.

For example, you can do the following:

```
var query =
    (from c in contact
    where c.FirstName.StartsWith("S")
    && c.LastName.StartsWith("K")
    orderby c.LastName
    select c);

dataGrid1.DataSource = query;
```

Likewise, you can bind data to a data source as follows (given the same query):

```
BindingSource bindsrc = new BindingSource();
bindsrc.DataSource = query;
dataGrid1.DataSource = bndsrc;
```

Implicit binding is available due to the fact that the Table<T> and DataQuery<T> classes have been updated to implement the IListSource interface.

Comparing DataRows

The last topic to be discussed in this chapter is the ability to use LINQ to DataSet to compare rows. As you learned in the early chapters of this book, LINQ provides several operators—`Distinct`, `Union`, `Intersect`, and `Except`—that provide comparison capabilities. These set operators compare source elements, checking for equality.

Elements can be compared for equality by calling the operators' `GetHashCode` and `Equals` methods. However, one of the things added to LINQ to DataSet is the `DataRowComparer` class. This class is used to compare two row values for equality using value-based comparison. It overcomes the need to do reference comparisons by executing value comparisons on the `DataRow` itself, enabling you to use this class against set operators.

Using the `DataRowComparer` class is preferable to using the `GetHashCode` and `Equals` methods because these operations perform reference comparisons, which is not ideal for set operations over tabular data.

One of the key things to remember about the `DataRowComparer` class is that it cannot be instantiated directly. The correct way to use this class is to use the `Default` property, which returns an instance of the class. You then use the `Equals` method to compare two `DataRow` objects. The two objects are used as parameters to the `Equals` method, which returns `true` if the two rows are equal, and `false` if they are not.

This type of comparison is illustrated in the following code. A DataSet is populated, and then two rows are identified for comparison. An instance of the `DataRowComparer` is then created, at which point the `Equals` method is called, passing the two rows as parameters for comparison. If the first row is the same as the second row, a message box displays a message indicating that they are equal; otherwise, a message box displays stating they are not equal.

```
try
{
    int salesPersonID = Convert.ToInt32(textBox3.Text);

    DataSet ds = new DataSet();

    string connectionInfo = "Data Source=avalonserver;Initial
        Catalog=AdventureWorks;Integrated Security=true";

    SqlDataAdapter da = new SqlDataAdapter(
        "SELECT SalesOrderID, OrderDate, " +
    "SalesOrderNumber, SalesPersonID, ContactID, TotalDue " +
    "FROM sales.salesorderheader " +
    "WHERE SalesPersonID = @ID; ", connectionInfo);

    da.SelectCommand.Parameters.AddWithValue("@ID", salesPersonID);
    da.TableMappings.Add("Table", "SalesOrderHeader");

    da.Fill(ds);

    DataTable header = ds.Tables["SalesOrderHeader"];

    DataRow first = (DataRow)header.Rows[0];
    DataRow second = (DataRow)header.Rows[1];

    IEqualityComparer<DataRow> comp = DataRowComparer.Default;

    bool isEqual = comp.Equals(first, second);
    if (isEqual)
        MessageBox.Show("they are equal");
    else
        MessageBox.Show("they are not equal");
}
catch (Exception ex)
{
    MessageBox.Show(ex.Message);
}
```

When you run this example, you get a message box stating that the rows are not equal. This is a simple example that compared the first row with the second row in the DataSet. This next example uses one of the set operators to determine equality.

```
try
{
    dataGridView1.Visible = false;
    listBox1.Visible = true;

    int salesPersonID = Convert.ToInt32(textBox3.Text);

    DataSet ds = new DataSet();

    string connectionInfo = "Data Source=avalonserver;Initial
        Catalog=AdventureWorks;Integrated Security=true";

    SqlDataAdapter da = new SqlDataAdapter(
        "SELECT SalesOrderID, OrderDate, " +
    "SalesOrderNumber, SalesPersonID, ContactID, TotalDue, CustomerID " +
    "FROM sales.salesorderheader " +
    "WHERE SalesPersonID = @ID; ", connectionInfo);

    da.SelectCommand.Parameters.AddWithValue("@ID", salesPersonID);
    da.TableMappings.Add("Table", "SalesOrderHeader");

    da.Fill(ds);

    DataTable header = ds.Tables["SalesOrderHeader"];

    IEnumerable<DataRow> query1 =
        from oh in header.AsEnumerable()
        where oh.Field<int>("SalesPersonID") == 288
        select oh;

    IEnumerable<DataRow> query2 =
        from oh2 in header.AsEnumerable()
        where oh2.Field<int>("CustomerID") == 555
        select oh2;

    DataTable dt1 = query1.CopyToDataTable();
    DataTable dt2 = query2.CopyToDataTable();

    var sales = dt1.AsEnumerable().Intersect(dt2.AsEnumerable(),
        DataRowComparer.Default);

    foreach (DataRow dr in sales)
    {
        listBox1.Items.Add(dr["SalesOrderID"] + "   " +
            dr["OrderDate"] + "   " + dr["SalesOrderNumber"] + "   " +
            dr["TotalDue"]);
    }

}
catch (Exception ex)
{
    MessageBox.Show(ex.Message);
}
```

In this example, the DataSet is filled with all records from the `SalesOrderHeader` table where the `SalesPersonID` = 288. From there, two tables are generated that contain a subset of that data. The first table contains those records from the DataSet whose `ContactID` = 30. The second table contains those records from the DataSet whose `CustomerID` = 555. The `Intersect` comparison operator is then used to return those records that are the same in each table. Those records are displayed in the list box.

When you run this example, the output should display three records, as shown Figure 14-4.

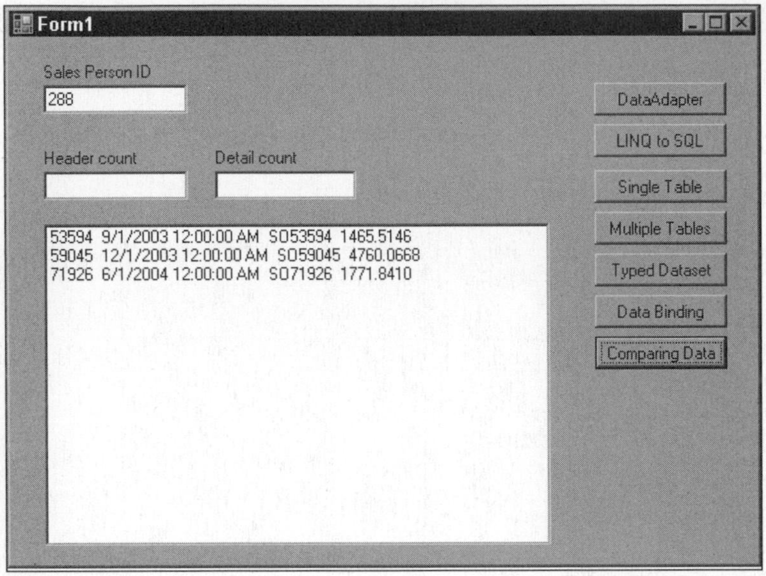

Figure 14-4

These comparison operators make it easy to compare elements and do set operations against data contained within DataSets. As you can see, working with DataSets with LINQ to DataSet is quite simple, whether you are comparing data, doing data binding, or just querying DataSets.

Summary

In ADO.NET programming, the DataSet is probably one of most commonly used components because of the functionality it provides when dealing with data caching and disconnected data manipulation. This chapter focused on the LINQ to DataSet features, the capability to query data cached in a DataSet object. These capabilities enable Visual Studio and developers to work more efficiently due to the benefits that the Visual Studio IDE provides, such as compile-time syntax checking, IntelliSense, and support for LINQ.

In this chapter, you got an overview of LINQ to DataSet and a look at the features and benefits that LINQ to DataSet provides. You also examined the steps necessary to create a LINQ to Dataset project in Visual Studio, and how to load data into a DataSet using the familiar `SqlDataAdapter` class as well as new approach using LINQ to SQL.

The heart of the chapter tackled querying DataSets, and you learned how LINQ to DataSet also supports data binding using DataSets. Finally, you saw how LINQ to DataSet supports the LINQ set operators to effectively compare source elements within a DataSet, whether they are in the same table or multiple tables within the DataSet.

So far, you've done everything in this book manually, such as create LINQ to SQL entity classes. The next chapter discusses several tools that make working with LINQ even simpler.

15

Advanced LINQ to SQL Topics

Visual Studio 2008 provides several tools to help facilitate the creation of entity classes and their mapping to relational objects in a database. These tools also help define the entity associations (database relationships) that the entity classes will use when working with two or more tables.

In essence, these tools help create an object model. The object model is defined within an application that will then be mapped to database objects. It is a fully functional object model, one that supports a mapping to stored procedures and user-defined functions as well as `DataContext` methods for data transport.

Equally important is the discussion of using LINQ to SQL in a multi-tier environment and other topics, such as external mapping with LINQ to SQL and entity classes.

Therefore, this chapter will discuss the following:

❑ Object Relational Designer

❑ SQL Metal tool

❑ External mapping

❑ Multi-tier operations

Object Relational Designer

The O/R Designer (Object Relational Designer) is a tool that provides the ability to create and manage LINQ to SQL entity classes, their associated relationships, and mappings through a graphical user interface. Through the O/R Designer you create an object model that maps entity classes within your application to objects within your database, such as tables and stored procedures. Instead of creating and defining these mappings by hand as you have done in previous chapters, the O/R Designer provides a graphical user interface in which you can accomplish these tasks.

Creating and Opening the O/R Designer

The Object Relational Designer is created by adding a specific file type to your Visual Studio project. Open Visual Studio, and create a new C# Windows project for .NET Framework 3.5. When the project is created, right-click on the project and select Add ➪ New Item from the context menu. In the Add New Item dialog, select the Data node under Categories, and then select the LINQ to SQL Classes under Templates, as shown in Figure 15-1.

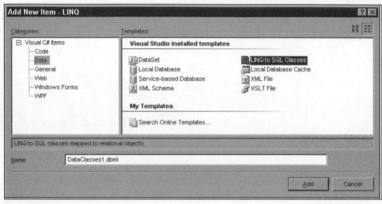

Figure 15-1

The LINQ to SQL classes are what define the Data (Entity) classes, such as the associations, mappings, and DataContext methods.

Provide a name for the LINQ to SQL class (this example uses the name AdventureWorksSales.dbml), and click the Add button. At this point, several files are added to the project:

❑ The .dbml file—The actual O/R Designer file.

❑ The .layout file—Contains the layout of the designer as you drag and drop objects onto it.

❑ The .cs file—Contains the designer code, such as the extensibility code definitions.

Figure 15-2 shows what the project should look like after the O/R Designer has been added to your project.

At this point the DataContext can be configured.

Creating/Configuring the DataContext

When you add the O/R Designer by adding the LINQ to SQL Classes item to your project, the designer opens in design mode automatically. Figure 15-3 shows what the O/R Designer looks like when it is first created. The O/R Designer design surface has two areas with which to work and design your data classes. The left pane is the Entities pane (or Entity Class pane), the main location where entity classes will be defined. The right pane is the Methods pane where DataContext methods are mapped to stored procedures and functions. The methods pane can be hidden; the entities pane cannot.

Figure 15-2

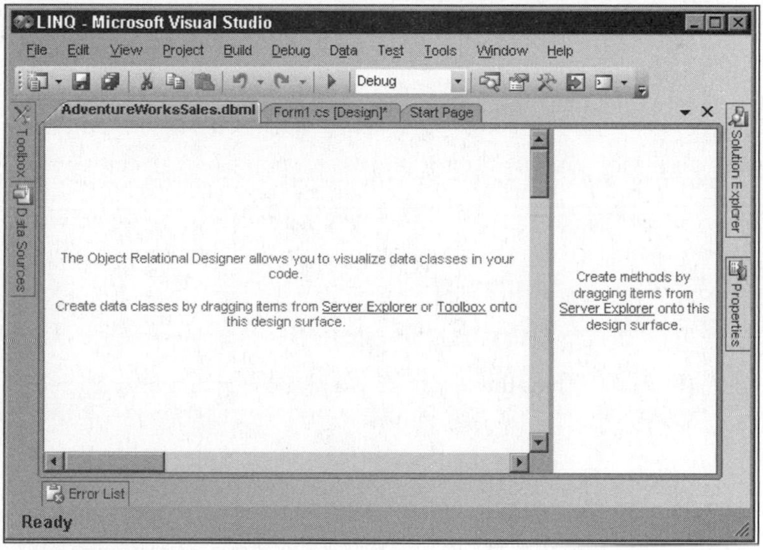

Figure 15-3

When the O/R Designer is first opened, it is empty of any objects, as Figure 15-3 shows. It represents an empty `DataContext` ready for configuration. Configuring the `DataContext` is as simple as dragging objects from the Server Explorer in Visual Studio to the Entities pane in the O/R Designer and setting the appropriate connection properties.

For example, the first time you drag a table from the Server Explorer to the Entities pane, you may receive a message (see Figure 15-4) asking if you want to save the connection information corresponding to this object and the Server Explorer Data Connection with the `DataContext` and the O/R Designer.

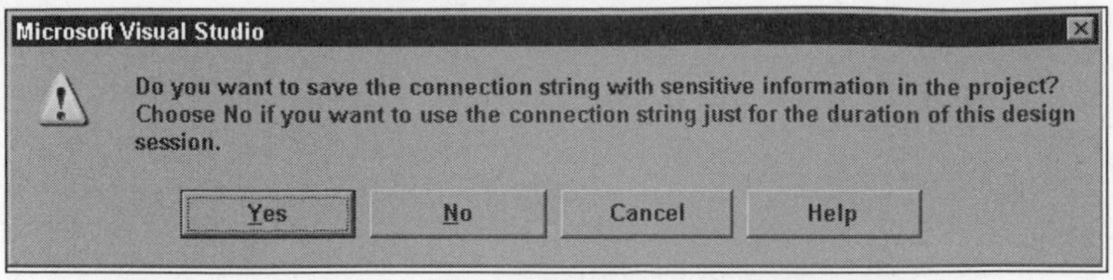

Figure 15-4

You get this message because the connection string used by select objects contains sensitive information. If you choose No, the connection string is stored as an application setting (except for the password) to be used only for the duration of the design session. Once the designer is closed, the connection information is no longer held.

Selecting Yes stores the connection string information as an application setting, such as the application configuration file. This is not secure because connection information is stored as plain text.

The connection information is obtained by making a connection in the Server Explorer window. From the View menu, select Server Explorer. In the Server Explorer window, you will see two nodes, one for Data Connections and one for Servers. Right-click the Data Connections node and select Add Connection. In the Add Connections dialog, enter the appropriate information to make a connection to your database server.

This connection information will be stored with the `DataContext` and O/R Designer. When you first drag an object from the Server Explorer onto the Entities pane, the information is used to provide the O/R Designer the necessary information that it needs to configure the `DataContext`.

The next section explains how to define entity classes that will be used to map to database tables and views, and you'll be dragging a table onto the designer to configure the `DataContext`.

Creating Entity Classes for Tables/View Mapping

When you drag a table from Server Explorer to the O/R Designer's Entities, you are creating an entity class that maps to a database table or view. Figure 15-5 shows what the O/R Designer looks like once you have dropped a table into that pane.

At this point you have created an entity class. The O/R Designer, behind the scenes, generates the appropriate classes and applies the appropriate LINQ to SQL attributes to those classes. This entity class now has all the appropriate properties that map the columns in the selected table. Also, the data connection information is provided to the designer and will be supplied to the `DataContext`.

These entity classes are updatable: They can save changes via the `SubmitChanges()` method of the `DataContext`.

Relationships between tables are also supported in the O/R Designer, and it is actually smart enough to pick them up automatically. For example, Figure 15-6 shows the defined relationship between the `SalesOrderHeader` and `SalesOrderDetail` when the `SalesOrderDetail` table is dropped onto the O/R Designer. Double-clicking the relationship line between the two tables opens the Association Editor dialog, which enables you to change the relationship (association) if necessary.

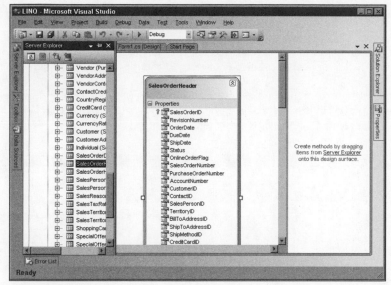

Figure 15-5

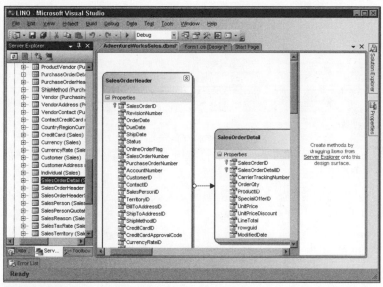

Figure 15-6

Keep in mind that the O/R Designer only reflects changes one way. That is, changes that you make via the designer are reflected in the code, but any code changes you make do not show up in the designer. This means that any code changes you make will be overwritten any time you make changes via the designer.

If you want to add code, read the section entitled "Extending O/R Designer-Generated Code" later in this chapter.

DataContext Mapping for Stored Procedures/Functions

DataContext methods are those methods of the DataContext class that run stored procedures and functions. In the context of the O/R Designer, the DataContext class is the LINQ to SQL class you just created; it acts as a channel between the database and the entity classes mapped to the database.

When a stored procedure or function is dragged from the Server Explorer and dropped onto the O/R Designer, it is displayed in the Methods pane, as shown in Figure 15-7. This pane lists all the DataContext methods you have created via the O/R Designer.

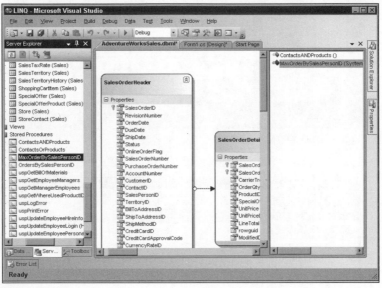

Figure 15-7

The return type of the generated DataContext method can depend on where you place the item in the O/R Designer:

❑ If you drop an item onto an existing entity class, the return type will be the type of that entity class for that DataContext method.

❑ If you drop an item onto an empty entity class or an empty area of the designer, the return type will be an auto-generated type for that DataContext method.

In other words, you can create DataContext methods that return auto-generated types by dragging a stored procedure onto an empty area of the O/R Designer. Likewise, you can create DataContext methods that return the type of the entity class by dropping a stored procedure on an existing entity class in the designer.

The return type of the DataContext method can be changed by opening the Properties window and changing the Return Type property for that method, as shown in Figure 15-8.

Once the DataContext method has been defined the method (stored procedure) can be called (which executes the stored procedure) passing the necessary parameters and return the data.

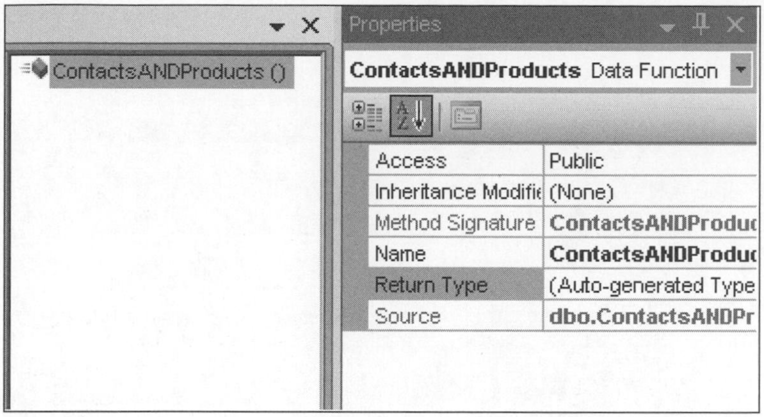

Figure 15-8

Calling Stored Procedures to Save Data Using Entity Classes

By default, the LINQ to SQL runtime handles the INSERT, UPDATE, and DELETE functions of an entity class. However, you can also use stored procedures to create DataContext methods to provide this functionality. These stored procedures can also be added to the O/R Designer as standard DataContext methods just like standard SELECT stored procedures.

Figure 15-9 shows the designer with the Properties page opened after clicking on the SalesOrderHeader entity in the entity class pane. Notice that the Properties page has Delete, Insert, and Update properties. The default value for these properties is Use Runtime.

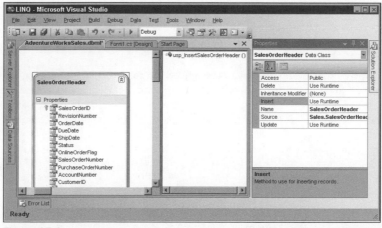

Figure 15-9

To change the default behavior and assign a stored procedure to perform the insert, update, or delete operation, drag and drop the stored procedure that performs the operation into the Methods pane on the designer. Next, click on the entity in the entity class pane of the designer, and on the Properties page, click the ellipsis button for the appropriate property (Delete, Insert, or Update) to the Configure Behavior dialog shown in Figure 15-10.

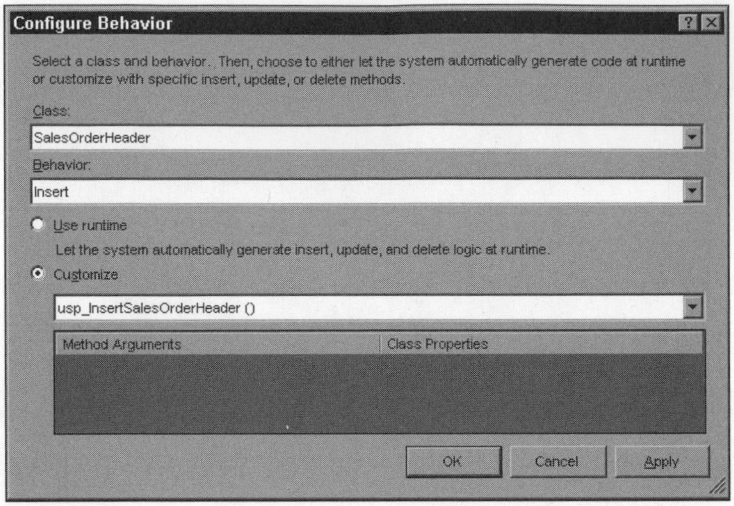

Figure 15-10

The Configure Behavior dialog enables you to override the default behavior by specifying the class in which to override the behavior, the type of behavior (Insert, Update, or Delete), and the method (stored procedure) to use to override the behavior. Select the Customize option to select the desired stored procedure (method), see the above figure. Once you have selected the appropriate information, click OK.

The Object Relational Designer currently supports a one-to-one (1:1) mapping relationship. It is a simple mapper, so complex mappings such as mapping an entity class to a joined table are not supported in this release.

Extending O/R Designer-Generated Code

LINQ to SQL realizes that there will always be a need for custom logic, so it provides a way to add validation logic to meet the demands of specific insert, update, and delete scenarios. The custom validation is provided by the capability to add a partial class, extending the `DataContext` class. The cool thing about this is that these custom methods are automatically called when the `SubmitChanges()` method is called.

When an entity is dropped onto the designer, partial classes are made available in which you can extend the validation logic. Figure 15-11 shows these partial class definitions within the `Extensibility Method Definitions` region.

You can easily add validation logic by implementing these classes. For example, to implement the custom Insert method, simply add the following code to the public partial class:

```
partial void InsertSalesOrderHeader(SalesOrderHeader instance)
{
    this.ExecuteDynamicInsert(instance);
}
```

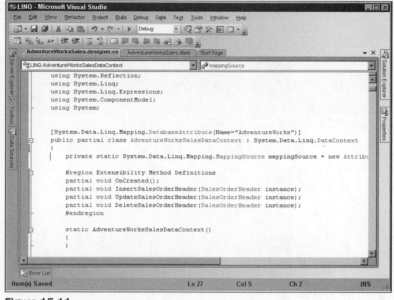

Figure 15-11

Notice that as you start typing, IntelliSense pops up and gives you the list of method definitions. Select the one you want and just add the appropriate custom validation logic to this method. Then add the appropriate call, such as the one shown in this example: `this.ExecuteDynamicInsert()`:

As stated before, these methods are automatically called when you call the `SubmitChanges()` method on your `DataContext`.

Figure 15-12

Pluralization of Classes in the O/R Designer

You might notice that as you drag-and-drop database objects onto the O/R Designer, the object names might change. This happens whenever your object name is a "plural," such as Contacts, Employees, or Categories. Any object name that ends in "s" or "ies" is automatically renamed from plural to singular. Thus, Employees becomes Employee, and Categories becomes Category.

The reasoning behind this is that it more accurately shows that the entity class maps to one record of data. That is, an Employee entity class contains data for a single employee.

However, object renaming can be turned off. To do so, in the Visual Studio EDI, select Tools ⇨ Options to open the Options dialog. Expand the Database Tools node, and select the O/R Designer option, shown in Figure 15-12. Then set the Enabled property to False to turn off pluralization of names.

Pluralization is available only in the English-language version of Visual Studio.

SQL Metal

SQL Metal is a command-line tool that generates the LINQ to SQL mapping code and other components necessary for LINQ to SQL. It performs a myriad of different functions, including the following:

❑   Generates source code and mapping attributes (or mapping file) from a database.

❑   Generates a custom DBML file from a database.

❑   Generates source code and mapping attributes (or mapping file) from a DBML file.

Because it's a command-line tool, it is necessary to supply options (parameters) when executing it. The following table lists the available options when using the SqlMetal tool.

Option	Description
/server:name	Denotes the database server name.
/database:name	Denotes the database (catalog) name.
/user:name	Denotes the logon user ID. By default, this option uses Windows Authentication.
/password:password	Denotes the logon password.
/timeout:timeout	The time-out value when accessing the database.
/views	Extracts database views.
/functions	Extracts database functions.
/sprocs	Extracts database stored procedures.
/dbml:file	Returns output as DBML. Not available for use with the /map option.
/code:file	Returns output as source code.

Option	Description
/map:file	Generates an XML mapping file instead of attributes. Not available for use with the /dbml option.
/language:language	Denotes the source code language.
/namespace:name	Denotes the namespace of the generated code. Default value: no namespace.
/context:type	Denotes the name of the data context class. Default value: Taken from database name.
/entitybase:type	Denotes the base class of the entity class.
/pluralize	Pluralizes or singularizes the class and member names.
/serialization:option	Generates serializable classes.
Inputfile	Denotes a SQL Server Express .mdf file.
/?	Outputs the most current option list.

The /language option has two available languages—C# and VB. If no value is specified, the default value is taken from the extension on the code filename.

The /serialization option has the available values of None and Unidirectional. The default value is None.

Using the SqlMetal tool is a two-step process:

1. Extract the database metadata into a specified .dbml file.
2. Generate the output code file using the appropriate options specified in the preceding table.

Here are a few notes of interest before you look at some examples:

❑ When you generate the code you can select C#, Visual Basic, or an XML mapping file.

❑ If the /server option is not specified, the default value of localhost/sqlexpress is used.

❑ Extracting metadata from an MDF file requires that the name of the MDF file be included after all the other options.

The SqlMetal tool is located in the \Program Files\Microsoft SDKs\Windows\v6.0A\bin *directory.*

OK, now for some examples. Like the process outlined, the first step is to extract the metadata into a .dbml file. So, the following example creates a .dbml file that contains extracted SQL metadata from the AdventureWorks database, creating a file called aw.dbml. This is achieved by executing the following

```
sqlmetal /server:avalonserver /database:AdventureWorks /dbml:aw.dbml
```

Figure 15-13 shows how this is executed in a command window.

Figure 15-13

After the command successfully executes, browse to the directory where the SqlMetal tool is located (\Program Files\Microsoft SDKs\Windows\v6.0A\bin), and you should see in the directory a filed called aw.dbml. You can also specify a location when generating the metadata, as illustrated in the following code:

```
sqlmetal /server:avalonserver /database:AdventureWorks /dbml:C:\wrox\aw.dbml
```

The next step is to generate the code, which is shown in Figure 15-14. This example specifies the language and the code file to generate.

```
sqlmetal /server:avalonserver /database:AdventureWorks /code:aw.cs /language:csharp
```

Figure 15-14 below shows how this is executed in a command window.

Figure 15-14

As with the previous example, after the command successfully executes, browse to the directory where the SqlMetal tool is located, and you should see in the directory a filed called aw.cs. You can also specify a location when generating the metadata, as shown here:

```
sqlmetal /server:avalonserver /database:AdventureWorks /code:↵
c:\wrox\aw.cs /language:csharp
```

Now that the two files are generated, you want to include them in the project. Right-click the project name, and select Add ➪ Existing Item from the context menu. Because no directories were specified for the generated files in the preceding examples, both files will be in the same directory as the SqlMetal.exe file, which is \Program Files\Microsoft SDKs\Windows\v6.0A\bin.

Browse to that directory, and add both the aw.cs file and the aw.dbml file. You'll notice that Visual Studio creates the same file structure that you saw when you added the LINQ to SQL class manually. Figure 15-15 shows this.

Figure 15-15

Now you are ready to go—you don't have to manually drag and drop tables onto the designer!

External Mapping

External mapping in LINQ to SQL is the act of utilizing an external file that contains the mapping information between the data model and your object model.

A mapping file is an XML file, but not just any XML file. It must be well formed and validated against the following schema definition (.xsd):

```
<?xml version="1.0" encoding="utf-16"?>
<xs:schema xmlns:xs="http://www.w3.org/2001/XMLSchema" ↵
targetNamespace="http://schemas.microsoft.com/linqtosql/mapping/2007" ↵
xmlns="http://schemas.microsoft.com/linqtosql/mapping/2007"
elementFormDefault="qualified" >
  <xs:element name="Database" type="Database" />
  <xs:complexType name="Database">
    <xs:sequence>
      <xs:element name="Table" type="Table" minOccurs="0" maxOccurs="unbounded" />
      <xs:element name="Function" type="Function" minOccurs="0" ↵
maxOccurs="unbounded" />
    </xs:sequence>
    <xs:attribute name="Name" type="xs:string" use="optional" />
    <xs:attribute name="Provider" type="xs:string" use="optional" />
  </xs:complexType>
  <xs:complexType name="Table">
    <xs:sequence>
      <xs:element name="Type" type="Type" minOccurs="1" maxOccurs="1" />
    </xs:sequence>
```

```xml
      <xs:attribute name="Name" type="xs:string" use="optional" />
      <xs:attribute name="Member" type="xs:string" use="optional" />
  </xs:complexType>
  <xs:complexType name="Type">
    <xs:sequence>
      <xs:choice minOccurs="0" maxOccurs="unbounded">
        <xs:element name="Column" type="Column" minOccurs="0" ↵
maxOccurs="unbounded" />
        <xs:element name="Association" type="Association" minOccurs="0" ↵
maxOccurs="unbounded" />
      </xs:choice>
      <xs:element name="Type" type="Type" minOccurs="0" maxOccurs="unbounded" />
    </xs:sequence>
    <xs:attribute name="Name" type="xs:string" use="required" />
    <xs:attribute name="InheritanceCode" type="xs:string" use="optional" />
    <xs:attribute name="IsInheritanceDefault" type="xs:boolean" use="optional" />
  </xs:complexType>
  <xs:complexType name="Column">
    <xs:attribute name="Name" type="xs:string" use="optional" />
    <xs:attribute name="Member" type="xs:string" use="required" />
    <xs:attribute name="Storage" type="xs:string" use="optional" />
    <xs:attribute name="DbType" type="xs:string" use="optional" />
    <xs:attribute name="IsPrimaryKey" type="xs:boolean" use="optional" />
    <xs:attribute name="IsDbGenerated" type="xs:boolean" use="optional" />
    <xs:attribute name="CanBeNull" type="xs:boolean" use="optional" />
    <xs:attribute name="UpdateCheck" type="UpdateCheck" use="optional" />
    <xs:attribute name="IsDiscriminator" type="xs:boolean" use="optional" />
    <xs:attribute name="Expression" type="xs:string" use="optional" />
    <xs:attribute name="IsVersion" type="xs:boolean" use="optional" />
    <xs:attribute name="AutoSync" type="AutoSync" use="optional" />
  </xs:complexType>
  <xs:complexType name="Association">
    <xs:attribute name="Name" type="xs:string" use="optional" />
    <xs:attribute name="Member" type="xs:string" use="required" />
    <xs:attribute name="Storage" type="xs:string" use="optional" />
    <xs:attribute name="ThisKey" type="xs:string" use="optional" />
    <xs:attribute name="OtherKey" type="xs:string" use="optional" />
    <xs:attribute name="IsForeignKey" type="xs:boolean" use="optional" />
    <xs:attribute name="IsUnique" type="xs:boolean" use="optional" />
    <xs:attribute name="DeleteRule" type="xs:string" use="optional" />
    <xs:attribute name="DeleteOnNull" type="xs:boolean" use="optional" />
  </xs:complexType>
  <xs:complexType name="Function">
    <xs:sequence>
      <xs:element name="Parameter" type="Parameter" minOccurs="0" ↵
maxOccurs="unbounded" />
      <xs:choice>
        <xs:element name="ElementType" type="Type" minOccurs="0" ↵
maxOccurs="unbounded" />
        <xs:element name="Return" type="Return" minOccurs="0" maxOccurs="1" />
      </xs:choice>
    </xs:sequence>
    <xs:attribute name="Name" type="xs:string" use="optional" />
    <xs:attribute name="Method" type="xs:string" use="required" />
```

```xml
      <xs:attribute name="IsComposable" type="xs:boolean" use="optional" />
    </xs:complexType>
    <xs:complexType name="Parameter">
      <xs:attribute name="Name" type="xs:string" use="optional" />
      <xs:attribute name="Parameter" type="xs:string" use="required" />
      <xs:attribute name="DbType" type="xs:string" use="optional" />
      <xs:attribute name="Direction" type="ParameterDirection" use="optional" />
    </xs:complexType>
    <xs:complexType name="Return">
      <xs:attribute name="DbType" type="xs:string" use="optional" />
    </xs:complexType>
    <xs:simpleType name="UpdateCheck">
      <xs:restriction base="xs:string">
        <xs:enumeration value="Always" />
        <xs:enumeration value="Never" />
        <xs:enumeration value="WhenChanged" />
      </xs:restriction>
    </xs:simpleType>
    <xs:simpleType name="ParameterDirection">
      <xs:restriction base="xs:string">
        <xs:enumeration value="In" />
        <xs:enumeration value="Out" />
        <xs:enumeration value="InOut" />
      </xs:restriction>
    </xs:simpleType>
    <xs:simpleType name="AutoSync">
      <xs:restriction base="xs:string">
        <xs:enumeration value="Never" />
        <xs:enumeration value="OnInsert" />
        <xs:enumeration value="OnUpdate" />
        <xs:enumeration value="Always" />
        <xs:enumeration value="Default" />
      </xs:restriction>
    </xs:simpleType>
  </xs:schema>
```

Keep the following in mind when applying external mapping:

❑   External mapping overrides any attribute-based mapping.

❑   External mapping and attribute-based mapping cannot be combined.

❑   You can use external mapping with a specific database provider, something that you cannot do with attribute-based mapping.

So how, then, do you generate a mapping file? The previous section discussed a tool that can be used just for this. SqlMetal is perfect for generating an XML mapping file. To do this, simply execute the following command:

```
SqlMetal /server:servername /database:databasename /map:mappingfile.xml
```

Figure 15-16 shows the first part of the result of this command run against the AdventureWorks database.

When is using external mapping useful? Typically, it's useful when you want to separate the layers, such as separating the mapping code from the application code.

Figure 15-16

Multi-Tier Operations

All of the LINQ to SQL examples you have seen so far have used a single DataContext. This is fine for a small, two-tier application but for larger applications where an n-tier approach is desired, you may need a distinct DataContext instance for queries and data manipulation operations.

N-tier support in LINQ to SQL is accomplished via the Attach method of the Table(of TEntity) class. This feature lets entities span different DataContexts. Why would you need different DataContexts? In a two-tier application, the UI typically needs a subset of data within a table. However, in a multi-tier environment, the BL (business logic) layer generally requires a large set of the data and thus a more complex (populated) DataContext. The need, then, is to have the DataContexts span the different application tiers.

The Attach method makes this happen, letting entities cross tiers. Although they have this capability, they can still be tracked and identified with the original DataContext instance. Typically, the purpose of attaching an entity to a different DataContext is to manipulate the object.

When manipulating the objects, such as performing insert and update operations, you need to know how each is handled. When inserting, you need to use the Add method; the Attach method is not supported for insert operations. For update operations, the Attach method should be used. For delete operations, the Attach and Remove methods are available.

Here's how the Attach method works:

```
AdventureWorksSalesDataContext aw = new
AdventureWorksSalesDataContext();

Contact con = aw.Contacts.Single(c => c.ContactID == 483);

AdventureWorksSalesDataContext aw2 = new
AdventureWorksSalesDataContext();

Contact con2 = new Contact();
```

```
con2.ContactID = con.ContactID;
con2.Title = "Head Geek";

aw2.Contacts.Attach(con2, false);

con2.MiddleName = "Calvin";

aw2.SubmitChanges();
```

This example creates two DataContexts. A single Contact is queried using the first DataContext, and a new Contact is created with no association to either DataContext. Properties of the second DataContext are set, one of which is the ContactID taken from the ContactID of the first DataContext. The Attach method is used to attach the second Contact object to the second DataContext, and then the changes are submitted back to the database via the second DataContext.

The previous example showed you how you can change an object using a different DataContext instance.

When working in a multi-tier environment, the entire identity is not usually sent across tiers for a number of reasons, including performance, interoperability, and simplicity. For example, the client application might show only a small portion of data of a Contact entity. So, before using the Attach method and sending members between tiers, the member must meet one or more of the following criteria:

❑   The member must have the entity's identity.

❑   The member must participate in an optimistic concurrency check.

❑   The member must be modified.

N-Tier Best Practices

This section details some of the important things to keep in mind when using n-tier operations.

Optimistic Concurrency

In optimistic concurrency, rows are not locked when being read. When a user wants to update a row, the application must determine whether another user has changed the row since it was read. Optimistic concurrency improves performance because no locking of records is required, and locking records requires additional server resources. Also, a persistent connection to the database server is required to maintain record locks. Because that's not the case in an optimistic concurrency model, connections to the server are free to serve a larger number of clients in less time.

The following items should be considered when you're thinking about using optimistic concurrency:

❑   When using a timestamp or version number for a concurrency check, the corresponding member needs to be set before the call to the Attach method is made.

❑   The shape of the data exchanged between tiers is not specified by LINQ to SQL.

❑   All of the original values that are used for concurrency checks can be kept using a number of methods that are outside of the LINQ to SQL API scope, such as a view state in an ASP.NET application.

❑   Minimal updates are used for concurrency checks, meaning that any member that is not set or that is not flagged for optimistic concurrency is ignored.

❑   Any table that used a timestamp or a version number data type must have those columns set before calling the Attach method.

Insertion/Deletion

As explained earlier, the Attach method is not used for insert and delete operations. Instead, the Add and Remove methods should be used. However, it is your responsibility to handle foreign-key constraints in a two-tier update. That is, you must delete any child records before deleting the parent record.

N-Tier Examples

The AttachAll method enables you to attach many entities all at once instead of singularly using the Attach method. The following example illustrates the use of the AttachAll method to take all of the sales for one salesperson and, in one line of code, attach them to another salesperson.

First, open SQL Server Management Studio and query the Sales.SalesOrderHeader table to get a count of the number sales for SalesPersonID 284 by executing the following query:

```
Select * FROM Sales.SalesOrderHeader WHERE SalesPersonID = 284
```

You should see roughly 39 rows returned. The following code assigns all of the sales orders for salesperson 284, returned in the previous query, to salesperson 276. It queries the SalesOrderHeader table for all orders assigned to salespersonid 276. The AttachAll method is then used by a second instance of the SalesOrderHeader table to take ownership of them. Once ownership has been transferred, a simple loop needs to be performed to update the records to the new SalesPersonID.

```
AdventureWorksSalesDataContext db = new
AdventureWorksSalesDataContext();

var sohQuery =
    from soh in db.SalesOrderHeader
    where soh.SalesPersonID == 284
    select soh;

List<SalesOrderHeader> sohList = sohQuery.ToList();

Using (AdventureWorksSalesDataContext db2 = new
AdventureWorksSalesDataContext)
{
    db2.SalesOrderHeader.AttachAll(sohList, false);

    foreach (SalesOrderHeader soh2 in sohList)
    {
        soh2.SalesPersonID = 276;
    }
    db2.SubmitChanges();
}
```

Slick. OK, here's one more example. It shows how you can delete a SalesOrderHeader object. As stated earlier, the Remove() method should be used for delete operations.

```
Using (AdventureWorksSalesDataContext db = new
AdventureWorksSalesDataContext)
{
    SalesOrderHeader soh = new SalesOrderHeader() {
        CustomerID = 21768, ContactID = 13278} ;

    db.SalesOrderHeader.Attach(soh);

    db.SalesOrderHeader.Remove(soh);

    db.SubmitChanges();
}
```

When this code executes, it removes two rows from the SalesOrderHeader table. Now modify the Remove() statement so that it reads as follows:

```
db.Customer.Remove(soh);
```

When this code is executed, it will cause an error. Why? Because there is a foreign key constraint between the Customer table and the SalesOrderHeader table on the CustomerID column.

Designer Example

Hopefully, the Visual Studio project that you created earlier is still open. In this example, you use the O/R Designer to create a LINQ to SQL entity and bind that entity to a Windows form.

First, open the O/R Designer by double-clicking the AdventureWorksSales.dbml file in the Solution Explorer. Now, as you learned previously, you can create entity classes based on objects in the database. Open the Server Explorer and expand the connection to the AdventureWorks database you created earlier. Expand the Tables node and drag the Contact table into the entity pane.

Next, from the Data menu on the main menu bar, select Add New Data Source. That opens the Data Source Configuration Wizard dialog shown in Figure 15-17.

The wizard enables you to create entity classes as a data source. Entity classes can be used as object data sources, and as such can be added to the Data Sources window and placed on forms like any other Windows Forms controls. By placing an entity-based data source on a Windows form, you can create databound controls.

On the first page of the wizard, choose a data source type (specify where your data for the data source will come from). By default, Database is selected, but what you want to select is Object because the data will be coming from an entity object. So, select Object and click Next.

The next page asks you to select the object that you would like to bind to. Listed on this page are those objects in the current assembly. Your project is listed, and you need to expand that node to get to the information you want. Expand the LINQ node and select the Contact object (see Figure 15-18).

Notice that all of the objects here are objects within your project plus entities you have defined in the O/R Designer.

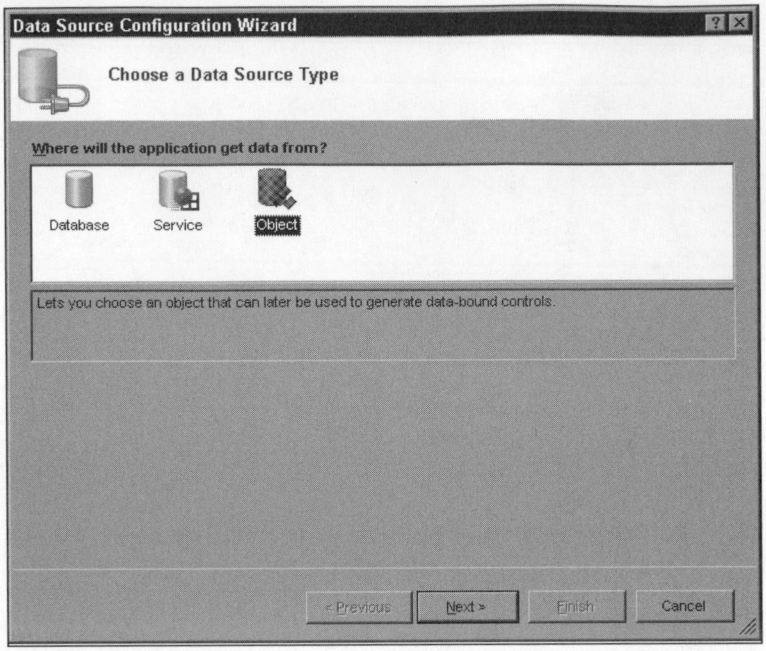

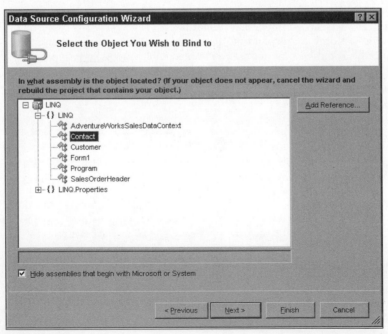

Figure 15-17

Figure 15-18

By default, the Hide Assemblies That Begin With Microsoft or System option at the bottom of the page is checked. If you uncheck this box, the list above it is repopulated with all assemblies that are referenced in your application.

Click Next.

The last step in the wizard is the summary page, which simply lists the objects that will be added to the data source. In this example, there's one object, Contact, as shown in Figure 15-19.

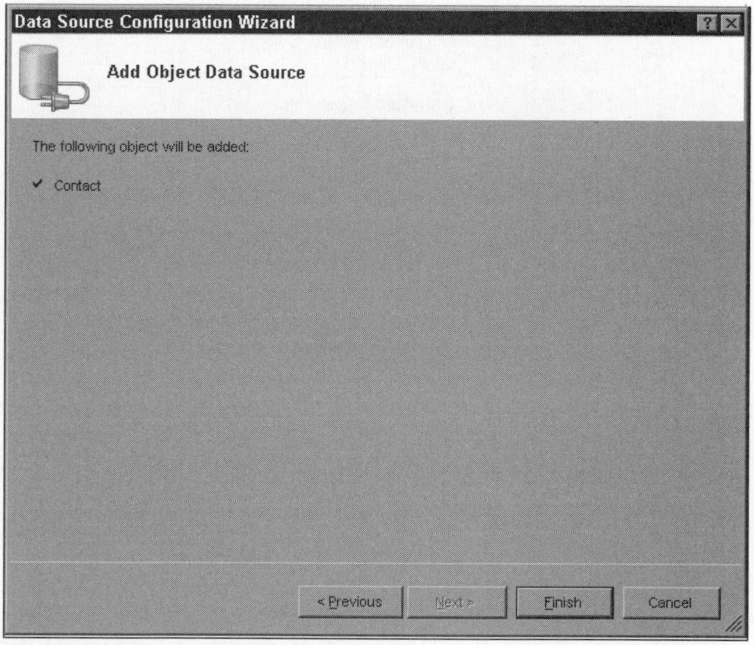

Figure 15-19

Click Finish. Your new data source is created. Open the Data Sources window (see Figure 15-20) to view the new data source.

Open `Form1` in design mode and from the Data Sources windows, drag the Contact node onto the form. Although you're dropping a single item on the form, you'll notice that two items are added to the form, as shown in Figure 15-21.

The control on the top of the form is a binding navigator control. The designer automatically names it `contactBindingNavigator`. It inherits from the Windows Forms `BindingNavigator` control that provides means for users to search and change data on a Windows Form, and it's composed of a tool strip that contains a number of common data-related objects such as buttons and record navigation objects.

A `BindingSource` component also was placed on the form. Typically, you will use a `BindingNavigator` component together with a `BindingSource` component to provide users with quick and easy navigation of data on a form. The `BindingSource` component encapsulates the data source for a form.

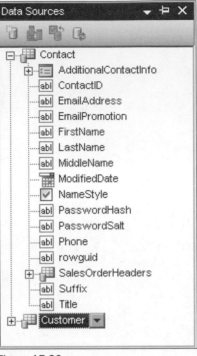

Figure 15-20

Figure 15-21

Select the `contactBindingSource` control and then open the Properties window (see Figure 15-22). You'll notice that the data source for this component comes from the data source defined previously.

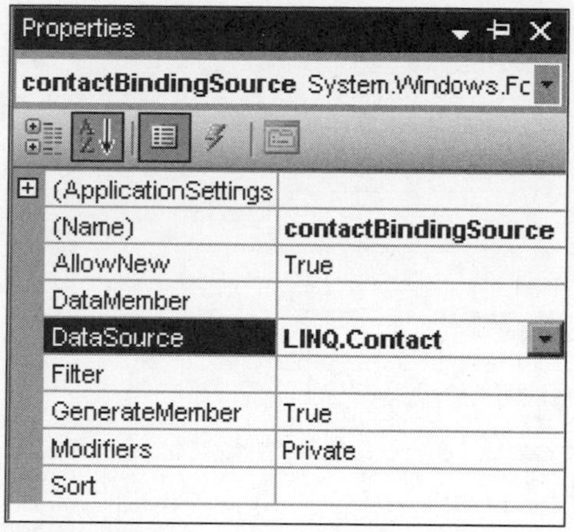

Figure 15-22

As the form sits right now, it is useless. The good news, however, is that it's easy to wire these controls. Right-click any gray area of the form, and select View Code from the context menu.

As with all of the other LINQ to SQL examples, you still need a `DataContext` reference, so after the partial class definition of `Form1`, add the following code:

```
private AdventureWorksSalesDataContext db = new
AdventureWorksSalesDataContext();
```

Next, in the `Form1 Load()` method, add the following code:

```
contactBindingSource.DataSource = db.Contacts
```

This code binds the data source of the BindingSource with the `Contacts` table, essentially providing the `LINQ.Contact` data source with the data it needs.

OK, time to test. Press F5 to compile and run the project. When the form loads, it will automatically load with data. You can use the navigation arrows on the navigator control (see Figure 15-23) to move between records, and you can also use the Add and Remove buttons to add new rows and delete existing rows.

If you delete or add a row, is it saved back to the database? No. Why? Remember that behind all of this is LINQ to SQL. You need to "submit changes" back to the database. Stop the project and select the Save button on the navigation control. Open the Properties window, and set the `Enabled` property for the Save button to `True`. Next, double-click the Save button to create a `Click()` event handler for the button.

Then, add the following code:

```
db.SubmitChanges();
```

Simple, isn't it? Now run the project again, and add and delete data. To verify that data is truly added and deleted, open a new query window in SQL Server Management Studio and execute the following T-SQL statement:

```
SELECT * FROM Person.Contact WHERE ContactID > 19990
```

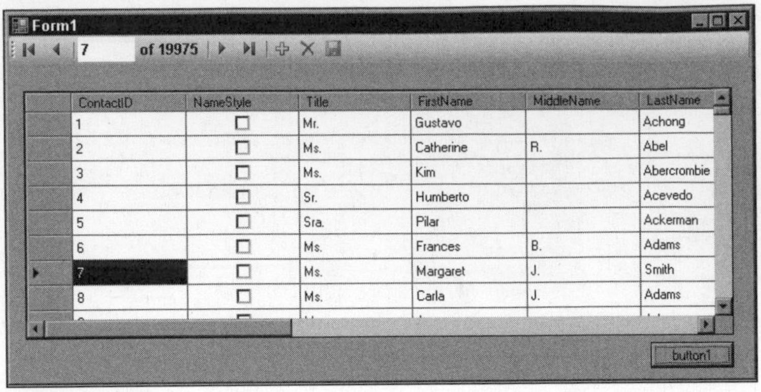

Figure 15-23

Awesome. But wait, it gets better. Stop the project and modify the code in the Load() method of the form, so that it looks like the following:

```
private void Form1_Load(object sender, EventArgs e)
{
    var conQuery =
        from con in db.Contacts
        select con;

    contactBindingSource.BindingSource = conQuery;
}
```

This illustrates that you can also bind a BindingSource directly to a LINQ to SQL query.

Summary

This chapter explored the Visual Studio O/R Designer and the associated SqlMetal utility. Each of these provide a great service in that you can quickly and easily create and manage LINQ to SQL classes, their associated relationships, and mappings. The purpose of doing things manually to begin with was to help lay the foundation and show how things are created, so that when an entity is created, you know what is going on behind the scenes.

This chapter also discussed external mappings with your object model. As stated earlier, external mapping provides the benefit of being able to separate the mapping code from the application code.

Last, the topic of building n-tier applications was discussed as used with LINQ to SQL. The key to using LINQ to SQL in an n-tier environment is utilizing multiple DataContext instances and taking advantage of the Attach method to efficiently span between the different DataContexts.

Appendixes

Case Study

Several years ago, Microsoft put out a demo application called Fabrikam (for the fictional company Fabrikam Fine Furniture) that was used quite heavily. It was a reference application for developers of Mobile PC applications and solutions, but it also had a server piece that tracked products and orders.

Well, it's time to dust off that old application and upgrade it to work with LINQ. If you have ever used Fabrikam, you know it is quite large because it deals with mobile components, SQL replication, and other technology components. This case study won't upgrade all of the application but will redo a portion that deals with Fabrikam's fine products, such as tracking (adding, updating, and deleting) products—enough to show you what you can do with a great new technology and a new or existing application.

> *The original Fabrikam application and code was downloaded from the Microsoft web site and was supplied "as is." Any modifications have been made by the author, and Microsoft holds no guarantees/warranties or support for this case study or sample, implied or explicit.*

The first thing to do is to build the database. The script (Fabrikam.sql) to build the database is available as part of the download for this book. (I thought about including the text here, but once I saw it was 25 pages, I changed my mind. It'll be much easier for you to simply use the download file.)

So, run Fabrikam.sql in SQL Server Management Studio. This script creates the database, all the necessary objects, and the data for this case study, so no extra work is needed. The following objects are created.

Object Type	Name
Table	Countries
Table	Customers
Table	Deliveries
Table	DeliveryDetails
Table	Employees
Table	Manufacturers
Table	OrderDetails
Table	Orders
Table	Products
Table	ProductTypes
Table	States
Stored Procedure	GetActiveCustomers
Stored Procedure	GetActiveDeliveries
Stored Procedure	GetActiveEmployees
Stored Procedure	GetActiveOrders
Stored Procedure	GetActiveProducts
View	vLoadMfrs
View	vProducts
View	vStates

Once the script finishes, you're ready to build the Fabrikam demo. Let's get started.

Open Visual Studio 2008 and create a new C# project; name it Fabrikam. When the project is created, ensure that the necessary LINQ references are included in your project:

```
System.Data.DataSetExtensions
System.Data.Linq
System.Xml
System.Xml.Linq
```

Then you have to add an application configuration file. In Solution Explorer, right-click on the solution and select Add ➪ New Item from the context menu. In the Add New Item dialog, select Application Configuration File. Make sure the name is App.Config and click OK.

Next, right-click on the solution and select Properties. In the Fabrikam solution Properties window, select the Settings tab along the left side of the window. Here you need to add a property for the Fabrikam application to use. Enter the information in the following table.

Setting	Value
Name	BusinessName
Type	string
Scope	Application
Value	Fabrikam Fine Furniture

Figure A-1 shows what the Settings page should look like.

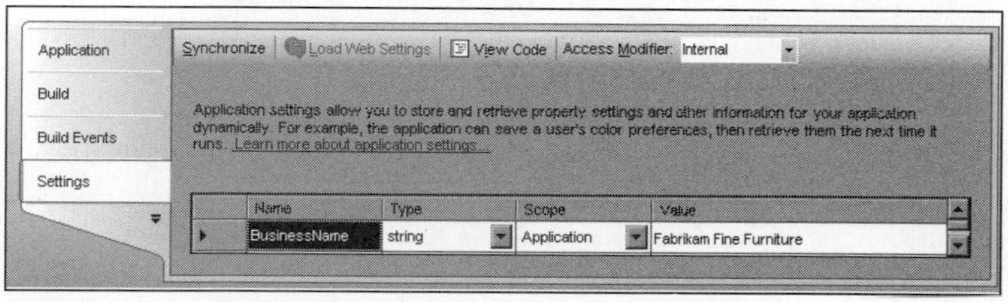

Figure A-1

This information will be stored in the application configuration file and you can change it to any value you want at a later date. Save your changes to the Properties by using the Ctrl+S key combination or by selecting Save from the File menu, and then close this window.

Now you create the mappings to the database objects (DataContext and associated entities), and the best way to do that is use the built-in LINQ templates. In Solution Explorer, right-click on the solution and select Add ⇨ New Item from the context menu. In the Add New Item dialog, select the Data node under Categories. The Templates section of the Add New Item dialog will display all available Data templates. In the Templates section, select LINQ to SQL Classes and name it Fabrikam. Click Add.

The Fabrikam Dataset Designer opens and displays an empty designer. It's time to add the server objects. In the Server Explorer window, right-click on the DataConnections node and select Add Connection. The Add Connection dialog displays. Enter the appropriate connection information to connect to your instance of SQL Server and the Fabrikam database. Click the Test Connection button to ensure that the connection information has been entered correctly and that Visual Studio can successfully connect to the Fabrikam database. If the connection test is successful, click OK.

Expand the new connection node in Server Explorer, and then expand the Tables and Stored Procedures nodes for the Fabrikam connection. Now drag and drop all the tables into the Entities pane of the O/R Designer. Next, drag all the stored procedures into the Methods pane of the O/R designer. Figure A-2 shows what the O/R Designer should look like when you're done.

Once you have added all of the objects, save the designer. As you know, the DataContext object and all mappings have now been created and you can now start writing code to access these entities.

When you dropped the first object onto the O/R Designer, it asked you whether you wanted to store the connection information. If you selected Yes, go back to the App.Config file and look at the information

LINQ added. There is a new `<connectionStrings>` section in which the connection to the Fabrikam database is stored. Pretty nifty.

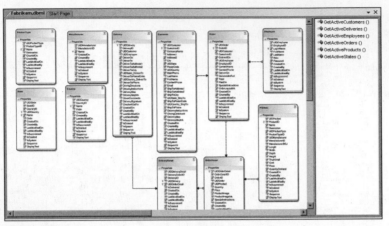

Figure A-2

You are now ready to start designing the UI. The first step is to create the main application form. `Form1` is already added to the project, so use that as the main form. On `Form1`, add the following (those blank cells in the tables throughout this appendix are blank on purpose, because those objects on the form do not require the object name to be changed or the `Text` values set).

Object Type	Name	Text
Panel		
Panel		
Button	cmdOrders	Orders
Button	cmdCustomers	Customers
Button	cmdSynchronize	Synchronize
Button	cmdDeliveries	Deliveries
Button	cmdProducts	Products
Label		Manage orders
Label		Manage customers
Label		Merge local DB w/Central DB
Label		Manage Deliveries
Label		Manage product catalog entries

You can place those objects anywhere on the form, but it should look something like Figure A-3. (Yeah, I added a pretty picture but it is not necessary.)

The next step is to add the login form. Add a new form to the project and call it `LoginForm`. Add the following objects to it.

Figure A-3

Object Type	Name	Text
Label		Enter user name and password
Label		Username:
Label		Password
TextBox	txtUsername	
TextBox	txtPassword	
Button	cmdOK	OK
Button	cmdCancel	Cancel

Figure A-4 shows what the login form should look like.

Figure A-4

Ready to start adding some code? Open Form1 in design mode and double-click on any gray area of the form to view the code. That also creates the `Load()` method for the form, which is what you need. In the `Load()` event for the main form, add the following code:

```
string s = System.Reflection.Assembly.GetExecutingAssembly().Location;
s = Path.GetDirectoryName(s);
Directory.SetCurrentDirectory(s);

string businessName = Properties.Settings.Default.BusinessName;

this.Text = "Switchboard = " + businessName;

LoginForm lf = new LoginForm();
if (lf.ShowDialog() != DialogResult.OK)
{
    Application.Exit();
}
```

For now, you are done with the main form. Open the login form in design mode, and double-click on the OK button. In the button's `Click()` event, add the following code:

```
string username = txtUsername.Text.Trim();
string password = txtPassword.Text.Trim();

if ((username.Length > 0) && (password.Length > 0))
{
    if (Authenticate(username, password))
    {
        DialogResult = DialogResult.OK;
}
```

```
        else
        {
            MessageBox.Show("Invalid username or password.", this.Text);
        }
    }
    else
    {
        MessageBox.Show("Enter a valid username and password.", this.Text);
    }
```

Below the `Click()` event of the OK button, add the following code. This code is what the `Click()` event will call to authenticate the user entered on the login form.

```
private bool Authenticate(string un, string pwd)
{
    bool isValid = false;

    FabrikamDataContext context = new FabrikamDataContext("user id=username;
password=password");
    IEnumerable<GetActiveEmployeesResult> result = context.GetActiveEmployees();
    foreach (GetActiveEmployeesResult emp in result)
    {
        if (emp.LoginName.ToLower() == un.ToLower() && emp.Password == pwd)
        {
            isValid = true;
            break;
        }
    }
    return isValid;
}
```

Before proceeding, compile the application to make sure that everything compiles OK. If there are no errors, press F5 to run the application. First, the login form will appear. For credentials, enter `RussellK` for the username and `password` for the password.

The `Authenticate` routine uses LINQ to SQL to call a mapped stored procedure to return all the existing employees. It then compares the usernames and passwords to those entered on the login form. Notice how easy it is to call the stored procedure using IntelliSense and dot notation. Sweet.

If the login is successful, the main form is displayed (you saw that in Figure A-3). It doesn't really do anything right now, so stop the application and add a new form to the project, naming it `SelectProduct`. On this form add the following controls (again, those blank cells in the tables throughout this appendix are blank on purpose because those objects on the form do not require that the object name to be changed or the `Text` value set).

Object Type	Name	Text
Label		Product Category
Label		Products in
Button	cmdNew	New

319

Object Type	Name	Text
Button	cmdEdit	Edit
Button	cmdDelete	Delete
ComboBox	cboProductType	
DataViewGrid	grdProducts	

This form, when laid out, should look something like Figure A-5.

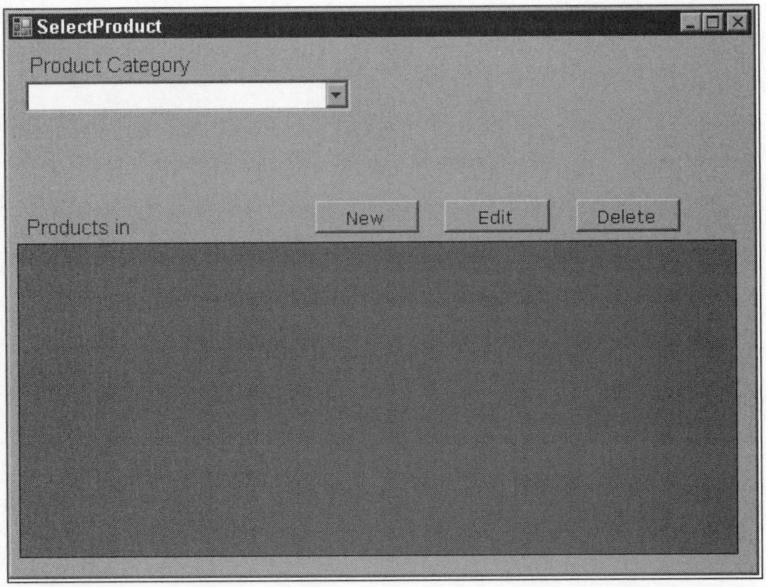

Figure A-5

Now add the following code to the Load() event of the new SelectProduct form. Be sure to use the correct username and password in the DataContext connection string.

```
FabrikamDataContext context = new FabrikamDataContext("user id↵
=username;password=password");

IEnumerable<ProductType> result =
    from prod in context.ProductTypes
    orderby prod.Name
    select prod;

DataTable dt = new DataTable("ProductType");
DataColumn dc;
DataRow dr;

dc = new DataColumn();
```

```
dc.DataType = System.Type.GetType("System.Int32");
dc.ColumnName = "ID";
dt.Columns.Add(dc);

dc = new DataColumn();
dc.DataType = System.Type.GetType("System.String");
dc.ColumnName = "Name";
dt.Columns.Add(dc);

foreach (ProductType product in result)
{
    dr = dt.NewRow();
    dr["ID"] = product.ProductTypeID;
    dr["Name"] = product.Name;
    dt.Rows.Add(dr);
}
cboProductType.DataSource = dt;
cboProductType.DisplayMember = "Name";
cboProductType.ValueMember = "ID";
```

Next, add the following code to the `SelectedIndexChanged` event of the `cboProductType` combo.

```
If (cboProductType.SelectedIndex > 0)
{
    int ProductID = Convert.ToInt32(cboProductType.SelectedIndex);
    DataSet ds = new DataSet();

    string connectionInfo = "Data Source=avalonserver;Initial Catalog=Fabrikam;
    user id=username;pwd=password";

    SqlDataAdapter da = new SqlDataAdapter("select ProductID, Name,
    Description, ManufacturerSKU, Cost, Price, QuantityOnHand FROM products
    WHERE ProductTypeID = @ID", connectionInfo);

    da.SelectCommand.Parameters.AddWithValue("@ID", ProductID);
    da.TableMappings.Add("Table", "Products");

    da.Fill(ds);

    DataTable dt = ds.Tables["Products"];

    IEnumerable<DataRow> prod =
        from p in dt.AsEnumerable()
        select p;
    if (prod.Count() > 0)
    {
        DataTable dat = prod.CopyToDataTable<DataRow>(); ↵
grdProducts.DataSource = dat;
    }
     else
    {
        grdProducts.DataSource = null;
    }
}
```

When the user selects a new product type, the corresponding products are retrieved from the database via a DataAdapter and used to fill a DataTable. A LINQ query is then executed to query the contents of the DataTable, at which point the CopyToDataTable method is used to return a DataTable with copies of the DataRow objects using an input IEnumerable<T> object.

The new DataTable is used as the data source for the products grid.

The SelectProduct form needs to be opened from the main form. To make that work, open the main form and add the following highlighted code to Products button's Click() event.

```
private void cmdProducts_Click(object sender, EventArgs e)
{
    SelectProduct selectProd = new SelectProduct();
    selectProd.Show();
}
```

To test what you have so far, compile the application to make sure that everything is good. Press F5 to run the application, and log in using the same credentials as last time (RussellK and password). When the main form appears, click the Products button, which opens the SelectProduct form (you saw it in Figure A-5). Select a product category from the Product Category combo—for this example, select the Chairs category. The grid is populated with two products associated with that product category, a secretary chair and a casual easy chair).

Now stop the application and create a new form called ProductMain. Add the following controls to it (as with the other forms, the same thing applies to the blank cells in the table below).

Object Type	Name	Text
Label		Name:
Label		Product ID:
Label		Description:
Label		Product Category:
Label		Manufacturer:
Label		Mfr.SKU (UPC):
Label		Length:
Label		Width:
Label		Depth:
Label		Height:
Label		Cost:
Label		Price:
Label		Qty on Hand:

Object Type	Name	Text
TextBox	txtName	
TextBox	txtProductID	
TextBox	txtDescription	
TextBox	txtManufacturerSKU	
TextBox	txtLength	
TextBox	txtWidth	
TextBox	txtDepth	
TextBox	txtHeight	
TextBox	txtCost	
TextBox	txtPrice	
TextBox	txtQuantity	
ComboBox	cboProductCategory	
ComboBox	cboManufacturer	
Button	cmdOK	OK
Button	cmdCancel	Cancel

Also, set the Enabled property of the txtProductID text box to False. When completed, the ProductMain form should look something like Figure A-6.

Before this form can be used a few changes need to be made. Open the form in design mode and double-click any gray area to view the code behind the form and to create the Load() event for this form. Next, add the following line of code directly above the ProductMain form constructor:

```
private int _productID;
```

A new constructor needs to be added so that a ProductID can be passed in, so add the following code below the default ProductMain constructor.

```
public ProductMain(int productID)
{
    InitializeComponent();
    _productID = productID;
}
```

Then, enter the following code in the ProductMain form's Load() event. It populates the form's two lookup combos.

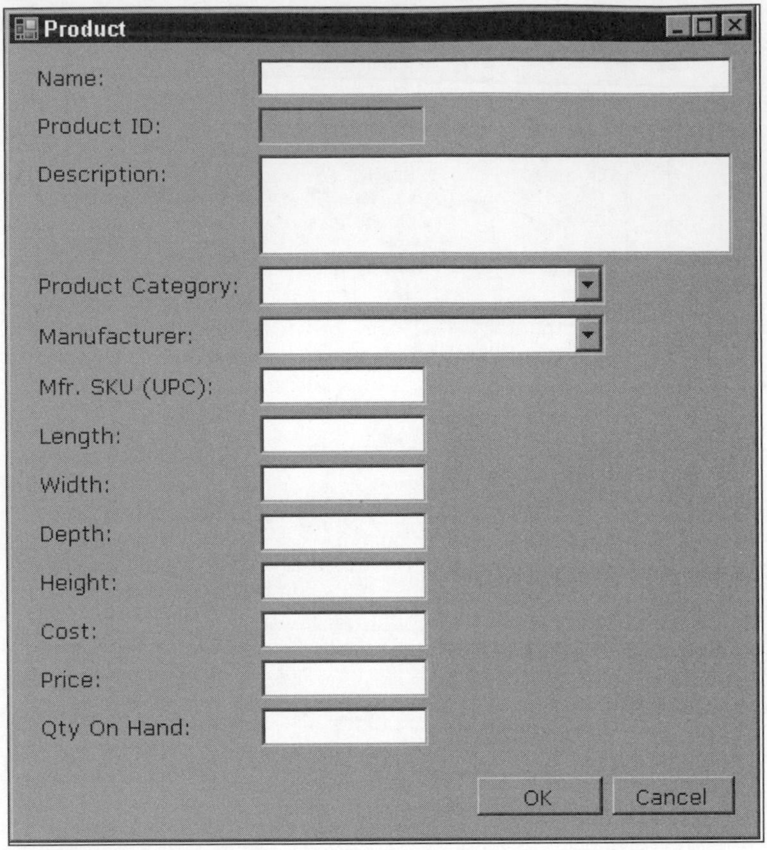

Figure A-6

```
FabrikamDataContext context =
    new FabrikamDataContext("user id=username;password=password");

//first, the producttypes
IEnumerable<ProductType> result =
    from prod in context.ProductTypes
    orderby prod.Name
    select prod;

DataTable dt = new DataTable("ProductType");
DataColumn dc;
DataRow dr;

dc = new DataColumn();
dc.DataType = System.Type.GetType("System.Int32");
dc.ColumnName = "ID";
dt.Columns.Add(dc);

dc = new DataColumn();
dc.DataType = System.Type.GetType("System.String");
```

```csharp
dc.ColumnName = "Name";
dt.Columns.Add(dc);
foreach (ProductType product in result)
{

    dr = dt.NewRow();
    dr["ID"] = product.ProductTypeID;
    dr["Name"] = product.Name;
    dt.Rows.Add(dr);
}


cboProductCategory.DataSource = dt;
cboProductCategory.DisplayMember = "Name";
cboProductCategory.ValueMember = "ID";
//now, the manufacturer info...
IEnumerable<Manufacturer> result1 =
    from manu in context.Manufacturers
    orderby manu.Name
    select manu;
DataTable dt2 = new DataTable("ProductType");
DataColumn dc2;
DataRow dr2;

dc2 = new DataColumn();
dc2.DataType = System.Type.GetType("System.Int32");
dc2.ColumnName = "ID";
dt2.Columns.Add(dc2);

dc2 = new DataColumn();
dc2.DataType = System.Type.GetType("System.String");
dc2.ColumnName = "Name";
dt2.Columns.Add(dc2);

foreach (Manufacturer man in result1)
{

    dr2 = dt2.NewRow();
    dr2["ID"] = product.ProductTypeID;
    dr2["Name"] = product.Name;
    dt2.Rows.Add(dr2);
}

cboManufacturer.DataSource = dt2;
cboManufacturer.DisplayMember - "Name";
cboManufacturer.ValueMember = "ID";
if (_productID > 0)
{
    this.GetProduct(_productID, context);
}
```

This code also looks to see if a `productID` was passed in. If a `productID` was passed in, you know that the user clicked the Edit button on the `SelectProduct` form and wants to display the product details of the product he selected in the grid; you want to call the `GetProduct()` method.

Well, the `GetProduct()` method has not been created yet, so add it now below the `Load()` event:

```
private void GetProduct(int productID, FabrikamDataContext context)
{
    var prodQuery = context.Products.Single(p => p.ProductID == productID);

    txtName.Text = prodQuery.Name;
    txtProductID.Text = Convert.ToString(prodQuery.ProductID);
    txtDescription.Text = prodQuery.Description;
    cboProductCategory.SelectedValue = Convert.Int32(prodQuery.ProductTypeID);
    cboManufacturer.SelectedValue = Convert.Int32(prodQuery.ManufacturerID);
    txtManufacturerSKU.Text = prodQuery.ManufacturerSKU;
    txtLength.Text = Convert.ToString(prodQuery.Length);
    txtWidth.Text = Convert.ToString(prodQuery.Width);
    txtDepth.Text = Convert.ToString(prodQuery.Depth);
    txtHeight.Text = Convert.ToString(prodQuery.Height);
    txtCost.Text = Convert.ToString(prodQuery.Cost);
    txtPrice.Text = Convert.ToString(prodQuery.Price);
    txtQuantity.Text = Convert.ToString(prodQuery.QuantityOnHand);
}
```

This code takes the `productID` that was passed in and uses LINQ to SQL to return a single product record. It then populates the `ProductMain` combo controls with the corresponding data.

Now add the following code to the OK button's `Click()` event. This code looks at the `txtProductID` control to see if there is a value. If not, it is a new product and a new instance of the `Product` entity is created, populated, and saved back to the database, all via LINQ to SQL. If there is an existing `productID`, the current record is updated and the changes are saved back to the database.

```
try
{
    FabrikamDataContext context =
        new FabrikamDataContext("user id=username;password=password");

    if (txtProductID.Text.Length == 0)
    {
        Product prod = new Product();
        prod.Name = txtName.Text.Trim();
        prod.Description = txtDescription.Text;
        Prod.ProductTypeID = Convert.ToInt32(cboProductCategory.SelectedValue);
        Prod.ManufacturerID = Convert.ToInt32(cboManufacturer.SelectedValue);
        prod.ManufacturerSKU = txtManufacturerSKU.Text;
        prod.Length = Convert.ToDecimal(txtLength.Text);
        prod.Width = Convert.ToDecimal(txtWidth.Text);
        prod.Depth = Convert.ToDecimal(txtDepth.Text);
        prod.Height = Convert.ToDecimal(txtHeight.Text);
        prod.Cost = decimal.Parse(this.txtCost.Text,
System.Globalization.NumberStyles.Currency);
        prod.Price = decimal.Parse(this.txtPrice.Text,
System.Globalization.NumberStyles.Currency);
        prod.QuantityOnHand = Convert.ToInt32(this.txtQuantity.Text);
        context.Products.Add(prod);
    }
```

```
        else
        {
            int productID = Convert.ToInt32(txtProductID.Text);

            var prodQuery = context.Products.Single(p => p.ProductID == productID);
            prodQuery.Name = txtName.Text.Trim();
            prodQuery.Description = txtDescription.Text;
            ProdQuery.ProductTypeID =
                Convert.ToInt32(cboProductCategory.SelectedValue);
            ProdQuery.ManufacturerID = Convert.ToInt32(cboManufacturer.SelectedValue);
            prodQuery.ManufacturerSKU = txtManufacturerSKU.Text;
            prodQuery.Length = Convert.ToDecimal(txtLength.Text);
            prodQuery.Width = Convert.ToDecimal(txtWidth.Text);
            prodQuery.Depth = Convert.ToDecimal(txtDepth.Text);
            prodQuery.Height = Convert.ToDecimal(txtHeight.Text);
            prodQuery.Cost = decimal.Parse(this.txtCost.Text,
System.Globalization.NumberStyles.Currency);
            prodQuery.Price = decimal.Parse(this.txtPrice.Text,
System.Globalization.NumberStyles.Currency);
            prodQuery.QuantityOnHand = Convert.ToInt32(this.txtQuantity.Text);

        }
        context.SubmitChanges();
    }
    catch (Exception ex)
    {
        MessageBox.Show(ex.Message.ToString());
    }
```

Next you need to put code behind the New, Edit, and Delete buttons on the SelectProduct form that will utilize the new ProductMain form. Open the SelectProduct form and add the following code to the cmdNew button's Click() event.

```
ProductMain prod = new ProductMain();
prod.Show();
```

This code opens the ProductMain form ready to add a new record.

Before you can add code behind the cmdEdit button, you have to declare a variable on the SelectProduct form that will hold the row index of the row selected in the grid. Add the following line of code above the SelectProduct() constructor on the SelectProduct form:

```
int selectedRow;
```

In the CellClick event of the Products grid, add the code that sets the variable declared you just declared:

```
private void grdProducts_CellClick(object sender, DataGridViewCellEventArgs e)
{
    selectedRow = e.RowIndex;
}
```

This code sets the row index so the application knows which row is selected.

Now add the following code to the cmdEdit button's Click() event on the SelectProduct form. Here is where the declared variable comes in because that variable is used to grab the ProductID value from the row that has been selected. This code then passes that value to the new constructor created on the ProductMain form, and opens the form.

```
int ProductID =
Convert.ToInt32(grdProducts.Rows[selectedRow].Cells["ProductID"].Value);
ProductMain prod = new ProductMain(ProductID);
prod.Show();
```

Last, wire the Delete button by adding the following code to the cmdDelete button's Click() event:

```
int productID =
Convert.ToInt32(grdProducts.Rows[selectedRow].Cells["ProductID"].Value);

FabrikamDataContext context =
    new FabrikamDataContext("user id=username;password=password");

var prodQuery = context.Products.Single(p => p.ProductID == productID);
context.Products.Remove(prodQuery);
context.SubmitChanges();
```

This code again gets the productID for the currently selected row in the Products grid and passes it to a LINQ query to return the item for the selected product. The Remove() method is called to remove that entity and then the SubmitChanges() is called to submit the changes back to the underlying database. That removes that record from the Products table.

OK, compile the application to make sure there are no coding errors. Press F5 to run the app, and have at it. The entire Products button on the main switchboard form has been wired up, and you can add, edit, and delete products.

Your homework assignment is to do the same thing for the Deliveries button. If you get stuck, the downloaded code for this appendix contains a fully functional copy (except for the replication part).

From this example, you can see how easy and efficient it is to use LINQ and LINQ technologies to upgrade an application.

LINQ to Entities: The ADO.NET Entity Framework

A lot of hype and information has come out of Microsoft regarding a technology called the ADO.NET Entity Framework. The ADO.NET Entity Framework is actually a set of technologies aimed at helping the developer be more productive and efficient. It was designed from day one to provide developers with the capability to create data access applications by programming against a known model over the existing method of accessing the database directly.

The ADO.NET Entity Framework is still in its development stages and won't be out until after the initial release of Visual Studio 2008. Because there might be some changes between now and when it is officially released, this appendix only introduces you to the technology and give you some insight as to what to expect when it does come out. The appendix provides an overview of the ADO.NET Entity Framework, including some background and some examples of how it can be used to benefit today's developers.

The ADO.NET Entity Framework has been scheduled to release after the release of Visual Studio 2008. At the time of this writing the current release of the Entity Framework is the ADO.NET Entity Framework Beta 2 dated August 27, 2007.

Overview

Today, the primary method of accessing data in a relational database is to write code that accesses that data directly. This requires developers who are used to working in an OO (object-oriented) environment to know the relational storage schema and takes much more code than is really needed.

The goal of the ADO.NET Entity Framework is to give developers the capability to create applications that access data in an OO fashion, meaning developers can now use a conceptual model in which to work with objects and properties. The benefits of this are much less code to write and developers who can work with technology that they know without needing to know the exact schema (such as tables and columns) in the underlying database.

ADO.NET Entity Framework addresses a number of developer issues that have been around for a while. For some time, developers have been struggling with how to model entities and relationships and at the same time work with the relational databases that store the data they need. It gets more difficult if the data spans multiple data stores. Add the OO layer to this puzzle, and you have the complexity of using OO technology to map to relational data stores, yet at the same time trying to make it easy (more efficient) for the developer.

For example, you can model a class to a relational data table, but how often is that a one-to-one situation? Typically, you have multiple tables that are mapped to a single class—and how do you represent relationships? Relationships between classes are certainly not the same as relationships between tables. You also have the problem of connecting objects with the data, meaning, how do you connect OO systems to relational data?

The good news is that the ADO.NET Entity Framework overcomes all of these issues and affords some additional features. To solve the problem of connecting OO systems to relational data, the Entity Framework maps relation objects (tables, columns, and primary and foreign keys) to entities and relationships in conceptual models.

The conceptual model comes from the division of the data model into three distinct parts:

- **Conceptual**—Defines the entities and relationships from the system being modeled.

- **Logical**—Normalizes the entities and relationships into "relational" tables and constraints.

- **Physical**—Handles the physical storage engine needs and capabilities of the particular data storage engine.

A developer need not be concerned about the physical aspects of the model. That is primarily the responsibility of a DBA. Today, developers typically focus their attention on the logical model by writing queries to access the data. Conceptual models are generally used as a data capture tool to gather requirements. Often you see developers completely skip the creation of the conceptual model by going right to the creation of the relational objects.

The ADO.NET Entity Framework puts more emphasis on the conceptual model by letting developers program directly against it. The ADO.NET Entity Framework conceptual model can be connected directly to the logical model, providing developers access to the conceptual entities and relationships. It is the job of the Entity Framework to map entity operations to their SQL counterparts. You can see the benefit of this: One model can be used across multiple storage engines.

The creation of the mapping between the application and the storage engine is the responsibility of the ADO.NET Entity Framework. The mapping requires the three parts discussed previously and are created and used within the application. Three physical components are created in the mapping:

- The conceptual schema definition language (a file with an extension of `.csdl`).

- The logical storage schema definition language (a file with an extension of `.ssdl`).

- The mapping specification language (a file with an extension of `.msl`).

The developer has a couple of options for creating these files. A set of classes is created with the files; the developer uses those classes to work directly with the conceptual model. Within Visual Studio

2008, you can use a wizard-driven Visual Studio template that creates the files automatically with the information you specify. The other option is a command-line tool the Entity Data Model Generator (EdmGen) that accomplishes the same thing. You'll look at the EdmGen tool later in this appendix, and you'll also see how to use the template.

Using the Entity Framework is quite simple because it consists of number of namespaces that construct and maintain the metadata information needed for models and mapping. `System.Data.Entity` uses the .NET Framework data provider and the `EntityConnection` class to accomplish this.

The great thing is that LINQ to Entities is fully supported by the Entity Framework. LINQ to Entities provides query support against the conceptual objects and strongly typed LINQ queries.

Installing the ADO.NET Entity Framework

Entity Framework is not installed when you install any beta of Visual Studio. It is a completely separate program, and there are actually two components that you need to install. The first is ADO.NET Entity Framework Beta 2 which can be found at:

```
http://www.microsoft.com/downloads/details.aspx?FamilyID=F1ADC5D1-A42E-40A6-A68C-
A42EE11186F7&DisplayLang=en
```

The file is a mere 1.2 megabytes, so it is a quick download.

The second download is the ADO.NET Entity Framework Tools, which you can get from:

```
http://www.microsoft.com/downloads/details.aspx?FamilyId=09A36081-5ED1-4648-B995-
6239D0B77CB5&displaylang=en
```

This download is a bit larger, roughly 6.6 megabytes.

Install the Entity Framework first, and then install the Entity Framework Tools. (If you attempt to install the Tools first, the install program tells you that you need to install the Entity Framework first and then exits the install.)

To begin, double-click the Entity Framework install file called `EFSetup-x86.exe`. At the Welcome screen, click Next. You'll need to select the I Agree option on the License Agreement screen before you can continue with the installation. Then click the Install button. Click Finish when the installation is complete.

The Tools installation (`EFToolsSetup-x86.exe`) is similar, but there are a couple of extra steps. At the Welcome screen, click Next. Again, you'll need to select the I Agree option on the License Agreement screen before you can continue. Click Next. The next step asks for the destination where you would like to install the product. Accept the default or enter a destination path, and then click the Install button.

Once the installation is complete, you'll notice a new Start menu option called ADO.NET Entity Framework Tools Preview. This new menu option includes several support documents along with a couple of great ADO.NET Visual Studio example projects. Very nice.

ADO.NET Entity Framework Example

The easiest way to get a feel for the ADO.NET Entity Framework and see what it can do is to run through an example. Fire up Visual Studio and create a new C# Windows forms project. Name the project `ProductSales` and click OK. Open the Solution Explorer, right-click on the solution name, and select Add ⇨ New Item from the context menu.

When the Add New Item dialog appears, select the ADO.NET Entity Data Model template (see Figure B-1).

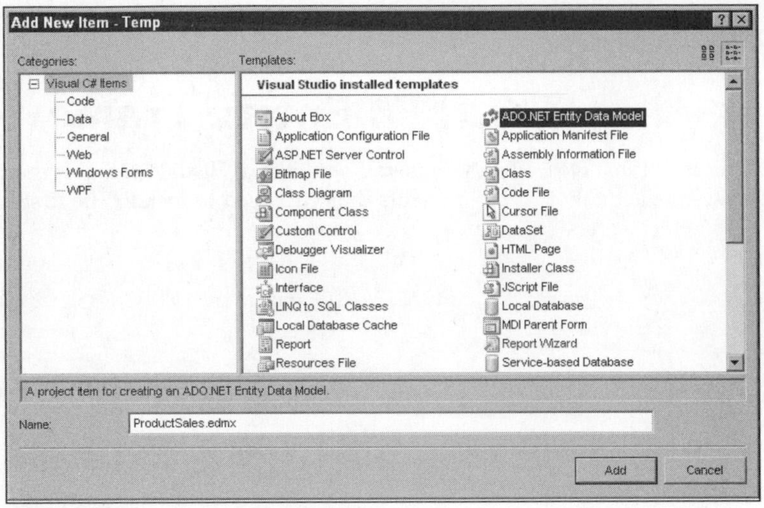

Figure B-1

Name the data model `ProductSales` and click Add. This launches the Entity Data Model Wizard. The first page of the wizard asks you to select the source that the model contents will come from. You can choose to generate a model from a database or to create an empty model.

If you choose to create an empty model, the Finish button appears. Click it, and an empty model is created, in which you can build a model manually using XML.

This example, however, won't put you through that, so select the Generate From Database option (see Figure B-2) and click Next.

The next page of the wizard lets you choose or create your data connection to the data store. Because no connection has been created, click the New Connection button to open the Connection Properties dialog (see Figure B-3).

In this dialog, select the server from which the Entity Framework will make its connection. Next, select how the Entity Framework will make its connection, via Windows Authentication or through SQL Server Authentication. This example uses SQL Server Authentication, but feel free to select Windows Authentication.

Next, choose the database from which the Entity Framework will connect to access the objects and create the entities and relationships. Select the AdventureWorks database, and then click the Test Connection button to ensure that the connection information has been entered correctly and that a connection can be made. Click OK.

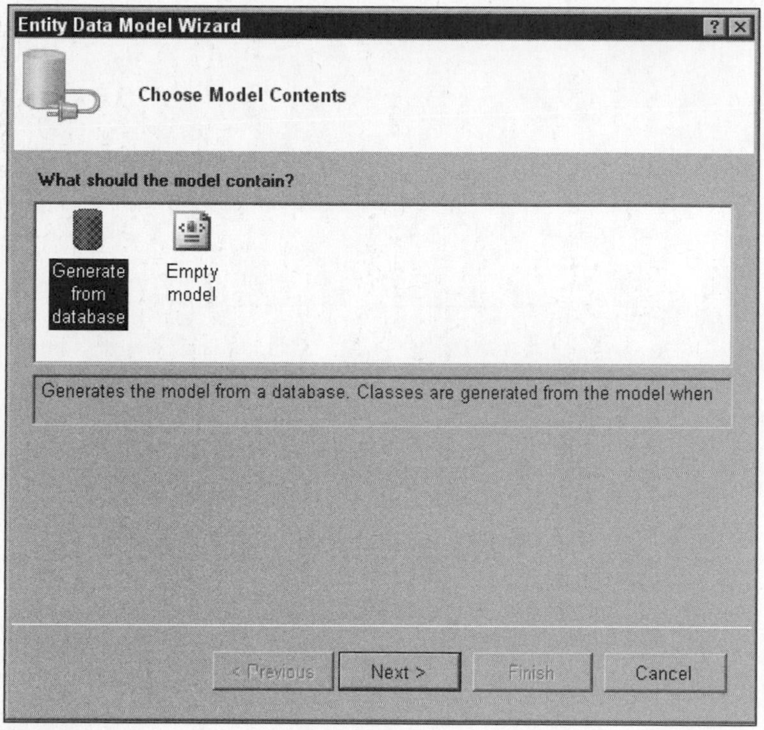

Figure B-2

The top part of the Data Connection Wizard step should look like Figure B-4.

Choose whether you want to store sensitive connection information in the connection string. For this example, select Yes.

Ensure that the Save Entity Connection Settings in the App.Config as check box is checked. The wizard requires that you provide a name for the connection settings. The best practice in naming is to include the word Entities at the end of the name. For this example, enter AdventureWorksEntities. Click Next.

The next page in the wizard asks you to select the database objects that you want to include in the model. By default, all the objects are selected including tables, views, and stored procedures. For this project, unselect all the objects, as shown in Figure B-5.

Now expand the Tables node, and select the following tables:

- ❑   Contact
- ❑   SalesOrderHeader
- ❑   SalesOrderDetail

- `SpecialOfferProduct`
- `Product`

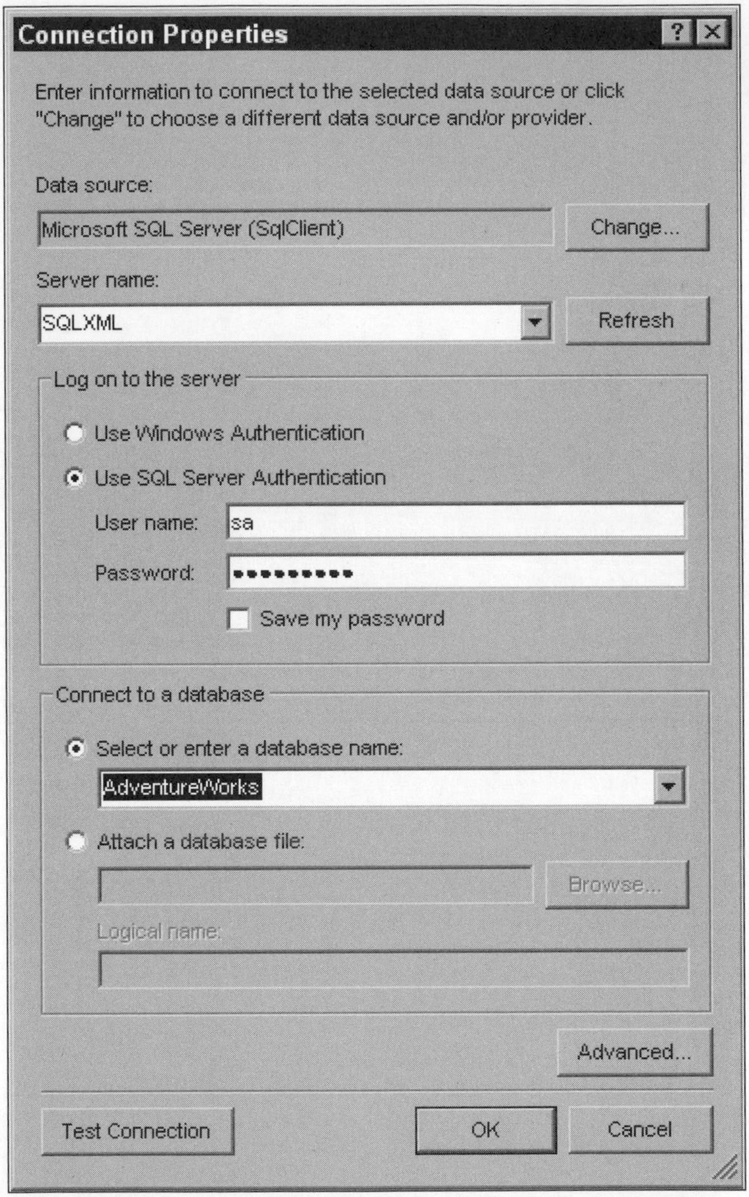

Figure B-3

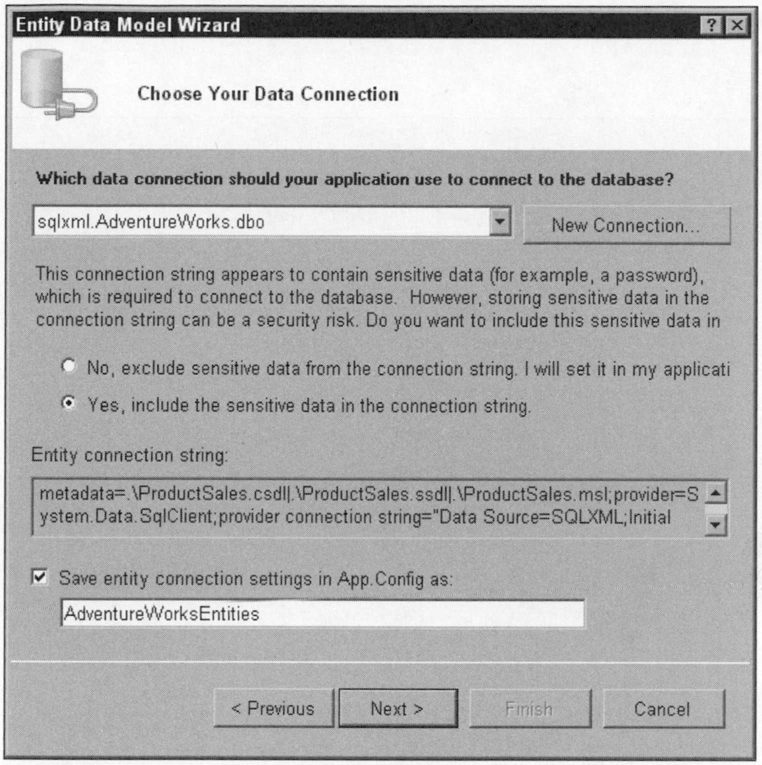

Figure B-4

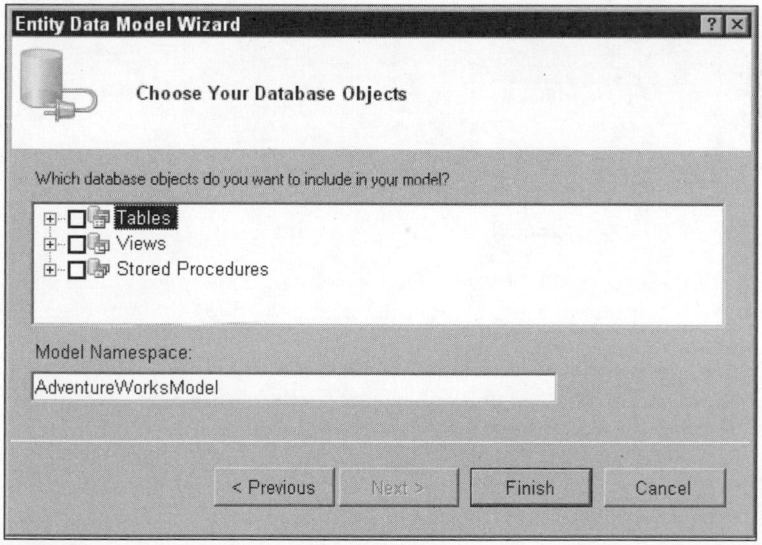

Figure B-5

At the bottom of the wizard page, name the Model Namespace. It is good practice to begin the name with the same name you gave the entity on the previous page. For this exercise, use the name AdventureWorksModel.

> The Model Namespace name and the Entity Connection Settings name must be different, like the ones in this example: AdventureWorksEntities and AdventureWorksModel. Giving them the same name will result in compile errors.

Click Finish. The Entity Data Model Wizard begins creating the entity data model for the objects that you selected. A mapping is created, and the mapping files and class definitions are generated. When the mapping generation is complete, the entity classes display in the designer (see Figure B-6). This view shows the entities that were created, the relationships between the entities that were created, and other pertinent information such as relationship names and navigation properties.

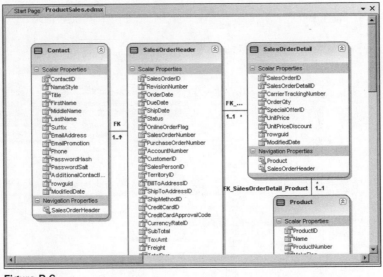

Figure B-6

You can see what files were created by going to the Solution Explorer and looking at the contents of the solution. Figure B-7 shows the files that were generated and added to the project.

In Solution Explorer, expand the ProductSales.edmx node. Underneath that node you'll see two files: a `.cs` file and a `.diagram` file. The `.cs` file contains the partial classes that contain the information that the programmer will interact with on the conceptual model level.

Open the .cs file and scroll down a tad (see Figure B-8). You will see that `ObjectContext` is used as well as the `EntityConnection` class (from the `System.Data.EntityClient` namespace).

You'll see that these classes derive from the `ObjectContext` class. The `ObectContext` in the ADO.NET Entity Framework represents the entity container in the conceptual model. Just like LINQ to SQL and the `DataContext`, the `ObjectContext` class exposes the `SaveChanges` method, which ushers changes back to the underlying database. It is the primary class for interacting with data as objects, serving as the pathway through which all CRUD (create, read, update, and delete) operations are passed and executed.

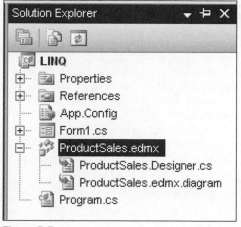

Figure B-7

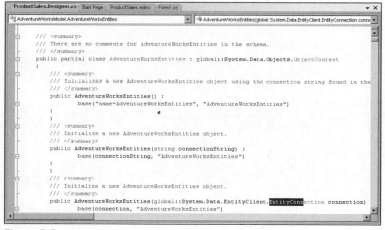

Figure B-8

As you scroll through the .cs file, you will see that it contains all the code necessary to manipulate the model-provided data, such as adding, deleting, and updating data.

Now you're ready to start adding code to utilize the Entity Framework. Open Form1 in design mode and add a button, a combo box, and a DataViewGrid to the form. Name the combo box salesPerson and name the grid grdOrderDetail. Next, double-click on the form itself to view the code behind. Add the following two statements to the top of the form:

```
using System.Data.Objects;
using AdventureWorksModel;
```

Add the following line of code to the top of the partial class for the form:

```
private AdventureWorksEntities productSalesContext;
```

Add the following code to the Load event of the form:

```
productSalesContext = new AdventureWorksEntities();

grdProducts.Columns.Add("OrderID", "Order");
grdProducts.Columns.Add("OrderQty", "Quantity");
grdProducts.Columns.Add("ProductID", "Product");
grdProducts.Columns.Add("UnitPrice", "Price");
grdProducts.Columns.Add("LineTotal", "Total");

ObjectQuery<Contact> salesPerson = productSalesContext.Contact.Where("it
.MiddleName IS NOT NULL").OrderBy("it.LastName");

this.cbosalesPerson.DataSource = salesPerson.Include
("SalesOrderHeader.SalesOrderDetail");

this.cbosalesPerson.DisplayMember = "LastName";
```

Finally, add the following code to the SelectedIndexChanged event of the combo:

```
grdProducts.Rows.Clear();

Contact person = (Contact)cbosalesPerson.SelectedItem;

foreach (SalesOrderHeader soh in person.SalesOrderHeader)
{
    object[] row = new object[4];

    row[0] = soh.SalesOrderDetail.SalesOrderID;
    row[1] = soh.SalesOrderDetail.OrderQty;
    row[2] = soh.SalesOrderDetail.ProductID;
    row[3] = soh.SalesOrderDetail.UnitPrice;
    row[4] = soh.SalesOrderDetail.LineTotal;

    grdOrderDetails.Rows.Add(row);

}
```

Compile the application to make sure everything is OK. Run the application, and when the form loads, the combo box will be filled with a list of contacts. Selecting a contact will display the order detail for that contact in the grid, as shown in Figure B-9.

Let's take a look on how this works. In the Load method, four columns are defined on the grid, but that is not the important code. The important code is the following lines:

```
private AdventureWorksEntities productSalesContext;

productSalesContext = new AdventureWorksEntities();
```

```
ObjectQuery<Contact> salesPerson = productSalesContext.Contact.Where↵
("it.MiddleName IS NOT NULL").OrderBy("it.LastName");

this.cbosalesPerson.DataSource = salesPerson.Include
("SalesOrderHeader.SalesOrderDetail");
```

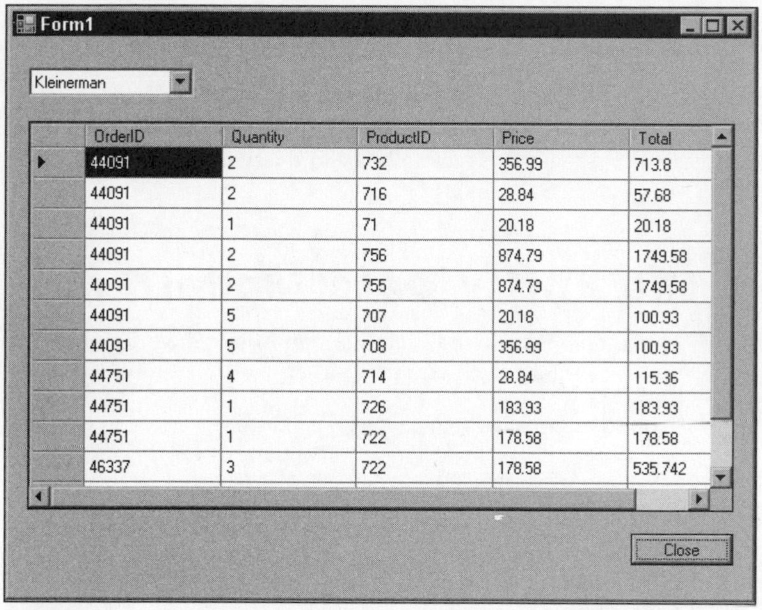

Figure B-9

The first line creates an instance of `ObjectContext` based on the defined entity. The second line initializes a new instance of the `ObjectContext` class. The third line uses the defined and mapped entities to return all contacts that have a middle name. The fourth line sets the data source of the combo box.

How about the `IndexChanged` event on the combo? The first line of the following code gets the selected contact from the combo. Because the ADO.NET Entity Framework handles the relationships, the rest of the code gets the sales order detail for the selected contact, and then populates the grid.

```
Contact person = (Contact)cbosalesPerson.SelectedItem;

foreach (SalesOrderHeader soh in person.SalesOrderHeader)
{
    object[] row = new object[4];

    row[0] = soh.SalesOrderDetail.OrderQty;
    row[1] = soh.SalesOrderDetail.ProductID;
    row[2] = soh.SalesOrderDetail.UnitPrice;
    row[3] = soh.SalesOrderDetail.LineTotal;

    grdOrderDetails.Rows.Add(row);

}
```

This last example is a simple one that builds on the first example. The previous example returned the `ProductID` from the `SalesOrderDetail` table. To return the actual product name instead of the just the ID, `Product` must be included in the join:

```
this.cbosalesPerson.DataSource = salesPerson.Include("SalesOrderHeader
.SalesOrderDetail").Include("SalesOrderHeader.Product");
```

With that, you can grab the product name and display it in the grid.

```
row[1] = soh.SalesOrderDetail.Product.ProductName
```

The following sections provide an overview of how to query the entity model and how to work with objects.

Querying the Entity Data Model

Querying the entity data model is really not that different from the work you did in LINQ to SQL. The best form is the `ObjectQuery` class, which you saw earlier:

```
private AdventureWorksEntities productSalesContext;

productSalesContext = new AdventureWorksEntities();

ObjectQuery<Contact> salesPerson = productSalesContext.Contact.Where
("it.MiddleName IS NOT NULL").OrderBy("it.LastName");
```

You can also do something like the following, which returns an entity type:

```
private AdventureWorksEntities productSalesContext;

string qry = @"SELECT VALUE Contact FROM AdventureWorksEntities.Contact";
ObjectQuery<Contact> con = new ObjectQuery<Contact>(qry, productSalesContext);
```

Likewise, you can create and use an `ObjectQuery`class with parameters:

```
private AdventureWorksEntities productSalesContext;

string qry = @"SELECT VALUE Contact FROM AdventureWorksEntities.Contact WHERE
Contact.LastName = @lastname AND Contat.FirstName = @fn";

ObjectQuery<Contact> con = new ObjectQuery<Contact>(qry, productSalesContext);

con.Parameters.Add(new ObjectParameter("ln","Klein"));
con.Parameters.Add(new ObjectParameter("fn","Jason"));
```

You can also use an `ObjectQuery` class to return primitive and anonymous types, and you can shape the results:

```
private AdventureWorksEntities productSalesContext;

ObjectQuery<Contact> con =  salesPerson.Include("SalesOrderHeader
.SalesOrderDetail");
```

```
foreach (SalesOrderHeader order in query.First().SalesOrderHeader)
{
    listbox1.Items.Add(String.Format("Order Date: {0}", order.PurchaseOrderNumber));
    listbox1.Items.Add(String.Format("Total: {0}",order.TotalDue.ToString()));
    foreach (SalesOrderDetail item in order.SalesOrderDetail)
    {
        listBox1.Items.Add(String.Format("Product: {0} "
            + "Quantity: {1}", item.Name.ToString(),
            item.OrderQty.ToString()));
    }
}
```

Querying the entity data model is quite easy and efficient.

Working with Objects

Let's take a look at working with objects that represent entity types defined by an entity data model.

The following example illustrates how to use the entity data model to update and insert data:

```
string ln = "Kleinerman";

productSalesContext = new AdventureWorksEntities();

Contact con = productSalesContext.Contact.Where("it.LastName = @lastname",
    new ObjectParameter("lastname", ln)).First();

con.EmailAddress = "";
con.EmailPromotion = 1;

Contact newcon = new Contact();

newcon.EmailAddress = "asdf";
newcon.EmailPromotion = 1;
newcon.FirstName = "Scott";
newcon.LastName = "Klein";
newcon.MiddleName = "L";
newcon.NameStyle = false;
newcon.PasswordHash = "asdf";
newcon.PasswordSalt = "adsf";
newcon.Phone = "555-555-5555";
newcon.Suffix = "Mr.";
newcon.Title = "Geek";

productSalesContext.SaveChanges();
```

As you saw earlier, you can also bind objects to controls, like this:

```
ObjectQuery<Contact> salesPerson = productSalesContext.Contact.Where
("it.ContactID < 5000").OrderBy("it.LastName");

this.cboSalesPerson.DataSource = salesPerson.Include("SalesOrderHeader
```

```
    .SalesOrderDetail");
    this.cbosalesPerson.DisplayMember = "LastName";
```

A best practice is to detach objects from the `ObjecContext` when they are no longer needed. Object Services lets you accomplish this via the `Detach` method. This decreases the amount of memory being used.

Object Services, implemented via the `System.Data.Objects` and `System.Data.Objects.DataClasses` namespaces, is a component of the .NET Entity Framework that enables you to perform CRUD operations that are expressed as strongly typed CLR objects. These objects are instances of entity types. Supporting both LINQ and Entity SQL queries, Object Services lets you query against defined types as well as track changes and bind objects to controls.

```
    productSalesContext.Detach(Contact.SalesOrderHeader);
```

Another good practice is to manage concurrency conflicts in an object context. Making changes back to the database could cause conflicts, so those need to be handled. In the following example, the `SaveChanges()` method is called to save any changes back to the database. If there are any conflicts, they are caught, the object context is refreshed, and `SaveChanges()` reapplied.

```
    try
    {
        //make changes..then save them
        productSalesContext.SaveChanges();
    }
    catch (OptimisticConcurrencyException oce)
    {
        productSalesContext.Refresh(RefreshMode.ClientWins, Contact);
        productSalesContext.SaveChanges();
    }
```

Hopefully, you can see that working with objects is just as simple as working with LINQ to SQL.

Entity Data Model Generator

The Entity Data Model Generator tool is one of the options available to the developer for generating the entity data model. It is a command-line tool that provides the following functionality:

- ❏ Create `.csdl`, `.ssdl`, and `.msl` files that are used by the entity data model.
- ❏ Validate existing models.
- ❏ Generate source code files containing object classes generated from a `.csdl` file.
- ❏ Generate source code files containing generated views from the `.ssdl`, `.csdl`, and `.msl` files.

The Entity Data Model Generator tool is located in `\Windows\Microsoft.NET\Framework\v3.5`. Its general syntax is:

```
    EdmGen /mode:choice [options]
```

The following table lists the available modes for the EdmGen tool. You must specify one of them.

Mode	Description
ValidateArtifacts	Validates the .cdsl, .ssdl, and .msl files. Requires at least one /inssdl or /incsdl argument. If /inmsl is specified, the /inssdl and /incsdl arguments are also required.
FullGeneration	Generates .cdsl, .ssdl, and .msl, object layer and view files. Updates the database connection information in the /connectionstring option. Requires a /connectionstring argument and either a /p argument or /outssdl, /outcsdl, /outmsdl, /outobjectlayer, /outviews, and /entitycontainer arguments.
FromSSDLGeneration	Generates .cdsl, and .msl, files. Requires the /inssdl argument and either a /p argument or /outcsdl, /outmsl, /outobjectlayer, /outviews, and /entitycontainer arguments.
EntityClassGeneration	Creates a source code file that contains generated classes from the .csdl file. Requires the /incsdl argument and either a /p or /outobjectlayer argument.
ViewGeneration	Creates a source code file containing views generated from the .ssdl, .csdl, and .msl files. Requires the /inssdl, /incsdl, /inmsl, and either the /p or /outviews arguments.

Along with the modes, you can specify one or more of the following options.

Option	Description
/p[roject]:	String value that specifies the object name.
/prov[ider]:	String value that specifies the name of the ADO.NET data provider. The default is System.Data.Sqlclient (the .NET Framework Data Provider for SQL Server).
/c[onnection]:	String value that specifies the string used to connect to the data source.
/incsdl:	Specifies the .csdl file or a directory where the .csdl files are located. Argument can be specified multiple times.
/refcsdl:	Specifies additional .csdl files used to resolve .csdl source file references specified by the /incsdl option.
/inmsl:	Specifies the .msl file or a directory where the .msl files are located. Argument can be specified multiple times.
/inssdl:	Specifies the .ssdl file or a directory where the .ssdl file is located.
/outcsdl:	Specifies the name of the .csdl file to be created.
/outmsl:	Specifies the name of the .msl file to be created.
/outssdl:	Specifies the name of the .ssdl file to be created.
/outobjectlayer:	Specifies the name of the source code file containing the generated objects fro the .csdl file.

Option	Description
`/outviews:`	Specifies the name of the source code file containing the generated views.
`/language:`	Specifies the language for the generated source code files. Options are VB and C#. Default is C#.
`/namespace:`	Specifies the namespace to use and set in the `.csdl` file when running in `FullGeneration` or `FromSSDLGeneration` mode. Not used in the `EntityClassGeneration` mode.
`/entitycontainer:`	Specifies the name to apply to the `<EntityContainer>` element in the EDM file.
`/nologo`	Hides the copyright message.
`/help`	Displays command syntax and tool options.

The following examples show how the EdmGen tool can be used. The first example uses the `FullGeneration` mode to generate all necessary files:

```
edmgen /mode:fullgeneration /c:"Data Source=AvalonServer;Initial
Catalog=AdventureWorks; Integrated Security=SSPI" /p:LINQProject
```

In this example, a C# object source code file is created from the `.csdl`:

```
edmgen /mode:entityclassgeneration /incsdl:c:\wrox\Appendix\LINQ\
AdventureWorksModel.csdl /outobjectlayer: c:\wrox\Appendix\LINQ\
AdventureWorksModel.cs /language:csharp
```

The ADO.NET Entity Framework clearly helps you work with relational databases as well as model entities and relationships.

LINQ to XSD

Any programming language that supports the .NET Framework will support LINQ. LINQ to XML is LINQ-enabled, meaning that you have access to all of the functionality of LINQ such as the standard query operators and the LINQ programming interface. Because of the integration into the .NET Framework, LINQ to XML can take advantage of functionality the .NET Framework provides, such as compile-time checking, strong typing, and debugging.

LINQ to XML makes working with XML much easier by providing a simple way to work directly with methods and properties, by programming against XML tree components such as elements and attributes, but in an untyped manner. This is where LINQ to XSD comes in. LINQ to XSD lets you work with typed XML.

Although LINQ to XSD is in its early stages, it'd be a shame not to include it in this book. It will probably change somewhat, but the purpose of this appendix is to provide you with an introduction to LINQ to XSD and show you some of its capabilities. This is a cool technology and makes working with XML a pleasure.

LINQ to XSD has been scheduled to release after the release of Visual Studio 2008. At the time of this writing the current release of LINQ to XSD is the LINQ to XSD Preview 0.2 that works with Beta 1 of Orcas. To work with the examples in this appendix, you need to install Beta 1 of Visual Studio codenamed Orcas.

LINQ to XSD Overview

LINQ to XSD is a new technology aimed at enhancing the great LINQ to XML technology by providing .NET developers support for typed XML programming. For example, in typical LINQ to XML programming, you would work with an XML tree as follows:

```
var total = (from item in SalesOrderHeader.Elements("Item")
    select (double)item.Element("UnitPrice")
        * (int)item.Element("OrderQuantity")
    ).Sum();
```

In this example, the developer is working with untyped XML, accessing the elements and attributes of the XML directly. However, LINQ to XSD lets you work with typed XML, like this:

```
var total = (from item in SalesOrderHeader.Item
            select item.UnitPrice * item.OrderQuantity
            ).Sum();
```

Working with typed XML is made possible by XML schemas that are mapped automatically to defined object models. Through this mapping XML data can be manipulated just like other object-oriented models. The result is that you are working directly with classes that can enforce validation through the use of the schema, plus you are working with XML objects generated from the XML schemas that provide a much more efficient XML development platform.

The benefit of working with typed XML is that it makes working with XML-related programming tasks much easier and makes for much more efficient code.

Installing LINQ to XSD

For now, LINQ to XSD is not installed when you install any beta of Visual Studio. It is a completely separate install and is currently found at the following location:

```
http://www.microsoft.com/downloads/details.aspx?FamilyID=e9c23715
    -9e71-47a7-b4db-363c2a68fab4&DisplayLang=en
```

At a mere 1.6 megabytes, it's a quick download. The install is simple. At the Welcome screen, click Next. On the License Agreement screen, select the I Agree option to continue with the installation, then click the Next button. The final screen of the installation wizard lets you know that the installer is ready to install LINQ to XSD. Click Next to begin the install.

Once the installation is complete, you'll notice a new Start menu option called LINQ to XSD Preview. You can tell that Microsoft is serious about this technology because not only does the LINQ to XSD installation install the necessary support files for LINQ to XSD, but it also installs several support documents along with a couple of great LINQ to XSD Visual Studio example projects. How cool is that?

LINQ to XSD Example

The easiest way to get a feel for LINQ to XSD and to understand what it can do is to tackle an example. You're going to need Beta 1 as stated earlier, but before you fire up Visual Studio, a little prep work needs to be done.

In the Wrox directory on your local hard drive, create a folder called AppendixC. Next, open your favorite text editor and enter the following XML. Save the file as Orders.xml. The data that this XML uses comes from the SalesOrderDetail table in the AdventureWorks database. Obviously it is not all the records from that table, but only a small subset of orders from a specific customer.

```
<Order>
  <OrderDetail>
    <CustID>676</CustID>
```

```
      <OrderID>43659</OrderID>
      <Item>
        <ProductID>709</ProductID>
        <UnitPrice>5.70</UnitPrice>
        <OrderQuantity>6</OrderQuantity>
      </Item>
      <Item>
        <ProductID>711</ProductID>
        <UnitPrice>20.18</UnitPrice>
        <OrderQuantity>4</OrderQuantity>
      </Item>
      <Item>
        <ProductID>712</ProductID>
        <UnitPrice>5.18</UnitPrice>
        <OrderQuantity>2</OrderQuantity>
      </Item>
      <Item>
        <ProductID>714</ProductID>
        <UnitPrice>28.84</UnitPrice>
        <OrderQuantity>3</OrderQuantity>
      </Item>
      <Item>
        <ProductID>716</ProductID>
        <UnitPrice>28.84</UnitPrice>
        <OrderQuantity>1</OrderQuantity>
      </Item>
      <Item>
        <ProductID>771</ProductID>
        <UnitPrice>2039.99</UnitPrice>
        <OrderQuantity>1</OrderQuantity>
      </Item>
    </OrderDetail>
  </Order>
```

Once you have created the Orders.xml file, fire up Visual Studio and create a new C# Windows project. In the Project types section, expand the C# node. Select the LINQ to XSD Preview project type, and then choose the LINQ to XSD Windows Application from the list of project templates (see Figure C-1).

Name the project LINQ, specifying the appropriate location in which to create the project. Click OK.

Now open the Solution Explorer and expand the References node. Besides the typical LINQ reference of System.Xml.Linq, you'll see a new reference to Microsoft.Xml.Schema.Linq, shown in Figure C-2. This namespace contains all the XML classes that provide the LINQ to XSD mapping functionality and XSD schema definition support.

Next, open Form1 in design mode and drop a couple of buttons and a text box on the form. Set the Text property of button1 to Untyped, and then double-click the button to view its Click event. Enter the following code in the button1 Click event:

```
var order = XElement.Load("C:\\Wrox\\AppendixC\\Orders.xml");

var total = (from salesOrder in order.Elements("OrderDetail")
    from item in salesOrder.Elements("Item")
```

```
    select (double)item.Element("UnitPrice")
        * (int)item.Element("OrderQuantity")
    ).Sum();

    textBox1.Text = total.ToString();
```

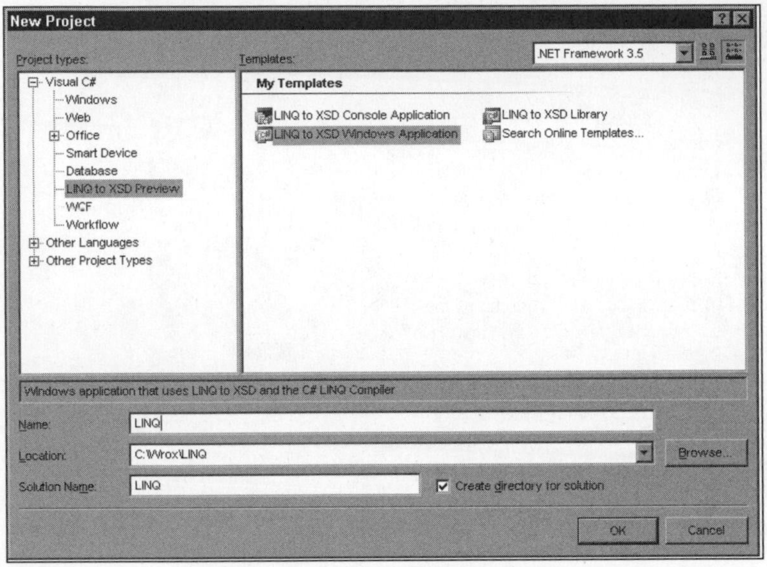

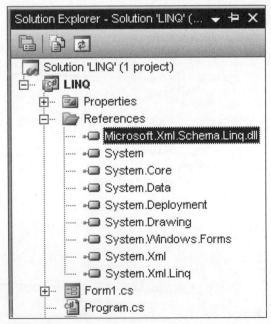

Figure C-1

Figure C-2

From the Build menu, select Build Solution to ensure that the project compiles. Then run the application and click the Untyped button. The text box should be populated with the value of 2280.63, as shown in Figure C-3.

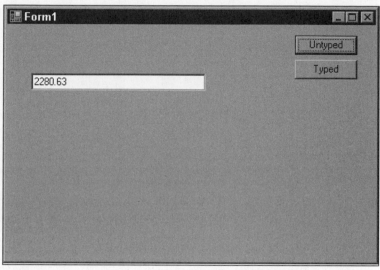

Figure C-3

This example is similar to the examples you worked with in the Chapters 5 through 9 in the LINQ to XML section. It uses the Load method of the XElement method to load an XML document into memory. A LINQ query expression is then executed against the XML document, using the sum( ) query operator to sum all the order totals. The results are the displayed in the text box.

Notice that because the XML document is untyped, the use of the Elements method is needed to specify the element you're looking for. Because no mapping taking place, you have to physically specify the element name.

Wouldn't it be nice to be able to use typed XML programming? Ah, yes, you can. First, open the Orders.xml file and add the following highlighted namespace to it:

```
<Order xmlns="http://www.AdventureWorks.com/Orders">
  <OrderDetail>
    <CustID>676</CustID>
    <OrderID>43659</OrderID>
    <Item>
      <ProductID>709</ProductID>
      <UnitPrice>5.70</UnitPrice>
      <OrderQuantity>6</OrderQuantity>
    </Item>
    ...
</Order>
```

Next, highlight the entire XML tree and copy it to the Clipboard. Go back to your Visual Studio project, and in the Solution Explorer window right-click the solution and select Add ➪ New Item from the context menu. In the Add New Item dialog, select XML File in the Templates section (see Figure C-4).

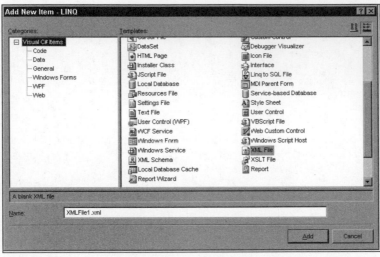

Figure C-4

For the purposes of this example, you can keep the name of XMLFile1.xml. Click Add.

XMLFile1.xml opens in the IDE and contains a single header line. Delete the XML that is there, and paste the XML that you copied from Orders.xml to the Clipboard. Save the new XMLFile.xml file.

Next, return to Solution Explorer and add a new item, this time selecting an XML Schema template from the Add New Item dialog. When the schema opens, delete the default contents of the file, add the following XML, and save it:

```xml
<xs:schema
  xmlns:xs="http://www.w3.org/2001/XMLSchema"
  targetNamespace="http://www.AdventureWorks.com/Orders"
  xmlns="http://www.AdventureWorks.com/Orders"
  elementFormDefault="qualified">

<xs:element name="Order">
  <xs:complexType>
    <xs:sequence>
      <xs:element ref="OrderDetail"
                  minOccurs="0" maxOccurs="unbounded"/>
    </xs:sequence>
  </xs:complexType>
</xs:element>
<xs:element name="OrderDetail">
  <xs:complexType>
    <xs:sequence>
      <xs:element name="CustId" type="xs:string"/>
      <xs:element ref="Item"
                  minOccurs="0" maxOccurs="unbounded"/>
```

```
        </xs:sequence>
      </xs:complexType>
    </xs:element>
    <xs:element name="Item">
      <xs:complexType>
        <xs:sequence>
          <xs:element name="ProductID" type="xs:string"/>
          <xs:element name="UnitPrice" type="xs:double"/>
          <xs:element name="OrderQuantity" type="xs:int"/>
        </xs:sequence>
      </xs:complexType>
    </xs:element>
  </xs:schema>
```

You're not quite done yet. Once you have created the schema, a property needs to be changed on it. Return to the Solution Explorer window, right-click on the XMLSchema1.xsd file, and select Properties from the context menu, as shown in Figure C-5.

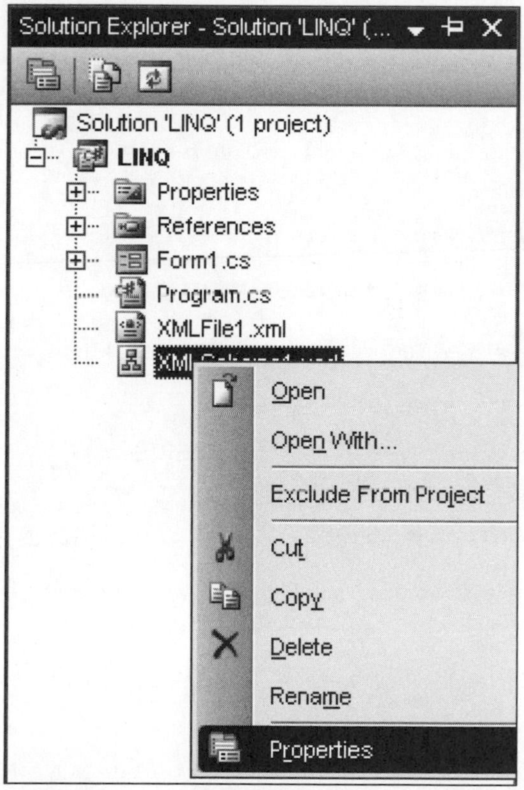

Figure C-5

In the Properties window for the schema, select the property called Build Action. The default value for this property is None; change it to LinqToXsdSchema, as shown in Figure C-6. This property informs the project that the schema will be included in the project's build process.

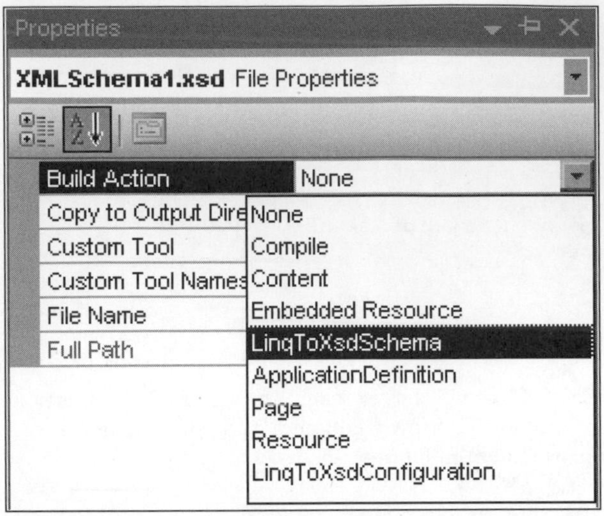

Figure C-6

The final step is to add some code behind the form. Set the Text property of the second button to Typed, and double-click the button to display the Click event code for that button.

Before you add the code to the Click event, scroll to the top of the code and add the following using statement:

```
using www.AdventureWorks.com.Orders;
```

Finally, in the Click event for button2, add the following:

```
var ord = Order.Load("C:\\Wrox\\AppendixC\\Orders.xml");

var total = (from purchaseOrder in ord.OrderDetail
             from item in purchaseOrder.Item
             select item.UnitPrice * item.OrderQuantity
             ).Sum();

textBox1.Text = total.ToString();
```

Notice that as you type, IntelliSense kicks in and displays the mapping between the XML and the XSD. You know typed XML programming is here, and now you only need to type order.OrderDetail.

Now, compile and run the application, and click the Typed button. You will get the same results in the text box that you did when you click the Untyped button.

Cool, huh? But wait. What is this Order object in the first line that the Load method uses? Where did that come from? Put your mouse cursor over the word Order and right-click. From the context menu, select Go To Definition (see Figure C-7).

A file called `LinqToXsdSources` opens, as shown in Figure C-8.

This file is an external mapping file created by LINQ to XSD when the project is compiled. As you can see, it is a fairly lengthy file, but it contains all the necessary mapping information to effectively provide typed XML programming.

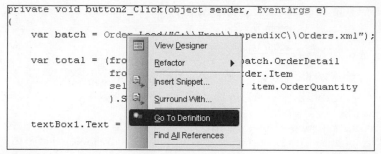

Figure C-7

Figure C-8

It is recommended that the generated code not be modified because it is quite complex and any changes made to the file would be lost during regeneration.

Instances of LINQ to XSD types are referred to as XML objects because the generated classes model typed views on untyped XML trees. Another way to say it is that the generated classes use properties to access the untyped XML trees.

An instance of LINQ to XSD is a set of classes that form wrappers around an instance of the LINQ to XML `XElement` class.

Mapping Rules

When a schema is mapped to an object type, LINQ to XSD requires that the mapping meet several constraints:

❑ The mapping is understandable to the developer.

❑ The mapping does not rely on any customization by default.

❑ The mapping must derive classes that are close to the expectation of an OO programmer.

❑ The mapping covers all of the XML schema.

❑ The mapping facilitates round-tripping of instance data.

❑ The mapping conveys, where possible, most schema objectives into the object models.

This systematic rule mapping ensures a clean, precise mapping, and is assumed by LINQ to XSD. The following is a list of most of the mapping rules that are utilized by LINQ to XSD to map XML schemas to .NET object models:

❑ XML names are mapped to CLR names.

❑ XML namespaces are mapped to CLR namespaces.

❑ Global element declarations are mapped to classes.

❑ Complex-type definitions are mapped to classes.

❑ Local declarations of elements, attributes, and references are mapped to properties.

❑ Named and anonymous types by default are not mapped to classes.

❑ Simple-type references are mapped to CLR value types or strings.

❑ Anonymous complex types for local elements by default are mapped to inner classes.

❑ Simple-type restrictions are mapped to element property preconditions.

❑ Complex-type derivation is mapped to object-oriented subclassing via extension and restriction.

❑ Substitution grouping is mapped to object-oriented subclassing.

❑ Redefinitions are carried out before mapping as applied by `System.Xml.Schema` rules.

LINQ to XSD-Generated API Class Methods

This section briefly discusses the methods of the API classes that LINQ to XSD generates from XML schemas. These methods should seem familiar because they are also methods within LINQ to XML. However, they are the typed version of the methods.

The current release of LINQ to XSD is in its early stages, so these API methods could change.

Load Method

You've seen the `Load` method used a couple of times in the example in this appendix. The first was the LINQ to XML's `Load` method on the `XElement`. The second time it was used was on the typed version of a generated class.

`Load` creates an instance of the generated class, letting the newly created instance serve as a typed view on an `XElement` instance. Take a look at the various overloads for the `Load` method. First, here's an example that takes a URI string as the data source:

```
public static val Load(string uri);
```

The next example is the same as the first, but it includes a parameter to control the preservation of whitespace.

```
static val Load(string uri, bool preserveWhitespace);
```

Here's how to use a TextReader as the data source:

```
static val Load(TextReader tr);
```

The following example is the same as the previous example except that it includes a parameter to control the preservation of whitespace. Notice that this example also uses a TextReader as the data source.

```
static val Load(TextReader tr, bool preserveWhitespace);
```

Here's how to use an XmlReader as the data source.

```
static val Load(XmlReader xr);
```

The following example, taken from earlier in the appendix, shows how the Load method is used on a typed `XElement`.

```
var ord = Order.Load("C:\\Wrox\\AppendixC\\Orders.xml");
```

Keep in mind that these overloads may change in the actual release of LINQ to XSD.

Parse

The `Parse` method of a generated class is the typed version of the LINQ to XML `XElement Parse` method. This method takes an XML string and parses it into an `XElement` instance, casting that instance into the requested type of the static method call. `Parse` has two overloads. The first takes a string parameter, as shown here:

```
public static XElement Parse(string text);
```

An optional parameter can be passed to preserve the whitespace:

```
public static XElement Parse(string text, bool preserveWhitespace);
```

The following example shows how to use the typed version of the `Parse` method.

```
var ord = Order.Parse("C:\\Wrox\\AppendixC\\Orders.xml");
```

Save

The `Save` method of a generated class is the typed version of the LINQ to XML `XElement` `Save` method. As with the LINQ to XML `Save` method, the typed version of the `Save` method takes the source XML tree and forwards it to the wrapped `XElement` instance for saving.

`Save` has several overloads. This first example shows the syntax to save the output to a text file:

```
public void Save(string filename);
```

The following example is the same as the first example but includes a parameter to control the preservation of whitespace:

```
public void Save(string filename, bool preserveWhitespace);
```

Here's an example that shows the syntax to save the output to a TextWriter:

```
public void Save(TextWriter tw);
```

The following example from earlier in the appendix shows how the `Save` method is used on a typed `XElement`.

```
public void Save(TextWriter tw, bool preserveWhitespace);
```

Here's how to write the output to an XmlWriter:

```
public void Save(XmlWriter xw);
```

The following example shows how to use the typed version of the `Save` method to save the output to a text file.

```
var ord = Order.Load("C:\\Wrox\\AppendixC\\Orders.xml");
// process the xml tree
order.Save("C:\\Wrox\\AppendixC\\Orders2.xml");
```

Clone

The `Clone` method clones the entire underlying untyped XML tree. The capability to clone is provided by the generated classes' base class, `XTypedElement`. The `Clone` method is quite simple to use, but the result of a clone is weakly typed and therefore a cast must be used to access the intended type.

For example, the following code shows the original XML tree being cloned into a second XML tree while being cast to the original type. Once the cast and clone are executed, it can be used just like the original XML tree.

```
var ord = Order.Load("C:\\Wrox\\AppendixC\\Orders.xml");
var ord2 = (Order)ord.Clone();

var total = (from purchaseOrder in ord2.OrderDetail
             from item in purchaseOrder.Item
             select item.UnitPrice * item.OrderQuantity
             ).Sum();

textBox1.Text = total.ToString();
```

Default Values

Default values affect the behavior of the getters for properties that implement declarations for elements or attributes for defaults. That is, when the element or attribute is not found in the XML tree, the getter for either the attribute or element returns the default value.

For example, the following XSD schema fragment contains an element declaration that also defines a default value for the Department element.

```
<xs: ComplexType name="EmployeeInfo">
  <xs:Sequence>
    <xs:element name="NationalIDNumber" type="xs:string" />
    <xs:element name="LoginID" type="xs:string" />
    <xs:element name="Title" type="xs:string" />
    <xs:element name="Name" type="xs:string" />
    <xs:element name="EmailAddress" type="xs:string" />
  </xs:Sequence>
  <xs:attribute name="Department" type="xs:string" default="Dev"/>
</xs:ComplexType>
```

You can build an XML tree that intentionally excludes the definition of a Department element:

```
var emp = new EmployeeInfo
{
  NationalIDNumber = "123456789",
  LoginID = "adventure-works\scott",
  Title = "Geek",
  Name = "Scott",
  EmailAddress = "scott@adventure-works.com"
};
```

When the getter for the Department element is called, the default defined by the schema is returned, as shown here:

```
<EmployeeInfo Department="Dev">
  <NationalIDNumber>123456789</NationalIDNumber>
```

```
        <LoginID>adventure-works\scott</LoginID>
        <Title>Geek</Title>
        <Name>Scott</Name>
        <EmailAddress>scott@adventure-works.com</EmailAddress>
    </EmployeeInfo>
```

Again, the current release of LINQ to XSD and the API of XML objects may, and probably will, change. For example, the current release of LINQ to XSD does not support defaults for elements, but it does support defaults for attributes (thus, the use of a default for an attribute in the previous example).

Also, the actual overloads for the API methods may differ.

Index

Index